Cooking Basics

FOR

DUMMIES®

3RD EDITION

**by Bryan Miller and Marie Rama
with Eve Adamson**

Foreword by Wolfgang Puck

WILEY

Wiley Publishing, Inc.

Cooking Basics For Dummies®, 3rd Edition

Published by
Wiley Publishing, Inc.
111 River St.
Hoboken, NJ 07030-5774
www.wiley.com

Copyright © 2004 by Wiley Publishing, Inc., Indianapolis, Indiana

Published by Wiley Publishing, Inc., Indianapolis, Indiana

Published simultaneously in Canada

For general information on our other products and services or to obtain technical support, please contact our Customer Care Department within the U.S. at 877-762-2974, outside the U.S. at 317-572-3993, or fax 317-572-4002.

Wiley also publishes its books in a variety of electronic formats. Some content that appears in print may not be available in electronic books.

Library of Congress Control Number: 2004112319

ISBN: 978-0-7645-7206-7

Manufactured in the United States of America

10 9 8 7

3B/RV/RR/QY/IN

WILEY

About the Authors

Bryan Miller is a former restaurant critic and feature writer for the *New York Times,* who also wrote *Desserts For Dummies* (with Bill Yosses), published by Wiley. He also has written nine other books, including three cookbooks with Pierre Franey (*Cuisine Rapide; The Seafood Cookbook — Classic to Contemporary;* and *A Chef's Tale,* also with Richard Flaste) and four editions of the *New York Times Guide to Restaurants.* Mr. Miller also collaborated for 13 years with Pierre Franey on the syndicated "60-Minute Gourmet" column, which appeared weekly in the *New York Times.* His eleventh book, *Cooking with the 60-Minute Gourmet,* was published in September 1999. He is the recipient of the "James Beard Who's Who Food and Beverage Award," which recognizes outstanding achievement in the field of food and wine.

Marie Rama is an independent food, beverage, and media consultant, who also wrote *Grilling For Dummies* (with John Mariani), published by Wiley. She has worked as a professional pastry chef and as a recipe developer for several food companies and associations, including the McIlhenny Company and the United Fresh Fruit and Vegetable Association. Ms. Rama has served as the Director of Weddings, Romance, and Entertaining for Korbel Champagne and as the "Lemon Lady" for Sunkist Growers, appearing on hundreds of television and radio shows around the United States and Canada. Ms. Rama lives in Bronxville, New York, with her husband, Mark Reiter, and their two sons, Nicholas and William.

Eve Adamson is an award-winning writer and the author or coauthor of over 25 books and hundreds of magazine articles on a variety of subjects, from cooking to yoga to pets. She is the author of *Dachshunds For Dummies* and the coauthor of *Labrador Retrievers For Dummies,* with trainer Joel Walton, both published by Wiley. She has coauthored or contributed recipes to several cookbooks, including the popular *The Mediterranean Diet: A Recipe for Wellness,* coauthored with nutritionist Marissa Cloutier. Eve is a member of the International Association of Culinary Professionals and a self-taught home cook. She lives (and cooks) with her two children and artist Ben Minkler in Iowa City, Iowa.

Publisher's Acknowledgments

We're proud of this book; please send us your comments through our Dummies online registration form located at www.dummies.com/register/.

Some of the people who helped bring this book to market include the following:

Acquisitions, Editorial, and Media Development

Senior Project Editor: Alissa Schwipps

(Previous Edition: Elizabeth Netedu Kuball)

Acquisitions Editor: Stacy Kennedy

Senior Copy Editor: Tina Sims

Assistant Editor: Holly Gastineau-Grimes

Technical Editor: Patty Santelli

Editorial Manager: Jennifer Ehrlich

Editorial Assistants: Courtney Allen, Melissa Bennett

Cover Photo: © StockFood/Green

Cartoons: Rich Tennant, www.the5thwave.com

Composition Services

Project Coordinators: Courtney MacIntyre, Erin Smith

Layout and Graphics: Joyce Haughey, Stephanie D. Jumper, Barry Offringa, Brent Savage

Special Art: Elizabeth Kurtzman

Proofreaders: Brian H. Walls, Aptara

Indexer: Aptara

Special Help
Carmen Krikorian

Publishing and Editorial for Consumer Dummies

Diane Graves Steele, Vice President and Publisher, Consumer Dummies

Joyce Pepple, Acquisitions Director, Consumer Dummies

Kristin A. Cocks, Product Development Director, Consumer Dummies

Michael Spring, Vice President and Publisher, Travel

Brice Gosnell, Associate Publisher, Travel

Kelly Regan, Editorial Director, Travel

Publishing for Technology Dummies

Andy Cummings, Vice President and Publisher, Dummies Technology/General User

Composition Services

Gerry Fahey, Vice President of Production Services

Debbie Stailey, Director of Composition Services

Contents at a Glance

Recipes at a Glance

Meat and Poultry

Fish and Shellfish

Meatless Main Dishes

Vegetables and Side Dishes

Sauces, Dressings and Garnishes

Desserts

Beverages

Table of Contents

Foreword

Cooking Basics For Dummies, 3rd Edition, may seem at first glance to be just a lighthearted romp through the culinary meadow, but in fact, beneath all the fun it is a serious book with solid learning tools that introduces readers to an impressively wide range of skills. Wonderful ingredients and good technique are what good food is all about, and because knowing how to bring out the best in food is what makes a meal memorable, technique is the foundation of all good cooking, professional or amateur. Every great chef starts somewhere, and Cooking Basics For Dummies, 3rd Edition, shows you where.

Spago Beverly Hills is the most well-known of my restaurants and there, like all of my other dining locations, we focus on grilling. Sure, we get our famous results partly by having a great staff and a professional kitchen, but Cooking Basics For Dummies, 3rd Edition, shows the home cook that superior grilling (as opposed to the ordinary backyard barbecue) lies in a number of easy-to-master techniques. Step-by-step recipes and illustrations walk you through different levels of sophistication, so you can see how all great food has the same beginnings.

Cooking is also about making wonderful food to share with family and friends, and Cooking Basics For Dummies, 3rd Edition, lets you do just that. Think of this book as a set of training wheels that prop you up as you learn all the twists and turns of the kitchen. Not only will you come away with plenty of exciting dishes, but you will also eventually take off the training wheels and set off on your own.

Cooking should be an adventure; more importantly, it should also be fun. Your series of small discoveries can lead to a lifetime of great meals. Cooking Basics For Dummies, 3rd Edition, gives you all the information and direction you need to set out on that adventure, confident and ready to cook great food!

— **Wolfgang Puck**

Introduction

. . . .

*W*hether you fancy yourself a hotshot home cook or someone who wouldn't know a whisk from a Weimaraner, *Cooking Basics For Dummies,* 3rd Edition, can help you. For the novice, our technique-oriented approach puts the tools in your hands and the knowledge in your head so that you can read a recipe and say to yourself, "Okay, I can do this." Dinner parties won't be so daunting. Family meals? A snap. You may even find yourself ready to tackle Thanksgiving dinner!

Even more experienced cooks may want to hone their basic skills, and the more than 200 recipes in this book offer plenty of food for thought.

Unlike most cookbooks, this one is more than a compilation of tasty recipes. We also focus on cooking techniques like broiling, steaming, braising, and roasting. After you master these techniques, you're no longer a slave to recipes. Once again, you can cook with imagination and creativity — and that's the sign of a skilled cook.

The best part about discovering how to cook this way is that, while you're practicing your techniques, you have all kinds of delicious food to eat. Sure beats trumpet lessons.

Furthermore, this book is structured around the way you live. For example, it includes information about cooking for guests when you have only one hour, cooking economically, and making a delicious meal when you don't even have time to get to the market. Watching carbs, or calories, or fat grams? Going vegetarian? No problem. We make special note of the recipes that fit into your healthy lifestyle, and also mention ways to adapt recipes for your individual dietary needs.

Most of all, you actually have fun as you explore the endless pleasures of cooking. And that, after all, is what food is all about.

The food revolution that began in the later years of the 20th century has made available to home cooks products that they had never dreamed of: truffles, flavored vinegar, exotic seafood, frozen stocks, goat cheese, and countless types of olive oil, to name just a few. At the same time, the technology of cooking equipment has narrowed the gap between home and professional kitchens.

Of course, new products and technology don't make a good cook. The requirements of a refined cook haven't changed since the 17th century: a sensitive palate, an understanding of cooking techniques and products, strong knife skills, and patience. These are skills we want to help you develop.

About This Book

We start at the very beginning: your kitchen and your equipment. What basic tools do you need? How do you use these things? We help you stock your pantry, refrigerator, and freezer with basic staples so you know what to have on hand. Then we move on to cooking techniques to get you up and running as soon as possible. Doing simple things well offers great personal satisfaction, as you will see.

Depending on your needs and cooking skills, you can start at the beginning of the book and work your way through, go straight to the chapters that interest you most (the table of contents and index point you in the right direction), or read the book Arab-style, from the back to the front.

Conventions Used in This Book

Here are some non-recipe conventions you should keep in mind to get the most out of this guidebook:

- ✔ *Italic* is used for emphasis and to highlight new words or terms that are defined.
- ✔ **Boldfaced** text is used to indicate the action part of numbered steps.
- ✔ Monofont is used for Web addresses.

Before charging ahead to make any of the recipes in this book, you should know a few things about the ingredients and instructions:

- ✔ **Milk is always whole.** You can substitute lowfat or skim milk, but these products give soups and sauces a thinner, less creamy consistency.
- ✔ **Use unsalted butter so that you can control the amount of salt in a dish.** We don't recommend substituting margarine, which has just as many calories per tablespoon (100) as butter. Margarine's flavor is inferior to butter as well.
- ✔ **Unless otherwise noted, all eggs are large.**
- ✔ **All dry ingredient measurements are level.** Brown sugar is measured firmly packed.

- ✔ **All salt is common table salt, and pepper is freshly ground.** We seldom specify measured amounts of salt and pepper because every cook has a different palate. Sample the recipe several times during preparation to taste for seasoning, and add salt and pepper to taste when we instruct you to do so.

- ✔ **All oven temperatures are Fahrenheit.**

And keep the following general tips in mind:

- ✔ Read through each recipe at least once to make sure that you have all the necessary ingredients and utensils, understand all the steps, and have enough preparation time. (We begin each recipe by listing the cooking utensils you need as well as the preparation and cooking times.)

- ✔ Be sure to use the proper size pan when a measurement is given.

- ✔ Preheat ovens, broilers, and grills at least 15 minutes before cooking begins. Place all food on the middle rack of the oven unless the recipe says otherwise.

- ✔ Most of the recipes in this book are written to serve four. You can reduce by half or double many of them to satisfy two or eight people.

- 🍅 If you're looking for vegetarian recipes, you can easily find them in the Recipes in This Chapter list, located at the beginning of every chapter. Vegetarian recipes are marked by the tomato bullet shown here, instead of the usual triangle.

What You're Not to Read

We've written this book so that you can 1) find information easily and 2) easily understand what you find. And although we'd like to believe that you want to pore over every last word between the two yellow covers, we actually make it easy for you to identify "skippable" material. This information is the stuff that, although interesting and related to the topic at hand, isn't essential for you to know. In other words, it won't be on the test!

- ✔ **Text in sidebars:** The sidebars are the shaded boxes that appear here and there. They offer personal observations, an occasional historical tidbit, or a fascinating fact, but they aren't necessary reading.

- ✔ **The stuff on the copyright page:** No kidding. You'll find nothing here of interest unless you're inexplicably enamored by legal language and Library of Congress numbers.

- ✔ **Our extraordinary biographies:** You don't need to know who we are to know that this is the best cookbook out there. After all, all *For Dummies* authors are considered experts in their fields. Still, aren't you curious?

Foolish Assumptions

We wrote this cookbook with some thoughts about you in mind. Here's what we assume about you, our reader:

- ✔ You love the *idea* of cooking. You're a crackerjack at boiling water. But you just aren't quite sure how to actually organize a meal, make lots of things at once, or combine foods or flavor meals in ways that make your family members sigh with satisfaction after they put down their forks.

- ✔ You've cooked before. Sometimes it was pretty darn good. Sometimes you were glad you didn't have company. Sometimes the fire department had to be called. But really, sometimes it *was* pretty darn good! You're pretty sure you have potential.

- ✔ You sometimes daydream about going to cooking school or impressing people with the way you chop garlic with your very expensive chef's knife. But you don't yet own a very expensive chef's knife.

- ✔ You have basic kitchen equipment on hand, including pots and pans and measuring cups, but you aren't sure whether you have all the right things you need for efficient cooking, and you probably don't know what all those different pots and pans are called.

- ✔ You love to eat at restaurants, and you often wonder if you could make that stuff at home.

- ✔ You bought this cookbook for yourself so you can finally gain the skills you need to earn the title of "really great cook."

- ✔ Somebody gave you this cookbook as a gift, and you assume that it was a hint somehow related to that interesting casserole-type thing you attempted last week.

Foolish of us, maybe, but we assume that you trusted us to do our very best when writing this cookbook, so that every time you open it, you'll enjoy reading it. Even more, we want you to enjoy the meals you will make from our recipes. Our promise to you is that if you read this book and try the recipes here, you will indeed master some very important cooking skills and you'll have a great time doing it, too.

How This Book Is Organized

This book is organized around cooking techniques and real-life situations. Major sections are called parts. Within each part are chapters that address specific subjects. Following is a rundown of each part and what you can read about there.

Part 1: Go On In — It's Only the Kitchen

What is this strange room? It's the most popular room in the house, where friends hang out as they help themselves to your food and drinks, where parties inevitably gravitate, and where couples have their best arguments. This part is designed to help you get over your fear of cooking. It touches on kitchen design and organization, helping you to arrange your appliances, kitchen space, counters, and cabinets for maximum efficiency. It also covers in detail necessary equipment like pots, pans, knives, and all kinds of gadgets. You find out which basic supplies you need to stock up on. Plus, we get you cooking right away in this part, with simple yet delicious recipes guaranteed to whet your appetite to cook even more.

Part II: Know Your Techniques

Part II is where the fun begins. Each chapter includes recipes that illustrate an essential cooking technique: braising, sautéing, roasting, grilling, and more. From that starting point, we take you through a number of recipe variations that show you how to improvise with confidence and skill.

Part III: Expand Your Repertoire

Part III looks at pasta, eggs, and larger categories of dishes like soups, salads, desserts, and one-pot meals. Here, you can read about how to make the perfect omelet, how to mix a balanced vinaigrette, and how to use seasonal fruits to create delectable desserts. Also included are illustrations and charts — like the one identifying different types of pastas (so that you know tagliatelle from linguine) — and, of course, dozens of delicious recipes.

Part IV: Now You're Cooking! Real Menus for Real Life

Part IV injects another dose of reality into the cooking experience. Most glossy cookbooks assume that you have all the time in the world to prepare a dish. Some books also assume that price is no object — "now take that loin of veal and sprinkle it with black truffles" — and that everybody lives next door to a gourmet market. In the real world, you have 45 minutes, if you're lucky, to prepare dinner while a 2-year-old is clinging to your leg and the cat is coughing up hairballs. At the same time, the local supermarket may be closing in 5 minutes. Now that's real-life cooking. And that's what these chapters are all about.

Part V: Special Occasions

Part V offers some great menus for popular special occasions. We give you everything you need to make your summer soiree a hit. We also cover Super Bowl parties, from the kickoff to the two-minute warning, and we provide a fantastic menu for a Thanksgiving dinner. If a holiday or special occasion is quickly approaching and you have no idea what to cook, turn to these chapters for some complete menus.

Part VI: The Part of Tens

Just when you thought that we had covered everything, we give you more! These quick lists include kitchen disasters and what to do about them, a few important reminders, and kitchen wisdom. Before you know it, you'll be thinking like a chef!

We round out the book with two helpful appendixes. This straightforward reference section gives you useful lists and charts, as well as a glossary. Here, you can find the meaning of more than 100 common cooking terms. We also provide common equivalents and substitutions for those emergency situations when you discover at the last minute that you don't have the ingredient you need.

Icons Used in This Book

Icons are those nifty little pictures in the margin of this book. They each grab your attention for a different reason, and we explain those reasons here.

When there's an easier way to do something, a step you can take to save money, or a shortcut you can take to get yourself to the dinner table faster, we let you know by marking the tip with this icon.

The kitchen can be a dangerous place. This icon, like a flashing yellow light, steers you clear of potentially dangerous mishaps.

We hope that you remember every valuable piece of information in this book, but if your brain can hold only so much, make sure that you hang on to the tidbits marked by this icon.

Where to Go from Here

You'll notice how easy it is to jump from chapter to chapter in our book without feeling lost. That's intentional, so you can start enjoying *Cooking Basics For Dummies,* 3rd Edition, with any chapter you like. Even if you know your way around a kitchen pretty well, we recommend that you start by reading two key chapters — Chapter 2, just to be sure you really do have all the equipment to cook the recipes in this book, and Chapter 3, which talks about all the basic ingredients every well-stocked kitchen pantry, freezer, and refrigerator should contain.

If you're in the process of buying a house, remodeling a kitchen, or just dreaming about your perfect kitchen, check out Chapter 1, where you can read all about kitchen design, from lighting to countertops to appliances. Wary about safety? Check out the end of Chapter 1, or skip on over to Chapter 22 for a list of ten common kitchen disasters and how to avoid them. Or, maybe you just want to start cooking. In that case, check out any of the other chapters in this book. Some are arranged around techniques, such as boiling or grilling or sautéing, with recipes to help you practice. Others are arranged around menus for parties, for economy, or for times when you need to prepare a meal on short notice. But all these chapters are chock-full of delicious recipes with simple instructions.

We know you'll enjoy cooking with us. Cooking doesn't have to be complicated, as long as you know the basics. So come on in to the kitchen, grab a pot (we tell you which one), and get cooking. We're getting hungry just thinking about it!

Part I
Go On In — It's Only the Kitchen

The 5th Wave   By Rich Tennant

@RICHTENNANT

"I'm sure there are some canned staples in the food pantry. That's what it's there for. Just look next to the roller blades, below the bike helmets above the back packs but underneath the tennis balls."

In this part . . .

There's no doubt about it: If you want to learn to cook, you have to go into the kitchen. But never fear! The kitchen may seem like it's full of strange appliances, oddly shaped tools, and bottles and jars and packages of ingredients you know nothing about, but as a beginning cook, this is where the fun begins! We help you navigate, utilize, and even enjoy your kitchen with organizational strategies, supply lists, and even a few remodeling tips, if you should need them. You'll even try your hand at a couple of recipes sure to please your family and friends.

Chapter 1

Cooking with Confidence

. . . .

In This Chapter

▶ Taking a good look at your kitchen

▶ Familiarizing yourself with some basic cooking techniques

▶ Figuring out your menus

▶ Making your kitchen safe and user-friendly

▶ Trying your hand at a simple recipe

Recipes in This Chapter

☉ Scrambled Eggs

. . . .

So you want to find out how to cook? Good for you! Cooking is fun, relaxing, exciting, and even therapeutic. It enables you to eat for less money than ordering take-out or dining in a restaurant every night, and it allows you to know exactly what you're eating and to make conscious, healthy food choices. Cooking lets you easily adapt your meals to suit your own nutritional and gastronomic preferences, whether you're eating low-carb or vegetarian, or you're determined to immerse yourself in classic French cuisine. Plus, cooking the food you eat puts you in closer touch to the process of nourishing your own body, and that can make you feel better about yourself, your health, your body, and your life. Yes, cooking can be that powerful!

We love to cook, and we're excited to share our knowledge with you, but we remember being beginning cooks, too. Sometimes you may not feel confident enough to try what looks like a complicated recipe, let alone figure out which equipment and supplies you need and how you should set up a kitchen that works for you.

In this chapter, we begin at the beginning: with your kitchen. Whether you have a cramped apartment kitchen with counter space the size of a cereal box, or a sprawling country kitchen with a commercial stove and a work island, this chapter helps you set up your kitchen in a way that will allow you to become a more productive cook. To be sure, space is great. But knowing how to use what you have efficiently is the real key. You would be surprised to see how small some restaurant kitchens are; they work, however, because everything is in its place and is easily accessible. Have you ever ricocheted around the kitchen desperately searching for a spatula while your omelet burned on the range? We want to ensure that you're never in that situation again.

To do that, in this chapter, we give you a broad overview of what you need to know to be an effective cook. We talk about how to set up your cooking space, introduce you to the major appliances of a kitchen, and give you a glimpse of some basic cooking techniques. Then we discuss menu planning, kitchen safety, and we even help you to get started with a nice, easy, practical recipe.

Warming Up to Your Kitchen

There it is: the kitchen. Maybe you don't go in there very much, or maybe you like to hang around watching other people cook. Or maybe you cook dinner in there every night, but you don't enjoy it very much. Never fear. Your kitchen can easily become a place you *love* to cook in and be in. It's all a matter of organization.

Setting up your cooking space

You don't need a fabulous kitchen to prepare fabulous food. But a well-designed workplace sure makes cooking easier and more pleasurable. Chances are, you aren't in the process of remodeling your kitchen, and you have to make do with the basic kitchen design you have. But if you are designing your cooking space, consider the concept of access. If you want to spend the day running, join a health club. If you want to enjoy an efficient and pleasurable cooking experience, put some thought into the organization of your workspace. Although nothing is wrong with a large, eat-in kitchen, the design of the cooking area should be practical. You shouldn't have to walk ten feet from the stove to get the salt, for example.

You should be able to move from your working counter space to the stove and the refrigerator in a smooth, unobstructed fashion. This working space actually has a name: the *kitchen triangle* (see Figure 1-1). If a table, plant, or small child is blocking the way, move it. For suggestions on designing your kitchen, check out *Kitchen Remodeling For Dummies,* by Donald R. Prestly (Wiley). But remember, even if you can't design your kitchen space, you can arrange what you need in a way that works for you. Here's how to do that.

Decluttering your countertops

First things first: Take a good hard look at your countertops. What's on them? Coffeemakers, blenders, food processors, stacks of bills, permission slips, and grade school art projects? Counter space is the single most overlooked item in many kitchens. The counter is where you set out and prepare food (often on a cutting board), stack plates, put kitchen machines, and lose car keys amid the clutter. A clean, clear counter space can inspire great meals. A cluttered one is more likely to make you want to pick up the phone and order a pizza. Try to keep your counters neat and clean. So many kitchen counters are cluttered with paraphernalia that they become nearly useless.

The most important key for organizing your counter space is to keep it clear of most stuff. Unless you use an appliance at least several times a week — the coffee machine, toaster, and blender, for example — put it away. That's precious work space you're filling up with all that stuff! Also remember that a kitchen counter is not a magazine rack, plant holder, wine bin, or phone book shelf, so try not to use it for these purposes if you actually want to cook!

In addition to keeping your countertops clutter free, take steps to care for them. Use cutting boards for cutting and trivets for hot pots and pans, and wipe up spills quickly to prevent stains. The nicer your counters look, the more you'll enjoy being in the kitchen. (Flip ahead to Chapter 22 for more information about countertop care.)

Let there be lighting

Kitchens should be well lit — the stove and workspaces most of all. If you have a combination kitchen/dining area, you may want to put the lights on a dimmer. That way, you can keep the kitchen bright while the dining area is dim. Lights under the stovetop hood can really help when stirring sauces or sautéing vegetables. You haven't replaced that burned-out bulb in a year? Time to do it!

Another option is to have special lighting for the cooking area, either inset into overhead cabinets or in the ceiling. Nothing is worse than trying to check your food in a dimly lit area. If your kitchen is poorly lit over the cooking area, the least expensive solution is a wall-mounted supplementary light.

Staple city: Organizing your pantry

The pantry is the place where you store your basic cooking staples, as well as other dry goods. Dry goods are foods that aren't refrigerated or frozen, including staples like flour and sugar, and packaged foods like crackers, cookies, pasta, and rice. If you're lucky enough to have an entire room or closet dedicated to a pantry, keep it well organized so that you can see and easily reach the staples you use most, like flour, sugar, and cooking oil. But even if you have only a cabinet or two for your pantry, organization is the key to efficiency. (For tips on what to keep in your pantry, turn to Chapter 3.)

The first thing to consider in organizing your pantry is the kind of closet or cabinet you decide to use and whether the food you store inside of it is easily accessible.

We've seen many ingenious kitchen cabinets on the market, such as those that have storage shelves on the swing-out doors as well as inside, Lazy-Susan-type cabinets that rotate for full access to round shelves, or cabinets with shelves that roll out on tracks so you can easily reach even those things you store at the back of the shelf. If your cabinets don't have these convenient features, you can improvise by mounting racks on the inside of the doors or installing those handy roll-out shelves yourself. Look for such kits in hardware or kitchen stores.

A good cabinet or closet system enables you to see exactly what's in your pantry, thus helping to inspire your culinary creativity and allowing you to grab what you need without knocking over vinegar bottles and stacks of spice jars. Store dried beans, pasta, different kinds of rice, flour, sugar, tea, and coffee in large glass or clear plastic jars with lids. This type of storage is practical and looks professional, too.

If you use something all the time, consider taking it out of the pantry and storing it closer to your stove or workstation, in a "satellite" pantry like a cabinet or shelf. You might want to do this with your cooking oils and sprays, your spice rack, or your baking supplies such as baking soda, baking powder, and vanilla.

Kitchen islands are extremely efficient in that they can have considerable storage space below. Moreover, they can double as a kitchen table. If you don't have an island (and you have the space), consider buying a butcher block table with shelving underneath.

Introducing major appliances: Friends, not foes

There they are, those formidable appliances that make your kitchen into a room custom-made for food preparation and storage. Your major appliances are capable of producing the most exquisite gourmet meals or the most horrible, burned disasters; of yielding fresh, glistening produce or slimy bags of who knows what?

Major appliances are your allies in good cooking. Until you make friends with your stove, your oven, your refrigerator, and small appliances (which we discuss in Chapter 2), you'll never really feel at home in the kitchen. To know your appliances is to love them, and knowing each appliance's relative strengths and weaknesses can help you make the most of what they can do for you.

Stovetop and oven

Whether you have an old gas stove that looks like it belonged to your grandma or a fancy space-age-looking glass cooktop, your stovetop may be the cooking appliance you use the most. Right under it, or sometimes over it, or possibly off to the side, is your oven, which you'll probably use almost as much for baking, roasting, and warming up leftovers. Your stove and oven are your best friends in the kitchen (see Parts II, III, IV, and V for recipes using your stove and oven), and if you're buying new ones, you have all kinds of new technology to choose from. Even if you won't be going appliance shopping any time soon, knowing exactly what kind of stovetop and oven you have and how to use them may help your cooking efforts.

Gas

Most serious cooks prefer gas stoves. You can turn a gas flame up and down quickly, which is important in sautéing and sauce making. You can adjust the flame in tiny increments, more so than you can with an electric stove with numbers on the dials. Commercial gas ranges are extremely powerful and can cut your cooking time by as much as one-fourth, but simple home ranges work just fine for most purposes. New cooks may feel intimidated by gas because of the flames, and gas stoves can produce higher heat than electric stoves, so those used to cooking on electric stoves will need to adjust so that they don't burn their food or destroy that expensive sauté pan. But with a little practice, you'll get the hang of cooking with gas. When you can confidently proclaim, "Oh, I like to cook only with gas," you know you've reached a whole new level of culinary prowess.

Newer gas ranges should not smell of gas from flaming pilot lights. Newer models no longer have standing pilots. They ignite electronically; therefore, gas doesn't flow through the system unless the range is turned on. If you do smell gas, you have a leak in your system. This situation is dangerous — call your gas company immediately. Do not use the stove or any other electrical appliances, even your lights, because doing so can spark an explosion.

Electric heat

Electric ranges became all the rage after World War II. They were considered clean, easy to use, and modern. The drawback to electric ranges is their slow response time. Reducing heat from high to low can take a minute; gas can do it in seconds. However, many professional chefs prefer electric ovens, especially for baking, because they're very accurate and consistent. Today's gas and electric ovens generally hold and maintain oven temperature within a variance of about 5 degrees.

Induction

Induction is a new form of kitchen heat. Some professional chefs are so impressed with it that they predict it will replace all other systems in ten years.

Whether that is true or not, induction cooking is impressive to watch. Basically, it works on a magnetic transfer principle — heat passes via magnetic force from the burner to the pan. If you place a paper towel between the burner and the pan, the towel does not get hot. A 2-quart pot of water comes to a boil in about a minute. However, an induction cooktop uses only selected metal pans to which a magnet adheres, such as stainless steel. Copper and glass cookware, for example, do not work. An induction cooktop is expensive, priced at over $800 for four burners.

Convection ovens

Chefs have used convection ovens for years. If we were to recommend an addition to your kitchen, a convection oven might be the one. A small fan in the rear of the oven circulates air all around the food to cook it rapidly and evenly. Cooking times and temperature settings are reduced by about 25 percent, so most manufacturers suggest that you reduce the cooking temperature given in the recipe by 25 degrees when baking. Some oven manufacturers offer both regular and convection cooking at the flick of a switch. Do you need a convection oven? No. But if you bake often, you might learn to love one.

If a convection wall oven is over your budget, consider the smaller, less expensive convection toaster oven, especially if you're cooking for one or two. It can toast, bake a cake, broil a burger, and roast a small chicken. And cooking times are shorter than in conventional ovens. Small convection ovens can cost as little as a few hundred dollars, while larger, full-sized convection ovens can range from a couple thousand dollars to $10,000 or more, depending on the model and brand.

How does a microwave cook?

Every microwave has an energy box called a *magnetron,* which produces microwaves (from electricity). The microwaves pass through materials like glass, paper, china, and plastic to convert to heat when they come in contact with food molecules. The microwaves cause the water molecules in the food to rotate so rapidly that they vibrate, creating friction and heat.

A major misconception is that microwaves cook from the inside out. They do not. Microwaves penetrate primarily the surface and no farther than 2 inches into the food. The heat spreads by conduction to the rest of the food.

Microwave ovens

Microwave cooking is unlike any other kind of conventional cooking. You must follow a different set of cooking rules. Although over 90 percent of American kitchens have a microwave, most people use the microwave only as a reheating and defrosting device. If this is your intention, purchase a simple unit with only one or two power levels. If you're short on counter or wall space, consider a microwave-convection oven combination that allows you to cook by using either method.

Microwaves can't pass through metal, so you can't cook with traditional metal cookware. You can, however, use flameproof glass, some plastics, porcelain, paper, ceramic, and plastic cooking bags. Some microwaves permit you to use aluminum foil to cover dishes, as long as the foil doesn't touch the oven walls or the temperature probe. Check your operating manual to see whether your appliance allows using foil in this way. Cookware placed in the microwave should not get hot. If it does, it's probably not microwaveable.

A microwave is not a replacement for conventional cooking of grilled meats, baked breads, cakes and cookies, and other foods that need browning — unless it has a browning unit. Use your microwave for what it does best in combination with other appliances. For example, you can precook chicken in minutes in the microwave and finish it under the broiler or on an outdoor grill. Following are some other microwave tips:

- Recipes that require a lot of water, such as pasta, don't work as well in a microwave and probably cook in less time on your stovetop.

- Foods must be arranged properly to cook evenly. Face the thickest parts, like broccoli stalks, outward toward the oven walls. Arrange foods of the same size and shape, such as potatoes, in a circle or square with space between them and no item in the center.

- Covering dishes eliminates splattering, and it also cuts down on cooking time. Frequently stirring, turning, and rotating foods ensures an even distribution of heat.

✔ As with conventional cooking, cutting foods into smaller pieces shortens cooking time.

✔ Before cooking, pierce with a fork foods that have skins, like potatoes, hot dogs, and sausages. Doing so releases steam that can lead to sudden popping and splattering.

✔ A number of variables, including the type of microwave, can affect a recipe's cooking time, so check for doneness after the minimum cooking time. You can always cook food longer. Also, always observe the recipe's "standing" time, because microwaved food continues to cook after you remove it from the oven.

✔ Be sure to use the defrost power setting (30 to 40 percent of full power) when thawing food to ensure slow and even defrosting; otherwise, the outside of the food may start to cook before the inside is thoroughly thawed.

Read your microwave manual carefully before using it. One woman we know ruined her microwave oven because she used the cooking-time button as a kitchen timer, not realizing that you should never run an empty microwave, a warning found in just about every manual.

Most major appliance companies, including General Electric (800-626-2000), Amana (800-843-0304), and KitchenAid (800-422-1230), have toll-free information numbers with appliance experts on hand to answer questions about using and caring for your microwave.

Refrigerator

Refrigerators are the black holes of the kitchen — objects drift in and are never seen again, at least until the next thorough cleaning. At that time, your leftovers may resemble compost. And what's in this little ball of aluminum foil? *Do not open!*

Refrigerators come in many sizes and shapes. A family of four needs a minimum of 16 cubic feet and should probably buy one that's at least 18 cubic feet (unless you have a teenage boy, in which case you need a second refrigerator). If you use the freezer a great deal, having the freezer compartment on the top, rather than the bottom, is more convenient. Make sure that the doors open in the most convenient way for your kitchen. Also check the door compartments to see whether space is available to place a bottle upright. The door should not be cluttered with little compartments that just eat up space.

Try not to pack the refrigerator too densely. This way, the cold air has sufficient space to circulate around and cool the food. Store foods in the same spot so that you don't have to search for that little jar of mustard or jelly every time you open the door. Clear shelves and bins make it even easier to see where everything is.

The bottom drawers are usually the coldest and should be used for storing meat, poultry, and fish. Fresh vegetables are usually stored in the *crisper* drawer, which is often located just above the meat bin. Salad greens and leafy herbs can be washed, thoroughly dried, and wrapped in paper towels to extend their storage life. Other vegetables, like broccoli and cauliflower, should be washed just before serving. Excess water on any vegetable in storage can hasten its deterioration.

Liberate old food from the refrigerator every two weeks or so, and give the fridge a good soap-and-water bath every few months. An open box of baking soda at the back of a shelf soaks up odors. Remember to replace the baking soda every few months.

Freezer

Your refrigerator and freezer hold what your pantry and cabinets can't: the stuff that has to stay cold. Your freezer can be a great storage space for food you buy in bulk, like meat, frozen vegetables, and bread, as well as leftovers like soup, chili, casseroles, and baked goods. Because your freezer space is probably relatively small, you can't store too much in there, however. To get the most use of the space, stack things neatly and use bins to keep things organized.

If you're lucky enough to have a stand-alone freezer, all the better! You can take advantage of sales on meat, frozen vegetables, and fruits, and can also cook in bulk, freezing leftover soups, stews, sauces, and desserts. You'll always have food handy at the touch of the microwave's defrost button. You can organize your stand-alone freezer more like your refrigerator, organizing food in bins and on separate shelves.

Finally, make sure that your refrigerator/freezer is within easy reach of your workspace. You can store a stand-alone freezer, however, in another room off the kitchen or even in the basement.

Dishwasher

Because you probably have better things to do with your evening than wash the dishes from dinner for eight, you'll probably want a dishwasher. Your dishwasher may be built in, or it may be portable. You can even buy tabletop dishwashers for modest dishwashing needs. Newer dishwashers require less prerinsing of dishes, and new dishwasher detergent formulas leave dishes spot-free. If you cook for a family, a dishwasher can save you a lot of time, but remember that dishwashers also use a lot of water and electricity. But for those who would rather spend time cooking than washing dishes, the expense is well worth it.

Garbage disposal

Garbage disposals are handy for the home cook. These grinders, housed in the underbelly of your sink drain, grind up the food that goes down the drain. If all you eat are frozen dinners and take-out, you probably won't need a disposal very often, but if you're always peeling, chopping, and wiping counters of the residue of cooking a good meal, you'll appreciate the convenience of a garbage disposal.

To keep your garbage disposal smelling good, grind up a few orange or lemon peels every so often. To keep the drain clean, once a month pour ½ cup baking soda down the drain, followed by 1 cup white vinegar. When the baking soda stops foaming, rinse with hot water. Better yet, let your kids do this kitchen chore. They love the volcanic action of the vinegar and baking soda.

Getting Acquainted with Basic Cooking Techniques

Recipes are full of terminology and techniques that new cooks might not be familiar with. At the heart of most recipes are some basic techniques, which we expand upon throughout this book in various sections. As a warm-up, however, here are the basic cooking techniques and what they involve. Become familiar with these terms, practice the techniques, and you'll realize that many recipes aren't as complicated as you thought.

- ✔ **Boiling, poaching, and steaming:** These terms involve cooking with water. *Boiling* is heating water so that it bubbles vigorously. *Poaching* is cooking fish, eggs, or vegetables in gently simmering water — water that is just beginning to bubble but not yet boil. *Steaming* is cooking food over, but not in, boiling or simmering water. We describe these techniques and more water-based cooking methods in detail in Chapter 4.

- ✔ **Sautéing:** This term refers to cooking food in a skillet or sauté pan quickly over high or medium-high heat, usually in heated oil or butter. Chapter 5 tells you all about sautéing.

- ✔ **Braising and stewing:** To *braise* is to cook food in a small amount of liquid, such as water or broth, for a long period of time. This technique results in particularly succulent meat. *Stewing* is cooking food (usually meat and veggies) in liquid flavored with herbs, broth, and sometimes wine until it is absorbed, to create a delectable, too-thick-to-be-soup concoction. For more on braising and stewing, check out Chapter 6.

Why everyone should learn to cook

Here are seven good reasons why everyone should learn to cook:

- ✔ When you dine in restaurants, you can complain with authority that particular dishes are not made the way you make them at home.

- ✔ You get to use all kinds of amusing implements — and actually know what to do with them.

- ✔ You can control your diet rather than depend on the dubious victuals churned out by carryout places or frozen food purveyors.

- ✔ At home, seconds and thirds are permissible.

- ✔ Feeding friends and loved ones is inherently more intimate than going to a restaurant.

- ✔ Establishing a connection with the food chain allows you to distinguish quality food from what's second rate. Who knows, you may even be inspired to plant a vegetable garden next spring.

- ✔ You start hanging around the cookbook section in bookstores — fertile terrain for opposite-sex encounters.

- ✔ **Roasting:** *Roasting* involves cooking food, uncovered, in a pan in the oven for a long period of time. This technique is usually used to describe cooking large pieces of meat, such as a pot roast or a turkey, or vegetables. Chapter 7 has lots more details about roasting.

- ✔ **Grilling:** If you like to spend as much time as possible outdoors, *grilling,* or cooking on a grate over hot charcoal or other heat element, is for you. Grill varieties include charcoal, gas, and electric. Chapter 8 goes into more detail about grill choices and grilling techniques.

Planning Your Menu

It's one thing to cook a recipe. It's another thing to plan a meal or a whole week's worth of meals! Menu planning, however, can be a lot of fun and a great way to experiment with new recipes and techniques. Planning your menu and writing out a shopping list assures that you have everything you need for your meals before you start cooking. Some cooks like to write down all the elements of each meal for an entire week at a time and then study recipes and make out a shopping list. To some people, this approach may sound tedious. To others, the chance to read all those recipes sounds like fun! But you don't have to be quite so formal, as long as you make sure you have all the necessary ingredients and equipment to cook all the elements of a meal before you begin.

But how do you know what to make? Formal dinners typically have several courses, including appetizers, salad, soup, a main course, a dessert, and sometimes even courses such as a cheese course, a pasta course, and a casserole course. It all depends on how fancy you want to get.

For most families, however, a simple meal with a main course (a meat or vegetarian dish, featuring ingredients separately or in a casserole form), accompanied by soup or a salad and bread, rice, pasta, or some other grain, make a filling and complete meal — with or without dessert. Healthy choices include lean meats and lowfat dairy dishes based on whole grains and legumes (such as lentils and white or black beans), lots of fresh vegetables, and sweetness from fresh fruit. Lunch can be even simpler: a hearty salad (see Chapter 12) or a big bowl of soup (see Chapter 11). And what about breakfast? See Chapter 10 for some delicious dishes based on eggs.

Holidays and special events offer opportunities to plan fancier or more elaborate meals or meals with a theme. Special dinners also provide an excuse to serve fancy desserts you may not want to indulge in every day (see Chapter 15 for dessert ideas of all kinds).

Menu planning is limited only by your imagination! See Part IV of this book for some specific ideas on menu planning, depending on the event, your budget, and how much time you have to prepare. Part V gives you more ideas for menus when you want to host a party.

Kitchen Safety 101

Cooking is fun, but it also requires certain precautions. You may think that the biggest danger in the kitchen is serving a meal that has guests roaring hysterically with laughter on their way home ("Can you believe he called that fiasco *dinner*?"). As humiliating as that can be, home cooks should be aware of other perils as well, so they can take the proper precautions and cook with no worries

Do you remember Dan Akroyd's classic skit on *Saturday Night Live,* in which he impersonates world-renowned chef Julia Child? In the middle of his cooking demonstration, he pretends to accidentally cut off his fingers: "Just a flesh wound," he warbles and continues cooking. Then he severs his wrist, his hand falling to the ground. Blood spurts everywhere. Pretty funny, huh?

That wildly exaggerated scene carries a cautionary note about razor-sharp knives: Always pay attention to what you're doing because one slip can cause great pain. (Keep in mind that dull knives can be dangerous, too, because they force you to apply more pressure, and your hand may slip while doing this.) For more on kitchen safety and preventing or dealing with kitchen disasters, check out Chapter 22. Some basic rules of safety include the following:

✔ Store knives in a wooden block or on a magnetic bar mounted out of reach of children, not in a kitchen drawer. For more information about knives and knife safety, see Chapter 2.

✔ Never cook in loose-hanging clothes that may catch fire, and keep long hair tied back for the same reason (not to mention keeping hair out of the food!).

✔ Never cook while wearing dangling jewelry that can get tangled around pot handles.

✔ Professional chefs have hands of asbestos from years of grabbing hot pots and pans. You do not. Keep potholders nearby and use them.

✔ Turn pot handles away from the front of the stove, where children may grab them and adults can bump into them.

✔ Don't let temperature-sensitive foods sit out in your kitchen, especially in warm weather. Raw meat, fish, and certain dairy products can spoil quickly, so refrigerate or freeze them right away.

✔ Wipe up spills immediately so that no one slips and falls.

✔ Don't try to cook if your mind is elsewhere, because your fingers may wind up elsewhere as well.

✔ Separate raw meat, especially poultry, from produce and other items in your refrigerator to avoid cross-contamination of harmful bacteria from one food to another. Never put cooked food or produce on a cutting board where you were just cutting raw meat.

✔ Wash your hands before handling food. Hands can be a virtual freight train of bacteria, depending, of course, on what you do during the day. Also wash thoroughly after handling meat or poultry.

✔ To avoid panic-stricken searches, always return utensils to the proper place. Always return a knife to its holder when you're finished with it.

✔ Clean up as you work. Obvious, no? Then why doesn't everyone do it? We know people who can make a tuna salad sandwich and leave the kitchen looking as if they had just served a lunch to the Dallas Cowboys. Put away dirty knives, wipe down counters, and return food to the refrigerator between steps in a recipe — doing so keeps you thinking clearly and discourages household pets from jumping onto countertops. Plus, cleaning up as you go frees up that spatula or whisk for the next step of the recipe.

✔ Every kitchen needs a fire extinguisher. It is inexpensive (about $15), easy to use, and mounts on the wall. This device may not do much for your cherries jubilee, but it can avert a disaster.

✔ The old wives' tale "Oil and water do not mix" happens to be true. Throwing water on a grease fire makes it worse by spreading it around. If the fire is contained in a pot or pan, cover it with a lid. For a fire in your oven or one that has spread to the floor, a few handfuls of baking soda or salt should cut off its oxygen supply while you grab the fire extinguisher.

Now Get Crackin'!

If you're eager to jump in and start cooking, try your hand at this quick and easy recipe for scrambled eggs, which you can enjoy for breakfast, lunch, or dinner. Eggs are a healthy and nutritious protein source, and cooking them is easy (see Chapter 10 for more egg recipes). This recipe for Scrambled Eggs is perfect for the beginner and loved by all. These eggs are sure to please and impress your family and friends.

If you want to make excellent scrambled eggs, don't overbeat the eggs before you cook them.

Scrambled Eggs

Some scrambled egg recipes call for cream, which adds a nice smoothness to the eggs; others call for water, which increases the volume by stimulating the whites to foam. You can use either ingredient, or just use milk, for the following recipe — try it different ways and see which you prefer.

Tools: *Medium bowl, fork, 10-inch (preferably nonstick) skillet or omelet pan, metal spatula or wooden spoon*

Preparation time: *About 5 minutes*

Cooking time: *About 4 minutes*

Yield: *4 servings*

8 eggs	*½ teaspoon salt (optional)*
¼ cup light cream, half-and-half, milk (whole or low-fat), or water	*Few dashes black pepper (optional)*
	2 tablespoons butter
2 tablespoons chopped chives (optional)	

1 Break the eggs into a bowl. With a fork or a wire whisk, beat the eggs until they're blended to incorporate the yolks and whites, but no more. Add the cream (or milk or water if you prefer), chives (if desired), salt (if desired), and pepper, and beat a few seconds to blend well.

2 Melt the butter in a 10-inch skillet over medium heat. (Don't let it burn.) Pour in the egg mixture. As the mixture begins to set, use a heatproof rubber spatula or wooden spoon to pull the eggs gently across the bottom and sides of the pan, forming large, soft lumps. The eggs are cooked when the mixture is no longer runny.

Vary It! *You can dress up this basic scrambled eggs recipe by adding different seasonings to the liquid egg mixture, such as a dash of Tabasco sauce, a sprinkling of dry mustard or grated Parmesan cheese, 2 tablespoons of chopped fresh parsley or basil, or a teaspoon or so of freshly grated lemon.*

Per serving: Calories 228 (From Fat 167); Fat 19g (Saturated 8g); Cholesterol 450mg; Sodium 133mg; Carbohydrate 2g (Dietary Fiber 0g); Protein 13g.

Chapter 2

Gathering the Tools You Need

Recipes in
This Chapter

▶ Tuscan Bread Salad

Kitchen equipment is sort of like a car. When you first get your driver's license, a dented ten-year-old Honda Civic is nirvana. But as you become a more experienced driver, you start dreaming of a better car, maybe a new Ford Explorer. When you enter the wonderful world of cooking, you really can do fine with just a few basic tools — the ride may not be as luxurious as a new Ford Explorer, but you'll still get to the prom on time.

This chapter is all about understanding and using kitchen equipment. Learning how to use kitchen equipment properly — say, a chef's knife — is time well spent.

If you are just getting started or are on a tight budget, we suggest some essential tools. As you become more proficient, you may want to expand your repertoire — and, for that reason, we let you know about more luxurious equipment, too.

In fact, we won't waste another moment, because we know how eager you are to hear what you absolutely *must have* in your kitchen.

Collecting Your Cookware Basics

Here is our short list of bare-bones-all-I-can-spend-now kitchen equipment (you can find more detailed descriptions of some of these items later in this chapter). See Chapter 1 for information on appliances. This is our list of pots, pans, and other tools no home cook should be without:

✔ **10-inch chef's knife:** You can perform more than 80 percent of all cutting and slicing chores with this knife.

✔ **9- to 12-inch serrated bread knife:** Invaluable for cutting slices of fresh bread without squishing the loaf, and also for slicing other delicate foods like fresh tomatoes.

✔ **Paring knife:** For peeling, coring, and carving garnishes from vegetables and fruits.

✔ **10-inch nonstick frying pan:** The all-around pan for sautéing, making egg dishes, braising small quantities of food, and more.

✔ **3-quart saucepan:** For cooking vegetables, rice, soups, sauces, and small quantities of pasta.

✔ **10-quart stockpot with lid:** For making stocks or large quantities of soup, pasta, and vegetables. You'll be surprised by how often you use this pot.

✔ **Heavy-duty roasting pan:** For cooking everything from beef brisket to your Thanksgiving turkey, roasting pans have high sides to keep in all those juices you can use to make gravy.

✔ **Liquid and dry measuring cups and measuring spoons:** So you don't botch up recipes by using too much or too little of something.

✔ **Strainer:** Essential for certain sauces, pastas, salads, and soups.

✔ **Meat thermometer:** Why guess?

✔ **Vegetable peeler, heatproof rubber spatula, and a few wooden spoons:** Don't go off the deep end buying little kitchen gizmos; these tools are all you need to get started.

Pots and Pans 101

Have you ever wondered what the difference is between a pot and a pan? If it has two opposite-set handles and a lid, it's classified as a *pot. Pans* have one long handle and come with or without lids. This section gives a rundown of important pots and pans and how to evaluate them, including the must-haves listed in the earlier section "Collecting Your Cookware Basics" and lots of other types of fancy pots and pans you don't need but may decide to acquire anyway.

Comparing cookware before you buy

Pots and pans come in all kinds of material, from aluminum with a nonstick coating to heavy-duty stainless steel to expensive copper to muscle-building cast iron coated with enamel. The more you cook, the more uses you'll find for different kinds of pots and pans, and the more you'll develop your own tastes and preferences for different types of pots and pans and different materials.

Here are some things to keep in mind when buying cookware:

- ✔ **Examine how you cook and how you'll use equipment.** For example, if you do a lot of fat-free and lowfat cooking, you'll want to invest in several nonstick pieces, which require less butter or oil during cooking because food tends not to stick to them, so your meals contain less fat.

- ✔ **Think twice about buying whole sets, even if they're on sale, unless you can use every piece.** Sets are limited to one type of material and one style, whereas you may be better off with various styles and materials. And why pay for three saucepans when you'll use only one?

- ✔ **Grasp the handle of the pan in the store.** It should sit comfortably in your hand. Ask yourself whether having a heat-resistant handle is important, or whether you will always remember to cook with a potholder.

Pots and pans have handles with varying degrees of heat resistance. Many pans with metal handles are made to withstand extreme temperatures. Sometimes cooking starts on top of the stove and finishes in the oven or under the broiler. Just to be sure, assume that every handle is roaring hot, no matter how well made; never grab one without a *real* potholder. Don't use a cotton dish towel as a substitute for a potholder; not only could a dish towel catch on fire, but it's also too thin to provide proper protection from a hot handle, and if it's even a little wet, it will conduct heat quickly and could cause a burn.

- ✔ **Buy the best equipment you can afford.** It's the same philosophy you use when buying a man's suit: One quality, durable suit is far preferable to two cheesy getups. Cheap, flimsy pots and pans need to be replaced after a few years of normal use.

- ✔ **Consider the appearance of your cookware.** Appearance is especially important if you decide to hang your pots and pans for decoration. Stainless steel and copper look great hanging from a sturdy pot rack in a gourmet kitchen.

Investing in the essentials . . . and then some

The following list of different kinds of pots and pans is not exhaustive, but it will get you started. We begin with the pots and pans we think you'll use the most — the essentials most home cooks will use again and again. We end the list with the pots and pans you won't use as often or probably don't need at all, unless you harbor dreams of having your own show on the Food Network. (It could happen!)

Heavy-gauge cast-iron skillet

The cast-iron skillet, shown in Figure 2-1, has been a standard in American and European kitchens for hundreds of years and still outperforms contemporary cookware in some respects (for example, browning, blackening, and searing). Better yet, a cast-iron skillet is one of the most inexpensive pans you can find, and it will outlast most other skillets as well. Tag sales and antique shops are loaded with them.

Figure 2-1:
You use a cast-iron skillet for browning, searing, and more.

Before using a cast-iron skillet for the first time, season it by wiping it with vegetable oil and then heating it on the range on a medium setting for about 2 minutes. In addition, you must thoroughly wipe the skillet dry after washing it to prevent rust. Clean the skillet gently with soap and water; never scour with metal pads. (Plastic pads are fine.) Look for a skillet with a spout for pouring off fat. Before storing, wipe the skillet with a few drops of vegetable oil to keep the surface seasoned and to help develop that characteristic non-stick coating of well-used cast iron. For recipes and more details on choosing and caring for cast-iron cookware, check out *Cast-Iron Cooking For Dummies* by Tracy Barr (Wiley).

Sauté pan

The sauté pan is one of the most basic pans. You'll probably use it all the time, so get a good, heavy-duty one. We recommend a heavy aluminum nonstick sauté pan or, if you prefer the kind of pans chefs tend to like, a heavy duty stainless steel pan, which requires the use of more oil and butter to keep food from sticking but also collects more bits of food for making delicious sauces. The choice is yours, but nonstick is also easier to clean (although not usually made for the dishwasher), if that is a consideration for you.

Your sauté pan should have straight or sloped sides (see Figure 2-2) and be at least 10 or 12 inches in diameter and 2 inches deep, which is ideal for sautéing, braising, frying, and making quick sauces. Look for one with a lid so that you can cover and simmer food in small amounts of liquid.

Figure 2-2:
You can use a nonstick sauté pan to sauté foods in just a little fat.

saute´ pan

Nonstick coatings are the best aid to novice cooks since grocery stores started selling spaghetti sauce in jars. Nonstick pans have great appeal with today's emphasis on lowfat cooking. You can sauté potatoes, vegetables, fish, poultry, and meats in very little oil or butter. Nonstick pans don't brown foods as well as regular pans do, but they're easier to clean, and the convenience may be worth it.

In recent years, nonstick pans have improved tremendously, and the linings last longer than before (ten years or more) — as long as you don't use metal utensils with them. A few new varieties even work with metal utensils and have lifetime guarantees so that if they do scratch, you can get new ones. So many brands exist that keeping track of them all is difficult. Look for well-known manufacturers, such as All-Clad, Calphalon, Cuisinart, and WearEver.

Don't buy an inexpensive pan (whether nonstick or regular) that is thin and light — it will warp over time. A good sauté pan should have some heft to it. Purchase pots and pans from a major manufacturer that stands behind its products and will quickly replace or repair damaged goods.

Saucepans

A saucepan can be stainless steel with a copper or aluminum core, heavy-gauge aluminum, or a combination of metals. It is an all-around pan used for cooking vegetables, soups, rice, and sauces for pasta and other dishes. (See Figure 2-3.) You'll want to own a number of saucepans in different sizes. A 1- to 1½-quart saucepan is perfect for melting small quantities of butter or chocolate or for warming milk. A medium 2- to 3-quart saucepan is essential for making sauces. And saucepans that are 4 quarts or larger are suitable for making soups, steaming vegetables, or boiling a moderate amount of pasta or rice.

Roasting pans

A well-equipped kitchen should have one oval roasting pan, about 12 inches long, and a large rectangular one, about 14 x 11 inches. An oval roasting pan is suitable for poultry and small roasts; a 14-inch rectangular one can handle two chickens or a large roast. The oval one should be enameled cast iron so that it can double as a gratin pan (see the following section); the rectangular pan can be heavy-gauge aluminum or stainless steel.

Figure 2-3:
You use a saucepan to boil foods and make sauces.

9-x-13-inch baking dish or casserole with lid

Another classic you'll want to own is the versatile 9-x-13-inch baking dish or covered casserole. Whether made of aluminum, glass, or ceramic, it's great for making casseroles, roasting winter vegetables, or baking brownies, other bar cookies, and cakes.

Enameled cast-iron stew pot (Dutch oven)

This attractive, all-around stew pot, also called a *Dutch oven,* is ideal for slow-cooking stews, soups, and all sorts of hearty winter meals. (See Figure 2-4.) Enamel doesn't brown food as well as cast iron that isn't coated or plain stainless steel, however. You may want to brown or sear meat in a separate pan before adding it to the Dutch oven. A 4-quart version made by Le Creuset and a similar one from Copco are excellent.

Figure 2-4:
An enameled stew pot, or Dutch oven, is best for cooking stews and soups.

Stockpot

A stockpot is indispensable in any kitchen. It can serve many functions: soup making, braising, steaming, and poaching, to name a few. Look for a tall, narrow, 10- to 14-quart heavy-gauge pot with a tight-fitting lid that can hold a steamer basket (see Figure 2-5). Inexpensive circular steamers open and close like a fan to fit different sizes of pots and pans. Heavy aluminum is fine for a stockpot; stainless steel costs twice as much.

Figure 2-5:
You make soups and much more in a stockpot. With a steamer basket, it doubles as a steamer.

stockpot

Rondeau (shallow, straight-sided pot)

A rondeau (pronounced *ron-DOE*) is great to have on hand when you entertain — and of course you will! A straight-sided pot with two handles and a lid, as shown in Figure 2-6, a 12-inch rondeau (the size we recommend) can hold enough food to serve eight people or more. If you just got a raise, splurge for heavy-gauge copper, which is expensive but beautiful to serve from. Stainless steel is good, too, but make sure that it has a copper or aluminum core for efficient heat conduction. Stainless steel alone is not an efficient heat conductor. (See the sidebar "Pros and cons of different materials," later in this chapter.)

Figure 2-6:
A rondeau can go from oven to table.

rondeau

A rondeau has many uses, among them braising, stewing, and browning large quantities of meat, poultry, or fish. Look for brands like All-Clad, Cuisinart, Sitram, Calphalon, Paderno, and Magnalite.

Sauteuse evasée (slope-sided saucepan)

This Gallic mouthful (also called a slope-sided saucepan) refers to a little pan that is the workhorse of the French kitchen. If you ever splurge on a piece of copper cookware, we recommend a sauteuse evasée (pronounced saw-TOOZ eh-va-SAY), which is 8 to 9 inches in diameter with a volume of about 3 quarts. (See Figure 2-7.) A sauteuse evasée may be referred to as simply a saucepan, which is its major role. Its sloped sides (*evasée* refers to the sloped sides) make for easy whisking.

Figure 2-7:
You use a
sauteuse
evasée
mainly as a
saucepan.

sauteuse evasée

Copper (lined with stainless steel or tin) provides the best heat control of all metals. That control is the secret of well-textured sauces. Stainless steel with copper or aluminum sandwiched in the base works very well, too, and is less expensive than the all-copper variety.

Wok or stir-fry pan

A wok is a large, bowl-shaped pan with a rounded bottom that sits inside a disk that fits over your heat source. Woks work best over a gas flame, but you can still use them if you have an electric stove. In a wok, the very bottom gets super hot, while the sides are cooler, so woks cook meat and vegetables very quickly, leaving vegetables bright and crispy and meats crisp on the outside and tender on the inside. You can cook meat and vegetables in a stir-fry-like technique by using a sauté pan, but for really authentically cooked Chinese food, only a wok will do.

Pasta pot

A large, 8-quart stainless steel pot fitted with a lid is the perfect size for cooking ½ to 2 pounds of pasta (or you can use your stockpot instead).

Pancake griddle

If you have hungry children around the house, this flat, nonstick griddle is well suited for pancakes, grilled cheese sandwiches, bacon, and the like. Of course, you can always use the sauté pan for these chores.

Omelet pan or skillet

A 10-inch omelet pan or skillet with curved sides, shown in Figure 2-8, is handy to have around. Contrary to what manufacturers say, reserving the omelet pan exclusively for eggs isn't necessary. An omelet pan is also excellent for sautéing potatoes and other vegetables. (See Chapter 4 for more information about sautéing.) But if you keep the pan (whether nonstick or untreated metal) in pristine condition and grease it well before cooking, you can make picture-perfect omelets.

Figure 2-8:
Omelet pans
are great for
making
scrambled
eggs, fried
eggs,
frittatas, and
more, but a
sauté pan
works, too.

Gratin pan

Novice cooks tend to make many one-pot dishes. To give these entrees a delicious finishing touch, often by broiling to crisp the top, you should have a gratin dish, shown in Figure 2-9. Unlike Dutch ovens, gratin dishes are shallow, measure from 10 inches long and up, and do not have a lid. A 12-inch dish can feed six or more people. These pans are ideal for macaroni and cheese, turkey casserole, gratin of potatoes, and many other simple dishes. Some are attractive enough to go from oven to table.

Figure 2-9:
A gratin pan
is handy for
finishing
one-pot
dishes.

Extras you may not want to live without

Just as you don't need but might enjoy a bread machine or pasta maker, you also don't need a pizza stone, fish poacher, or other similar kitchen luxuries. But that doesn't mean you won't want them!

A pizza stone is a clay disk that you use in place of a metal pizza pan, and it cooks pizza crust just right, whether its homemade or the frozen kind. You can also buy other disks, planks, and baking or roasting implements made from atypical materials, designed to cook in different ways, such as cedar baking planks, which chefs sometimes use for cooking fish.

A fish poacher is a typically steel or copper pot that is a long, thin oval, perfectly sized to hold a fish. It has a lid and poaches fish nicely, but of course you can also do this job in a regular large pot with a lid. The fish poacher, however, requires less liquid because the pot fits snugly around the fish.

For more on the many, many options in baking pans, see the section "Tools for Mixing and Baking," later in this chapter.

If you browse your favorite kitchen store or kitchen Web site, you'll likely see even more different kinds of pots, pans, and other cooking implements. We recommend that you start with the basics and then expand as your skills and interests grow.

From Slicing to Dicing: Knives for All Occasions

Investing in quality knives yields dividends for years. A good chef's knife will be your constant companion in the kitchen, but you will use other knives again and again, too. This section tells you what you need to know about knives.

Selecting the knives you need

Knives are often sold in sets of six to eight, which can be a bargain. But think twice. Do you really need a boning knife or a filleting knife right now? Sometimes buying what you need as your skills progress makes more sense.

Home cooks really need only three essential knives: a 10- to 12-inch chef's knife, a 9- to 12-inch serrated (bread) knife, and a small paring knife.

A *chef's knife* (shown in Figure 2-10) is generally 10 to 12 inches long and can be used for all sorts of chopping, slicing, dicing, and mincing. This knife is really the workhorse of the kitchen, so investing in a great chef's knife always pays off.

Figure 2-10:
A chef's knife is handy for all sorts of chopping chores.

chef's knife

Here is a dish in which the chef's knife goes into action — chopping, slicing, and trimming.

Tuscan Bread Salad

This wonderful salad, typical of the Tuscan countryside in Italy, is ideal for entertaining. Serve it with grilled fish or chicken, or as a light lunch all on its own. If you have leftovers, you can refrigerate it overnight; more than that and it gets soggy.

Tools: *Chef's knife, bread knife, cotton towel, two large bowls*

Preparation time: *15 minutes, plus 30 minutes for marination*

Yield: *Serves 4*

1 country loaf of bread (or 1½ baguettes), sliced thinly and left out overnight

½ cup red wine vinegar

4 scallions, trimmed and chopped (including green part)

1 cucumber, peeled and sliced crosswise (⅛ inch thick)

1 red or yellow bell pepper, cored, seeded, and sliced into thin strips

3 tomatoes, halved and chopped

20 fresh basil leaves, sliced thinly, or 1 teaspoon dried basil

8 to 12 anchovy fillets, rinsed and chopped (optional)

6 ounces canned tuna (in oil), drained and flaked

6 tablespoons olive oil

1½ teaspoons salt

1½ teaspoons black pepper

1 teaspoon chopped fresh marjoram (or ½ teaspoon dried marjoram)

1 Tear the bread roughly and soak it in ¼ cup of the vinegar mixed with enough water to soak it through. After 2 minutes, place it in a paper towel and press to squeeze out as much liquid as possible. Place the bread in a large bowl with the scallions, cucumber, bell pepper, tomatoes, basil, anchovies (if desired), and tuna.

2 In a separate bowl, combine the olive oil, the remaining ¼ cup vinegar, salt, and pepper. Stir to combine well. Add this dressing to the vegetable-bread mixture and toss well. Let sit for 30 minutes at room temperature. Taste for seasonings — it may need more salt and pepper. Sprinkle the marjoram over the top and serve.

Tip: *Nothing evokes the fresh flavors of summer like fresh basil. But basil is very fragile. Shortly after you chop it, the pieces start to darken — the flavor is still there, but the appearance is off-putting. Always chop basil just before using it.*

Per serving: *Calories 559 (From Fat 240); Fat 27g (Saturated 3g); Cholesterol 11mg; Sodium 1,597mg; Carbohydrate 67g (Dietary Fiber 9g); Protein 20g.*

Have you ever tried to slice a baguette with a regular knife? It's not only frustrating, but also dangerous. So, to remedy that situation, we put a serrated knife on our list of essential knives.

A *serrated knife* (shown in Figure 2-11), generally with an 8- to 10-inch blade, is essential for cutting bread. Hard-crusted French or Italian bread dulls a chef's knife quickly. Look for a serrated knife that has wide teeth.

A *paring knife* (shown in Figure 2-12), with a blade from 2 to 4 inches long, is for delicate jobs like peeling apples and other fruits, trimming shallots and garlic, removing stems from strawberries, coring tomatoes, or making vegetable or fruit decorations.

Be sure to keep the following ideas in mind when you select knives:

- ✔ Every department store carries kitchen knives these days, and some knives look quite impressive. But don't buy knives on appearance alone. Hold a knife. If it's well constructed, it should feel substantial in your hand. The handle should be comfortable. The knife should be *balanced* — that is, the handle should not be significantly heavier than the blade or vice versa.

- ✔ Home cooks should buy high-carbon stainless steel knives with riveted wooden handles. These knives are durable and don't rust the way carbon steel knives do.

- ✔ The best knives have a tapered blade that runs from the tip to the base of the handle — the technical term is *forged*.

✔ The most reputable knife brands include the following:

- Chef's Choice
- Global
- Henckels
- Hoffritz
- International Cutlery
- Sabatier
- Wüsthof

Using knives safely

Every year, hundreds of thousands of people wind up in hospital emergency rooms as a result of kitchen accidents involving knives. Many injuries have resulted from time-pressed, hungry people trying to pry apart frozen hamburgers or slice through hard bagels. Don't make their mistake! Slice away from your hand, keep your fingers clear of the blades, and don't ever use the palm of your hand as a cutting board.

When using your chef's knife to mince things like garlic or parsley, keep the tip on the cutting board and pump the handle up and down quickly. (You've probably seen professional chefs do this on television.) However, because that knife is moving fast, be extra careful about your fingers. Keep your fingertips curled under when holding the food you are chopping, so that if you do misfire, you're more likely to hit a hard knuckle than a soft fingertip. Practice makes perfect when using a chef's knife, so practice, but practice safely.

Always use a cutting board when using your knife, and be sure the board doesn't slide around the counter. Use a cutting board with rubber feet that help the board grip the counter, or put your slippery plastic cutting board on a towel for traction.

Home cooks may want to have their knives (especially high-carbon stainless, the most common type) professionally sharpened only twice a year, because oversharpening wears down the blade. Your local butcher or gourmet retailer may sharpen them for free. Electric home sharpeners are okay, but they can't match a professional using a rotating stone.

To get the best from your knife, run the blade over a *steel* (a 12-inch-long steel shaft with a handle) every time you use it. Doing so realigns the molecules on the blade and restores the sharp edge. See the sidebar "Honing a knife with a steel" for illustrated instructions.

Honing a knife with a steel

Really good knives are only as good as their sharpened cutting edges, and those edges don't stay sharpened by themselves. To keep your knives in peak cutting condition, here's how to sharpen them:

1. **Grab the steel firmly and hold it slightly away from your body and at a slight angle, as shown in the accompanying figure.**

2. **Hold the knife firmly with the other hand and run the blade down the shaft at about a 30-degree angle.**

3. **Start near the tip of the steel and, as you move down the steel, run the blade from near handle to tip.**

4. **Repeat on the other side of the blade and keep alternating until you've honed each side of the blade (about ten times).**

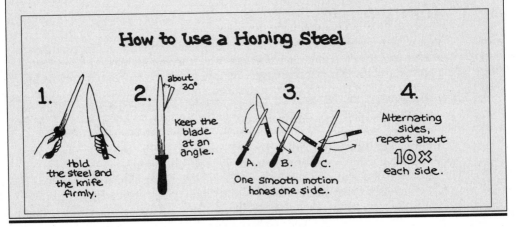

How to Use a Honing Steel

1. Hold the steel and the knife firmly.

2. about 30° Keep the blade at an angle.

3. A. B. C. One smooth motion hones one side.

4. Alternating sides, repeat about 10X each side.

Tools for Mixing and Baking

Baking requires a unique set of pots, pans, bowls, spoons, whisks, and spatulas. While there is some crossover — for instance, you might make a lasagna in your 9-x-13-inch baking pan— you'll probably reserve many of your baking pans, mixing bowls, and stirring equipment for baking because baking tools and equipment are designed specifically for that purpose.

Whether you're making bread, birthday cake, chocolate chip muffins, or your mother's killer recipe for homemade brownies (or try our recipe for homemade brownies in Chapter 14), the right baking equipment makes these jobs easier. Here's what you need:

Stainless steel, glass, or ceramic mixing bowls: Mixing bowls are among the most frequently used items in every kitchen. Buy bowls with flat bottoms for good balance in these sizes: 8 quarts, 5 quarts, 3 quarts, and 1½ quarts. Buy them in sets that stack and store easily. You can use these bowls to mix batters for cakes, cookies, or muffins; whip egg whites or whipped cream; let bread dough rise; or even toss salads, whip up sauces and dressings, or store leftovers.

Whisks: Whisks should be made of stainless steel. You use a stiffer *sauce whisk,* about 8 to 10 inches long, to blend sauces, such as béchamel and some cream sauces. You use a larger, rounder one, sometimes called a *balloon whisk,* generally 12 to 14 inches long, for whipping eggs and heavy cream.

Spoons, spatulas, long-handled forks, and tongs: Look for a variety of spoons. A solid, one-piece stainless steel spoon, about 12 to 15 inches long, fills most needs. Buy wooden spoons of various sizes for hand-mixing batters, scraping food bits off the bottom of a simmering casserole, or stirring anything cooking in nonstick cookware. A slotted, stainless steel spoon removes food solids that are cooking in hot liquid, such as ravioli.

You can use a long-handled, stainless steel ladle with a 4- to 6-ounce bowl to dole out soups and pour pancake batter onto a griddle. Buy at least two rubber spatulas and a square-tipped hard plastic turner to flip burgers and other foods. You need metal tongs for turning over tender pieces of meat or fish. Inexpensive plastic spaghetti tongs are useful for serving cooked pasta.

Baking (or cookie) sheet: For baking cookies, biscuits, and breads, a heavy-duty steel or nonstick baking sheet with ½-inch flared edges (they prevent butter and juices from spilling onto your oven) is essential. Baking sheets come in different sizes. Buy two large ones that fit in your oven, leaving a 2-inch margin on all sides to allow an even flow of heat during baking.

Jelly roll pan: This 15-x-10-inch shallow rectangular baking pan holds cake batters and egg batters that are filled and rolled. If you ever saw a Yule Log and wondered how the filling ends up swirled into the center, this pan is the answer. (You spread the filling over the cake and then roll it up, starting with one of the short sides.) Buy one made of heavy aluminum.

Round cake pans: Standard layer cake recipes call for two 8-x-2-inch or 9-x-2-inch pans. Choose anodized or nonstick aluminum.

Square cake pan: For making brownies or gingerbread, you need an 8- or 9-inch square, 2-quart capacity pan. Anodized aluminum and other nonstick materials make removing the brownies easier.

Muffin tins: For baking quick breads and muffins, you need a 12-cup tray of nonstick or heavy-gauge aluminum. It's handy to have a box of paper muffin liners so you don't have to grease and flour each metal cup.

Pie pan: A glass or aluminum pan that is 9 inches in diameter suits most standard recipes.

Rolling pin: You don't need an arsenal of rolling pins like professional pastry chefs have. For home baking, get a two-handled, hardwood rolling pin that is about 15 inches long.

Cooling racks: Cookies and cakes removed from the oven need to cool. Racks allow air to circulate around them and vent steam. They come in many shapes and sizes. Buy two 12- to 14-inch racks made of chromed steel.

Pastry board: A pastry board is a marble board that looks like a really fancy cutting board. It's not for cutting, though. The marble stays cool so when you knead or roll out pastry dough (such as pie crust or biscuit dough), it won't stick as easily and the butter or shortening will stay cooler, which translates to flakier pastry.

Loaf pan: For baking breads, terrines, and meat loaf, you want a sturdy, 6-cup loaf pan. (See Figure 2-13.)

Figure 2-13:
You can bake all sorts of foods in a loaf pan.

loaf pan

Springform pan: With its hinged-release, detachable bottom, a springform pan easily unmolds cheesecakes, delicate tarts, and cakes with crumb crusts. Get a 9- to 10-inch pan of heavy-gauge aluminum. (See Figure 2-14.)

Figure 2-14:
Use a springform pan to make delicious desserts.

springform pan

Flour sifter: Not all baking recipes call for sifted flour, but when they do, you need a sifter to aerate the flour and eliminate lumps. A 3-cup stainless steel sifter with a rotating handle is a good choice.

If you don't have a sifter and need sifted flour for a recipe, you can use a strainer. (See Figure 2-15 for instructions.)

How to Sift Flour If You Don't Have a Sifter

1. Pour flour into a strainer.

2. Use your hand to lightly tap the strainer

– OR – tap the strainer on the inside of the bowl.

Figure 2-15:
In a pinch, you can sift flour by using a strainer.

Pastry brush: To apply glazes and coatings to breads and cakes, use an all-purpose, 1½-inch pastry brush with natural bristles. Pastry brushes are also essential for basting food with pan drippings or sauces. Buy several brushes at a time because they wear out quickly. Clean the brushes with a mild dish soap, rinsing thoroughly.

Cake tester: A cake tester helps you determine whether your cake is finished. Pierce the cake with the needle-thin tester; if it comes out free of sticky batter, the cake is done. In a pinch, you can use a toothpick instead.

Metal or plastic dry measuring cups: To follow precise recipes, you need a set of dry measuring cups — ¼ cup, ⅓ cup, ½ cup, and 1 cup. Metal is better than plastic, which isn't as durable.

Glass or plastic liquid measuring cup: Get one with a 1-cup and one with a 2-cup capacity, each with a spout for pouring liquids. Four-cup and 8-cup liquid measuring cups come in handy, too.

Metal measuring spoons: These items are essential for many recipes, especially baking. Make sure that the set you purchase comes with ¼ teaspoon, ½ teaspoon, 1 teaspoon, and 1 tablespoon capacities.

Small Appliances: Necessity or Luxury?

Some of your most useful kitchen appliances won't be large (we discuss large appliances in Chapter 1). In fact, they may be quite small, like a coffee grinder or blender. But small appliances can make a large impact on your cooking efficiency, not to mention the fun quotient! For example, cutting butter into flour for a pie crust with a cumbersome pastry blender or a couple of knives can be cumbersome, but whirling everything with a few pulses of the button on your food processor — woo-hoo! Look at that butter crumble!

You don't need to own every small appliance on the market, but you may find that some small appliances can benefit your cooking efforts and make cooking fun! If you do decide to invest in any or all of these small appliances, read product reviews on the Web first and be sure you have the storage space to keep them during the 360 days in the year when you *don't* use them. If you're like us, you'll find that you won't use some of them even weekly and that you use some of them only seasonally.

Here's something else to consider before purchasing small appliances. You can't very easily make juice or ice cream or waffles without a juice maker or ice cream maker or waffle iron. You can, however, make bread, pasta, and sandwiches without their respective appliances, so if this makes a difference to you about which items to buy, or which to buy first, great. We're glad to help.

This section is your guide to the basic small appliances. We include helpful information about what they do and whether you *really* need them.

Slow cookers and pressure cookers

Slow cookers are stoneware crocks nestled in a slowly heated metal container that cook foods for long periods at low temperatures. With a slow cooker, you can put a chicken. a roast, or a pot of rice and veggies and broth on in the morning, turn it on low, and come home eight to ten hours later to a piping hot, savory meal that fills the whole house with irresistible aromas. Although you don't *need* a slow cooker, it's great for busy people who work all day but still want a home-cooked meal when they get home. Turn to Chapter 14 for some slow cooker recipes.

On the opposite end of the scale, a pressure cooker cooks foods at extremely high pressure so that the temperature of cooking can rise beyond the boiling point of 212 degrees to a temperature up to 250 degrees! This means you can cook food very fast. Every pressure cooker is different, so follow the manufacturer's instructions, but you can expect to use less liquid and less time than you would use in cooking on the stove. Pressure cookers are also a non-necessity, but they can cook a hot meal so quickly that they provide instant gratification for those who don't like standing over the stove stirring the sauce for an hour. For more info about pressure cookers, see Chapter 14.

Toasters and toaster ovens

Everybody needs a toaster or toaster oven. You probably don't need both, and a toaster oven is more versatile but takes up more counter space. If you use your toaster for, well, toast (or bagels, English muffins, toaster pastries, and so on), then go with the one that matches your kitchen décor. If you also want to be able to broil little meals for yourself, the toaster oven is nifty.

Electric griddles and stovetop grills

Electric griddles and stovetop grills make certain jobs easier, but they also take up space and mean extra cleaning. An electric griddle plugs in to an outlet and heats up without the need for the stove. This grill is handy if you frequently make pancakes, bacon, or burgers for a crowd. A stovetop grill sits over your stove burner but can give you the feel of grilling outdoors. It catches the grease in a pan below the grill plate, but then you have to clean out all that grease and you still won't get that smoky taste. Do you need these appliances? We say probably not, unless you like variety in your cookware and you have cabinet space to spare.

Mixers, beaters, and blenders

Mixers, beaters, and blenders *are* necessary for the home cook. You'll use these all the time, to mix up cake and cookie batters, blend homemade smoothies or milkshakes, or whip up a fluffy meringue. We use our stand mixers and blenders so much that we keep them out on the counter, and you may want to do that, too, if you find that you use them almost every day.

Mixers are stand-alone contraptions that hold a bowl and also hold a beater, wire whisk, or dough hook over the bowl. Get an industrial-strength stand mixer, and it will last for years. Use the beater for batters, the whisk for egg whites and homemade whipped cream, and the dough hook to knead bread dough while you kick back and read a magazine.

Beaters, or hand mixers, are like manual stand mixers. You hold the mixer in your hand, insert the two beaters or whips, and hold it in the batter, egg whites, or whipped cream. Most hand mixers aren't sturdy enough to handle bread dough or thick cookie dough, which is why we use our stand mixers more often, but they are handy when you need something quick and portable. You can get by without a hand mixer, but they can be awfully convenient at times.

Immersion blenders are like a cross between a hand mixer and a blender. You immerse them in a saucepan of soup or anything else you want to purée right there in the pan without pouring it into the blender, blending, and returning to the heat. These tools are also great for blending smoothies or milkshakes right in the glass. They're not a necessity, but they can be useful.

The blender is definitely a must-have. Even if you don't enjoy protein shakes for breakfast or daiquiris on the weekends, you'll certainly use your blender for many kitchen chores, from chopping a cup of walnuts to making home-made salsa. Blenders and food processors can do many of the same chores, but for beverages and really smooth purées, you can't beat a blender. Go for the high-quality, heavy-duty blender because it will last for years. A cheap plastic blender can burn out in a few months.

Food processors, choppers, dicers, and slicers

A food processor (see Figure 2-16) is a versatile kitchen machine that used to be a luxury but has become a necessity for anybody who cooks a lot. Food processors have steel blades that can whip up pie crust dough in seconds, not to mention sauces, soups, and finely chopped nuts, herbs, or vegetables. Other attachments on the same machine can grate cheese or carrots, slice tomatoes, and chop celery, onions, garlic, or just about anything else you need chopped, diced, sliced, minced, or puréed. While your blender can do some of these things and can purée soups and beverages beautifully, blenders aren't as versatile. We recommend owning both, if for no other reason than to make great smoothies (see Chapter 19 for a recipe) *and* flaky pie crust (turn to Chapter 17 for an apple pie recipe).

Figure 2-16: Food processors can do a wide variety of tasks.

food processor

Small choppers can be handy for herbs, nuts, and garlic, but they're almost more trouble to clean than to do these small jobs by hand with your lovely chef's knife. Hand graters and *mandolines* (rectangular manual slicers) do these jobs without the need for electricity.

Java station: Coffee makers and grinders

If you are a coffee drinker or host parties to which you invite coffee drinkers, you'll want to have a coffee maker. Because coffee brewed from freshly ground beans is far superior, especially to the coffee aficionado with the refined java palate, anybody really serious about her cup o' joe also needs a grinder. One of our favorite appliances is a beautiful coffee maker/grinder combination. Put in the coffee beans, pour in the water, press a button, and the grinder grinds the beans, shoots them into the filter, and brews the coffee. Talk about fresh! Or, for a more European flair, use a French press, a simple device consisting of a glass carafe and a plunger. Put in ground coffee, add almost-boiling water, stir, steep, and slowly press the plunger. Voila — coffee! Everybody will be knocking on your door, coffee cakes and muffins in hand. Forget the local coffeehouse!

If you never drink coffee and don't associate with anyone who does, ignore the preceding advice and instead invest in a nice teapot to boil water for your herbal tea or hot cocoa.

Specialty appliances: Help or hype?

Now we're getting into the really fancy stuff. You don't need a juice maker, a bread maker, a pasta maker, an ice cream maker, or a sandwich maker any more than you need another pair of shoes or a jazzy yellow sports car. But maybe you want those things anyway! Maybe you're a creative type who just loves to invent all kinds of homemade ice creams or fresh juices. Bread makers fill your house with the aroma of home-baked bread with barely any effort. Homemade pasta is delicious and sure to impress your dinner guests. Maybe your kids always enjoy the whimsy of the sandwich maker or the Belgian waffle iron. Maybe you'll want to choose just one or two specialty appliances that suit your needs. We won't argue with you!

Miscellaneous Gizmos and Gadgets

Just when you thought you had everything you need, we're giving you more! These miscellaneous tools can be useful for all kinds of reasons, and we recommend you add them to your kitchen.

Kitchen timer: Don't stand in front of the oven staring at the clock like a monk at the shrine of Buddha. Set a timer and go watch *Jeopardy!* or read a book. Today, many ovens and microwaves have built-in kitchen timers, so you may not even need to buy a separate one.

Colander: Buy one made of stainless steel or plastic for draining pasta and rinsing salad greens, vegetables, and berries.

Cutting boards: Use cutting boards to save your counters from sharp knives and hot pots and pans. Plastic or composite boards are easier to clean than wooden ones and can be washed in the dishwasher. Chefs clean their wooden boards with a solution of water and bleach or rub them with lemon juice. Excessive soaking or placing wooden boards in the dishwasher causes them to splinter, warp, and crack.

Meat thermometer: Unlike great chefs, most people can't tell that a roast has finished cooking by pressing its surface. You can use two types of meat thermometers to check: An instant-read thermometer, our favorite of the two kinds, has a thin rod that lets you pierce into the roast periodically to test for doneness. An ovenproof thermometer remains inside the meat or poultry from beginning to end of cooking. See Figure 2-17 for an illustration of both kinds of meat thermometers.

Figure 2-17: Meat thermometers are essential for determining whether a roast is done.

meat thermometers

Bulb baster: Using this tool is the most convenient way to coat a roast or chicken with pan juices. A large spoon also works as a basting tool, but a bulb baster is quicker and safer for removing hot grease from the bottom of a roasting pan.

Following are 11 more handy utensils to have around your kitchen:

- Chinois (a cone-shaped sieve)
- Citrus juicer
- Lemon and cheese grater
- Multipurpose kitchen shears
- Oven thermometer
- Pepper mill
- Pie server
- Potato masher
- Salad spinner
- Shrimp deveiner
- Vegetable peeler

Chapter 3

The Bare Necessities: Stocking Your Pantry

• •

In This Chapter

▶ Getting the essential dried goods, herbs, spices, and canned and bottled goods

▶ Adding condiments and baking ingredients to your cupboard

▶ Finding out what you need in your refrigerator and freezer

▶ Selecting and storing vegetables, fruits, meats, and fish

• •

*Y*ou could probably survive for quite some time on a diet of peanut butter, canned tuna, and saltines, but eventually you'd get bored. This chapter helps to alleviate the boredom of stocking your pantry. Shopping thoughtfully not only cuts down on trips to the market but also saves you money — those 8 p.m. dashes to 7-Eleven for grated cheese add up quickly. And when you don't have time to make it to the market, what's for dinner often depends on the ingredients you have in the fridge and cupboard.

The payoff for keeping a well-stocked kitchen, with only enough perishables that you can eat in a week, is that you can whip up satisfying meals on short notice. Add some vegetables and meat to a can of chicken broth for soup or to pasta or rice for a quick and delicious dinner. Add a salad, some bread, and a glass of good wine, followed by cheese and fruit for dessert, and you'll see how wonderful it is to have your pantry at your service.

Following are a series of checklists of pantry basics. Foods such as milk, cheese, eggs, and bread are obvious items to keep stocked. Less common staples such as sun-dried tomatoes, fruit chutney, dry sherry, anchovies, and artichoke hearts are important, too, because they can instantly impart flavor and dress up everyday dishes like tossed salads, omelets, and pasta. You won't need all of these, but if you always have a few exotic ingredients on hand, you'll feel ready for just about anything!

Dry Goods: The Pantry's Backbone

Every pantry should be well stocked with dry goods. You probably consume these foods at least once a week, so buy them in bulk to save on packaging costs:

- **Assorted breads and English muffins:** All breads can be frozen. Yeast breads freeze well for 6 to 8 months. Quick breads (baked with baking powder or soda) freeze without losing flavor for 2 to 4 months.

- **Assorted coffees:** You can freeze ground or whole beans for long storage.

- **Cold and hot cereals:** Always tightly reseal cereal boxes after opening to keep them fresh.

- **Dry beans and grains:** See Chapter 16 for more information about the various types of dried beans and Chapter 4 for more information about the various types of grains.

- **Herbal and regular teas:** Store in a sealed canister in a cool, dry place.

- **Macaroni and other pasta:** See Chapter 13 for a complete pasta chart.

- **White and brown rice, wild rice, and Arborio (an Italian rice used for making risotto):** See Chapter 4 for more information about the various types of rice.

Spicing Up Your Life with Dried Herbs, Spices, and Seasonings

Herbs and spices are essential flavoring ingredients. Herbs are produced from the leaves and stems of a variety of plants; spices can come from a plant's roots, seeds, bark, buds, or berries. Here are the herbs, spices, and seasonings you should stock regularly:

- **Dry herbs:** Basil, bay leaves, dill, marjoram, oregano, rosemary, sage, tarragon, thyme, and parsley

- **Salt and pepper:** Table salt, whole or ground black pepper, whole or ground white pepper, cayenne pepper, and red pepper flakes

- **Spices:** Allspice, chili powder, cinnamon, whole and ground cloves, ground cumin, curry powder, ginger, dry mustard, nutmeg, and paprika

Purchase dried herbs and spices in small quantities. After a year or so of storage, their potency diminishes drastically. Keep all dried herbs and spices tightly sealed and away from direct heat (don't store them near the stove) and sunlight.

To get the most flavor from dried herbs, crush them briefly between your fingers before adding them to a dish. Whole spices, such as peppercorns and nutmeg, have much more aroma and flavor than those sold preground, so try grinding or grating them yourself as needed. A coffee grinder reserved for spices works well for this purpose.

Table 3-1 can help you decide which herbs go best with which kinds of dishes. (Also see Figure 3-1.) After you become familiar with the properties of these flavor enhancers, you can toss the chart and navigate on your own.

Table 3-1	A Few Fresh Herbs You Should Know
Herb	*Description*
Basil	Pungent, sweet flavor. Most fresh varieties are dark green, except for the purple-leafed opal basil. Available as fresh sprigs or crumbled dry. Essential to Mediterranean cooking, especially Italian and French cuisine. Excellent with tomatoes, eggs, pasta, poultry, fish, and green salads, and in vinaigrettes.
Bay leaf	Strong, herbaceous taste. Sold as a whole, dried leaf. Excellent in long-cooking dishes like soups, stews, poaching liquid, marinades, pot roasts, rice casseroles, stuffings, and barbecue sauces. Remove the leaf before serving the dish.
Chervil	Quite aromatic, with delicate licorice-like flavor. Available as fresh sprigs (mostly in summer) or crumbled dry. Use with fish and shellfish, eggs, chicken, tomatoes, asparagus, summer squash, eggplant, herb butters, sauces, green salads, and soups.
Chives	Delicate mild-onion flavor. Sold in thin fresh stalks, chopped, or dried. Wonderful in cream sauces or soups, with chicken, eggs, shellfish, or marinated salads, or as a plate garnish.
Cilantro or Chinese parsley	Extremely pungent and aromatic. Sold in fresh, curly-leafed bunches. Found in Mexican and Asian dishes and works well with rice, fish, pork, ham, salsa, avocado, and tomato.
Dill	Delicate caraway flavor. Sold in feathery, fresh bunches or as dried seeds. Use seeds in pickling recipes; use fresh leaves with fish and shellfish, omelets, chicken, turkey, dressings and vinaigrettes, cold salads and marinades, fish mousses, and pâtés.
Marjoram	A little like oregano in taste, but much milder and sweeter. Sold fresh or crumbled dry. Extremely versatile herb. Add to almost any vegetable dish. Especially good with sweet potatoes, squash, tomatoes, corn, stuffings, stews, omelets, soups, herb butters, rice, pork, lamb, beef, poultry, or any fish.

(continued)

Table 3-1 *(continued)*

Herb	Description
Mint	Fresh scent and a sweet, pungent flavor. Most common varieties are standard peppermint and spearmint. Sold in fresh bunches or crumbled dry. Terrific in cold grain and rice salads, with fresh fruit, in cold fruit soups and sauces, and with marinated vegetable salads of cucumber or tomato; also good with grilled chicken, pork, lamb, and shellfish and in cold drinks like iced tea.
Oregano	Intense flavor. Sold fresh or crumbled dry. An essential ingredient in Italian and Greek cooking. A little goes far with poultry, tomato sauces, egg dishes, vegetable stews, and stir-fries.
Parsley	Fresh-flavored and slightly tart. Available year-round in fresh bunches or crumbled dry. Two common fresh varieties are the stronger-flavored Italian flat leaf and the curly leaf. An all-purpose herb; use in savory soups or stocks in bouquet garni, stews, dressings, stuffings, and frittatas, with fish, poultry, beef, pork, lamb, veal, game, and all vegetables. Also a pretty plate garnish.
Rosemary	Quite aromatic, needle-shaped leaves smell a little like lemon and pine. Sold as fresh sprigs or dried. Use sparingly with vegetables and in stuffings, rice dishes, and stews. Excellent with game, meats (especially grilled), chicken, halibut, salmon, tuna; in herb breads; or to flavor oils and marinades. The stem of the rosemary herb is rather tough and woody. Pull the needles or leaves off the stem, and mince them finely before using. Discard the tough stem.
Sage	Green-gray or purple oval leaves with a slightly bitter mint taste. Available in fresh sprigs, crumbled dry, and ground. Use sparingly. Excellent in poultry stuffings, pâtés, fish and chicken stews, chicken salads, meat loaves, and herb butters, with halibut and salmon, and for seasoning meat and poultry roasts.
Savory	Full-bodied herb that some people say tastes like a cross between mint and thyme. Fresh sprigs available in two varieties: winter savory and milder summer savory. Crumbled dry available year-round. Excellent with fresh or dried bean salads, most fish and shellfish dishes, omelets, soufflés, rice dishes, stuffings, meat and poultry, tomatoes, potatoes, artichokes, and onions.
Tarragon	Aromatic herb with assertive, licorice-like flavor. Sold as fresh whole sprigs, crumbled dry, and whole dried leaves. Fresh tarragon, widely available in the summer months, has the most subtle flavor. Use with chicken, pork, lamb, veal, fish, shellfish, omelets and other egg dishes, dips and dressings, mayonnaise, vegetable casseroles and salads, herb butters, and as flavoring for white vinegar and hot or cold potato dishes.

Herb	Description
Thyme	Tiny leaves with minty aroma and tealike taste. Sold as fresh sprigs and crumbled dry. Fresh varieties include lemon, orange, and French (the common variety). Add to vegetables, meat, poultry, fish, egg dishes, soups, stews, cream sauces, meat loaf, pâtés, chowders, stuffings, and bouquet garni.

Figure 3-1:
Types of
herbs.

Spices, which are almost always sold dried, have been a vital element in international cooking since Byzantine times. Most spices come from the East, where they were introduced to Europe during the Crusades.

Dried spices are generally more concentrated than dried herbs, so use them carefully. If a recipe calls for 1 tablespoon of fresh oregano, you need only use ½ teaspoon dry oregano. After you become familiar with the qualities of different spices, your cooking repertoire expands exponentially.

The flavor of freshly ground spices is much more potent than those sold already ground. Whenever possible, buy whole spices, like nutmeg and peppercorns, and grate or grind them yourself before using them. You can purchase a small spice grater for just this purpose.

Whole spices also can be wrapped and tied in a piece of cheesecloth, added to soups and stews, and then removed before serving. Cloves are often stuck into an onion and then added to a stew.

Store spices in a cool, dry place and try to use them within 6 to 10 months. Table 3-2 lists the more common spices.

Table 3-2	A Few Spices You Should Know
Herb	*Description*
Allspice	Spice berries of the evergreen pimiento tree with tastes of cinnamon, nutmeg, and cloves — hence the name. Sold as whole, dried berries or ground. Excellent in both sweet and savory dishes — pâtés, stews, chili, poached fish, meat loaf and meatballs, pumpkin and fruit pie fillings, barbecue sauce, stuffed cabbage, winter squash, chutneys and preserves, and gingerbread.
Caraway	Has a nutty, faint anise flavor and is commonly used in German cooking. Sold as dried seeds. Found in rye bread and also in cakes, stews, and some European cheeses.
Cardamom	Pungent, spicy-sweet flavor. Sold as whole dried seeds and ground. Excellent in baked goods, fruit salads, pumpkin pie, and Indian curries, one of the main ingredients in garam masala, an essential spice mixture in Indian cooking.
Cayenne or red pepper	A hot, powdered mixture of several chile peppers. Sold ground. Use sparingly. Especially good in dishes with eggs, cheese, rice, fish, chicken, or ground beef.
Chili powder	A hot and spicy mixture of dried chiles, cumin, oregano, garlic, coriander, and cloves. Sold ground. A multipurpose hot seasoning; use sparingly in stews, soups, chili, egg dishes, dressings, guacamole and bean dips, barbecue sauces, and rice and bean casseroles.

Herb	Description
Cinnamon	Sweet and aromatic spice from the bark of a tropical tree. Sold whole, in dry sticks or ground. Primarily a baking spice in cakes, cookies, and pies, but also adds a savory touch to stews, curries, baked sweet potatoes, and yellow squash.
Clove	Sharp and deeply fragrant. Sold as whole dried buds or ground. Use much like cinnamon, but more judiciously. Excellent in stocks, vegetable soups, and glazes.
Coriander	Similar in flavor to caraway. Sold as whole dried seeds and ground. Seeds used for pickling; powder used for curries, lamb, pork, sausage, and baked goods.
Cumin	Slightly acidic aroma; nutty-flavored seed. Sold as whole dried seeds and ground. Essential to Middle Eastern and Asian cooking. Use in curries, chili, and bean dips and with fish, lamb, poultry, and beef.
Curry powder	A spice blend that can include more than a dozen different herbs and spices, often with cinnamon, cloves, cardamom, chiles, fenugreek seeds, mustard seeds, turmeric (which gives curry its distinctive golden color), and red and black pepper. Commercial blends tend to lose their flavor fast and should be used within 2 months of purchase. Use to season lamb, pork, chicken, rice, stuffings, and sautéed vegetables like onions, cabbage, and baked squash.
Ginger	Sharp and faintly sweet flavor; intensely aromatic. Sold dried ground, crystallized, preserved, and fresh. Use ground sparingly in curries, spice cakes, and marinades and with pork, chicken, and seafood. Use crystallized (candied) in fruit syrups and glazes and with pies and cakes. Grate fresh ginger into stir-fries of pork, chicken, beef, and fresh vegetables.
Nutmeg	Pleasing aroma; slightly sweet and nutty taste. Sold as whole seeds and ground. Delicious in white sauces, sweet sauces, and glazes, puréed vegetables and soups, eggnog, fruit pies, spice cakes, and pumpkin pie. Best freshly grated. Use very sparingly.
Paprika	Beautiful red powder; varieties range from sweet to hot. Sold ground (the Hungarian variety is considered the best). Accents dips, creamy salads, dressings, stews (like goulash), sautéed meats, chicken, and fish. Imparts rusty red color to creamed dishes and sauces.
Peppercorns	Black peppercorns are intense, hot, and aromatic. Sold cracked, finely ground, or as whole peppercorns in black and white, with black being the strongest. (All are berries from the same vine, picked at various stages of maturity.) Black pepper is perhaps the world's most popular spice, used to accent nearly every savory dish. Use freshly ground peppercorns for best effect — ground pepper quickly loses its intensity. Use white pepper to enrich cream sauces and white dishes if you don't want the pepper specks to show.

(continued)

Table 3-2 *(continued)*	
Herb	*Description*
Saffron	The world's most expensive spice. Made from dried stigmas hand picked from a special variety of purple crocus flowers. Available as powder or whole red threads (which are of better quality). A little goes a long way. Essential to classic dishes like bouillabaisse and paella, but also delicious in rice casseroles, creamed dishes, risotto, and with seafood. Imparts a pale yellow color to cream sauces and rice dishes.
Turmeric	Yellow-orange powder that is intensely aromatic and has a bitter, pungent flavor; gives American-style mustard its color. Sold as a powder. Essential ingredient in curries; use in rice and chili and with lamb and winter squash.

Peanut Butter and Beyond: Bottled and Canned Goods

Obvious bottled and canned items include canned tuna, jellies and jams, peanut butter, and cans of chicken, beef, and vegetable broth. In addition, always stock the following essentials:

- **Assorted oils and vinegars:** See Chapter 12 for a complete list.

- **Tomato paste and canned tomatoes:** For flavoring stews and sauces. You'll be glad to have canned Italian plum tomatoes and crushed tomatoes for making pasta sauces when fresh tomatoes are pale and tasteless.

- **Wines:** A dry white and a dry red wine for adding to sauces, stews, and long-simmering casseroles and soups. Dry sherry, port, and Madeira are nice to have, too. See the "Matching Wine with Food" sidebar in this chapter for info about what wines to pair with what foods.

Following are other items that can help make your cooking more inspired:

- **Anchovies:** For salad dressings and simple sauces, anchovies can lend subtle depth of flavor. They also enhance store-bought pizza or pizzas you make on a store-bought crust. (See Chapter 16 for more information about anchovies.)

- **Artichoke hearts marinated in olive oil:** Great tossed into green salads, marinated vegetable salads, and even cooked pasta.

Wining and dining: Knowing what to serve

Many a gracious host has at least a rudimentary wine cellar, whether this consists of built-in shelves in a damp basement or a simple metal wine rack on the kitchen counter. But what wines should you stock, and how do you know which wines to serve with what foods?

The best wine for a meal is the one you think tastes good with that food. In fact, a French saying confirms this: *A châque son gout,* or "personal taste rules." That being said, a few tried and tested concepts apply when pairing wine with food: walnuts and Port, lamb and red Bordeaux, salmon and Pinot Noir, dark chocolate and California Cabernet Sauvignon, to name just a few. More generally, you may have heard that white wines go with fish and poultry and other light dishes, like soup and salad, while red wines go with beef, pork, and other heavier foods such as rich casseroles and heavily sauced pasta.

Food can exaggerate, underplay, or enhance the taste of a wine or certain aspects of its taste, and wine can do the same thing for food. A classic example is a strongly flavored red wine with a light, delicate fish. The wine will overwhelm the fish, and you won't be able to appreciate the food's delicate flavor. An opposite example is a light, delicate white wine paired with a thick cut of rare steak covered in a rich sauce. The food will overwhelm the wine, and you won't be able to appreciate the wine. But again, we remind you that personal taste rules. If you like a rich buttery Chardonnay with your filet mignon, or an effusive red Italian table wine with your grilled chicken, more power to you! For much more detailed information about wines, see *Wine For Dummies,* by Ed McCarthy and Mary Ewing-Mulligan (Wiley).

Now, what should you keep in your collection for casual dinners and entertaining? Here's what you might choose for an adequately stocked wine cabinet, with a few general statements about what foods typically go with which wines. (We won't be offended if you experiment or even disagree with our suggestions.)

- Easy-to-drink, lighter red wines go well with meat, poultry, and oily fish like salmon. Examples include Merlot, Pinot Noir, Syrah (called Shiraz in Australia), Beaujolais, and those small-winery offerings labeled simply "red table wine."

- Richer, more fully-flavored red wine can accompany rich meats and sauces, heavy casseroles, and other strongly-flavored foods. Examples include Cabernet Sauvignon, red Zinfandel, and red Bordeaux.

- Easy-to-drink, light white wines match light dishes such as delicate fish, salads, and broth-based soups that aren't too highly spiced. Examples are dry Riesling, Sauvignon Blanc, Chablis, and Pinot Grigio.

- Rich, oaky, buttery California Chardonnay pairs with more strongly flavored fish, poultry, salads, and soups. A gutsy Chardonnay can also taste good with the leaner cuts of pork and beef.

- Sweet wines are suitable for serving with dessert (or *as* dessert). Try Riesling, Gewürztraminer, White Zinfandel, Vouvray, and fortified dessert wines like sherry and Port.

- Champagne or other sparkling wines are good to keep on hand because you never know when you might have cause for celebration! We think champagne goes with just about any food.

- **Beans:** Kidney, garbanzo, and baked beans for soups, salads, and quick side dishes. Refried beans for tacos, burritos, nachos, omelet fillings, and side dishes come in handy, too.

- **Canned clams and clam juice:** For quick pasta sauce or as a substitute for homemade fish stock.

- **Capers (pickled flower buds of the caper bush):** For making quick, tangy sauces for meats and poultry.

- **Cranberry sauce:** Serve with grilled meats and poultry or use as a basting sauce.

- **Hoisin sauce:** A favorite of Chinese cuisine that is made from soybeans, garlic, chile peppers, and spices. Terrific in marinades and with spareribs, roast duck, or poultry.

- **Olives:** Green, black, and stuffed for appetizers and slicing into salads and pasta dishes.

- **Roasted peppers:** For adding to marinated vegetables, tossed green salads, and creamy dips.

Condiments to Fancy-Up Any Meal

Having quality condiments and sauces — mustards, chutneys, salsas, hot sauces, barbecue sauce, and more — is always wise. Make sure to stock the following:

- **Dijon-style mustard:** Good for adding to salad dressings, dips, and sauces and for garnishing hot or cold meats and sandwiches. To produce a flavored mustard, add herbs or spices, citrus juice or zest, or a little honey to the Dijon base.

- **Ketchup:** For hamburgers and as an ingredient in fish and barbecue sauces and baked beans.

- **Mayonnaise:** A basic ingredient for many salad dressings, as well as meat and egg salads. Plus, it tastes great on a sandwich.

These items are also good to keep on hand:

- **A good bottle of mango or tomato chutney:** Chutney is a sweetened fruit condiment for broiled chicken, lamb, pork, or duck. Try using it as a basting sauce for roasting meats or poultry or for spreading on cold sandwiches of hard-cooked eggs, tuna, chicken, or turkey. Also good in yogurt-based dips and in omelet fillings.

- **Assorted relishes:** Relishes such as corn, tomato, cranberry, and onion are good for spreading on cold sandwiches and grilled and roasted meats.

- ✔ **Dill and sweet pickles:** For serving with sandwiches and also for chopping into potato, chicken, and egg salads. *Cornichons* are crisp, tiny pickles made from small gherkin cucumbers. Serve them with cheeses, roasted meats, and pâtés, or chop them into vinaigrettes or creamy dressings.

- ✔ **Horseradish:** For sandwiches, salad dressings, roast beef, ham sandwiches, raw oysters and clams, and certain cream and tomato-based sauces.

- ✔ **Pesto (jarred, or homemade and frozen):** For pasta, grilled meats, fish, poultry, or vegetables.

- ✔ **Salsa:** With grilled meats and fish, omelets and other egg dishes, salads, and traditional Mexican foods.

- ✔ **Soy sauce (dark and light, Chinese and Japanese):** For marinades, salad dressings, stir-fries, sushi, and sauces. Chinese soy sauce is stronger and saltier than the Japanese variety. Light soy sauces are for seasoning shrimp, fish, and vegetables, such as stir-fried snow peas or broccoli. Dark soy sauce, flavored with caramel, is delicious with broiled meats.

- ✔ **Sun-dried tomatoes in olive oil:** Enhance sauces (especially for pasta), tossed salads, and dressings.

- ✔ **Tabasco sauce:** For adding flavor and heat to savory dishes. Use in omelets, on steaks and French fries, and in marinades, soups, stews, and casseroles.

- ✔ **Worcestershire sauce:** For hamburgers, steak, marinades, sauces, baked clams, and Bloody Marys.

Condiments such as relishes, jellies, pickles, mayonnaise, mustard, and salsa keep for months in the refrigerator after you open them. Steak sauce, peanut butter, oil, vinegar, honey, and syrup do not require refrigeration after you open them and can be stored on a shelf or in a cool cabinet for months, away from heat and sunlight. When in doubt, always follow the storage instructions on the product's label.

Stocking Up on Baking Supplies

No one expects you to bake a cake when you get home from work at 7:30 p.m. But sometimes you need a quick dessert or sweet and have the zeal to do it yourself. If you already have everything you need, you're in business for baking! Having the ingredients on hand makes baking so much easier. Always keep these items in stock:

- ✔ **All-purpose flour (5-pound bag):** For dredging meats, fish, and poultry, and for pancakes, biscuits, and waffles, as well as baking. Store flour in a tightly covered canister, where it stays fresh for months.

- ✔ **Baking powder:** A leavening agent used in some cake, cookie, and quick bread recipes to lighten texture and increase volume. Check the sell-by date to ensure that the powder is fresh before buying. (Baking powder loses its effectiveness sitting on the shelf.) Buy a small container and keep it tightly sealed. To test whether powder is still potent, mix 1 teaspoon baking powder with ⅓ cup warm water. The solution fizzes if the powder is good.

- ✔ **Baking soda:** Used as a leavening agent in baked goods and batters that contain an acidic ingredient such as molasses, vinegar, or buttermilk. Also good for putting out grease fires and flare-ups in the oven or on the grill. Keep an open box in the refrigerator to absorb odors. (Change the box every 3 months, or it may become one of the foul odors.)

- ✔ **Granulated sugar (5-pound bag):** An all-purpose sweetener. Store in a canister with a tight-fitting lid.

Having the following items increases your range of possibilities:

- ✔ **Chocolate:** Unsweetened and bittersweet squares, semisweet chips, and cocoa powder for chocolate sauces, chocolate chip cookies, and hot chocolate. (You can find recipes for chocolate sauce in Chapter 9.)

When the temperature climbs above 78 degrees, chocolate begins to melt, causing the cocoa butter to separate and rise to the surface. If the cocoa butter separates, the chocolate produces a whitish exterior called *bloom*. Though it looks a little chalky, bloomed chocolate is perfectly safe to eat. To prevent bloom on chocolate, store it in a cool, dry place (not the refrigerator), tightly wrapped.

- ✔ **Confectioners' sugar (1-pound box):** For sprinkling over baked goods and cookies or for quick frostings.

- ✔ **Cornmeal:** Yellow or white for corn muffins and quick bread toppings for stews and baked casseroles. Keep in a canister or tightly sealed bag.

- ✔ **Cornstarch:** For thickening soups, stews, sauces, and gravies.

- ✔ **Cream of tartar:** For stabilizing egg whites.

- ✔ **Dark and light brown sugars:** For baking and making barbecue sauces and glazes for ham and pork. Dark brown is more intense in flavor than light. To keep brown sugar soft after you open it, store the whole box in a tightly sealed plastic bag. If it hardens, place half an apple in the bag for several hours or overnight and then remove the apple. This little trick softens the brown sugar.

- ✔ **Gelatin:** Unflavored and powdered for molded salads and cold dessert mousses.

- **Honey:** For sweet glazes, dressings, and syrups. To thin crystallized honey, set the bottle in a pan of hot tap water.

- **Muffin mixes in assorted flavors:** For when you don't have time to make them from scratch.

- **Vanilla and almond extract:** For flavoring whipped cream, desserts, and baked goods. (Other handy extracts include orange, lemon, and hazelnut.) Don't buy imitation vanilla extract. It's a poor substitute for the real thing.

- **Vanilla bean:** For dessert sauces and vanilla sugar. (See the Vanilla Sauce recipe in Chapter 9.) To store, wrap tightly in plastic wrap, place in an airtight container, and refrigerate. It will keep for about 6 months.

Cooling It with Refrigerated and Frozen Staples

Following are a few essential items to stock in the refrigerator or freezer:

- **Eggs:** Never be without them, for omelets, breakfast foods, and quick dinners. (See Chapter 10 for handy egg recipes and other egg tips.) Refrigerate eggs in the shipping carton to keep them from picking up odors and flavors from other refrigerated foods, and use them before the expiration or "use by" date stamped on the carton.

- **Milk:** We make our recipes with whole milk, which has about 3.5 percent butterfat. If you prefer, use 1 percent (lowfat), 2 percent (reduced fat), or skim (nonfat) milk, with the understanding that the recipe may not have as creamy a consistency. Whole milk keeps for about a week after the store expiration date. Skim milk has a shorter shelf life. Some markets sell sterilized milk in vacuum packages that last for months unrefrigerated. After you break the seal, however, vacuum-packed milk is just like any other milk and must be refrigerated. Some people also choose to stock soy milk in addition to or instead of milk. You can buy soy milk in the refrigerated section near the regular milk and also in vacuum-packed cartons. The preceding shelf-life rules apply to soy milk.

- **Pastas:** Stock various stuffed pastas, such as ravioli, in the freezer for quick dinners. You can wrap fresh pasta in freezer bags and store it for 6 to 8 months. Do not defrost before cooking. Simply drop frozen pasta into boiling water and cook until *al dente* (or tender but still pleasingly firm to the bite).

- **Sweet (unsalted) butter:** Use sweet butter in all recipes so that you can control the amount of salt. Butter has a refrigerator shelf life of about 2 to 3 weeks and can be frozen for 8 to 12 months in the original unopened carton or, if opened, in plastic freezer bags.

These items are nice to have, too:

- ✔ **Bagels, English muffins, hamburger buns, and other specialty breads:** For breakfasts and sandwiches. All bread products can be frozen in freezer bags. Thaw on the counter, in the microwave, or in the oven at 300 degrees (but take the bread out of its plastic bag first!).

- ✔ **Cottage cheese, ricotta, and cream cheese:** For adding to dressings and dips, snacking, spreading on bagels or toast, and for cheesecakes. Store in the original, covered container or foil wrapping and consume within 1 to 2 weeks.

- ✔ **Hard and semihard cheeses:** Mozzarella, Parmesan, cheddar, and blue cheeses for salads, casseroles, omelets, white sauces, and sandwiches, to grate into pasta, and just to snack on! (See the sidebar "Cheese: Milk gone to heaven" for more cheese choices.)

  Wrap all cheese in foil, a resealable plastic bag, or plastic wrap after opening. Trim off any mold that grows on the outside edges of hard cheeses. Depending on its variety, cheese keeps in the refrigerator for several weeks to months.

  We don't normally recommend buying pregrated Parmesan or Romano cheese. It quickly loses its potency and absorbs the odors of other refrigerated foods. Instead, keep a piece of cheese for grating in the fridge to use as needed. Grating your own cheese really is easy and makes a big difference in taste. Or, if you'll use it all right away, you can save time with a high-quality Parmesan or Romano that has been freshly grated at the deli.

- ✔ **Heavy cream, light cream, or half-and-half:** For making quick pan sauces for fish, poultry, and pasta. Use within a week of purchase or freeze for longer storage. Heavy cream (not half-and-half or light cream) is used for making whipped cream.

- ✔ **Ice cream or frozen yogurt:** Instant dessert; for eating guiltily in bed at midnight. After you open it, you should eat ice cream and frozen yogurt within 2 weeks. You can freeze unopened containers for up to 2 months.

- ✔ **Pie crusts:** Keep frozen shells in the freezer for up to 6 to 8 months to fill with fresh fruits and pudding fillings when you need a dessert in a hurry, or to make a quick quiche. (See Chapter 10 for a recipe for Classic Quiche Lorraine.)

- ✔ **Plain yogurt:** Good for quick dips and low-fat sauces, especially if mixed with dry mustard and various herbs. Also makes pancake batters lighter. Follow the expiration date on the package.

- ✔ **Sour cream:** You can use standard (18 percent fat), low-fat, and nonfat sour cream interchangeably in recipes. As with all dairy products, buy the container with the latest store expiration date. Sour cream should keep for about 2 weeks.

Cheese: Milk gone to heaven

Compared to most European countries, America is not a major cheese consumer. That is, cheese is not routinely part of a meal, either in addition to or in place of dessert. But if you get to know your cheeses, eating it can be a tantalizing change of pace, especially with wine.

Cheese is a perfect after-dinner course, especially if you don't have time to fuss with dessert. Serve it with fruit or with neutral crackers that don't interfere with the flavor. Let cheese reach room temperature before serving.

Trying to define which cheeses are best for dessert is sort of like saying which cars are best for driving to the supermarket — most of them can do the job, but some do it with more style. Foremost, think of what is harmonious with the meal. Strong cheeses follow strongly flavored meals, while mild cheeses go well after more delicately flavored fare. For example, you don't want to serve a very potent blue cheese after a subtle dinner of grilled chicken breasts and summer vegetables.

Wine also is a consideration. For example, sharp cheddars and tart goat cheeses go best with assertive red wines (Bordeaux, California Cabernet Sauvignons, Zinfandels, ports, and even bitter beer). You want a wine that can stand up to the potent cheese. Light cheeses like Gouda, Havarti, Monterey Jack, and Muenster call for equally delicate wines so that you have a balanced taste: Beaujolais, lighter Côtes-du-Rhône, and Barbarescos. Ask your local wine merchant for advice when choosing a wine to match cheese. For more information about wines, see *Wine For Dummies,* by Ed McCarthy and Mary Ewing-Mulligan (Wiley).

When buying cheese, remember that there's a big difference between aged cheese and old cheese. Old cheese looks fatigued and has discoloration, maybe a cracked rind, and signs of overdryness. Old cheese makes your car smell like a locker room. If cheddars look darker around the periphery than at the center, they are probably dried out. Inspect these cheeses extra carefully. Your best bet is to go to a store that sells a large volume of cheese because the inventory changes quickly and the selection is better and fresher.

As for the type of cheese to choose, here is a brief summary of some of the more common types of gourmet cheeses available on the market today. Everyone has different tastes, so try them all and see what you like:

- **Brie:** Almost a cliché because it was the first "gourmet" cheese for many American palates, spawning wine-and-cheese cocktail parties across the land. This soft, creamy cheese is generally mild tasting and goes well with most light red wines.

- **Camembert:** French, from Normandy. A creamy cheese not unlike Brie. When ripe, it oozes luxuriously. (No, really, in the world of cheese, oozing is a *good* thing.)

- **Cheddar:** One of the world's most popular cheeses. Made all over the world, but originally from England, where much of the best cheddar comes from. The flavor of this semifirm cheese ranges from rich and nutty to extremely sharp.

- **Fontina Val d'Aosta:** Italian cow's milk cheese, semifirm, subtle, nutty, and rich.

- **Goat cheese (chèvre in France):** Goat cheese ranges from mild and tart when young to sharp and crumbly when aged.

- **Gorgonzola:** From the Lombardy region of Italy. This blue-veined cheese is popular in the United States. Gorgonzola is rich and creamy yet pleasantly pungent. Creamier than Roquefort.

(continued)

(continued)

- **Gruyère:** Sort of a more gutsy version of Swiss cheese, from Switzerland. Faint nuttiness. The classic fondue cheese.

- **Mascarpone:** An Italian cow's milk cheese that has the consistency of clotted cream. Often used in cooking but can be seasoned with fresh herbs and used as a delicious dip. The cheese used in authentic tiramisù.

- **Monterey Jack:** A California cow's milk cheese in the cheddar family that is semi-soft, smooth, and very mild when young, and sharper when aged.

- **Mozzarella:** Familiar to all from pizza and lasagna fame. Mozzarella is often breaded and fried for an appetizer, called *Mozzarella in Carozza*. It's also great in salads or layered with sliced tomatoes and basil.

- **Pecorino Romano (or Romano):** A sheep's milk Italian cheese (all sheep's milk cheese in Italy is called pecorino). Pecorino Romano is soft and mild when young, with a touch of tartness. Quite tart when older, mostly grated over pasta.

- **Roquefort:** Made from ewe's milk and aged in the famous caves of Roquefort, France. Roquefort is among the most intense of all blue-veined cheeses. Has a creamy texture at its best. For Americans not used to strong cheeses, this cheese is an acquired taste.

Squeezing the Melon: Buying and Storing Fruits and Vegetables

Fruits and vegetables add color, flavor, vitamins, minerals, and fiber to the foods you eat. The quality of the produce you buy directly impacts the quality of the dishes you cook with that produce. Who wants to eat a wilted salad or a dingy bowl of fruit? The sign of a truly committed home cook is the quality of the fruits and vegetables you buy. Always seek out the best sources for produce. If you have a local farmer's market featuring seasonal produce, browse the stalls and choose what looks best. You can plan a whole meal — or at least a memorable side dish — around a really ripe carton of tomatoes and a dewy bin of fresh lettuce, or what about those blushing peaches bursting with juice for dessert? Sometimes, though, the only outlet you will have for fresh produce is your local grocery store. If so, here are some hints and tips for which items to pick. We also give you some ideas on which produce items you should always have on hand, and how to store them so they last the longest and stay the freshest.

Picking your produce

When choosing fruits and vegetables, a few rules apply across the board. Avoid fresh produce with brown spots or wrinkled skin or produce that doesn't look . . . well . . . fresh! Here are a few other produce rules to live by:

✔ Onions, shallots, garlic, and potatoes should feel very hard. Soft ones are probably overripe.

✔ Avocados and melons should feel slightly soft. Smell the stem-end of a cantaloupe and if it smells like cantaloupe, it's ripe. If it smells like nothing, it's not ripe yet.

✔ Apples and Bosc pears should be crisp and hard.

✔ Summer fruits, including peaches, nectarines, and apricots, are ripe when they give just a little when pressed and smell like peaches, nectarines, or apricots.

✔ Look for green and red grapes with a bloom or white powdery finish, which tells you they're fresh.

✔ Do we need to tell you not to buy slimy lettuce?

Stocking your produce bin like a pro

Every well-stocked cook should have on hand the following produce staples:

✔ Carrots

✔ Garlic

✔ Onions

✔ Potatoes

✔ Salad greens

You also may want to stock the following produce items, which can add flair to salads both savory and sweet, serve as tasty snacks when sliced and eaten raw, or for adding flavor to cooked dishes, from soups to stir fry:

✔ Apples, grapes, peaches, or whatever else is in season

✔ Assorted citrus fruits, such as lemons, limes, oranges, and grapefruit

✔ Bananas (available year-round)

✔ Celery

✔ Cucumbers

✔ Green onions

✔ Mushrooms

✔ Red and green bell peppers

Storing produce to last

Most fruits and vegetables are quite perishable and require refrigeration. Here are some general suggestions on storing fruits and vegetables:

- **Apples:** Refrigerate or store in a cool, dark place. Keep for several weeks.

  Apples release a gas that makes other fruits ripen more quickly, so if you don't want your fruit to ripen too fast, keep it away from the apple bowl and don't store it with apples in the refrigerator.

- **Artichokes and asparagus:** Refrigerate and use within 2 to 3 days of purchase.

- **Avocados, papayas, kiwis, and mangoes:** Keep at room temperature until fully ripened and then refrigerate them to keep for several more days.

- **Bananas:** Refrigerate to slow down their ripening. Their peel continues to darken, but not their flesh.

- **Bell peppers:** Store in the refrigerator for up to 2 weeks.

- **Broccoli and cauliflower:** Refrigerate and consume within a week.

- **Cabbage:** Keeps for 1 to 2 weeks in the refrigerator.

- **Carrots:** Keeps in the refrigerator for several weeks.

- **Celery:** Keeps for 1 to 2 weeks in the refrigerator.

- **Cherries and berries:** Keep refrigerated. For best flavor, consume them the same day you purchase them.

- **Citrus fruits (such as lemons, grapefruits, and oranges):** Refrigerated, citrus fruits, which don't ripen further after they're picked and are relatively long-storage fruits, keep for up to 3 weeks.

- **Corn:** Refrigerate and use the same day of purchase. After corn is picked, its sugar immediately begins converting to starch, diminishing its sweetness.

- **Cucumbers and eggplant:** Keep for 1 week in the cold crisper drawer of the refrigerator.

- **Garlic:** Keep garlic at room temperature, in a small bowl within reach of your food preparation area, to encourage you to use the fresh stuff. Garlic will last longer in the refrigerator, however, so if you don't use it often, keep it chilled.

- **Grapes:** Keep in the refrigerator for up to a week.

- **Green beans:** Refrigerate and use within 3 to 4 days of purchase.

- **Leaf greens (beet tops, collards, kale, mustard greens, and so on):** Very perishable. Refrigerate and consume within 1 to 2 days.

- **Mushrooms:** Store in a paper bag in the refrigerator. Use within a week.

- **Onions, potatoes, shallots, and hard-shelled winter squash (like acorn and butternut):** Keep at room temperature for several weeks to a month. Store onions, potatoes, and winter squash in a cool, dry, dark drawer or bin.

- **Pineapple:** Doesn't ripen after it's picked, and is best if eaten within a few days of purchase. Keep at room temperature, away from heat and sun, or refrigerate whole or cut up.

- **Salad greens:** Rinse thoroughly, trim, and dry completely before storing wrapped in paper towel or in plastic bags in the refrigerator crisper drawer. Keeps for 3 to 4 days. (See Chapter 12 for more information.)

- **Spinach:** Trim, rinse, and dry thoroughly before storing in the refrigerator for 2 to 3 days.

- **Summer squash (zucchini and yellow squash):** Store in the refrigerator for up to a week.

- **Tomatoes:** Store at room temperature for more flavor. Keep in a cool, dark place or in a paper bag to ripen fully. Refrigerate them after they ripen to keep them from spoiling. Then return to room temperature before eating.

- **Unripe melons and tree fruits (such as pears, peaches, and nectarines):** Keep at room temperature so that they can ripen and grow sweeter. After they're fully ripe, you can store them in the refrigerator for several more days.

Selecting, Buying, and Storing Meat, Poultry, and Fish

Meat, poultry, and fish are highly perishable foods that need to be stored in the coldest part of your refrigerator. Keep them tightly wrapped, preferably in their own drawer, to prevent their juices from dripping onto other foods.

Always check expiration dates (avoid items that are older than your car's last oil change). And never allow meat, poultry, or fish to thaw at room temperature, where bacteria can have a field day. Always thaw them in the refrigerator, which takes more time (and planning), but is by far the safest method.

Beef

Beef is rated according to the animal's age, the amount of fat, or *marbling,* in the cut (the more marbling, the more moist and tender), as well as its color and texture. *Prime* meat is the highest grade and the most expensive. In general, the most tender and flavorful meat falls under this category. But aging has a lot to do with it. Years ago, all beef aged "on the hoof," or the whole carcass, before it was shipped. Today, most meat is cut up and shipped in vacuum-sealed Cryovac containers. The aging takes place in the wrapping. Buy from butchers in your area who still age their own beef, if possible. You pay a little more, but the taste is worth the price. Aged meat is more tender and has more flavor.

Choice is the second tier of meat grading, leaner than prime. *Select* meats are best for stewing and braising.

The more tender cuts of meat include steaks such as porterhouse, sirloin, shell, New York strip, Delmonico, and filet mignon, as well as roasts like rib, rib eye, and tenderloin. Tender meats are usually cooked by the dry heat methods of roasting, broiling, grilling, and sautéing. (See Chapter 7 for roasting, Chapter 8 for broiling and grilling recipes, and Chapter 5 for sautéing recipes.)

Less tender cuts that have more muscle tissue and less fat are usually cooked by braising and stewing. (See Chapter 6 for braising and stewing recipes.) Tougher cuts include brisket, chuck, shoulder, rump, and bottom round. Figure 3-2 illustrates where the various cuts come from.

Figure 3-2:
Various cuts of meat come from different parts of a steer.

Look beyond ratings to judge meat. Meat should look bright red, never dull or gray. Excess juice in the package may indicate that the meat has been previously frozen and thawed — do not purchase it. Boneless, well-trimmed cuts are slightly more expensive per pound but have more edible meat than untrimmed cuts, so in the long run they can cost about the same.

Store meat in the meat compartment or the coldest part of the refrigerator, securely wrapped so the raw meat juices don't drip onto ready-to-eat foods. Use raw meat within two days, or by the "use by" date on the package, or freeze it. To freeze, rewrap in aluminum foil, heavy-duty plastic wrap, or freezer bags, pressing out as much air as possible and dating all packages. Freeze ground meat for a maximum of 3 months; freeze other cuts for up to 6 months. Defrost in the refrigerator or microwave.

Chicken

The tenderness and flavor of fresh poultry vary somewhat from one commercial producer to the next, so you should buy and taste a few different brands to determine which you like. Grade A poultry is the most economical because it has the most meat in proportion to bone. Skin color is not an indication of quality or fat content. A chicken's skin ranges from white to deep yellow, depending on its diet.

Most supermarkets carry five kinds of chicken:

- ✔ **Broiler/fryer:** A 7- to 9-week-old bird weighing between 2 and 4 pounds. Flavorful meat that is best for broiling, frying, sautéing, or roasting. A whole broiler/fryer is always less expensive than a precut one.

- ✔ **Capon:** A 6- to 9-pound castrated male chicken. Excellent as a roasting chicken because of its abundance of fat. Just to be sure, pour off or scoop out excess melted fat as the chicken roasts — especially if you do not have an exhaust fan — or your kitchen will resemble the Towering Inferno. Not widely available in supermarkets (it usually needs to be special-ordered).

- ✔ **Roaster or pullet:** From 3 to 7 months old and between 3 and 7 pounds. Very meaty, with high fat content under the skin, which makes for excellent roasting.

- ✔ **Rock Cornish game hen:** A smaller breed of chicken weighing 1 to 2 pounds. Meaty, moist, and flavorful for roasting.

- ✔ **Stewing chicken:** From 3 to 7 pounds and at least 1 year old. Needs slow, moist cooking to tenderize. Makes the best soups and stews.

How free is free range?

Compared to cooped-up, hormone-blasted, sunshine-deprived regular chickens, free-range chickens have a pretty cozy life. But *free range* is a bit of exaggeration in most cases. These privileged chickens do not pack lunches and take daily outings across the vast countryside, stopping for a couple of pecks in fields of clover on the way home. Most free-range chickens are enclosed in fenced areas with very limited room to maneuver. They do get some sunshine, at least, and a little exercise. And in most cases, they're chemical-free. Because it costs more to produce free-range chickens, the chicken usually costs more — sometimes just a little more, sometimes a lot more, depending on the store, the brand, and the source. Try both kinds and decide for yourself whether the taste difference is worth the price difference.

Remove the package of giblets (the neck, heart, gizzard, and liver) in the cavity of a whole bird and then rinse under running cold water and dry before cooking it. Also trim away excess fat. After preparing poultry, wash your hands and work surfaces (counters and cutting boards) with soap and water to prevent cross-contamination from bacteria.

Consume whole or cut-up poultry within 1 to 2 days of purchase. A whole, raw chicken may be wrapped and frozen for up to 12 months; parts can be frozen for up to 9 months. Defrost in the refrigerator, never at room temperature. Be sure to place the thawing package in a pan or on a plate to catch any dripping juices. A 4-pound chicken takes 24 hours to thaw in the refrigerator; cut-up parts between 3 and 6 hours. If you use your microwave to defrost poultry, do so on a very low setting and be sure to cook the poultry immediately after thawing it.

Fish

Fish falls into two broad categories: lean and oily. Lean fish include mild-tasting sole, flounder, snapper, cod, halibut, and haddock. Oily fish have more intense flavor, higher levels of heart-healthy omega fatty acids, and generally darker flesh. These include bluefish, mackerel, salmon, swordfish, and tuna. In general, you should purchase fillets of oily fish with the skin intact. That way, the fish holds together better during cooking. Lean fish usually come without the skin from the supermarket or fish counter.

Here are some of the more reasonably priced types of fish that you can try in lieu of expensive gray sole, swordfish, and the like. Always ask your fish dealer what is the freshest that day.

- ✔ **Bluefish:** Rich flavor, especially when fresh and under 2 pounds. Bake or broil.

- ✔ **Catfish:** Dense, relatively mild fish. Usually cooked in a strong sauce or deep-fried.

- ✔ **Cod:** Mild-flavored, white, firm flesh. Can be broiled, baked, fried, or braised.

- ✔ **Haddock:** Meaty, white flesh, mild flavor. Good pan-fried or braised.

- ✔ **Porgy:** Firm, low-fat, white-fleshed fish with delicate flavor. Excellent grilled or broiled.

- ✔ **Tilapia:** An increasingly popular and affordable farm-raised fish with a mild flavor. Tilapia holds together well and can therefore be cooked in many different ways, making it a favorite of restaurant chefs.

- ✔ **Whiting (silver hake):** Fine, semifirm white flesh. Subtle and delicious when broiled or pan-fried.

Freshness is the most important factor in purchasing fish. Learn to recognize it. In a whole fish, the eyes should be bright and clear, not cloudy. The gills of fresh fish are deep red, not brownish. The skin should be clear and bright with no trace of slime. Really fresh fish shouldn't smell like fish, either. Fish might smell briny but should not smell fishy. Fishy-smelling fish (ironically) isn't fresh.

If possible, have your fishmonger cut fresh fillets from whole fish while you wait. Purchase precut fillets only if they're displayed on a bed of ice, not sealed under plastic, which can trap bacteria and foul odors. Fillets should look moist and lie flat, with no curling at the edges. Consume fresh fish and seafood as soon as possible and ideally on the day of purchase. You can freeze freshly caught and cleaned fish for 2 to 3 months if they're wrapped well in two layers of freezer wrap. Although some fish merchants will tell you that you can refreeze shrimp, salmon, and other types of seafood, refreezing compromises the flavor and texture of many kinds of fish. We recommend never refreezing fish after thawing it.

Shellfish should be firmly closed and odorless when purchased. If clams or mussels don't close when tapped on the counter, toss them. Eat fresh clams, oysters, and mussels as soon as possible. Store for no more than 24 hours in the refrigerator in a plastic bag poked with small holes, allowing air to circulate. It's best to purchase shrimp in the shell. Eat shrimp the same day you purchase it. Most of all, never overcook shellfish because it gets rubbery.

Part II
Know Your Techniques

The 5th Wave   By Rich Tennant

"Why don't you start with some guacamole and I'll finish charring the peppers."

In this part . . .

The focus of this book is cooking techniques — chopping, slicing, sautéing, braising, poaching, roasting, and a whole lot more. Granted, you have a lot to absorb, but you already exhibited superior intelligence by buying this book, so the rest should be a cakewalk.

The goal of this part — and indeed this book — is to give you the basic tools you need to cook from a recipe. We explain each technique from the ground up, giving you a variety of recipes to practice with. As you gain experience, you'll learn to improvise and maybe even invent some recipes yourself.

Chapter 4

Boiling, Poaching, and Steaming

"I can't even boil water" is the would-be cook's lament. Well, grab a pot so we can tell you about this bubbly experience — and faster than you can say "instant coffee."

In this chapter, we cover three vital cooking techniques: boiling, steaming, and poaching. We concentrate here on vegetables because there are no better ways to enjoy their fresh flavors and textures. We also tell you about the different types of rice, an incredibly versatile staple, and how to cook and season them. And who can forget potatoes? In addition, we talk about poaching seafood, a surprisingly simple technique for cooking tender, succulent fish.

Cooking Food with Water: The Techniques Defined

Relax; even home ec dropouts can figure out the basic cooking techniques that involve the use of water. Cooking with water is simple, but it helps to have a little knowledge about the process so you don't overboil your vegetables to mush or serve up crunchy rice. Here are some basic terms to know:

✔ *Boiling* is bringing water to 212 degrees Fahrenheit for cooking. You don't need a thermometer. Let the water come to a *full rolling boil* (when the bubbles are rapidly breaking the surface). Covering the pot speeds the process by trapping surface heat. And no one knows why, but watching the pot really does seem to slow down the boiling process!

✔ *Parboiling* and *blanching* mean pre-cooking tough or salty foods to soften their textures and rinse out excess flavor to keep it from overwhelming a dish. Rice is sometimes parboiled (or "converted") and then packaged to shorten cooking time and retain nutrients. Bacon may be blanched to soften the flavor. Tomatoes can also be blanched to loosen their skins.

✔ *Simmering* is like a gentle pre-boil. In a simmer, tiny bubbles break the surface gently — like a soft summer shower on a still lake. (Are we going overboard? That really is what it looks like!) Simmering occurs at a lower temperature — just below a boil — and is used for long, slow cooking and braising. (Chapter 6 talks more about braising.) *Poaching* and *simmering* are virtually identical; cookbook writers use the terms interchangeably just to confuse you.

A soup or stock recipe often combines the techniques of boiling and simmering, instructing you to bring the liquid to a full boil and then to lower the heat and simmer, sometimes for a long time.

✔ *Reducing* means boiling stock or liquid to thicken and intensify the flavor, typically for use in a sauce. Reducing actually reduces the volume of the liquid by boiling off the water, leaving a thicker, more richly flavored liquid behind. Many sauce recipes ask you to reduce the stock or liquid.

✔ *Steaming* is the gentlest way to cook and is better than boiling or poaching for retaining a food's color, flavor, texture, shape, and nutrients. Steaming often involves placing food over simmering water on a perforated rack in a covered pot. When you steam foods set in a pan of water in the oven, it's called a *water bath.* Cheesecakes and custards are often baked this way. Sometimes this is also called a *bain marie,* or Marie's Bath.

You need to monitor dishes that are boiled, simmered, steamed, or poached to make sure that the water or other liquid doesn't steam away. (Otherwise, your pot will not be a pretty sight.) If necessary, add a little more liquid to prevent the food from burning.

How would you like your meat boiled?

Boiling is an ancient method of cooking. Thank your lucky stars that you didn't live in medieval times when they boiled just about everything. Meat was boiled to kill germs in food that sat out on a counter for days. Boiling also washed off salt, which was used heavily to preserve meat.

Making Rice Just Right

Before we get into recipes that demonstrate boiling, simmering, poaching, and steaming techniques, we say a few words about rice, an incredibly versatile food that is usually boiled and then simmered. Rice has an affinity with countless boiled and steamed foods, and you can season it to create exciting taste sensations.

The world is home to thousands of strains of rice. India alone has more than 1,100 types, which must make shopping a confusing endeavor. Many different cultures also have their own characteristic way of flavoring rice. To give your rice dishes an international flair, try these flavoring combinations:

- **France:** Garlic, tomatoes, fresh herbs (thyme, tarragon, basil), and vegetables or seafood

- **India:** Curry and hot spices, chicken, or vegetables

- **Mexico:** Garlic, hot peppers, onions (sometimes dried beans)

- **Middle East:** Onions, raisins, cinnamon, allspice, turmeric, cardamom

- **Southern United States (Louisiana):** Pork sausage, onions, garlic, cayenne; also with seafood

- **Spain:** Saffron, nuts, bell peppers, and other vegetables; also chicken, sausage, and seafood

While we won't expect you to memorize every type of rice on the planet, you will benefit from knowing the five basic types common to cooking today:

- **Converted or parboiled rice:** Basic white rice used for home cooking in much of the Western world; medium to long grain

- **Long-grain rice:** Includes the Indian basmati

- **Short-grain rice:** The family of Italian Arborio, used to make risotto; also used in sushi

- **Wild rice:** Not really rice at all (we get to that later)

- **Brown rice:** Healthful, unrefined rice (that means it still has the bran and germ that are removed from white rice) with a slightly nutty flavor

Each type has its textural and flavor differences, as the following sections explain.

Converted or parboiled rice

You've probably seen converted rice in the supermarket. The term *converted* doesn't mean that your rice has undergone some sort of spiritual transformation, but rather it refers to a process by which whole grains of rice are soaked in water, steamed, and then dried. This precooking, also called parboiling, makes milling easier and also conserves nutrients that are otherwise lost. Steaming also removes some of the rice's sticky starch, leaving each grain smoother in texture. This process also shortens the time you have to spend cooking the rice.

 Rice absorbs its cooking water while simmering, so getting your proportions right is important — too much water leaves the rice soupy, and too little water leaves it dry. If the rice is cooked but the cooking liquid isn't completely absorbed, place it in a colander to drain off any excess liquid. If the liquid is completely absorbed before the rice is cooked, add a little more water or stock, about ¼ cup at a time, and continue to cook until the grains are tender.

To practice, try the following simple recipe for converted rice.

☜ Converted Rice

Cooking converted rice is quick and simple. Make this often for an easy and delicious side dish to accompany just about any kind of meat or vegetables, including the Pork and Noodle Stir-Fry in Chapter 18 and the Tuna Steaks with Ginger Chili Glaze in Chapter 5).

Tools: *Medium (3-quart) saucepan fitted with a lid*

Preparation time: *About 5 minutes*

Cooking time: *About 25 minutes*

Yield: *4 servings*

2¼ cups water	*1 tablespoon butter*
1 cup converted rice	*½ teaspoon salt, or to taste*

1 Bring the water to a boil in a medium saucepan. Add the rice, butter, and salt. Stir and cover.

2 Reduce the heat to low and simmer for 20 minutes.

3 Remove from the heat and let stand, covered, until all the water is absorbed, about 5 minutes. (If you have excess water, strain it off; if the rice is too dry, add a little boiling water and stir. Let sit for 3 to 5 minutes.) Fluff the rice with a fork and check the seasoning, adding more salt and pepper to taste, if desired.

Vary It! *Basically, the more flavor in the cooking liquid, the better the rice tastes. The flavors permeate the grains, making them a superb complement to steamed vegetables or sautéed meats or poultry. To boost the flavor of your rice, replace some or all of the water for cooking the rice with chicken, beef, or vegetable broth. You can also add seasoned herbs, a dash of saffron, lemon zest or juice, or any combination of herbs and spices you like to flavor the cooking liquid. If adding fresh herbs, do so in the last 10 minutes of cooking so the herbs retain their flavor.*

Per serving: *Calories 195 (From Fat 26); Fat 3g (Saturated 2g); Cholesterol 8mg; Sodium 291mg; Carbohydrate 38g (Dietary Fiber 0g); Protein 4g.*

You can add flair to the Converted Rice recipe in many different ways. Some ideas include

- ✔ **Turmeric rice:** Use chicken broth instead of water, and then add chopped onion, minced garlic, turmeric, thyme, and a bay leaf to the broth along with the rice.

- ✔ **Sweet rice:** Add chopped onion, minced garlic, raisins, rice, chicken broth, and pine nuts or almonds just before serving.

- ✔ **Creole rice:** While the rice is cooking, place butter and chopped onion in a sauté pan and cook until the onion wilts. Add diced tomatoes and salt and pepper, cooking and stirring for 1 to 2 minutes. Add the cooked rice to the tomato mixture with chopped fresh basil, 1 tablespoon fresh lemon juice, and ½ teaspoon grated lemon zest.

- ✔ **Curried rice:** Cook chopped onions in butter in a skillet. Add the rice and chicken or vegetable stock, curry powder, salt and pepper, and ½ cup currents or chopped dried apricots. Cover and cook until done.

Long-grain and short-grain rice

Because rice goes with almost everything, making it well is a very important skill to master. Follow these tips for perfect long-grain rice:

- ✔ Always read package cooking directions.

- ✔ Always measure the amounts of rice and liquid.

- ✔ Time your cooking.

- ✔ Keep the lid on tightly to trap steam.

- ✔ At the end of cooking time, test for doneness. If necessary, cook for 2 to 4 minutes more.

- ✔ Fluff cooked rice with a fork to help separate the grains.

The term *pilaf* refers to a dish in which the grain (rice or other whole grains) is browned slightly in butter or oil and then cooked in a flavored liquid, like chicken or beef stock. After you get the technique down, you can add any flavors you like.

Basic Rice Pilaf

This rice pilaf recipe — seasoned with cumin, almonds, and raisins — gives this basic pilaf recipe a special flair.

Tools: *Medium (3-quart) saucepan fitted with a lid, chef's knife, wooden spoon*

Preparation time: *About 5 minutes*

Cooking time: *About 25 minutes*

Yield: *4 servings*

1 tablespoon olive oil	*1 cup converted rice*
½ medium yellow onion, minced	*2¼ cups chicken broth*
½ red bell pepper, minced	*½ cup chopped almonds (optional)*
1 teaspoon cumin powder	*¼ cup currants or raisins (optional)*
½ teaspoon salt, or to taste	*Black pepper*

1 In a medium saucepan, heat the olive oil over medium-high heat. Add the onion, bell pepper, cumin powder, and salt. Sauté until the onion begins to soften, about 5 minutes.

2 Add the rice and cook, stirring until the rice is coated, about 3 minutes. Pour the chicken broth into the sauté pan and bring to a boil. Stir and cover.

3 Reduce the heat to low and simmer for 20 minutes.

4 Remove from the heat and let stand, covered, until all the chicken broth is absorbed, about 5 minutes. (If the rice is too dry, add a little boiling water and stir. Let sit for 3 to 5 minutes.) Fluff the rice with a fork. Stir in the almonds and/or raisins, if desired. Taste and add black pepper to taste.

Go-With: *This slightly sweet, starchy side dish is delicious with Osso Buco (see Chapter 17), Easy Coq Au Vin (see Chapter 6), or Roasted Pork Ribs with Country Barbecue Sauce (see Chapter 7).*

Per serving: *Calories 311 (From Fat 114); Fat 13g (Saturated 2g); Cholesterol 3mg; Sodium 854mg; Carbohydrate 43g (Dietary Fiber 2g); Protein 8g.*

○ Basic Wild Rice

Wild rice may seem exotic, but it's easy to cook. Don't let the "wildness" of this dish throw you off. It has only three steps!

Tools: *Colander, medium saucepan fitted with a lid*

Preparation time: *About 15 minutes*

Cooking time: *About 50 minutes*

Yield: *4 servings*

1 cup wild rice	*2 tablespoons butter*
2½ cups water	*Salt and black pepper*

1 Wash the wild rice thoroughly before you cook it: Place the rice in a pot filled with cold water and let stand for a few minutes. Pour off the water and any debris that floats to the surface. Drain well in a colander.

2 Fill a medium saucepan with the 2½ cups of water, cover, and bring to a boil over high heat. Add the rinsed rice, butter, and salt and pepper to taste. Stir once. Reduce the heat to low and simmer, covered, for 45 to 55 minutes or until the rice is tender.

3 Fluff the rice and add more salt and pepper, if desired, before serving.

Go-With: *Basic Wild Rice tastes great with highly flavored meats. Try it with The Perfect Steak (see Chapter 7) or Glazed Leg of Lamb with Pan Gravy and Red Currant Glaze (see Chapter 7).*

Per serving: *Calories 211 (From Fat 56); Fat 6g (Saturated 4g); Cholesterol 15mg; Sodium 151mg; Carbohydrate 34g (Dietary Fiber 3g); Protein 6g.*

The technique for cooking long-grain rice and short-grain rice is essentially the same, except when making risotto, the creamy, long-stirred specialty of northern Italy. This dish uses the short-grained rice called Arborio rice (available in gourmet markets).

⏱ *Risotto*

When making risotto, you want the rice to slowly absorb enough of the hot broth to form a creamy blend of tender yet still firm grains. Giving an exact amount of liquid for making risotto is difficult. The key is to keep stirring the rice over low heat, adding only enough liquid (a little at a time) so that the rice is surrounded by, but never swimming in, broth. Make this basic recipe once or twice until you have the technique down. Then you can alter it by using the suggestions that follow the recipe or by improvising on your own.

Your risotto will be only as good as the chicken stock it absorbs. Make your own stock or buy the best commercial brand you can.

Tools: *Chef's knife, skillet or sauté pan, small saucepan with lid, wooden spoon*

Preparation time: *About 15 minutes*

Cooking time: *About 35 minutes*

Yield: *4 servings*

1 teaspoon olive oil	*About 5 cups chicken or vegetable stock*
3 strips lean bacon, cut into 1-inch pieces	*1½ cups Arborio rice*
½ cup chopped shallots or yellow onions	*Salt and black pepper*

1 Place the olive oil and bacon in a large skillet or sauté pan and cook over medium heat, stirring occasionally until the bacon is brown, about 2 to 3 minutes. Add the chopped shallots (or onions) and lower the heat to medium-low. Cook the shallots until golden but not browned, stirring occasionally.

2 While the shallots are cooking, bring the stock to a boil in a small, covered saucepan. Reduce the heat to a simmer.

3 When the shallots are golden, add the rice to the skillet. Raise the heat to medium and cook 1 to 2 minutes, stirring constantly, until the rice is well coated with the oil.

4 Add ½ cup hot stock to the rice and stir it in with a wooden spoon. When most of the liquid is absorbed (and it will be absorbed quickly), add another ½ cup stock to the rice, stirring constantly. The rice should be surrounded by liquid but never swim in the stock. Be sure to loosen the rice from the bottom and sides of the pan to keep it from sticking.

5 Continue cooking, stirring and adding ½ cup stock after most of the broth is absorbed. (You may not need all the broth.) The risotto should be creamy and tender but still firm to the bite after about 25 to 30 minutes. During the last 10 minutes, add only ¼ cup stock at a time so that most of the cooking liquid is absorbed when the rice is done.

6 Remove from the heat. Taste for seasoning and add salt and pepper, if desired. Serve immediately.

Tip: *Risotto can be a course on its own or served as a side dish with entrees like Roast Loin of Pork (see Chapter 7) or Roasted Chicken (see Chapter 7).*

Vary It! *You can add an endless variety of ingredients to risotto. A few minutes before it's done, try stirring in l cup fresh or frozen peas or ½ cup chopped parsley. Or add chopped fresh kale, spinach leaves, sliced mushrooms, or broccoli rabe to the pan after browning the shallots. Small shrimp or bits of crab can make risotto into a special main course.*

Per serving: Calories 406 (From Fat 92); Fat 10g (Saturated 3g); Cholesterol 10mg; Sodium 1,477mg; Carbohydrate 68g (Dietary Fiber 1g); Protein 12g.

Wild rice

Wild rice is a remote relative of white rice, actually a long-grain, aquatic grass. The wild version (it is now cultivated) grows almost exclusively in the Great Lakes region of the United States and has become quite expensive because of its scarcity. You can reduce the expense by combining it with brown rice. Wild rice is especially good with robust meat dishes, game, and smoked foods because of its more intense flavor.

Brown rice

If you associate brown rice with bare-wood, macramé-festooned health food cafes, think again. Brown rice can be cool; brown rice can be elegant. Brown rice has more substance and flavor than white rice, and it lends itself well to lots of spices, nuts, fruits, and other embellishments.

Mise en place

The French term *mise en place* (meeze-on-plahs) means to have on hand all the ingredients that you need to prepare a dish. For example, onions and herbs are chopped, garlic is minced, vegetables are rinsed, ingredients are measured, and so on, all ahead of time. This preparation allows you to cook efficiently and without interruption, the way real restaurant chefs do it. Practice *mise en place* by having all your prep work completed right up to the point of cooking.

The term brown rice refers to rice that has not been "polished"; that is, nothing but the tough, outer husk has been removed. With its bran layer intact, brown rice is superior in nutrition to polished rice and is also a little more expensive. Brown rice has a faintly nutty flavor and a shorter shelf life than white rice. You can store white rice almost indefinitely, but brown rice should be consumed within 6 months of purchase.

Working with Other Whole Grains

Most grains, like rice, cook quickly in boiling water or flavored boiling liquid, like beef stock or chicken stock. They usually don't need to be soaked before cooking, but they should be rinsed to remove any surface grit. Here are some of the more common whole grains, other than rice:

- **Barley:** A great substitute for rice in soups and side dishes, barley is commonly sold as "pearl" barley, with its outer hull and bran removed. It cooks relatively quickly — about 25 minutes in boiling water or stock. Season with butter, salt, and pepper.

- **Buckwheat:** Although buckwheat isn't really a grain, we treat it like one. Buckwheat is really a grass and a cousin of the rhubarb plant. It has an earthy, almost nutlike flavor and tastes more like brown rice than other grains — an acquired taste. Kasha, also called buckwheat groats, is simply buckwheat that has been roasted.

- **Bulgur:** Wheat grains that are steamed and then hulled, dried, and cracked, bulgur cooks very quickly. In fact, in some recipes, like tabbouleh, you don't have to cook it at all (although you do soak it in water to soften it).

- **Polenta:** Basic cornmeal is often called by its Italian name, polenta. While it is a less common grain-based side dish in this country than rice and pasta, it tastes delicious. Grits, that southern specialty often served with breakfast, is also made of cornmeal, but polenta needn't be relegated to the morning hours. Cornmeal comes finely ground and coarsely ground. The finely ground type cooks much faster than the coarsely ground meal. The latter has a nuttier texture and takes longer to cook. Try both to see which you prefer.

- **Quinoa:** A small grain that is power-packed with nutrients, quinoa (pronounced keen-wah) is available in most health food stores, Middle Eastern shops, and quality supermarkets. You must rinse quinoa a few times before cooking. Like rice, it takes about 2 parts liquid to 1 part quinoa, and cooks in about 15 minutes.

In the following recipe, the bulgur wheat is rehydrated with boiling water and mixed with some simple ingredients for a fresh grain salad with a Middle Eastern flair.

☜ *Tabbouleh Salad*

This salad is great at room temperature or chilled, and it makes a delicious, nutritious, and slightly exotic lunch. Make it the night before so the flavors have time to meld, and then enjoy it the next day.

Tools: *Large bowl, chef's knife*

Preparation time: *1 hour (mostly waiting for the bulgur to absorb water and to chill)*

Yield: *4 servings*

½ cup bulgur wheat

1 cup boiling water

2 tomatoes, coarsely chopped

3 scallions, chopped, including green parts

½ medium cucumber, peeled and chopped

1 cup fresh parsley or cilantro leaves, or a combination of both, minced

½ teaspoon dried mint leaves or 1 tablespoon minced fresh mint leaves

¼ cup lemon juice (fresh or bottled)

¼ cup extra-virgin olive oil

2 cloves garlic, minced or put through a garlic press

½ teaspoon salt

Few dashes black pepper

1 Put the bulgur wheat in a large bowl. Add the boiling water. Let sit until all the water is absorbed, about 25 minutes.

2 Fluff the bulgur with a fork. Stir in the tomatoes, scallions, cucumber, parsley, mint, lemon juice, olive oil, garlic, salt, and pepper. Cover and chill for at least 30 minutes. Serve cold or at room temperature.

Per serving: Calories 213 (From Fat 128); Fat 14g (Saturated 2g); Cholesterol 0mg; Sodium 312mg; Carbohydrate 21g (Dietary Fiber 5g); Protein 4g.

For a change of pace, try polenta with your meal. If you don't have time to make polenta from scratch, you can buy it ready-made, wrapped in a tube of plastic that looks like a fat sausage; it's available in most supermarkets. Ready-made polenta is good sliced, brushed with a little butter or olive oil, and grilled on both sides until lightly browned. Use polenta in any form — homemade or store-bought — as a base for grilled chops, chicken or sausages, and vegetables.

Making polenta from scratch doesn't actually take much time at all. Try this recipe as a side dish.

⏱ Polenta with Herbs

This simple dish is a delightful change from pasta or rice; it's a quick and tasty light meal in itself when covered with a good tomato-meat sauce. This recipe works well with chicken stock or water — but stock adds more flavor. If you want a more garlicky finish, add a minced clove to the cooking liquid.

Continuous stirring helps prevent polenta from getting lumpy. If lumps form, stir with a wire whisk to break them up. Also, polenta hardens very quickly after it's cooked and removed from the heat, so be sure to bring it to the table steaming.

Tools: *2- or 3-quart heavy-bottom saucepan, wooden spoon, chef's knife*

Preparation time: *5 minutes*

Cooking time: *3 to 5 minutes for precooked or fine-grained polenta*

Yield: *4 servings*

3¼ cups chicken stock or water	*1 tablespoon butter*
1 cup precooked polenta	*1 tablespoon fresh, chopped tarragon, marjoram, or thyme, or 1 teaspoon dried*
⅛ cup freshly grated Parmesan cheese (optional)	*Salt and black pepper*

1 In a heavy, deep pot, bring the stock or water to a boil.

2 Slowly stir in the polenta. Reduce the heat to low and continue stirring until the mixture thickens to a porridge consistency, about 3 to 5 minutes. Stir in the cheese, if desired, and then the butter, tarragon (or marjoram or thyme), and salt and pepper to taste. (If using salted chicken broth, you may need little or no salt.)

Vary It! *Add sautéed onion and garlic along with the butter and herbs. You can also blend in cooked carrots, celery, turnips, broccoli rabe, or even hot Italian sausages. After the polenta is cooked, spread it over a greased baking pan, brush it with melted butter or olive oil (flavored, if you like), and place it under a broiler to brown. Then cut it into squares and serve like bread.*

Go-With: *This recipe is delicious as a side dish with chicken, pork, or veal stews; as a base for grilled vegetables; or smothered with any tomato-based meat sauce.*

Per serving: *Calories 219 (From Fat 55); Fat 6g (Saturated 3g); Cholesterol 12mg; Sodium 958mg; Carbohydrate 36g (Dietary Fiber 4g); Protein 5g.*

Boiling and Steaming Delicious Vegetables

All the different techniques we talk about earlier in the "Cooking Food with Water: The Techniques Defined" section apply to cooking vegetables, and even fruits.

Sometimes a recipe calls for parboiling vegetables. Certain dense vegetables, such as carrots, potatoes, and turnips, are sometimes *parboiled*, or cooked briefly in boiling water, to soften them slightly before another method finishes cooking them. This technique guarantees that all the ingredients in the dish finish cooking at the same time. You might, for example, parboil green peppers before you stuff and bake them. Or you might parboil pieces of broccoli, carrots, and cauliflower before tossing them into a stir-fry of egg noodles and shrimp. (See Crispy Roasted Root Vegetables in Chapter 7 for a recipe that uses this technique.)

Blanching, or briefly plunging vegetables or fruits into boiling water for a few seconds and then into cold water to stop the cooking process, helps cooks remove the skins from tomatoes, nectarines, and peaches. (See Chapter 11 for instructions for removing the skins of tomatoes.) Some vegetables, like green beans, are blanched before they're frozen or canned to help retain their color and flavor.

Steaming is the gentlest way to cook vegetables and seafood. It's also one of the most healthful because nutrients aren't lost in the cooking liquids. This method is a particularly good way to cook delicate seafood, especially shellfish like shrimp, scallops, and mussels.

You can steam in two ways: in a perforated steamer set over simmering water (and covered) or in a deep, covered pot or saucepan holding about 1 to 2 inches of water. The latter method works especially well for vegetables like broccoli and asparagus.

If you steam foods often, you may want to invest in some sort of steamer. The conventional steamer model is a pair of pots, the top one having a perforated bottom and a lid. You can also buy bamboo steamers or little metal steamer baskets that fit inside saucepans you already own.

Ready to try cooking vegetables in water? The following recipes show you how to boil potatoes for mashed potatoes and steam broccoli for a bright green, crisp-tender, super-nutritious side dish.

⏱ Homemade Mashed Potatoes

Although it sounds like a contradiction, "baking" potatoes (often referred to as Idaho potatoes) actually make fluffier, lighter mashed potatoes than "boiling" potatoes. Boiled potatoes get dense and gluey when mashed but are great for recipes in which they need to hold their shape — such as in potato salad.

When mashing potatoes, the slow way is the best. Mashed potatoes are much better when mashed by hand with a potato masher or fork or when pressed through a *ricer* (a round, metal device with small holes through which foods are pressed). Blenders and food processors whiz too fast and can leave you with excellent wallboard paste. Even when mashing by hand, don't overdo it. Mash just enough to get rid of the lumps.

Tools: *Chef's knife, medium saucepan fitted with a lid, potato masher or ricer, colander*

Preparation time: *About 15 minutes*

Cooking time: *About 20 minutes*

Yield: *4 servings*

4 large Idaho potatoes, about 2 pounds	½ teaspoon salt, or to taste	3 tablespoons butter
	½ cup milk	Black pepper

1 Peel the potatoes and cut them into quarters.

2 Place them in a medium saucepan with cold water to barely cover and add the ½ teaspoon salt, or to taste.

3 Cover and bring to a boil over high heat. Reduce heat to medium and cook, covered, for about 15 minutes or until you can easily pierce the potatoes with a fork.

4 Drain the potatoes in a colander and then return them to the saucepan. Shake the potatoes in the pan over low heat for 10 to 15 seconds to evaporate excess moisture, if necessary.

5 Remove the pan from the heat. Mash the potatoes a few times with a potato masher, ricer, or fork. (You can use a handheld mixer to mash them on low speed if you don't have a potato masher, but be careful not to overdo it!) Add the milk, butter, and salt and pepper to taste and mash again until smooth and creamy.

Go-With: *Mashed potato fiends think that mashed potatoes go with everything short of oatmeal. Try these potatoes with Roasted Fillet of Beef or Smoked Ham with Apricot Glaze (both in Chapter 7), and don't forget to serve them with the Thanksgiving turkey!*

Vary It! *For garlic mashed potatoes, wrap a whole, medium head of garlic (not just a clove — a whole head) in aluminum foil and roast it in a 350-degree oven for 1 hour. Remove the foil, allow the cloves to cool slightly, and then press the soft cloves to release the pulp. Mash the pulp into the potatoes with the butter and milk; then season with salt and pepper to taste. You can mash other cooked vegetables, such as broccoli, carrots, turnips, or sweet potatoes, and blend them into the potato mix.*

Per serving: Calories 263 (From Fat 88); Fat 10g (Saturated 6g); Cholesterol 27mg; Sodium 315mg; Carbohydrate 41g (Dietary Fiber 4g); Protein 5g.

⟲ *Steamed Broccoli with Lemon Butter*

Steamed broccoli is a classic, and this most nutritious of vegetables is delicious with a little lemon butter or, alternatively, a dash of olive oil and some hot pepper flakes. You also can substitute vegetables like cauliflower, kale, and asparagus for the broccoli in this recipe. Make sure that you trim and cut the vegetables into equal-sized pieces so that they cook evenly.

Tools: *Paring knife, deep 3- or 4-quart saucepan fitted with a lid, tongs, small saucepan*

Preparation time: *About 15 minutes*

Cooking time: *About 10 minutes*

Yield: *4 servings*

1 head broccoli	*3 tablespoons butter*
Salt and black pepper	*Juice of ½ lemon*

1 Wash the broccoli thoroughly. Trim off only the thickest part of the stems and the large leaves. Divide the larger florets by slicing through the base of the flower and straight down through the length of the stem. All pieces should be roughly the same size.

2 Place the broccoli in a deep 3- or 4-quart saucepan holding about 2 inches of water. (The stalks should stand on the bottom with the florets facing up.) Add salt and pepper to taste and cover the pan.

3 Bring to a boil over high heat and then reduce the heat to low and simmer, covered, for about 8 minutes or until the stalks are tender but not soft. When done, the stalks should be firm but easy to pierce with a sharp knife.

4 While the broccoli steams, melt the butter in a small saucepan and add the lemon juice. Stir to blend.

5 Using tongs, carefully remove the broccoli to a serving dish. Pour the lemon-butter sauce over the broccoli and serve.

Go-With: *Fresh broccoli adds color and flavor to innumerable meals, including Roasted Fillet of Beef and Glazed Leg of Lamb with Pan Gravy and Red Currant Glaze (both in Chapter 7).*

Per serving: Calories 109 (From Fat 80); Fat 9g (Saturated 5g); Cholesterol 23mg; Sodium 176mg; Carbohydrate 6g (Dietary Fiber 3g); Protein 4g.

Simple tips for boiling and steaming a dozen fresh vegetables

Boiling other vegetables is as easy as boiling potatoes. Following are specific instructions for boiling and steaming common vegetables:

- ✔ **Artichokes:** Lay the artichokes on their side on a wooden cutting board. Using a sharp chef's knife, trim about ½ inch off the top. Use scissors to trim the prickly tips off each leaf. Pull off any very thick or tough leaves (but no more than 3 or 4) at the bottom of the artichoke. Place the artichokes in a deep pot with cold water to cover. (They should fit snugly to keep them from bobbing in the water.) Add salt and pepper and lemon juice to taste and bring to a boil. Boil gently for 30 to 40 minutes, depending on size. When the artichokes are done, you should be able to pierce the bottom with a fork or easily pull off a leaf. Use tongs to remove the artichokes and drain upside down on a plate or in a colander. Serve hot with a sauce of lemon juice and melted butter. Or marinate for several hours in a vinaigrette dressing (see Chapter 12) and serve at room temperature.

- ✔ **Asparagus:** Snap off the thick, woody stems at the natural breaking point. (If very coarse, use a vegetable peeler to remove some of the outer green layer at the thick end of each spear.) Rinse the stalks under cold water or soak them for about 5 minutes if they seem especially sandy. Place the spears in a wide, shallow pan in one layer, if possible (and never more than two). Add boiling water to cover and salt to taste. Cover and boil gently until crisp-tender, about 8 minutes for medium spears. Cooking time varies with the thickness of the stalks. Drain and serve immediately with butter, lemon juice, salt and pepper, and, if desired, grated Parmesan cheese.

- ✔ **Brussels sprouts:** With a sharp paring knife, trim off the tough outer leaves. Using a paring knife, trim a very thin slice off the stem end. Then cut an X in the stem end to ensure even cooking of the stem and leaves. Boil gently in about 1 inch of water for about 8 to 10 minutes or until crisp-tender. Test for doneness by tasting. Drain and serve with a simple lemon-butter sauce.

   To steam Brussels sprouts, place trimmed sprouts in a steaming basket over about 1 inch of boiling water. Cover the pot and steam for about 8 minutes, depending on size.

- ✔ **Cabbage:** Cut the head into quarters and cut out the hard core. Add the quarters to a large pot of lightly salted boiling water, cover, and boil gently for about 12 minutes. Cabbage should remain somewhat crisp.

   To steam, place the quarters in a large deep skillet or saucepan with about ½ inch of water and cook, covered, over low heat until crisp-tender. Cabbage is also quite delicious when braised. (See Chapter 17 for a recipe for Braised Cabbage with Apple and Caraway.)

✔ **Carrots or parsnips:** Trim off the ends and peel with a vegetable peeler. Place them sliced into a pot with lightly salted water to just cover. Cover the pot and boil gently for about 12 to 15 minutes for sliced carrots, or about 20 minutes for whole ones. Or place in a steaming basket and steam in a covered pot over about 1 inch of boiling water. Sliced carrots or parsnips steam in 5 minutes; whole and large, 2- to 3-inch pieces need about 12 minutes. Serve with butter sauce flavored with lemon juice and grated lemon or orange zest, or a sauce of melted butter and minced fresh dill.

✔ **Cauliflower:** To boil, cut a whole head into florets and boil gently in enough lightly salted water to cover the cauliflower for about 8 to 10 minutes or until crisp-tender. Adding the juice of half a lemon to the cooking water helps to retain cauliflower's whiteness.

To steam, place florets in a steaming basket over about 1 inch of boiling water. Cover pot and steam for about 5 minutes or until desired doneness. Toss in a sauce of melted butter, lemon juice, and chopped fresh parsley.

✔ **Corn:** Don't husk or remove the ears from the refrigerator until you're ready to boil them. (The sugar in corn rapidly turns to starch at room temperature. To retain sweetness, keep ears cold and cook the same day of purchase.) Heat a large pot filled with enough water just to cover the corn, add the husked corn, cover the pot, and boil for about 5 minutes. Remove with tongs and serve immediately with butter.

✔ **Green beans:** Trim by snapping off the stem ends. Add the beans to lightly salted boiling water to cover and cook for 8 to 10 minutes, or until crisp-tender. They should retain their bright green color.

To steam, place steaming basket over about 1 inch of boiling water. Add beans, cover the pot tightly, and check for doneness after 5 minutes. Serve hot beans with a simple butter sauce or toss in a vinaigrette dressing and chill before serving.

✔ **Pearl onions:** Peel and boil in a covered pot with lightly salted water to just cover for about 15 minutes or until tender but still firm. Don't overcook, or they'll fall apart. Serve smothered in a sauce or gravy, or mixed with other vegetables.

✔ **Snow peas:** Rinse the peas, snap off the stem ends, and lift the string across the top to remove it. Place in boiling water to cover and cook for 2 minutes. Drain in a colander and run cold water over them to stop the cooking and retain their green color.

✔ **Sweet potatoes:** Scrub the potatoes well, trim the tapered ends, and cut out any bruised spots. (Cut very large sweet potatoes in half crosswise, or quarter them.) Place in a large pot, add cold water to cover the potatoes, cover the pot, and simmer for about 35 to 40 minutes for whole potatoes or 20 to 25 minutes for halved or quartered potatoes. Potatoes are done when you can pierce them easily with a fork. Don't overcook, or they'll fall apart in the water. Drain and cool slightly before peeling. Mash or serve in large chunks with butter, salt, pepper, and ground ginger or nutmeg to taste, if desired.

✔ **Yellow squash and zucchini:** Scrub clean and trim the ends. Slice into ½-inch-thick rounds. Place in a steaming basket over about 1 inch of boiling water and steam in a covered pot for about 4 minutes or just until crisp-tender. These tender vegetables are also delicious sautéed.

Fresh vegetables have more flavor and retain their nutrients better if you cook them only until *crisp-tender,* or firm to the bite. The B vitamins and vitamin C are water soluble and leach into the cooking water as the vegetables cook, so save the vitamin-packed cooking liquid to add to other dishes you're cooking, such as soups and stews.

Trying something new: Vegetable purées

Vegetable *purées* are simply cooked vegetables (usually boiled or steamed but sometimes roasted) that are mashed, blended, or processed to a thick consistency. Starchy root vegetables like potatoes, sweet potatoes, rutabagas, parsnips, and carrots generally make the best purées, but broccoli, cauliflower, and roasted red peppers are also wonderful, especially when mixed with a dense root vegetable. Thick purees make a great side dish; when thinned with water, broth, or sauce, they make delicious toppings for meat, potatoes, pasta, or rice. Try the following recipe for a bright, colorful, flavorful purée.

☺ Red Pepper Purée

This red pepper purée brightens up any mild meat or fish, or try it on baked potatoes or steamed asparagus.

Tools: *Chef's knife, medium skillet, food processor*

Preparation time: *10 minutes*

Cooking time: *About 20 minutes*

Yield: *6 servings*

1 tablespoon olive oil	2 garlic cloves, peeled and minced or put through a garlic press	Juice of ½ lemon
3 medium red bell peppers, cored, seeded, and chopped (see Figure 4-1)		½ teaspoon salt
	1 teaspoon paprika	Few dashes black pepper
¼ cup chopped red onion	1 tablespoon fresh chopped or 1 teaspoon dried cilantro	

1 Heat the olive oil in the skillet over medium-high heat until you begin to smell the oil, about 3 minutes.

2 Add the peppers, onion, and garlic. Sauté until the vegetables are soft but not browned, about 15 minutes.

3 Put the vegetables in the food processor with the paprika, cilantro, and lemon juice. Process until smooth, about 15 seconds. Stir in the salt and pepper. Serve warm over meat, fish, or vegetables. (You can warm it up for about 15 to 30 seconds in the microwave or for about 5 minutes in a saucepan over low heat on the stove, if you want to make it ahead of time and serve it later.)

Vary it: *Try mixing this purée with a little cream or half-and half and serve over pasta.*

Per serving: *Calories 42 (From Fat 22); Fat 2g (Saturated 0g); Cholesterol 0mg; Sodium 196mg; Carbohydrate 5g (Dietary Fiber 1g); Protein 1g.*

How to Core and Seed a Pepper

Figure 4-1: Removing the seeds and core from a pepper.

1. Cut out stem. twist and pull out.

2. Cut in ½ ... ...and remove membranes.

3. Cut into lengthwise strips.

4. For cubes, hold strips together and cut crosswise.

Poaching Seafood

Poaching seafood is a fabulous way to preserve its flavor and texture. You just have to watch the clock to prevent overcooking and keep the poaching liquid to a gentle simmer. Vigorous boiling breaks up the fish's tender flesh.

If you poach seafood in vegetable broth, the seafood will take on a subtle, herby flavor, but you can always use water, too. Poaching works best with firm-fleshed fish: salmon, tuna, cod, halibut, and the like.

Poached Salmon Steaks with Béarnaise Sauce

This recipe takes light but richly flavored salmon and pairs it with its classic partner, béarnaise sauce, for a sensational, velvety, delicious dish. Salmon contains omega-3 fatty acids for heart health, and the béarnaise sauce makes this dish suitable for even the most finicky dinner guests.

Tools: *Chef's knife; large, deep skillet*

Preparation time: *About 25 minutes*

Cooking time: *About 10 minutes*

Yield: *4 servings*

1½ quarts (6 cups) vegetable broth or water

4 salmon steaks or fillets, about 6 ounces each, with skin

Water (if necessary)

Béarnaise sauce (see Chapter 9 for a recipe)

1 Bring the vegetable broth or water to a boil over high heat in a large skillet. Submerge the salmon steaks or fillets in the boiling liquid. Add more water only if there is not enough stock to just cover the steaks.

You might have to cook the fish in more than one batch, if the steaks or fillets don't all fit in your skillet (you can use the same cooking liquid).

2 Return to a boil; then lower the heat to a simmer and cook, uncovered, for about 5 minutes.

3 Turn off the heat and let the steaks stand in the poaching liquid about 3 to 5 minutes longer or until done. Don't let them sit too long or they'll get overcooked. Cut into the center delicately to check for doneness. (See the sidebar "Is that fish done or just resting?" for details.) Remove the poached steaks to a platter.

4 Drizzle some béarnaise sauce over each salmon steak and serve immediately.

Go-With: Serve this delicate, light dish with Basic Rice Pilaf (see the recipe earlier in this chapter) or a salad and a simple pasta with butter.

Per serving: *Calories 340 (From Fat 177); Fat 20g (Saturated 9g); Cholesterol 207mg; Sodium 201mg; Carbohydrate 0g (Dietary Fiber 0g); Protein 38g.*

Is that fish done or just resting?

One traditional guideline for cooking fish is the so-called Canadian Fish Rule. Measure the whole fish steak or fillet at its thickest point and cook it (whether you're boiling, steaming, baking, broiling, or poaching) for precisely 10 minutes per inch, although we've found that 8 to 9 minutes per inch works a little bit better. After about 8 minutes, check for doneness. If the thickest part of the fish is ¾ inch thick, for example, cook it for 6 to 7 minutes.

Whole fish is easiest to check. If the dorsal fin comes out easily, it's done; if not, it needs more cooking. However, as a beginning cook, you probably won't be cooking a whole fish just yet.

A fish fillet or steak is done when it flakes easily with a fork. Scallops turn opaque when done, and shrimp, which takes only a couple of minutes to cook, turns pink. Salmon and tuna are darkish pink at the center when medium. White fish should be glistening and wet looking only at the innermost core. Unless the recipe instructs you to do otherwise, remove all cooked fish from the heat or the poaching liquid immediately.

Mussels, clams, and oysters give you a clear indication that they're cooked: Their shells open when they're done, no matter how you cook them — like a built-in kitchen timer.

Chapter 5

Sautéing

The common technique of sautéing, or panfrying, as many hip restaurants call it today, is generally associated with French cuisine. But in fact, many other nationalities sauté routinely to sear steaks, cook fillets of fish, glaze vegetables, and quick-cook shellfish.

Sautéing is nothing more than cooking food in a hot pan, usually with a little fat (butter or oil, for example) to prevent sticking. Sautéing imparts a crispy texture to foods and brings out all sorts of flavors from herbs and spices.

The French word sauté translates literally as *to jump*. Chefs shake the sauté pan back and forth over the heat, tossing the food without using utensils, to keep the food from burning and to expose all sides to the intense heat. Practice this technique in an empty cold skillet by using small candies, such as M&M's.

Because sautéing is done at high or medium-high heat, be careful not to leave food in the pan too long. For example, if you drop a steak onto a roaring-hot pan (maybe with a little oil to prevent sticking), it develops a dark crust in a few minutes. This effect is desirable because you want to trap the juices inside the steak. If you do not flip the steak quickly to sear the other side, however, it may blacken and burn.

After your steak is browned on both sides, you should turn down the heat to medium to finish cooking. Doing so gives you the best of both worlds — a crispy outside and juicy inside.

Seafood benefits from sautéing in the same way; sautéing gives it texture and flavor. Likewise, sautéed vegetables become glazed with butter and absorb seasonings — that is, the seasonings are cooked into the vegetable, not added at the table.

In this chapter, we discuss sautéing and provide some helpful tips and delicious recipes for practice. You'll be sautéing vegetables, meat, chicken, and seafood like a pro in no time.

Knowing When to Use Oil or Butter

When you sauté a food, you need to use some kind of fat, but which should you choose — butter or oil? Each is best suited for different kinds of sautéing. When you're using very high heat, use oil, which is less likely to burn. When you're sautéing with medium-high heat, you may opt for butter, which adds a nice flavor, but the milk solids in the butter can burn, or brown, affecting the color and taste of your food.

Typically, meats are sautéed in oil because they need a higher heat, while vegetables are sautéed in butter to impart a pleasant buttery flavor. Seafood may be sautéed in either one, and many chefs opt to use half butter and half oil when sautéing: they get the benefit of the buttery flavor, but the added oil helps to keep the butter from burning as easily.

If you do decide to use oil in your sautéing, it is helpful to know that some oils have a higher *smoke point* than others, which means they will start to smoke at a hotter temperature, and so are preferable for cooking with high heat, such as with sautéing. Good oils for sautéing include canola oil, corn oil, olive oil, and peanut oil. If the recipe doesn't specify what type of oil to use, you can use any of these. Canola oil is a good standby to have around because its bland flavor and high smoke point make it suitable for all kinds of sautéing, and it won't flavor food strongly so it can be used in most dishes.

Oil should be hot but not smoking in the pan before you add food. Butter should foam at its edges but not brown. Some chefs insist on using only *clarified butter* (or butter that has been heated to separate out the milk solids, which are skimmed off, making it more like cooking oil with a higher smoke point) when sautéing because it won't burn as quickly when the milk solids are removed, but retains the buttery flavor. Clarified butter is, in other words, more like oil. Sound interesting? Here's how to *clarify* butter for sautéing:

1. **Melt the butter in a saucepan to separate its milk solids, which sink to the bottom of the pan.**

2. **Transfer the butter to a small bowl and let it sit for a minute to let the solids (foam) rise to the surface.**

3. **Use a spoon to skim off the foam and discard it.**

What's left is the clarified butter.

Making Great Sauce from Bits in the Pan: Deglazing

A very hot sauté pan begins to cook meat, poultry, or fish right away, browning the juices that flow from it and leaving bits of food sticking to the bottom of the pan. These browned bits are loaded with flavor. If *deglazed* (moistened and scraped up) in the pan, they become transformed into a delicious sauce.

Just follow these easy steps if you want to deglaze:

1. **Remove the meat, poultry, or fish from the pan onto a serving platter and immediately add liquid — you can use water, wine, stock, or a combination.**

   The liquid should be twice the amount of sauce you want to make. For example, if you want to make one cup of sauce, add two cups of wine.

   As a rule, the wine you use for deglazing depends on what you're sautéing: Use white wine for poultry and seafood, and red wine for meat.

2. **Raise the heat to high, bringing the liquid to a boil while you stir and scrape the browned bits off the bottom of the pan until they dissolve into the sauce.**

   This stirring and scraping is the key to deglazing — all those delicious little caramelized bits of cooked meat infuse the liquid, making it taste fantastic.

3. **Keep boiling and stirring until the sauce is reduced by half the volume or, in other words, until those two cups of wine (or water or broth) have boiled down to about one cup.**

   How can you tell? Just eyeball it. When it looks like you have half as much liquid as you did, it's time to take a taste.

And the verdict? Does your sauce taste delicious, or does it need more salt and/or pepper? Maybe a dash of fresh herbs? Add more seasoning if you think the sauce needs more flavor. You might also stir in a teaspoon or more of butter or olive oil for flavor and to add a smooth texture. (Lots of professional chefs do this.) Then spoon the sauce over the cooked meat, poultry, or fish and serve. Aren't you a pro! (See Figure 5-1.)

Deglazing a Pan

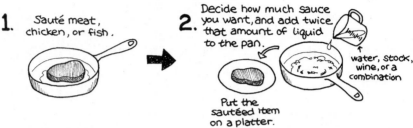

1. Sauté meat, chicken, or fish.

2. Decide how much sauce you want, and add twice that amount of liquid to the pan.

water, stock, wine, or a combination

Put the sautéed item on a platter.

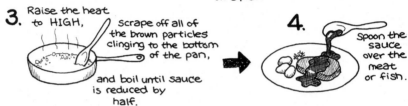

3. Raise the heat to HIGH, scrape off all of the brown particles clinging to the bottom of the pan,

and boil until sauce is reduced by half.

4. Spoon the sauce over the meat or fish.

Mincing Onions and Garlic

Although you need to mince onions and garlic for many different cooking techniques, not just for sautéing, onions and garlic often form a basis of flavor for sautéed meats and vegetables alike.

No matter how you slice it, an onion releases intense flavor and juice, which is why so many recipes call for chopped, minced, or diced onion. The fumes they emit can be very irritating to your eyes, however. To avoid chopped onion tears, the best strategy is to use a sharp knife that reduces cutting time and to frequently rinse off the onion in cold water as you go.

Follow these steps (shown in Figure 5-2) to mince an onion:

1. **Cut the onion in half lengthwise through the bulbous center, peel back the papery skin, and chop off the top, leaving the root end intact.**

   As you slice through the onion, the intact root end helps you to keep the slices from slipping out from under the knife.

2. **Place each half cut side down and, with your knife tip just in front of the root end, slice the onion lengthwise in parallel cuts, leaving ⅛ to ¼ inch between the slices.**

3. **Make several horizontal cuts of desired thickness, parallel to the board.**

4. **Cut through the onion at right angles to the board, making pieces as thick as desired, and, finally, cut through the root end.**

How to Mince an Onion or Garlic:

Cut off the stem, then cut in half through the root.

Peel off the skin.

Place one of the halves flat on a cutting board.

Make parallel, lengthwise cuts. DON'T cut through the root end!

Cut horizontal slices from top to bottom.

STOP!

Cut through the onion at a right angle to the cutting board, making pieces as thick or thin as desired. FINALLY cut off the root!

Now, repeat these steps with the other half!

Figure 5-2:
Mincing an onion.

Just as with onions, garlic releases its pungent juices when you slice, chop, or mince it. The more you chop it, the stronger its flavor becomes. Raw, mashed garlic carries the biggest punch, while whole roasted garlic cloves release a nutty, slightly sweet flavor. Here's how to mince a clove of garlic:

1. **Peel the garlic by whacking it with the side of your chef's knife as it sits on a cutting board and then slipping off the skin.**

2. **Hold the garlic clove on the cutting board, with the knuckles of your index finger and middle finger leaning against the side of the blade.**

   Keep your fingertips folded over inward to prevent cutting yourself.

3. **Using mostly the tip of your knife, work your chef's knife up and down, slowly moving your knuckles toward the other end of the garlic as you chop.**

   This takes practice, so don't go too fast.

If Steps 1 to 3 sound like too much work, use a garlic press! This handy gadget squeezes the clove of garlic through tiny holes, doing the mincing for you.

Getting Versatile with Your Sautéing

You can sauté just about any meat, fish, or vegetable, so experiment and enjoy some delicious meals. This section contains some recipes to get you started. Notice how the following recipes use the same basic sautéing technique and change only the types of fat and seasonings.

Vegetables

Vegetables are excellent when boiled or steamed until about 90 percent done and then transferred to a skillet to be finished in butter and maybe fresh herbs. Many classic recipes for potatoes call for sautéing; thinly sliced raw potatoes are delicious when cooked this way. In the following recipe, you cut the potatoes into fine cubes and toss them in a hot pan until crispy.

Be very careful when you put rinsed vegetables (or other foods) into a pan of hot fat. The water that clings to the vegetables makes the fat splatter, which can cause serious burns.

☞ Sautéed Skillet Potatoes

These potatoes, an excellent accompaniment to steak or veal chops, are cubed and sautéed in oil and butter until well browned. By using a combination of butter and oil, you give them a rich flavor and eliminate the risk of burning.

Tools: *Chef's knife, vegetable brush, colander, large nonstick skillet, slotted spoon*

Preparation time: *About 15 minutes*

Cooking time: *About 20 minutes*

Yield: *4 servings*

2 large baking potatoes, about 1½ pounds total	*1 medium yellow onion, peeled and chopped*	*½ teaspoon or less of salt*
¼ cup canola or corn oil	*½ green bell pepper, cored, seeded, and chopped*	*Few dashes black pepper*
2 tablespoons butter	*½ teaspoon dried oregano*	*⅛ teaspoon cayenne pepper or red pepper flakes (optional)*

1 Cut any eyes and bad spots out of the potatoes. Scrub them well with a vegetable brush to remove any dirt, but leave them unpeeled. Cut each into cubes of about ¼ inch.

2 Place the cubes in a colander in the sink. Run very hot water over the potatoes for about 10 seconds. (The hot water rinses off the starch so that the potatoes don't stick together in the pan and removes any discoloration from peeling and cutting the potatoes.) Drain well and dry on paper towels.

3 Heat the oil in a large nonstick skillet over high heat until it is hot. Add the potatoes, and cook, stirring often (to brown them evenly) for about 10 minutes. With a slotted spoon, remove the potatoes from the pan to a large bowl. Pour all the fat out of the pan and wipe out the skillet with paper towels.

4 Melt the butter in the skillet over medium-high heat. Do not let it burn. Sauté the onion, bell pepper, oregano, salt, black pepper, and cayenne pepper, if desired. Cook, stirring occasionally, for 4 to 5 minutes or until the vegetables begin to get soft. Add the potatoes back into the skillet and sauté everything together until the potatoes are browned and crisp, about 5 more minutes. Serve immediately, removing the potatoes with a slotted spoon.

Go-With: *These potatoes are a delicious side dish to omelets (see Chapter 10), Roasted Fillet of Beef (see Chapter 7), or Roasted Loin of Pork (see Chapter 7).*

Per serving: *Calories 325 (From Fat 180); Fat 20g (Saturated 5g); Cholesterol 15mg; Sodium 307mg; Carbohydrate 35g (Dietary Fiber 4g); Protein 4g.*

○ Sautéed Spinach Leaves

This quick and healthy side dish is a fine match with the Tuna Steaks with Ginger-Chili Glaze recipe later in this chapter. You may find yourself liking spinach again!

Tools: *Large sauté pan or skillet fitted with a lid*

Preparation time: *About 15 minutes*

Cooking time: *About 4 minutes*

Yield: *6 servings*

1½ pounds fresh spinach	*1 tablespoon butter*	*Salt and pepper*
1 tablespoon olive oil	*¼ teaspoon ground nutmeg*	

1 Cut away and discard any tough spinach stems and blemished leaves. Wash the spinach thoroughly in cold water and drain well. (See Chapter 12 for complete instructions for rinsing and trimming greens.)

2 Heat the oil and butter in a large sauté pan or skillet over medium heat. Add the spinach, nutmeg, and salt and pepper to taste.

3 Stir the spinach leaves to coat with the oil. (The spinach wilts so fast that you may think you barely have enough for one portion — don't worry, you do.) Cover and cook over medium-high heat for about 2 to 3 minutes or until the spinach leaves wilt thoroughly. Remove from heat and serve.

Go-With: *Sautéed spinach also complements Poached Salmon Steaks with Béarnaise Sauce (see Chapter 4), Grilled Swordfish Steaks with Lemon and Thyme (see Chapter 6), Barbecued Chicken (see Chapter 7), or the following recipe for Tuna Steaks with Ginger-Chili Glaze.*

Per serving: *Calories 55 (From Fat 40); Fat 5g (Saturated 2g); Cholesterol 5mg; Sodium 162mg; Carbohydrate 3g (Dietary Fiber 2g); Protein 2g.*

Firm, rich fish

Rich fish, with a high fat content, such as salmon, tuna, and bluefish, are exceptionally good when sautéed. And you can enhance them with countless sauces that you can make in 15 minutes or less. Because these fish have relatively high fat contents, they also stand up to spicy sauces.

However, a spicy sauce paired with a delicate fish, like sole or snapper, can be a culinary train wreck. In general, firm-fleshed fish (or rich fish) stand up best to spiciness.

Binding a sauce means simply pulling together sauce ingredients in the pan and creating a smoother and thicker texture by stirring in butter, cream, or starch, like cornstarch or flour. Binding is done at the very end of the sauce-making process, just before serving.

Tuna Steaks with Ginger-Chili Glaze

In this easy recipe, which is faintly sweet from the brown sugar in the glaze and heartily spicy due to the chili paste, note that you sear the tuna to seal in moisture and then remove it from the pan. You make the quick sauce in the same pan, and then you return the fish to the sauce for the rest of the cooking. This technique helps to keep the tuna moist and infuses it with some of the sauce flavors. If you don't have a pan big enough to cook all the tuna steaks at once, use a smaller skillet and cook the tuna in batches. If you cook the tuna in batches, be sure to save enough sauce for all the steaks.

Tools: *Paring knife, chef's knife, large nonstick skillet or sauté pan*

Preparation time: *About 15 minutes*

Cooking time: *About 15 minutes*

Yield: *4 servings*

4 tuna steaks, each about 6 to 7 ounces and ¾ inch thick	*1 tablespoon red chili paste (find it with the Asian food ingredients in your grocery store)*
Few dashes of salt and pepper for each steak	*½ teaspoon dried ground ginger*
2 tablespoons butter	*1 tablespoon brown sugar*
1 cup white wine or white grape juice	*1 tablespoon dark sesame oil*

1 Season both sides of the tuna steaks with salt and pepper. Melt the butter over medium-high heat in a large nonstick skillet or sauté pan large enough to hold the steaks in one layer.

2 Add the tuna to the pan and cook until lightly browned on both sides, about 3 minutes per side.

3 Transfer the steaks to a warm platter and cover with foil. Leave the cooking butter in the skillet and scrape the bottom of the pan with a wooden spoon to loosen the browned bits clinging to the pan. Add the wine, turn up the heat to high, and cook until about half the liquid in the pan evaporates (should take less than a minute, so be ready!). This step intensifies the flavor of the sauce.

4 Lower the heat to medium. Add the chili paste, ginger, brown sugar, and sesame oil. Stir continuously until the ingredients are well combined.

5 Add the tuna steaks back into the pan, along with any juices that have accumulated around the steaks, and bring to a simmer. Cook for about 1 minute more or until warmed through, turning once to coat the steaks in the glaze. Do not overcook.

6 Using a flat metal spatula, remove each tuna steak to an individual plate. Spoon a little of the sauce over each serving and serve immediately.

Per serving: Calories 274 (From Fat 96); Fat 11g (Saturated 4g); Cholesterol 89mg; Sodium 305mg; Carbohydrate 4g (Dietary Fiber 0g); Protein 38g.

Chicken

Sautéing is a great way to impart flavor to chicken. The chicken stays juicy with a flavorful outside, especially with the addition of different herbs and spices. You can also make a delicious sauce with the leftover oil or butter and herbs by adding wine, juice, or chicken broth to the pan after cooking the chicken and reducing the liquid to concentrate the flavor. Some potatoes or rice and a salad rounds out a delicious chicken dinner.

Sautéed Chicken Breasts with Tomatoes and Thyme

This simple recipe combines chicken with the sweet flavors of onions and tomatoes. It's easy to modify, to suit your own tastes, by changing the vegetables and/or the herbs, but try this basic version first, to work on your sautéing technique.

Tools: *Chef's knife, large sauté pan or skillet, meat mallet or heavy pan, waxed paper, aluminum foil*

Preparation time: *About 20 minutes*

Cooking time: *About 10 minutes*

Yield: *4 servings*

4 boneless, skinless chicken breast halves

Salt and pepper

2 tablespoons olive oil

1 medium yellow onion, chopped

1 large clove garlic, chopped

2 medium tomatoes, peeled, seeded, and chopped (see Chapter 13 for instructions)

1 teaspoon chopped fresh thyme, or ¼ teaspoon dried

2 tablespoons chopped fresh or 2 teaspoons dried basil (optional)

⅓ cup white wine or chicken stock

1 Place the chicken breasts on a cutting board, season generously on both sides with salt and pepper, cover with waxed paper, and pound them lightly so that they're of equal thickness. (Use the bottom of a heavy pan or a meat mallet.)

2 Heat the olive oil in a large sauté pan or skillet over medium-high heat. Add the chicken and sauté for about 4 to 5 minutes per side or until done. (To test for doneness, make a small incision in the center of each piece. The meat should be white, with no trace of pink.) Remove the pieces to a platter and cover with aluminum foil to keep warm.

3 Add the onion to the pan over medium heat. Stir for 1 minute, scraping the bottom of the pan. Add the garlic, stirring occasionally for another minute. Add the tomatoes, thyme, basil (if desired), and salt and pepper to taste. Stir for 1 minute. Add the white wine or stock, increase the heat to high, and cook, stirring occasionally, for about 2 to 3 minutes or until most of the liquid evaporates. (The mixture should be moist but not soupy.)

4 Place the chicken on 4 plates. Spoon equal portions of sauce over each piece.

Vary It! *You can modify this recipe in many ways. For example, use turkey breasts or slices of veal instead of chicken; add 1 cup fresh, frozen, or canned corn kernels with the chopped tomatoes; add 2 tablespoons heavy cream with the stock or wine; substitute tarragon, marjoram, or other herb of choice for the thyme; or grate some Parmesan cheese over the top of each serving.*

Go-With: *You can serve the chicken with side dishes of Mashed Potatoes or Wild Rice (both in Chapter 4) and a simple green salad (see Chapter 12).*

Per serving: *Calories 170 (From Fat 47); Fat 5g (Saturated 1g); Cholesterol 63mg; Sodium 203mg; Carbohydrate 6g (Dietary Fiber 1g); Protein 24g.*

Beef

Beef is excellent meat for sautéing. Steaks get dark and crisp on the outside, but stay tender and juicy on the inside. Whether you are sautéing bite-sized pieces of steak for a stir-fry or searing a big juicy T-bone in a hot pan, sautéing is the technique to use for beef.

The doneness of steaks is defined by the meat's interior color. Rare meat is bright red and juicy. Medium meat has a light pink center with light brown edges. Well-done, which we don't recommend, is brown-gray and dry throughout. While some people prefer their steaks well done, meat with a pink center is typically much juicier and more tender.

Sautéed Peppered Sirloin of Beef

One of the most popular beef dishes in restaurants is what the French call *steak au poivre,* in which beef is coated liberally with cracked black pepper before it's cooked in a hot pan. This recipe is our version of the classic French dish. The sauce is usually made with beef stock, shallots, red wine, and maybe a little brandy. The combination is compelling if the cook skillfully balances the pepper with sweet elements. We'll help you do just that!

Tools: *Chef's knife, large cast-iron skillet or other heavy-bottomed skillet, mortar and pestle or heavy pan*

Preparation time: *About 20 minutes*

Cooking time: *About 15 minutes*

Yield: *4 servings*

3 to 4 tablespoons black peppercorns, or to taste	*2 tablespoons butter*
	¾ cup dry red wine
2 boneless sirloin steaks, trimmed, each about 1 pound and 1¼ inches thick	*2 tablespoons brandy or apple juice*
2 tablespoons vegetable oil	*¼ cup homemade or canned beef or chicken stock*
3 tablespoons minced shallots	*1 teaspoon tomato paste*
2 tablespoons minced yellow onion (see the earlier section "Mincing Onions and Garlic")	*Salt*

1 Crush the peppercorns finely by using a mortar and pestle or on a hard surface (such as a wooden cutting board) with the bottom of a heavy pan, as shown in Figure 5-3. To prevent peppercorns from flying all over the place when you crush them, wrap them first in aluminum foil. Crushing them shortly before cooking gets the most potency from the pepper.

2 Press the steaks into the peppercorns, covering both sides evenly. (Three to four tablespoons of peppercorns makes for a wonderfully hot and spicy sauce, but if you prefer a milder sauce, use only 2 to 3 tablespoons.)

3 Heat the oil in a large cast-iron skillet over high heat. When the pan is very hot, lay the steaks in and cook for about 2 to 3 minutes per side to sear. Lower the heat to medium and cook another 6 to 7 minutes, flipping periodically to finish. Cooking times vary with the thickness of the meat, so make a small incision in the meat and check for the desired degree of doneness. Medium doneness has a slightly pink center with soft-brown edges. (For medium-well or rare doneness, cook a minute or two more or less per side.)

4 Remove the steaks from the pan and set aside on a plate. Cover the plate with foil to keep the steaks warm. Let the cooking pan cool slightly and remove any little burned particles, but do not rinse under water!

5 Return the pan to medium heat and add the shallot, onion, and 1 tablespoon of the butter. Cook for about 1 minute, stirring. Add the red wine and brandy. Raise the heat to high and boil the sauce to evaporate, or reduce, to about half its original volume, stirring often. Add the stock and tomato paste. Stirring, reduce the sauce again until it is about ½ cup total. Lower the heat to medium.

6 Add the remaining 1 tablespoon butter and stir well until it melts to finish, or pull together, the sauce. Spoon the sauce over the steaks. Check for seasoning, adding salt if necessary, and serve immediately.

Vary It! *If you'd like to flambé the steaks, bring the steaks and the pan to the table. Pour 2 tablespoons of brandy over the steaks and ignite them with a match (be sure to tie back your hair and roll up your sleeves first so nothing catches fire but the steak). Even if you don't taste the difference, your guests will be impressed. After the flame dies out, distribute the sauce over the steaks. You may want to practice this once before attempting it in front of a hungry audience.*

Go-With: *We recommend serving this with a side of Mashed Potatoes (see Chapter 4) and Sautéed Spinach Leaves (see the recipe in this chapter).*

Per serving: Calories 358 (From Fat 256); Fat 28g (Saturated 10g); Cholesterol 77mg; Sodium 357mg; Carbohydrate 3g (Dietary Fiber 1g); Protein 21g.

How to Crush Peppercorns

Figure 5-3: Crushing peppercorns with a heavy pan.

1. Gather whole peppercorns in the middle of a cutting board.

2. Use the heel of your hand to press the bottom edge of a pan.

3. Repeat steps 1 & 2 until peppercorns are crushed to desired size.

Chapter 6

Braising and Stewing: Now That's Home Cookin'

1 f you're like most people, you have precious little time, especially during the week, to stand over a pot. This chapter is for you. Braising and stewing are slow cooking methods that allow you to put all the ingredients in a pot, turn the heat to low, and do something else for an hour or two — maybe dust the TV or return the neighbor's newspaper that your dog retrieves every day.

Yet braising and stewing produce food that tastes like you've slaved over a hot stove all day long. This is the kind of food your grandma used to make, the kind of food that makes you feel all warm and cozy inside and hum happily for the rest of your day. It's comfort food.

Because braising and stewing dishes take so much time (even though a lot o f that time doesn't require you to do anything but keep an eye on the stove), they're best when you cook them the day before and reheat them — the flavors are actually more pronounced that way. They're also great for parties because they're easy to make in large batches and they're inexpensive (usually using less expensive cuts of meat).

Most meat dishes in this chapter use the less expensive front cuts of beef: the chuck, brisket, shank, and plate. (See Chapter 3 for an illustration of the various cuts of beef.) These more muscular cuts don't make much of a steak, but when you braise them for hours, their fibers break down and they become succulent. In some ways, these cuts are more flavorful than expensive tenderloin.

Where does a fricassee fit in?

A *fricassee* is a variation on stew. A traditional fricassee is made with poultry, usually chicken. Moreover, the poultry in a fricassee is not seared and browned first, as in a stew. The lack of browning makes the sauce paler than that of a stew, with a slightly milder flavor.

Slow cookers and pressure cookers also use the concepts of braising and stewing, but they do it automatically for you. We talk about those techniques in Chapter 13. (And if you want even more information, check out *Slow Cookers For Dummies,* by Tom Lacalamita and Glenna Vance, and *Pressure Cookers For Dummies,* by Tom Lacalamita, both published by Wiley.) In this chapter, we talk about how to do the braising and stewing yourself, the old-fashioned way. (And just to warn you, the neighbors may start hanging around your kitchen because it smells so good.)

Braising versus Stewing

Both braising and stewing involve long, slow cooking in liquid. The major difference is that in *braising,* foods lie in a few inches of liquid, not quite submerged, so that they stew and steam at the same time. When braising meat, the meat is usually browned in hot oil first, to give it an appealing color.

TIP

To seal in the moisture of meat, fish, or poultry before sautéing in oil prior to braising, you can *dredge,* or coat, the pieces with flour. Simply drag or roll the food in flour to coat all sides, and then pat or shake the pieces gently to remove excess before cooking. Or, for an even neater and easier method, put flour and meat in a plastic freezer bag and shake!

Stewing involves submerging ingredients in a liquid and simmering the mixture for a long time. Also, sometimes some of the ingredients (such as beef for a beef stew) are dredged in flour and browned in oil first, depending on the recipe.

Larger cuts of meat — and the very toughest — tend to be braised, whereas cut-up meat is stewed. For example, you braise a pot roast but stew cubed beef. Both methods make meat very, very tender.

Try Braising — It's Easy!

Braising is so easy to do that you may as well jump right in and try it. One of the easiest and most basic things to braise is a good old classic pot roast. You can braise a beef roast, a pork roast, or any other large piece of meat, including a whole chicken, by browning it on all sides in hot oil first to color it and add flavor, and then braising it in the liquid, as we explain in the following recipes.

Cooking with wine

An adage goes, "If you wouldn't drink it, don't cook with it." That is really the only rule you need to remember when cooking with wine. If you see a bottle in the store labeled *cooking wine,* keep walking.

Fortified wines, such as Madeira, Port, sherry, and Marsala, can add a lovely touch to stews and braised dishes. All have their places in certain recipes.

Note: In an episode of the 1950s television show *The Honeymooners,* Alice Kramden says that her husband, Ralph, has so little tolerance for alcohol that he gets tipsy eating rum cake. Although some residual alcohol may be found in rum cake, none survives in a long-cooked stew. What you get are flavors from the wine or spirit and maybe some added body. If you want to have a wild and crazy night, you'll have to drink lots of wine along with the stew. For information on pairing wine with food, see Chapter 3. (Or check out *Wine For Dummies* by Ed McCarthy and Mary Ewing-Mulligan [Wiley] for even more detailed information about which wines go with which foods.)

Pot Roast with Vegetables

The best cut of beef for a pot roast is the *first-cut* brisket. Sometimes referred to as the *flat cut,* the first-cut brisket has just the right amount of fat so it's not too dry after it's cooked. Ask your butcher for the first cut.

Pot roast is relatively inexpensive. You can make this dish for less than $20, with an individual serving costing about $2.50. This rich and satisfying dish is excellent served hot or cold with Dijon-style mustard or horseradish sauce.

Tools: *Large Dutch oven, chef's knife*

Preparation time: *About 20 minutes*

Cooking time: *About 3 hours*

Yield: *8 servings*

2 tablespoons vegetable oil	*¼ teaspoon dried thyme*
4 pounds first-cut beef brisket	*Salt and pepper*
2 large yellow onions, chopped	*4 large Idaho potatoes, peeled and cut into bite-size chunks*
3 large cloves garlic, chopped	
½ cup dry white wine	*3 large carrots, peeled and sliced crosswise into 2-inch pieces*
½ cup water, more if needed	
1 bay leaf	*3 tablespoons chopped fresh parsley*

1 Heat the oil in a large (preferably cast-iron) Dutch oven over high heat; add the brisket and brown on both sides, about 7 to 8 minutes. Allow the meat to sear to a golden brown without burning. Remove the brisket from the pot and set aside on a large plate.

2 Reduce the heat to medium-high; add the onions and garlic, and sauté until the onions are lightly browned, stirring frequently. (Do not let the garlic brown.)

3 Return the brisket to the pot. Add the wine, water, bay leaf, thyme, and salt and pepper. Cover, bring to a boil, adjust heat as necessary, and simmer for 2¾ to 3 hours, turning the meat several times and adding ½ to 1 cup water as necessary if the liquid evaporates.

4 About 10 minutes before the end of the cooking time, add the potatoes and carrots to the pot.

5 When the meat is so tender that you can pierce it easily with a fork, carefully remove it to a carving board with a long-handled fork; cover with foil and let it rest for 10 to 15 minutes. Continue cooking the potatoes and carrots in the covered pot, for about 10 to 15 minutes more, or until tender.

6 To assemble the meat and vegetable platter, slice the brisket across the grain, as shown in Figure 6-1. (If you cut with the grain, which is the visible layers of muscle tissue that holds the meat together, you'll shred the meat.) Arrange the slices on a serving platter.

7 Remove the cooked potatoes and carrots from the gravy and spoon them around the meat. Skim off the fat from the surface of the remaining juices, remove the bay leaf and discard, heat the juices through, and spoon over the meat and vegetables. Sprinkle with the chopped parsley. Serve the extra gravy in a sauceboat or gravy boat.

Go-With: *Pot roast is delicious served with a mixed green salad and country bread.*

Per serving: *Calories 546 (From Fat 199); Fat 22g (Saturated 7g); Cholesterol 133mg; Sodium 199mg; Carbohydrate 38g (Dietary Fiber 5g); Protein 47g.*

Cutting Pot Roast Across the Grain

Figure 6-1:
Cut across the grain to avoid shredding the meat.

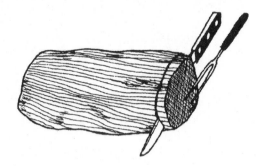

Easy Coq au Vin (Chicken in Wine)

Chicken braised in wine is a classic French dish. We make it easy to do with this simple recipe. Impress your date by making this one, being sure to mutter a few random French phrases under your breath as you're cooking. Depending on how big a pan you use, you may need to cook the chicken in batches. If so, cook the chicken breasts (white meat) together, and then cook the thighs and legs (dark meat) together. The thick meat on the breasts may need to cook slightly longer. Cut into the chicken to check for doneness.

This recipe tastes even better the next day after the sauce has a chance to thicken and the chicken soaks up even more of the savory flavor. Consider making the recipe a day ahead and storing it in the refrigerator. Simply reheat in a large sauté pan on the stove over medium heat until heated through.

Tools: *Large sauté pan with lid, chef's knife, vegetable peeler, slotted spoon*

Preparation time: *About 25 minutes*

Cooking time: *About 1 hour*

Yield: *4 servings*

1 whole chicken, cut in pieces, about 2½ to 3 pounds total	*1 medium yellow onion, peeled and chopped*	*1 750-ml bottle full-bodied, fruity red wine (like Pinot Noir or Cabernet Sauvignon)*
Salt and pepper	*2 ribs celery, trimmed and chopped*	*3 carrots, scrubbed clean, ends removed, and diced*
1 cup flour	*2 cups sliced white mushrooms*	*½ teaspoon salt (optional)*
1 tablespoon olive oil	*1 clove garlic, minced*	*¼ cup chopped fresh parsley leaves, for garnish*
1 tablespoon butter	*1 teaspoon dried thyme*	
4 strips thick-cut bacon, cut into 1-inch strips	*1 bay leaf*	

1 Rinse the chicken parts under cold running water and pat dry. Trim off any excess flaps of skin and fat. Sprinkle with salt and pepper on both sides. Put the flour in a shallow dish and coat each chicken piece lightly with flour.

2 Heat the oil and butter together in a heavy sauté pan that is large enough to hold the chicken pieces in one layer. Place the chicken pieces in the pan and cook over medium-high heat until they're a nice golden color on one side, about 5 minutes. Turn the chicken pieces over and continue cooking about 5 minutes more, or until golden. Remove the chicken pieces to a large platter.

3 Add the bacon, onions, and celery to the pan and cook about 4 to 5 minutes, turning occasionally. Add the mushrooms and cook about 3 minutes more, or until nicely browned, turning occasionally.

4 Return the chicken to the pan over medium heat. Add the garlic, thyme, and bay leaf and cook for 1 minute, stirring often. Do not brown the garlic. Add the wine and carrots, raise the heat, and bring to a boil.

5 Cover tightly, lower heat to medium, and simmer for 25 to 30 minutes, or until the chicken and vegetables are tender.

6 Transfer the entire mixture to a serving dish. Discard the bay leaf. If the sauce looks too watery to pour nicely over the chicken, turn up the heat to medium-high and stir until the sauce thickens just a little, about 2 to 3 minutes. Taste and add the ½ teaspoon salt and season with pepper, if desired. Pour the sauce over the chicken and sprinkle with the chopped parsley.

Vary It! *To give the chicken sauce a rich, smooth texture, stir in 2 to 3 tablespoons light cream after reducing the sauce and heat through. To reduce the number of calories in this dish, remove all skin from the chicken pieces before serving.*

Per serving: Calories 807 (From Fat 448); Fat 50g (Saturated 16g); Cholesterol 199mg; Sodium 597mg; Carbohydrate 35g (Dietary Fiber 4g); Protein 51g.

Time to Stew

Dollar for dollar, meat goes a long way when you stew it. For instance, few dishes are more economical than beef stew, yet who would know it from the taste? Not us! More expensive ingredients such as seafood can make a stew seem luxurious, but you don't need nearly as much shrimp, crab, or fish per person as you would if you were serving these dishes on their own. You can also cut up boneless chicken or turkey breasts, cubed pork, or sliced sausage. If you choose to make a stew with ground meat, be sure to brown it well first.

Getting acquainted with herbs and spices

Because the rainbow of herbs and spices available to home cooks is so exciting (see Chapter 3), you can easily overdo it. The best way to get to know herbs and spices is to cook dishes that contain only one herb or spice — see how it interacts with different foods, watch how it intensifies with cooking, and find out whether you really like it.

For example, with rosemary, you can make a quick sauce for sautéed or grilled chicken breast by combining 3 parts chicken stock to 1 part white wine in a saucepan. Then add a teaspoon of minced fresh rosemary (or ½ teaspoon dry), some very thin slices of garlic, and salt and black pepper to taste. Cook down the liquid until it's reduced by three-quarters. Then strain the sauce and serve it over the chicken.

This dish gives you a pure rosemary flavor. If you like it, you can refine it by adding more or less rosemary or even by adding a complementary herb, such as thyme, tarragon, or chives.

Old-Fashioned Beef Stew

Lean, boneless chuck is one of the least expensive cuts of beef, and the root vegetables (carrots and turnips) that surround it are as economical as they are healthful. Other good cuts to ask for when stewing are the neck, brisket, and shank. This recipe lets you give stewing a try.

If you don't have a stew pot big enough to brown the meat in one layer, cook the meat in batches, a little at a time, moving the pieces to a platter as they brown. Return the pieces to the pot after they're all browned.

This recipe serves 8 to 10 and is a perfect make-ahead meal for a small party. To reduce the yield to serve 4 or 5, use half the ingredients. But remember, stews are always better the next day after the seasonings have a chance to permeate the meat. If you make too much, you'll have delicious leftovers. You also can store meat stews in the freezer in tightly covered containers for up to six months.

Tools: *Chef's knife, stew pot (cast iron is best), large spoon, long tongs*

Preparation time: *About 25 minutes*

Cooking time: *About 1 hour and 40 minutes*

Yield: *8 servings*

¼ cup olive or vegetable oil	*2 bay leaves*
4 pounds lean, boneless chuck, cut into 2-inch cubes	*4 sprigs parsley, tied together (see the tip at the end of the recipe)*
2 large yellow onions, coarsely chopped	*4 sprigs fresh thyme, or 1 teaspoon dried thyme*
6 large cloves garlic, chopped	
6 tablespoons flour	*1 tablespoon minced fresh rosemary, leaves only, or 1 teaspoon dried and crumbled rosemary*
Salt and pepper	
3 cups dry red wine	*1 pound small turnips, trimmed and cut into 2-inch pieces*
3 cups homemade or canned beef or chicken stock	*6 large carrots, trimmed and cut into 1-inch lengths*
2 tablespoons tomato paste	
4 whole cloves	

1 Heat the oil in a large stew pot over medium-high heat, and then add the beef cubes Cook, stirring and turning the meat as necessary, for 5 to 10 minutes or until evenly browned. ***Warning:*** Meat or poultry browned in hot oil or fat of any kind splatters hot grease. Use long tongs to turn the meat carefully. If the oil becomes too hot, lower the heat to medium for the remainder of the browning.

2 Add the onion and garlic and cook over medium heat, stirring occasionally for about 8 minutes. Sprinkle the flour and salt and pepper and stir to coat the meat evenly.

3 Add the wine, stock, and tomato paste, and stir over high heat until the cooking liquid thickens as it comes to a boil. Add the cloves, bay leaves, parsley, thyme, rosemary, and turnips. Cover and reduce the heat to low. Simmer for 1 hour, occasionally stirring and scraping the bottom of the pot. Add the carrots and cook until the meat and carrots are tender, about 20 minutes more. Remove the herb sprigs and bay leaves before serving.

Tip: If using fresh herb sprigs, tie them together with a little kitchen twine. Doing so makes removing the herb sprigs easier, and you get the benefit of parsley flavor without stringy stems.

Go-With: You can serve this stew with country bread and Tomato, Red Onion, and Basil Salad (see Chapter 12).

Per serving: Calories 409 (From Fat 155); Fat 17g (Saturated 5g); Cholesterol 119mg; Sodium 237mg; Carbohydrate 18g (Dietary Fiber 4g); Protein 43g.

Before adding a dried herb, like rosemary, to a stewing pot, crush the brittle leaves in a mortar and pestle or with your fingers into smaller, more palatable pieces. Doing so also releases more of the herb's flavor.

Leftover terminology

The term *leftover* is unfortunate in some cases. Its unsavory connotation — something you "left," like your briefcase — hardly does justice to foods that can be just as good, or better, the next day, such as stews, soups, and certain one-pot dishes.

We invite you to join our campaign to find a new term for *leftovers*. Possibilities include

✔ Previously prepared

✔ Tested

✔ Enjoyed again

✔ Golden oldie

✔ Broken in

Mediterranean Seafood Stew

This fish stew combines different compatible flavors in one pot. Like other stews, you can prepare it several hours ahead of serving time. Simply complete the recipe up to Step 3. Five minutes before you want to serve the stew, add the fish and finish cooking.

Note that you add cilantro to this dish at the very last minute — fresh herbs are at their most fragrant that way. Cooking delicate chervil, cilantro, or parsley mutes its flavors. Moreover, herbs are more colorful when added at the last minute.

Tools: *Large, deep sauté pan or skillet, chef's knife, shrimp deveiner (optional)*

Preparation time: *About 30 minutes*

Cooking time: *About 25 minutes*

Yield: *4 servings*

3 tablespoons olive oil

2 large leeks, white and light green parts only, washed and cut into ½-inch pieces (see Figure 17-5 in Chapter 17)

2 large cloves garlic, chopped

1 red bell pepper, cored, seeded, and diced

¾ teaspoon ground cumin

¼ to ½ teaspoon red pepper flakes, or to taste

3 ripe plum tomatoes, cored and diced

1 cup dry white wine

1 cup water

Salt and black pepper

1 pound medium shrimp, shelled and deveined (see Chapter 14)

¾ pound sea scallops, cut in half

¼ cup coarsely chopped cilantro or parsley

1 Heat the oil in a large, deep sauté pan or skillet over medium heat. Add the leeks and cook, stirring occasionally, about 4 minutes, or until they wilt. Add the garlic and cook, stirring often, for another 1 to 2 minutes, or until just golden. (Don't let the garlic brown.)

2 Add the red bell pepper, cumin, and red pepper flakes and cook over low heat about 8 minutes, or until the peppers are tender, stirring occasionally.

3 Add the tomatoes, wine, water, and salt and pepper to taste. Cover and raise the heat to bring the mixture to a boil. Reduce the heat to medium and cook, partially covered, for 6 to 8 minutes.

4 Add the shrimp and scallops and cook, partially covered, about 5 minutes more, or just until the shrimp is evenly pink and the scallops are opaque. Remove from the heat, stir in the cilantro or parsley, and serve.

Vary It! *You can make fish stew with species such as cod, halibut, porgy, squid, tilefish, and weakfish, some of which are quite inexpensive. Think of the texture and flavor of different fish. In stew, you want a relatively firm-fleshed fish that doesn't fall apart. Sole, for example, would be too delicate. Dark-fleshed fish, like mackerel, would overpower the stew.*

Vary It! *Not sure about using leeks, or can't find any? You can substitute one medium white onion, chopped, for the leeks in this recipe.*

Go-With: *Serve this dish with noodles or rice. A salad and good bread are also great accompaniments to this dish.*

Per serving: Calories 318 (From Fat 111); Fat 12g (Saturated 2g); Cholesterol 210mg; Sodium 551mg; Carbohydrate 13g (Dietary Fiber 2g); Protein 36g.

Solving cooking woes

What do you do if a stew or a braised dish is . . .

✔ **Flat-tasting?** Add salt and pepper. Or try a little sherry or Madeira.

✔ **Tough?** Cook it longer. Additional cooking breaks down the sinew in muscular cuts of meat. You may want to remove the vegetables in the dish with a slotted spoon to prevent them from overcooking.

✔ **Burned on the bottom?** Carefully scoop out the unburned portion of the stew into a separate pot. Add water or stock to stretch it if necessary, and add sherry and a chopped onion. (The sweetness in an onion can mask many mistakes.)

✔ **Too thin?** Blend 1 tablespoon flour with 1 tablespoon water. Mix this mixture with 1 cup stew liquid and return to the pot with the rest of the stew. Stir well. Heat slowly until thickened.

Chapter 7

The House Sure Smells Good: Roasting

A roast in the oven perfumes the house with the aroma of comfort. Whether you are preparing a fancy roast for a holiday or a simple roast for a small family meal, whether you are roasting meat or poultry, fish or vegetables, roasting is a delicious way to prepare food in the oven. It brings out the flavors, the textures, and the juices in many foods, and roasting a meal can also be very satisfying, from the initial preparation to the final presentation at the table.

The strict definition of *roasting* is cooking uncovered in an oven in which heat emanates from the walls. When it comes to ease and simplicity, roasting is a valuable technique. You simply buy a big hunk of meat or a variety of vegetables, crank up the oven, and toss it in (well, almost). Whole fish are sublime when seasoned well and roasted. And root vegetables — carrots, onions, and beets, for example — become particularly sweet and succulent when you roast them.

The art of roasting is 90 percent timing and 10 percent patience. And if you use a meat thermometer when roasting meats, fouling up is almost impossible. After you understand timing, you can focus on the finer points of roasting.

This chapter provides you with a few recipes to get you started.

Roasting 101

Roasting is easy, but knowing a few techniques can help you to make the most of your roast! Roasted meats, fish, and vegetables taste even better with the right seasonings. Some roasts are best seared in a hot pan before baking to seal the juices inside the meat. And finally, some roasts should "rest" after roasting and before eating. Here's what you need to know.

Seasoning a roast

Have you ever eaten a superb, charbroiled steak that lingers on the palate like an aged wine? Part of its appeal comes from being seasoned before cooking. You can season meat, poultry, fish, and vegetables with salt, pepper, herbs, and spices, but the trick is to know how much of which seasonings to use.

The most basic seasoning is probably salt. Salt is a flavor enhancer that brings out the best in many foods. For that reason, salting meat, fish, poultry, and vegetables before roasting is important. However, it's easy to overdo the salt, and while a nicely salted roast is delicious, an overly salted roast is unpleasant. We advise using no more than a teaspoon of salt per two pound roast, and many people would choose to use much less than this amount, or no salt at all. Some people are advised to limit salt in their diets, so you should ask guests ahead of time about their dietary restrictions. Others simply choose to enjoy the flavors of other herbs and spices.

Fresh herbs, dried herbs, and ground spices can all enhance the flavor of a roast, but overdoing the seasoning by including too many different flavors can also be detrimental to your final result. In addition to salt, limit yourself to no more than three or four different seasonings. For instance, you might combine oregano, basil, thyme, and parsley to season a pot roast. You might enhance a roasted chicken with tarragon and lemon pepper, or rosemary and white pepper. Cumin or chili powder can add punch to a roasted turkey. Or you might season a fish with paprika, black pepper, and dill. The possibilities are endless, and while some seasonings are traditionally used with certain kinds of foods (see Chapter 3 for more on which seasonings to use where), you can experiment to find the combinations you like. Seasoning is an art, and the more you practice, the more accomplished you will become.

To sear or not to sear?

Searing refers to the technique of heating oil in a very hot pan and then rolling a cut of meat (commonly roast) around to brown the entire surface, which seals in the juices and adds flavor before roasting. You can also sear steaks and chicken pieces by placing them in a very hot pan with oil and then turning them all around until a crust forms on the surface. The advantage to searing is not only that it locks the juices inside the meat, but that it adds a nice golden brown color to a roast that might not color so nicely on its own in the oven. The added flavor of oil used in searing can also enhance the flavor of the roasted meat.

However, searing isn't a requirement. If you don't sear your roast, it may be lighter in color and lighter in flavor, but you can still add seasonings. Searing adds one more pan to clean at the end of the meal, so skipping it saves not only an extra step in cooking but an extra step in cleaning up. The roast won't have the same crisp outer layer when it isn't seared first, but you might like your roast better this way. You might try roasting meat with searing, and the next time, without, just to see which you prefer. If you don't sear you might consider basting instead, which we discuss in the next section.

Basting

Many recipes call for *basting* the roast, which means brushing or pouring pan juices over it during cooking. Basting helps to color a roast evenly and keep the surface moist, and can be a good way to add flavor to the outer surface of a roast if you decide not to sear it first. The juices don't penetrate to the inside of the roast, as some people might tell you. The purpose in basting is purely for the benefit of the roast's surface.

To baste, use a large spoon, bulb baster, or basting brush to coat the roast's surface with the pan juices or oil. Baste the meat every 15 to 30 minutes throughout the roasting process. Basting keeps the meat or vegetables moist, prevents shrinkage, and gives the crust or skin an even brown color, but it isn't necessary. Some people never baste their roasts and they turn out just fine. Try basting and see if it improves your roasts. (Some people just do it because it's fun!)

Be careful when basting, however, because you will be reaching into a hot oven. You can pull out the oven rack to minimize the chances of burning your hands on the oven coils, but remember, you are still handling sizzling-hot juices, and a spill or a too-vigorous squeeze of the bulb baster could result in spattering juices and burns. Baste with care!

Resting your roast

If you're like us, by the time a roast emerges from the oven, the intoxicating aroma has you so hungry that you could tear at it like a dog. Instead, take a deep breath, have some brie and crackers, and let the roast sit out, covered with aluminum foil, for 15 to 20 minutes (if the cut of meat is large). Even a roast chicken or duck should sit for 10 minutes out of the oven before you carve it. Sitting lets the meat *rest:* that is, loosen up a bit, allowing the internal juices to distribute more evenly and settle into the meat. Resting makes for a juicier roast that won't lose so much juice when you cut into it. Resting the roast also allows it to come to a temperature that is better for carving and for eating. So patience, patience! When dinner is finally served, it will all be worth the wait.

Roasting times and temperatures

Tables 7-1 through 7-4 give approximate cooking times and temperatures for various roasts and weights. Remember to remove a roast when its internal temperature is 5 to 10 degrees *less* than final internal temperature, and then let it rest for about 15 minutes. During the resting time, the roast cooks 5 to 10 degrees more. None of this is an exact science, though; you have to use a meat thermometer to get the results you like. See Figure 7-1 for illustrated instructions for using a meat thermometer.

When inserting a meat thermometer into a roast, do not let the metal touch the bone — the bone is hotter than the meat and registers a falsely higher temperature.

Where to put a Dial (or Oven-proof) Meat Thermometer

Figure 7-1:
How to insert a meat thermo- meter in various roasts.

Boneless Roast

Insert to core

Poultry

Insert inside of the thigh

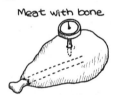

Meat with bone

Insert into the thickest part of the meat

✳ For an accurate reading, do NOT touch the bone, fat, or bottom of the pan with the thermometer.

Table 7-1	Beef Roasting Chart			
Beef Roast	*Preheated Oven Temperature (°F)*	*Weight*	*Approximate Total Cooking Time*	*Remove from Oven at This Meat Temperature*
Boneless rib-eye roast (small end)	350°	3 to 4 pounds	Medium rare: 1½ to 1¾ hours	135°
			Medium: 1¾ to 2 hours	150°

Beef Roast	Preheated Oven Temperature (°F)	Weight	Approximate Total Cooking Time	Remove from Oven at This Meat Temperature
Boneless rib-eye roast (small end)	350°	4 to 6 pounds	Medium rare: 1¾ to 2 hours	135°
			Medium: 2 to 2½ hours	150°
		6 to 8	Medium rare: 2 to 2¼ hours	135°
			Medium: 2½ to 2¾ hours	150°
Bone-in rib roast (chine bone removed)	350°	4 to 6 pounds (2 ribs)	Medium rare: 1¾ to 2¼ hours	135°
			Medium: 2¼ to 2½ hours	150°
		6 to 8 pounds (2 to 4 ribs)	Medium rare: 2¼ to 2½ hours	135°
			Medium: 2¾ to 3 hours	150°
		8 to 10 pounds (4 to 5 ribs)	Medium rare: 2½ to 3 hours	135°
			Medium: 3 to 3½ hours	150°
Round tip roast (sirloin tip)	325°	3 to 4 pounds	Medium rare: 1¾ to 2 hours	140°
			Medium: 2¼ to 2½ hours	155°
		4 to 6 pounds	Medium rare: 2 to 2½ hours	140°
			Medium: 2½ to 3 hours	155°

(continued)

Table 7-1 *(continued)*

Beef Roast	Preheated Oven Temperature (°F)	Weight	Approximate Total Cooking Time	Remove from Oven at This Meat Temperature
Round tip roast (sirloin tip)	325°	6 to 8 pounds	Medium rare: 2½ to 3 hours	140°
			Medium: 3 to 3½ hours	155°
Tenderloin roast	425°	2 to 3 pounds	Medium rare: 35 to 40 minutes	135°
			Medium: 45 to 50 minutes	150°
		4 to 5 pounds	Medium rare: 50 to 60 minutes	135°
			Medium: 60 to 70 minutes	150°

Medium rare doneness: 140° to 145° final meat temperature after 10 to 15 minutes standing time
Medium doneness: 155° to 160° final meat temperature after 10 to 15 minutes standing time
Allow ¼ to ⅓ pound of uncooked boneless beef per serving and ½ to 1 pound of bone-in meat per serving, depending on the cut.
Source: National Cattlemen's Beef Association

Table 7-2   Poultry Roasting Chart

Bird	Weight	Preheated Oven Temperature	Cooking Time
Chicken, broiler/fryer (unstuffed)	3 to 4 pounds	350°	1¼ to 1½ hours
Chicken, roaster (unstuffed)	5 to 7 pounds	350°	2 to 2¼ hours
Whole turkey (thawed and unstuffed)	8 to 12 pounds	325°	2¾ to 3 hours
Whole turkey (thawed and unstuffed)	12 to 14 pounds	325°	3 to 3¾ hours
	14 to 18 pounds	325°	3¾ to 4¼ hours
	18 to 20 pounds	325°	4¼ to 4½ hours

Bird	Weight	Preheated Oven Temperature	Cooking Time
Duck (whole, unstuffed)	4 to 5½ pounds	325°	2½ to 3 hours

Depending on the size of the bird, allow 15 to 20 minutes additional cooking time if stuffed. Internal temperature for stuffing should be 165°. Internal temperature for meat should be minimum 180° in the thigh. Allow about ¾ to 1 pound of uncooked chicken or turkey on the bone per serving.
Source: National Chicken Council

The associations and companies that produce and market poultry use these roasting tables only as a rough guideline. For actual cooking times, they recommend always using a meat thermometer when cooking poultry of any kind.

Table 7-3	**Pork Roasting Chart**		
Cut	*Thickness/Weight*	*Final Internal Temperature*	*Cooking Time*
Loin roast (bone-in)	3 to 5 pounds	155° to 160°	20 minutes per pound
Boneless pork roast	2 to 4 pounds	155° to 160°	20 minutes per pound
Tenderloin (roast at 425° to 450°)	½ to 1½ pounds	155° to 160°	20 to 30 minutes
Crown roast	6 to 10 pounds	155° to 160°	20 minutes per pound
Boneless loin chops	1 inch thick	155° to 160°	12 to 16 minutes
Ribs		Tender	1½ to 2 hours

Roast in a shallow pan, uncovered, at 350°.
Allow about ¼ to ⅓ pound of uncooked boneless meat per serving and about ½ to 1 pound of bone-in meat per serving, depending on the cut.
Source: National Pork Producers Council

Every oven is different, no matter how much you spend for it. Some ovens are off by as much as 50 degrees, which can be like trying to make gourmet coffee with hot tap water. Baking can be a disaster without precision. Investing in an oven thermometer is worthwhile.

Table 7-4		Lamb Roasting Chart	
Roast	*Weight*	*Final Internal Temperature*	*Approximate Cooking Time Per Pound*
Leg (bone-in)	5 to 7 pounds	Medium rare: 145° to 150°	15 minutes
		Medium: 155° to 160°	20 minutes
Boneless (rolled and tied)	4 to 7 pounds	Medium rare: 145° to 150°	20 minutes
		Medium: 155° to 160°	25 minutes
Sirloin roast (boneless)	about 2 pounds	Medium rare: 145° to 150°	25 minutes
		Medium: 155° to 160°	30 minutes
Top round roast	about 2 pounds	Medium rare: 145° to 150°	45 minutes
		Medium: 155° to 160°	55 minutes

Preheat oven to 325° and remove from oven about 10° below desired temperature.
Allow ¼ to ⅓ pound of boneless lamb per serving and ⅓ to ½ pound of bone-in lamb per serving.
Source: American Lamb Council

Don't keep opening the oven door to see whether the roast is done. Your kitchen will get hot, and the meat or vegetables will take longer to cook.

Roasting Poultry

Roasting poultry may seem challenging, but don't be intimidated. Although it's not just a matter of tossing it in the oven and mixing a gin and tonic, attention to a few details will yield a memorable result, whether you're roasting a 3-pound chicken or a 20-pound turkey.

Before you roast poultry, remove the packaged giblets (the neck, heart, gizzard, and liver) inside the cavity and save them. Rinse the bird thoroughly, inside and out, under cold running water. Then pat the skin dry with paper towels and season. The following recipe uses the giblets to make a delicious pan gravy.

As you cook the bird, use a meat thermometer! (When you feel feverish, which would you prefer: a doctor who places a hand on your forehead or one who uses a thermometer?) Whatever the type of thermometer you use (instant-read, which you can stick in the meat when you suspect it is nearing doneness to get an immediate temperature reading) or ovenproof (the kind you stick in the meat when you first put it in the oven and keep an eye on while cooking), insert it deep into the flesh between the bird's thigh and breast. If you don't have a thermometer, insert a knife into the thick part of the thigh; if the juices run clear, the bird is thoroughly cooked. If they run pink, let the meat cook for another 15 minutes or so before testing for done-ness again. Then go buy a thermometer so that you have one next time!

If you want your bird to hold its shape perfectly while roasting, you can truss it. You can do without this step if you're in a hurry, but we explain the tech-nique anyway. See Figures 7-2 and 7-3 for illustrated instructions. For more on cooking a large turkey for Thanksgiving, see Chapter 21.

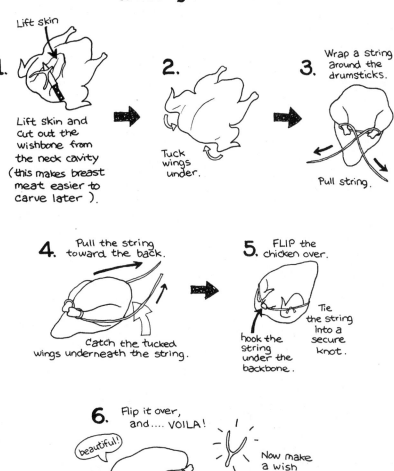

Trussing a Chicken

1. Lift skin
Lift skin and cut out the wishbone from the neck cavity (this makes breast meat easier to carve later).

2. Tuck wings under.

3. Wrap a string around the drumsticks.
Pull string.

4. Pull the string toward the back.
Catch the tucked wings underneath the string.

5. FLIP the chicken over.
hook the string under the backbone.
Tie the string into a secure knot.

6. Flip it over, and.... VOILA!
beautiful!
Now make a wish with that wishbone you took out!

Figure 7-2: Trussing helps poultry keep its shape.

TIP

Eat your chicken liver

A cardinal rule of many chefs (who hate to throw out food of any kind) is to never discard the giblets. You can add giblets to homemade soup or to canned stock to enrich its flavor.

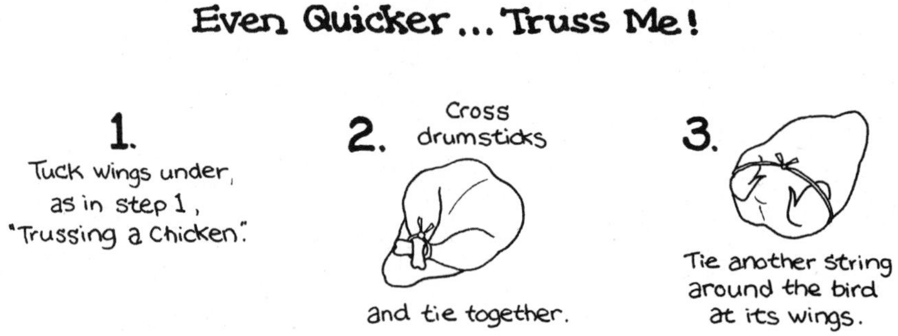

Even Quicker... Truss Me!

1.
Tuck wings under, as in step 1, "Trussing a Chicken."

2. Cross drumsticks
and tie together.

3.
Tie another string around the bird at its wings.

Figure 7-3:
How to truss a bird the fast way.

Roasted Chicken

The most common mistake home cooks make when roasting chicken is using an insufficiently hot oven. This recipe calls for a 425-degree oven, which yields a crispy, golden-brown skin. Irresistible!

Tools: *Chef's knife, large metal roasting pan, roasting rack, meat thermometer, kitchen string (if trussing)*

Preparation time: *About 15 minutes (or 20 if trussing)*

Roasting time: *About 1 hour and 15 minutes, plus 15 minutes resting time*

Yield: *4 servings*

1 chicken, 4 to 4½ pounds, with giblets	1 medium yellow onion, quartered
Salt and pepper	½ cup homemade or canned chicken stock
1 lemon, pricked several times with a fork	½ cup water, or more as necessary
2 sprigs fresh thyme, or ½ teaspoon dried thyme	2 tablespoons butter
1 clove garlic, peeled whole	Parsley, rosemary, tarragon, or other fresh herbs to taste (optional)
2 tablespoons olive oil	

1 Preheat the oven to 425 degrees. Remove the giblets from the chicken's cavity; rinse and reserve. Rinse the chicken under cold running water, inside and out, and pat dry with paper towels.

2 Sprinkle the chicken inside and out with salt and pepper to taste. Insert the lemon, thyme, and garlic into the cavity of the chicken. Rub the outside of the chicken all over with the olive oil.

3 Truss the chicken with string, if desired. (Refer to Figures 7-2 and 7-3 for instructions.)

4 Place the chicken, breast side up, on a rack in a shallow metal roasting pan. Scatter the giblets and onions on the bottom of the pan.

5 Place the chicken in the oven and roast for 45 minutes.

6 Carefully remove the roasting pan from the oven and close the oven door. Using a large spoon, skim any fat from the roasting pan juices. Add the chicken stock, water, and butter to the pan. Roast for another 20 to 30 minutes.

When cooked, the chicken should be golden brown all over, and no red juice should flow when you pierce the joint between the thigh and leg with a knife. A meat thermometer in the thigh should read 180 degrees (refer to Figure 7-1) before you remove the bird from the oven. Lift up the chicken to let the cavity juices (which should be clear, not pink) flow into the pan. Transfer to a carving board or serving platter, cover with aluminum foil, and let rest for 10 to 15 minutes.

7 Meanwhile, place the roasting pan on top of the stove. Using a slotted spoon, remove and discard any pieces of giblets or onion. Add water or stock if necessary to make about 1 cup liquid. (You can pour the juices into a glass measuring cup to gauge how much liquid is in the pan.) Bring to a boil and reduce for 1 to 2 minutes (letting the sauce evaporate and condense as it cooks over high heat), stirring and scraping the bottom of the pan. If desired, add fresh parsley, rosemary, tarragon, or other fresh herbs to taste. Turn off the heat when the sauce is reduced to about ¾ cup. Strain the sauce into a gravy boat or a small bowl just before serving.

8 Untruss the chicken (if necessary), cutting the string with a sharp knife or kitchen shears. Remove and discard the lemon and thyme sprigs.

9 Carve the chicken into serving pieces, as shown in Figure 7-4, and serve with the hot pan juices.

Vary It! *Roasted chicken, either hot or cold, goes well with a mildly spicy mustard mayonnaise. Blend Dijon mustard to taste into ½ cup of mayonnaise. (Start with about a teaspoon and work your way up if it isn't zippy enough for you.) Season with salt and pepper and freshly chopped herbs, such as tarragon, basil, chervil, parsley, or oregano. This is also good with cold pork, poultry, fish, and grilled meats.*

Go-With: *Serve this dish with any of the following side dishes: White Beans with Tomato and Thyme, Carrots with Cumin Butter, Southern Greens (all in Chapter 16), or with any kind of potato and a green salad.*

Per serving: *Calories 636 (From Fat 395); Fat 44g (Saturated 13g); Cholesterol 194mg; Sodium 395mg; Carbohydrate 0g (Dietary Fiber 0g); Protein 57g.*

Carving a Chicken

1. Place the chicken, breast side up, on a carving board.

Remove the leg by pulling it away from the body and cutting through the ball joint.

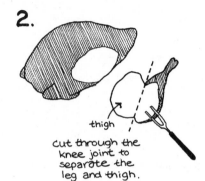

2.

thigh

Cut through the knee joint to separate the leg and thigh.

3.

Figure 7-4: How to carve a chicken.

Remove the wing, cutting as close to the breast as possible, through the joint that attaches it to the body. (cut off the wing tips, if desired.)

4.

Carve the breast meat parallel to the ribs, slicing toward the top of the breast. Keep the slices as thin as possible.

(Now get someone else to carve the other side, exactly the same way.)

Roasting Your Veggies

All kinds of vegetables, either alone or in combination with others, can be roasted by using the simple technique here — in fact, this is so convenient for home cooks that we decided to give you two recipes, one for summer vegetables and one for winter root vegetables.

If you combine different vegetables on the same roasting pan, be sure to choose those that will cook in about the same amount of time — for example, tomatoes cook much faster than carrots. Another way to achieve even cooking is to cut the hardest vegetables (carrots, parsnips, potatoes, and so on) into smaller pieces than the soft vegetables (celery, bell peppers, eggplant, and so on).

○ Crispy Roasted Root Vegetables

You can serve this dish separately with many entrees. But if you're roasting a side of beef or a chicken, scatter a variety of root vegetables (such as cut-up carrots, onions, and peeled potatoes) in the roasting pan. Turn them every so often in the pan drippings so they cook evenly. This makes for a great presentation at the table — that is, if you don't eat them all in the kitchen.

If you have leftover roasted vegetables, use them the next day in a salad, rolled in a tortilla with hot sauce, or in an omelet. If you want to make them crisp again, before serving, place them in a 400-degree oven for about 5 minutes.

Tools: *Vegetable peeler, chef's knife, large mixing bowl, baking dish*

Preparation time: *About 10 minutes*

Cooking time: *About 30 minutes*

Yield: *4 servings*

4 medium carrots, washed (skins on), halved, and chopped crosswise into about 4 pieces	*3 medium red potatoes, quartered*	*2 small bulbs fennel, trimmed and quartered*
	3 small turnips, peeled and quartered	*1 tablespoon minced fresh rosemary, or ½ tablespoon dried rosemary*
2 red or yellow bell peppers, cored, seeded, and sliced into ½-inch strips	*2 medium yellow onions, quartered*	*¼ cup olive oil*
		Salt and black pepper

1 Preheat the oven to 400 degrees.

2 Place the carrots, bell peppers, potatoes, turnips, onions, fennel, and rosemary in a large mixing bowl. Pour the olive oil over them. Season generously with salt and pepper. Toss well to blend. Transfer to a roasting pan that can hold them in one layer. Place the pan in the oven and roast for 25 to 30 minutes, turning the vegetables several times. (If after 25 minutes the vegetables are tender but not browned, place them under the broiler for a minute or two — but don't let them burn).

Go-With: *These vegetables go well with all sorts of roasted meats, like Roasted Fillet of Beef and Roasted Chicken, both in this chapter.*

Per serving: *Calories 334 (From Fat 127); Fat 14g (Saturated 2g); Cholesterol 0mg; Sodium 252mg; Carbohydrate 48g (Dietary Fiber 9g); Protein 6g.*

🍅 *Roasted Summer Vegetables*

Summer vegetables release quite a bit of water when roasted. To get them brown and crisp, be sure to place them on the lowest oven rack, close to the heating element. You may also sprinkle a little brown sugar over the vegetables; this brings out their natural sweetness and counterbalances the tastes of fresh ginger, garlic, and hot pepper.

If you have any leftovers, serve them as a side dish the next day with sandwiches, or roll them in soft flour tortillas, maybe with some lettuce and hot sauce; they're also great over pasta with a little grated Parmesan cheese.

Tools: *Vegetable peeler, chef's knife, spatula or wooden spoon*

Preparation time: *About 15 minutes*

Cooking time: *About 25 minutes*

Yield: *4 servings*

3 medium carrots, peeled and cut into ¼-inch slices

2 to 3 tablespoons olive oil

1 red or yellow bell pepper, cored, seeded, and cut into ½-inch cubes

1 small zucchini, halved lengthwise and cut into ½-inch-thick slices

1 small yellow squash, halved lengthwise and cut into ½-inch-thick semi-round slices

½ pound asparagus, trimmed of thick stems and cut diagonally into 1-inch pieces

1 small red onion, chopped into ⅛-inch cubes

1 large clove garlic, chopped

½ to 1 jalapeño pepper or small red chile pepper (according to taste), seeded and minced

1 tablespoon chopped fresh basil, marjoram, or thyme (or 1 teaspoon dried)

2 teaspoons peeled and minced fresh ginger

1 teaspoon brown sugar (optional)

Salt and black pepper

1 Preheat the oven to 425 degrees.

2 Scatter the carrots over a large roasting pan. Drizzle them with 1 tablespoon of the olive oil; toss to coat. Place the pan on the oven rack closest to the heating element, and roast for 10 minutes.

3 Take the pan from the oven and add the bell pepper, zucchini, squash, asparagus, onion, garlic, and jalapeño. Sprinkle with the basil, ginger, brown sugar (if desired), and salt and pepper to taste; drizzle the remaining 1 to 2 tablespoons of olive oil over the vegetables, using only enough to lightly coat them. Toss well, spreading the vegetables out in a single layer.

4 Return the roasting pan to the oven and roast about 20 to 25 minutes, or until tender, turning once with a spatula or wooden spoon after 15 minutes so the vegetables brown evenly. If after 25 minutes the vegetables are tender but not browned, place them under the broiler for a minute or two — but watch carefully that they don't burn.

Go-With: Serve these vegetables, hot or cold, with Grilled Swordfish Steaks with Lemon and Thyme or The Perfect Hamburger, both in Chapter 8.

Per serving: Calories 123 (From Fat 63); Fat 7g (Saturated 1g); Cholesterol 0mg; Sodium 181mg; Carbohydrate 14g (Dietary Fiber 4g); Protein 3g.

Roasting the Big Guns: Beef, Pork, Lamb, Ham, and Ribs

Americans have two immutable love affairs: automobiles and meat. We doubt anything will ever change that! Sure, people have become more health-conscious, and many seek leaner cuts of meat, but the beef and pork industries have responded, making great strides in breeding leaner animals without sacrificing tenderness. Add to that America's recent obsession with low-carb protein diets, and meat is where it's at! If you're looking for more low-carb recipes, check out *Low-Carb Dieting For Dummies,* by Katherine B. Chauncey, Ph.D. (Wiley).

Concerning pork or other meats, good butchers are also knowledgeable cooks. They can offer recipes, tips, and information on preparing your roast so that it is "oven-ready." For example, an oven-ready roast is trimmed of excess fat and sometimes tied with butcher's string to make it as uniform as possible for even cooking. A leg of lamb should have its fat and shank bone removed. The skin and rind of a smoked ham are trimmed away, leaving just a thin layer of fat that you can score to make a diamond pattern on the meat's surface for a pretty effect.

Pork paranoia

Cooks used to believe that if you ate pork that's cooked at less than 185 degrees, you could contract *trichinosis.* The average person didn't know what that was — or how many days of school kids could miss because of it — but it sure sounded unpleasant. Thus, for years, everyone ate overcooked pork. About a decade ago, scientists discovered that harmful trichinae are killed at 135 degrees. Cooking pork to 155 degrees is considered plenty safe and yields a much juicier result than the 185 degrees of the past.

Roast Loin of Pork

Compared to some types of roasts, pork remains a relative bargain. Pork is lighter and leaner than ever before, and you can assemble this uncomplicated dish in about a half-hour and then pop it in the oven.

Tools: Chef's knife, vegetable peeler, large roasting pan, meat thermometer, cutting board

Preparation time: About 25 minutes

Roasting time: About 1 hour and 5 minutes, plus 15 minutes resting time

Yield: 6 servings

Center-cut boneless loin of pork, about 3 pounds	6 medium red potatoes, peeled and halved lengthwise	2 large cloves garlic, finely chopped
4 tablespoons olive oil	3 medium yellow onions, peeled and quartered	½ cup water
2 tablespoons chopped fresh thyme, or 1 teaspoon dried thyme	4 carrots, peeled and cut into 2-inch pieces	¼ cup chopped fresh parsley
Salt and pepper	1 bay leaf	2 cups applesauce (optional)

1 Preheat the oven to 400 degrees.

2 Place the pork in a large roasting pan (without a rack) and brush or rub the meat all over with 3 tablespoons of the oil. Season with the thyme and the salt and pepper to taste. Roast, fat side up, for 15 minutes.

3 Remove the pan from the oven and scatter the potatoes, onions, carrots, and bay leaf around the roast. Drizzle the remaining 1 tablespoon of oil over the vegetables and, using a large spoon, turn the vegetables in the cooking juices. Sprinkle the garlic over the vegetables, and season the vegetables with salt and pepper to taste. Add the water to the pan.

4 Reduce the oven temperature to 350 degrees and roast for 45 to 50 minutes or until a meat thermometer registers 155 degrees in the thickest part of the roast.

5 Remove the pan from the oven, and transfer the roast to a cutting board. Cover with aluminum foil and let rest for 15 minutes before carving. Reduce the oven temperature to 300 degrees and place the pan with the vegetables in the oven to keep warm.

6 To serve, transfer the carved meat and vegetables to a large platter. (Pour any juices that have collected around the meat into the roasting pan.) Remove the bay leaf from the pan, and place the pan over two burners on high. Bring the juices to a boil, stirring and scraping the bottom and sides of the pan with a wooden spoon. Cook about 1 to 2 minutes or until the sauce is reduced and slightly thickened. Pour the juices over everything, sprinkle with the chopped parsley, and, if desired, serve with applesauce.

Go-With: This hearty dish is delicious with winter vegetables like Southern Greens (see Chapter 16) or Sautéed Spinach Leaves (see Chapter 5), or a simple salad of mixed greens (see Chapter 12).

Per serving: Calories 574 (From Fat 175); Fat 20g (Saturated 5g); Cholesterol 150mg; Sodium 244mg; Carbohydrate 43g (Dietary Fiber 5g); Protein 54g.

Roasted Fillet of Beef

This savory dish, although on the pricey side, is fast, simple, and always delicious — a real last-minute party saver. Serve it with simple dishes like garlic-flavored mashed potatoes and Steamed Broccoli with Lemon Butter (see Chapter 4). The roast called "fillet" is also called "tenderloin," so you can use these terms interchangeably. The fillet roast is different than the cut called "filet mignon."

Tools: *Roasting rack, roasting pan, meat thermometer, carving board*

Preparation time: *About 10 minutes*

Roasting time: *About 45 minutes, plus 10 minutes resting time*

Yield: *8 servings*

1 beef fillet (tenderloin) roast, oven-ready from the butcher, about 4 pounds	2 tablespoons vegetable oil
Salt and pepper	Herb butter (optional)

1 Preheat the oven to 425 degrees.

2 Sprinkle the fillet of beef with salt and pepper to taste.

3 Place the meat on a rack in a heavy roasting pan and brush or rub it with the oil. Roast for about 45 minutes for medium rare or until desired doneness. A meat thermometer should read 135 to 140 degrees for medium rare and 150 to 155 degrees for medium. Halfway through the roasting time, invert the meat and baste once with the pan juices.

4 Transfer to a carving board, cover with aluminum foil, and let stand for 10 minutes before carving.

5 Carve the fillet into approximately ½-inch-thick slices and serve immediately, topped with a pat of butter and a sprinkle of herbs (try fresh chopped or dried basil), if desired.

Go-With: *You can serve fillet of beef (tenderloin) with almost anything, from a simple avocado and tomato salad (see Chapter 17) to a fancy risotto (see Chapter 4).*

Per serving: Calories 528 (From Fat 356); Fat 40g (Saturated 15g); Cholesterol 135mg; Sodium 176mg; Carbohydrate 0g (Dietary Fiber 0g); Protein 40g.

You overcooked the roast beef

Unfortunately, ovens do not have reverse gears. But you can salvage overcooked roast beef in many tasty ways. You can always make roast beef hash or beef pot pie, various soups such as the Vegetable Beef Soup in Chapter 10, or beef stroganoff. Any recipe that calls for liquid or a cream-based sauce is good, too, for using over-cooked beef.

Glazed Leg of Lamb with Pan Gravy and Red Currant Glaze

This delicious but basic recipe for leg of lamb can benefit even more from the addition of root vegetables like carrots, onions, and potatoes. Add these to the pan during the last hour of cooking. If you enjoy your lamb cooked medium to well, just roast it a little longer, until the internal temperature reaches 155 or 160 degrees or more. But you may not need to. A roasted leg of lamb offers meat of varying degrees of doneness. The meat at the thin, shank end, very close to the bone, is browned and well done, and the meat at the thicker end ideally is quite pink and medium rare. Use the drier meats for hash or to train your dog to separate the sports section from the newspaper and bring it to you.

If you're lucky, a whole leg of lamb will leave you with delicious leftovers. You can make cold lamb sandwiches, Shepherd's Pie (see Chapter 14), or substitute lamb for the beef in Vegetable Beef Soup (see Chapter 11). Or turn to Chapter 18 for a delicious Lamb Curry recipe using leftover cooked lamb.

Tools: *Paring knife, roasting pan, roasting rack, basting brush, meat thermometer, small saucepan*

Preparation time: *About 15 minutes for the lamb, about 5 minutes for the glaze*

Roasting time: *About 1 hour and 40 minutes, plus 20 minutes resting time*

Yield: *10 servings*

1 leg of lamb (6 to 7 pounds), well trimmed and ready for roasting

3 cloves garlic, thinly sliced

1 tablespoon vegetable oil

½ teaspoon ground ginger

Salt and pepper

1 Preheat the oven to 425 degrees.

2 With a paring knife, make small incisions along the leg and then insert the garlic slivers into the incisions.

3 Rub the lamb with the olive oil and place it on a rack in a shallow roasting pan, fat side up. Sprinkle the meat with the ginger and salt and pepper to taste.

4 Roast the lamb for 20 minutes; reduce the heat to 350 degrees and roast for an additional 1 hour and 20 minutes, or until a meat thermometer registers 145 degrees in the thickest part of the leg for medium rare or 155 degrees for medium.

5 During the last 30 minutes of roasting, brush the top and sides of the lamb every 10 minutes with Red Currant Glaze and pan juices. (Start brushing when the meat thermometer in the lamb registers about 115 degrees.)

6 Remove from the oven, cover with foil, and let rest for 20 minutes. Carve (see Figure 7-5) and serve with some of the pan juices spooned over the top of the slices.

Go-With: *Serve with Crispy Roasted Root Vegetables (earlier in this chapter) and a tossed green salad (see Chapter 12).*

Red Currant Glaze

¼ cup red currant jelly

Juice and grated peel of ½ lemon

1½ teaspoons Dijon-style mustard

Combine all the ingredients in a small saucepan and heat until the jelly is melted (about 1 minute). Use as a basting sauce for a leg of lamb, brushing every 10 minutes during the last 30 minutes of roasting.

Per serving: Calories 287 (From Fat 105); Fat 12g (Saturated 4g); Cholesterol 117mg; Sodium 168mg; Carbohydrate 6g (Dietary Fiber 0g); Protein 37g.

A Sunday dinner winner

A *round tip roast,* also referred to as a *sirloin tip roast,* is leaner and less tender than a more expensive roast, such as prime rib. However, it is very economical, and, if cooked properly, makes a great family dinner.

To serve a tip roast for 6 people, follow these steps:

1. **Purchase a 3- to 4-pound sirloin tip roast.**

2. **Rub it with fresh chopped garlic, a little olive oil, salt, pepper, and your favorite herbs.**

3. **Place it on a rack in a shallow roasting pan in a preheated 325-degree oven and cook**

until a meat thermometer inserted into the center of the roast registers 140 degrees for medium-rare, or 150 degrees for medium.

Remember that a resting roast continues cooking, adding about 5 degrees on a meat thermometer. A 3- to 4-pound roast will cook to medium-rare in between 1¾ and 2 hours and to medium in between 2¼ and 2½ hours.

4. **Remove the roast from the oven and let stand, loosely covered with foil, for 15 minutes before carving.**

Carving a Leg of Lamb

1.
Cut out a narrow wedge of meat.

2.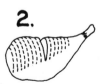
Carve the meat from either side of the wedge, down to the bone.

3.
Slice through cuts to form pieces.

4.
Turn the leg over. Trim off the fat and carve off slices parallel to the bone.

Figure 7-5: The proper technique for carving a leg of lamb.

Hams have more identities than an international spy. Sorting them all out is not terribly complicated, however. Remember that all hams are cured (which means seasoned and aged), and some are also smoked. The two most common methods of preparing a ham are *dry curing* and *wet curing.* In the dry method, a ham is rubbed with salt and seasonings and hung in a cool, dry place to age, anywhere from a few weeks to a year or more. Wet cured hams are soaked in brine, or injected with brine, to give them more flavor.

Here is a primer on some other terms for hams:

- **Country ham:** This is a dry cured ham that is smoked, salted, and then aged for at least 6 months.

- **Sugar-cured ham:** This is a ham that is rubbed with salt and brown sugar or molasses before aging.

- **Canned ham:** Cured but not always smoked, these cooked hams are ready to eat. A little cooking, though, improves the flavor.

- **Fully cooked hams:** These are the same as "ready-to-eat" hams. You can eat them without cooking.

- **Aged ham:** These are heavily cured and smoked hams that have been dry-aged at least one year.

- **Half ham:** These come from the shank bone, butt, or ham end. The shank portion is best and easiest to deal with.

- **Bayonne ham:** A dry-cured ham from the Basque country of France, specifically the city of Bayonne.

- **Prosciutto:** Strictly speaking, this is ham from Parma, Italy. It is seasoned, salt cured, air dried, and pressed to make the meat very firm. It is usually eaten in very thin slices over bread.

- **Westphalian ham:** A rosy, sweetish, German ham made from hogs that are fed sugar beet mash. It is usually eaten like prosciutto.

- **Smithfield ham:** The pride of Smithfield, Virginia, this salty, wonderfully flavorful ham is seasoned, smoked, and hung for at least a year.

- **Virginia ham:** Another salty, dry-cured ham; it is made from hogs that eat peanuts, acorns, and other high-protein foods.

Sweet little piggies

Baked hams — more accurately called "roasted hams" — are often brushed with a sweet marmalade or other glaze that counterbalances the saltiness of the meat. The thick skin, or rind, is first cut away to expose a thin layer of fat. This fat can be trimmed and then scored and studded with whole cloves for a pretty effect. The glaze is applied during the last 30 minutes of baking, or when the ham has reached an internal temperature of 120 degrees; if applied sooner, the glaze could burn. Glazes can be mixtures of all sorts of flavors: jams, brown sugar, molasses, corn syrup, mustard, cinnamon, cloves, ginger, whiskey, rum, orange juice, Port, or white wine. Some producers douse the ham with Coca-Cola to produce a syrupy coating — no kidding.

Smoked Ham with Apricot Glaze

In this recipe, the ham is brushed with an apricot-and-mustard glaze and then served with a pan sauce made from the luscious drippings. Ham and fruit make a natural pairing, and you can use this combination to good effect not only in the glaze but in the garnish. Decorate your platter with pieces of fruit, such as pineapple slices, apricot halves nestled in pear halves, or slices of oranges (shown in the color section). Brush fruits with glaze for beautiful presentation.

Tools: *Roasting pan, chef's knife, meat thermometer, brush for applying glaze, carving board, gravy skimmer (optional), fine strainer, wooden spatula*

Preparation time: *20 minutes*

Cooking time: *About 2 hours and 15 minutes*

Yield: *14 servings*

½ of a smoked cooked ham, bone-in (7 to 9 pounds)

About 30 whole cloves (optional)

About 1 cup water

½ cup apricot preserves or orange marmalade

2 tablespoons Dijon-style mustard

1 tablespoon dark rum (optional)

Pepper

1 cup homemade or canned chicken stock

1 Preheat the oven to 325 degrees. Remove the rind from the ham with a sharp knife and discard. It should have a thin layer of fat underneath.

2 Using a sharp knife, *score* the meat by making small cuts in the fat all over the ham, as shown in Figure 7-6 — this helps the glaze penetrate the meat. (If you want to add a decorative effect, insert a clove into the center of each diamond cut.) Place the ham in a heavy roasting pan; add ½ cup of water to the pan and bake until a meat thermometer inserted into the center registers 120 degrees — about 1½ to 2 hours. (Add an additional ½ cup of water to the roasting pan if it gets dry.)

3 Meanwhile, prepare the glaze. In a small pan, heat the apricot preserves over low heat; mash any large pieces of fruit with a fork. Stir in the mustard and, if desired, the rum. Season with pepper to taste. Boil, stirring occasionally, until the mixture thickens enough to coat a spoon, about 3 minutes.

4 When the ham reaches an internal temperature of 120 degrees, increase the oven temperature to 400 degrees. Pull out the ham and brush or spoon the glaze all over. Return the ham to the oven and bake for another 20 to 25 minutes, or until a thermometer inserted in the center registers 140 degrees (be careful not to burn the glaze). Place the ham on a large carving board; cover with foil and let rest 15 minutes.

5 While the ham rests, prepare the pan sauce. Pour the juices from the roasting pan into a small shallow bowl. Tilt the bowl and skim the fat that accumulates on the surface with a spoon (or use a skimmer, as shown in Figure 7-7). Return the skimmed juices to the pan and place it over a burner on high heat; add the chicken stock. Cook, stirring and scraping up browned bits on the bottom of the pan (a wooden spoon or spatula will not scratch your pan), until the liquid is reduced and slightly thickened. Pass the sauce through a fine strainer before serving with the ham.

6 Thinly slice the ham (see Figure 7-8); serve with pan juices and, if desired, a good mustard.

Vary 1t! You can flavor a ham's pan sauce in many ways. Try adding 2 to 3 tablespoons of dark raisins, 2 tablespoons of dark rum, or some dry white wine or apple cider. Grated orange zest and freshly squeezed orange juice also give the sauce a clean, citric edge.

Go-With: Ham always goes well with cabbage (cooked with caraway seeds and vinegar or shredded in coleslaw), but try other side dishes too, like Southern Greens (see Chapter 16) or Basic Wild Rice (see Chapter 4).

Per serving: Calories 435 (From Fat 253); Fat 28g (Saturated 10g); Cholesterol 103mg; Sodium 2,076mg; Carbohydrate 8g (Dietary Fiber 0g); Protein 36g.

♪ Score That Ham! ♪

Use a sharp knife to make shallow, even cuts across the top of the ham.

Then, make cuts in the opposite direction.

I'm scored

Decorate if you like, by sticking cloves in the middle of the diamonds made by the scores.

Figure 7-6: How to score a ham.

fat skimmer

2 cups

FAT

Figure 7-7: A fat skimmer.

Carving a Ham

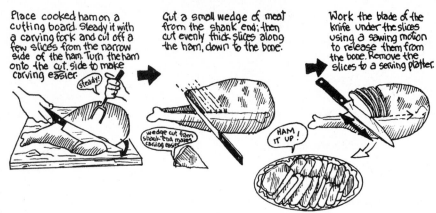

Place cooked ham on a cutting board. Steady it with a carving fork and cut off a few slices from the narrow side of the ham. Turn the ham onto the cut side to make carving easier.

steady!

Cut a small wedge of meat from the shank end; then cut evenly thick slices along the ham, down to the bone.

wedge cut from shank-end makes carving easier

Work the blade of the knife under the slices using a sawing motion to release them from the bone. Remove the slices to a serving platter.

HAM IT UP!

Figure 7-8:
How to carve a ham.

Roasted Pork Ribs with Country Barbecue Sauce

Whether done over a grill or in an oven, ribs need long, slow cooking. Some recipes call for parboiling ribs before roasting or grilling, but we have found that a lot of the flavor winds up in the cooking water when you do it this way. The best alternative we've found is roasting spareribs in a 300-degree oven for 2 hours, which leaves them succulent and flavorful.

Ribs are delicious when rubbed with spices before cooking. The recipe here calls for brown sugar, salt, and pepper. A sweet element always give the ribs a seductive flavor; the other ingredients can vary according to your taste. If you like them spicy, add a little cayenne pepper to the mix (about ¼ teaspoon or more if you like it extra hot). Other seasonings you could experiment with include sweet paprika, onion powder, garlic powder, ground cumin, ground coriander, cinnamon, dried thyme, and dried basil.

This dish, which is featured in the color section, is great for casual entertaining. Just be sure to have lots of moist towels around. Ribs get messy! (But that's half the fun.)

Tools: *Chef's knife, cutting board, roasting pan, basting brush*

Preparation time: *About 20 minutes, plus 30 minutes refrigeration*

Cooking time: *About 2 hours and 30 minutes (including making the sauce)*

Yield: *4 servings*

1 tablespoon brown sugar, packed	*1 teaspoon pepper, or to taste*
1½ teaspoons salt, or to taste	*3 to 4 pounds pork spareribs*

1 Preheat the oven to 300 degrees. Make a spice rub by combining the brown sugar, salt, and pepper in a small bowl. Stir well. Trim excess fat from the ribs. Place the ribs on a cutting board. Cut the slabs into pieces of one to two ribs each.

2 Arrange the spareribs in one layer on a roasting pan. Sprinkle the ribs with the spice rub, pressing the seasonings firmly onto the meat all around. Cover loosely and refrigerate about 30 minutes.

3 Roast in the oven for 1½ hours, turning them over after 45 minutes. (While the ribs cook, make the barbecue sauce.)

4 Increase the oven temperature to 350 degrees. Remove the roasting pan from the oven; carefully pour off all the fat (or transfer ribs to a clean roasting pan). Brush the ribs generously on all sides with the barbecue sauce and roast another 25 to 30 minutes, or until the meat is so tender it easily "wiggles" or pulls away from the bone. Serve the ribs with extra sauce on the side.

Country Barbecue Sauce

This sauce also works exceptionally well with barbecued chicken and beef.

2 tablespoons vegetable oil	*⅓ cup ketchup*	*1 tablespoon Worcestershire sauce*
1 small yellow onion, minced	*½ cup dark brown sugar, packed*	
2 cloves garlic, minced		*1 tablespoon molasses*
¾ cup water	*6 tablespoons cider vinegar*	*1 teaspoon ground cumin*
		Salt and pepper

1 Heat the oil in a saucepan over medium heat. Add the onion and cook, stirring often, until it starts to soften; add the garlic and continue cooking and stirring for about 1 minute longer.

2 Add the water, ketchup, brown sugar, cider vinegar, Worcestershire sauce, molasses, cumin, and salt and pepper to taste, and stir well. Increase the heat to high and bring to a boil. Reduce the heat and simmer 25 to 30 minutes, or until thickened, stirring occasionally. (The sauce may be prepared a day or two in advance, refrigerated, and reheated before using.)

Go-With: *These succulent ribs are great with Roasted Winter Vegetables (see the recipe earlier in this chapter) or White Beans with Tomato and Thyme (see Chapter 16).*

Tip: *As pork ribs cook, they leave a good amount of fat in the roasting pan. This fat should be carefully poured off and discarded before the ribs are brushed with barbecue sauce. Never pour hot fat down the sink drain or into a garbage disposal, where it could clog the lines. Pour it into an empty soup or coffee can, let it cool and harden, and then throw it out.*

Per serving: *Calories 875 (From Fat 495); Fat 55g (Saturated 19g); Cholesterol 191mg; Sodium 1,699mg; Carbohydrate 47g (Dietary Fiber 1g); Protein 47g.*

Chapter 8

Coals and Coils: Grilling and Broiling

An interesting thing about cooking is that a single food can be exposed to various cooking techniques and take on different characteristics. This difference is most dramatically evident in charcoal grilling and oven broiling, which impart very different flavors to foods than roasting does (we cover roasting techniques in Chapter 7).

Loosely speaking, the terms *grilling* and *broiling* are almost interchangeable. In grilling, which is done on a barbecue grill, the heat source is below; in oven broiling, it's above. Because both methods involve intense heat, they're best reserved for relatively thin pieces of meat, poultry, or vegetables — thick cuts of meat can burn on the outside before cooking sufficiently in the middle. The advantage of grilling or broiling is that the surface of the food being cooked, especially meat, turns dark brown and develops a characteristic "charcoal" flavor.

You do most broiling about 4 to 6 inches from the heat source. It is always best to put the food, whatever it is, on a broiler pan, which has a grated top that allows juices to fall into a pan below. And watch out for flare-ups, either in the oven or on the grill. Flare-ups not only pose a fire danger, but they also can burn meat and give it an acrid flavor. Use the grill's cover to extinguish flames, and keep a box of baking soda or salt handy in the kitchen for broiler flare-ups.

The grilled recipes in this chapter work for broiling as well. Because you can't see food that is broiling as readily as food on a grill, check it more often until you get used to the timing. Just watch and vary your cooking times because broiler heat is slightly more intense and the food generally cooks more quickly.

Preparing for Grill Time

Something about making a fire and cooking food out in the great wide open appeals to basic human instinct. Grilling is fun and imparts a unique, smoky flavor to food, but it also requires a little bit of know-how to get it right. Here are some basics, so you can brush up on grilling before giving it a try, from what kind of grill to use, to preheating, to marinating.

Choosing charcoal, gas, or electric

About 80 percent of all American households do some kind of grilling at home or on vacation, whether it is with a $12 hibachi or a $500 "grilling unit" that is roughly the size of a Fiat and sports everything from gas burners (for sauce-making and so on) and cutting boards to rotisseries and satellite TV (just kidding . . . . we think). Are the pricey models worth it? Or are you good to go with the hibachi? Look more closely at some of your grill options before you shell out the big bucks. Although the type of grill you choose is mostly a matter of personal preference, we give you some information to help you decide which way to go.

Charcoal grilling

Many hard-core barbecue experts prefer charcoal grilling over any other type because of the flavor it imparts to meat and vegetables. Charcoal grills can be short or tall, large or small, but they all have one thing in common: Instead of turning a switch or lighting a gas flame, you actually light briquettes or wood and cook your food over this sometimes temperamental heat source.

Charcoal grilling does produce a unique flavor you can't get from a gas or electric grill, and charcoal grills are usually much less expensive than gas or electric grills. Some double as smokers. Charcoal grills are the closest thing to cooking over a campfire. Charcoal grills have other advantages over gas and electric. They take longer to get to cooking temperature, but they can cook food more quickly because they can exceed the temperature of gas or electric grills. While coals may require replenishing, you don't have to worry about buying and/or refilling a propane tank. Charcoal grills can get messier than gas and electric grills, and you can't adjust the heat with a dial, but the main reason charcoal aficionados prefer them is because of the taste of food cooked over charcoal and/or wood.

For charcoal grilling, you can use charcoal briquettes or real wood briquettes (which are dense chunks of wood). Some briquettes are pre-treated with lighter fluid so they are easy to light. Others aren't. Real wood used as briquettes and/or soaked and used to add smoke to the cooking process can flavor meat and vegetables like mesquite, hickory, or other flavors.

If you add wood chips to a barbecue grill, soak them first in water for about 15 minutes. Doing so makes them smolder and smoke rather than burn up in a flash, and that translates to a delicious smoky taste in your food.

The key to successful charcoal grilling is the same as for stovetop cooking: an even source of heat. Probably the most common failing of amateur cooks is trying to work with a charcoal fire that is too hot. The following list provides additional tips for having the perfect charcoal grilling experience:

- ✔ As a general rule, 30 charcoal briquettes cook about 1 pound of meat. If you're cooking 2 pounds of meat, you need around 45 briquettes. Don't overload your grill with charcoal — too hot a fire will char food before it is fully cooked.

- ✔ Spread the coals in a solid layer about 4 to 6 inches below the food grate.

- ✔ Never light cooking fires with kerosene, gasoline, or other chemicals unless you have a terrific home insurance plan. Dry newspaper and a little patience work wonders. A good alternative is the *plug* — an electric rod that you place in the center of a charcoal pile until it ignites. Using lighter fluid (or charcoal presoaked in lighter fluid) remains the most popular way of starting a fire.

- ✔ Allow 30 to 35 minutes for the coals to burn to medium (the coals should be about 75 percent white). To gauge the temperature of the coals, place the palm of your hand just about the grill's grid. If you can hold your hand in that position for 2 seconds, the coals are hot; a 3-second hold tells you the coals are medium-hot; 4 seconds is medium; and 5 indicates low heat.

- ✔ If you're cooking a large quantity of food and the fire begins to fade before you finish, add a small amount of fresh charcoal from time to time to keep the fire alive.

- ✔ Store your charcoal in a dry place to help it light faster and burn more quickly.

Axioms of outdoor grilling

When it comes to grilling, you can count on the following:

✔ The fire is always at its peak 15 minutes after you finish cooking the food.

✔ If you overhear the cook say, "No problem, I'll just dust it off," it's time to visit the salad bowl.

✔ The chances of getting good food at a home barbecue are in inverse proportion to the silliness of the chef's apron. If the apron is plain and solid in color, you have reason for hope; if it says, "Who Needs Mom?" or "Kiss the Cook," hit the onion dip fast.

✔ Barbecues benefit from the "Hot dogs taste better at the ballpark" syndrome. That is, the very nature of having a barbecue somehow makes all the food taste better.

Gas grilling

Gas grills can get pretty fancy . . . and pretty expensive! But they look impressive on the patio. Thankfully gas-powered grills have become increasingly popular and more affordable in recent years. And they have several advantages over charcoal grills:

✔ They heat up quickly.

✔ The heat is adjustable, which means you can maintain high heat without fading.

✔ They cook food evenly.

✔ They are easy to clean and maintain.

Of course, you don't get to make a big fire in a gas grill, but if that doesn't bother you, gas may be your grill of choice. But some gas grills use lava rocks to simulate charcoal, which works exceedingly well. The cooking technique is the same as for charcoal grills, but the flavor is somewhat different.

One major difference between a gas and a charcoal grill is that gas grills run off a propane tank. That means you need to buy propane, attach it to your grill, and refill it when it runs out. Some people don't like working with propane, but if you follow the directions for your grill, propane is safe. And keep an eye on how much propane you have! Nothing dampens a party like a trip to the store for a propane refill while your guests stare longingly at a grill full of half-cooked pork chops.

Electric grilling

The electric grill is easy to operate and some models work inside, such as the George Foreman grill. Indoor/outdoor versions also exist. Electric grills are essentially like portable electric stoves. Some contain smokers. The main advantage of an electric grill is that you can use it indoors if you want to but still have the grease-draining effect of an outdoor grill. Electric grilling is safe and easy, but the grills will be more expensive than charcoal hibachis and won't cook food with the same flavor as a charcoal grill.

Grilling tips

Before you fire up the grill, keep in mind the following tips:

- ✔ Clean the grill grate well with a wire brush between uses. A dirty grate can affect the taste of your food.

- ✔ Before igniting the fire, brush some vegetable oil over the grates to prevent food, particularly fish, from sticking.

- ✔ Trim meat of excess fat to avoid grease flare-ups that blacken the meat and give it a burned flavor.

- ✔ Cooking times in outdoor grill recipes are approximate; don't throw the meat on and jump in the pool for 15 minutes. Many variables affect cooking time: wind, intensity of coals, thickness of meat, and your fondness for dancing every time a Supremes song comes on.

- ✔ Use the grill lid. Many barbecue grills come with lids, which, when secured, create an oven that can exceed 450 degrees. Certain foods that take a relatively long time to cook — chicken legs, thick slices of steak, and so on — grill faster and better with the lid on. Essentially, you're grilling and roasting at the same time. A lid traps much of the heat, directing it into the food rather than allowing it to blow away. The lid also creates a smoky effect that envelops the food with delicious aroma and flavor. But be sure to lift the lid frequently to check on (and avoid burning) your food.

- ✔ Do not apply sweet barbecue sauces to meat until the last 10 minutes or else the sugar in them may burn.

- ✔ Grilling is easier if you're organized. Set up a small table right next to the grill with all of your ingredients, utensils, serving platters, and so on.

- ✔ Marinate, marinate, marinate — to add moisture and flavor to almost all foods.

- ✔ Be sure to shut off the valve that leads gas into your grill after you turn off the burners. On a charcoal grill, close all the vents after grilling and close the lid to extinguish the hot coals.

Barbecuing doesn't equal grilling

The terms *barbecuing* and *grilling* are often incorrectly interchanged. Grilling, like broiling, is a quick technique that cooks relatively small, tender pieces of food (such as chicken breasts, pork kebabs, or skewered shrimp) directly over the heat source. Barbecuing is more like oven roasting and almost the opposite of grilling. With barbecuing, larger cuts of meat (such as spare ribs, pork butts, or whole turkeys) are slowly roasted over an indirect fire, in a covered grill,

sometimes for hours, until the food is very tender and succulent. To make an indirect fire, the coals are moved to one side of the grill in the fire box. (On a gas grill, only one side of the grill is heated.) The food is cooked opposite the fire and covered, to trap the heat and smoke. This chapter focuses on grilling only. For barbecuing information, tips, and recipes, check out *Grilling For Dummies,* by Marie Rama and John Mariani (Wiley).

Marinating myths and facts

A common misperception is that marinades tenderize meat. They don't. A marinade barely penetrates the outer ⅛ inch of meat, poultry, or game. What a marinade can do is add flavor to the surface, which is, of course, the first thing you taste.

We could write a whole book about marinades. Suffice it to say that most marinades involve an acidic ingredient (vinegar, lemon, or some kinds of wine), oil, herbs, and perhaps a base flavor ingredient (beef or chicken stock, for example). You want to end up with a marinade that is well balanced and flavorful. The only way to know what you have made is to taste it.

Consider this example: You have a chuck shoulder steak. Ask yourself whether you want to add a hot, medium, or sweet flavor. Much of this depends on the main ingredient. You may not want a sweet flavor on fish, for example. With pork, though, you may.

Say for now that you want a hot marinade for the steak. You want to give the steak some zip. Start with red chile flakes (carefully!). Then what? You need a liquid that goes with beef as well as chiles. You can use beef stock (home-made or canned beef broth) or red wine. Suppose that you choose red wine. So you have the foundation of your hot marinade, which you can now jazz up. What goes well with hot things? Minced garlic and black peppercorns maybe. Chopped cilantro adds flavor, too. (As you begin to cook, you'll discover more about ingredients in the supermarket and how to blend them.) Depending on your taste, you may want to add a little dried cumin or coriander seed. Then, at the end, add 2 to 3 tablespoons of good olive oil, salt, and black pepper.

So there you have your basic hot marinade for steak, which you can vary as you go along to make it hotter, milder, or whatever. Now you try!

Be sure to marinate meats, fish, poultry, and vegetables in the refrigerator. Bacteria forms on the surface of room-temperature food very quickly. And don't reuse marinade from pieces of raw chicken or fish unless you bring it to a boil first.

Get to Grilling!

Following are some recipes to get you started grilling. Novice cooks should follow the recipes exactly before modifying them to fit personal tastes.

Grilling vegetables

When it comes to vegetables, even those that you're not wild about can taste terrific when grilled. Charcoal imparts an alluring texture and a smoky essence that is irresistible. Moreover, preparation is easy and quick. Here are some examples:

✔ **Eggplant and zucchini:** Cut them lengthwise into 1-inch-thick slices before grilling. Brush with oil, season to taste, and grill for 15 to 20 minutes or until charred and tender, turning occasionally. For additional flavor, marinate first in a 3-to-1 oil/vinegar mixture with salt and pepper and maybe Dijon-style mustard for about 15 minutes before grilling.

✔ **Corn:** Pull back the husks to remove the silk, but leave the husks attached to the base of the ear. Wrap the husks back around the corn and tie at the top with string or a strip

of husk. Grill 20 minutes or until tender, turning frequently. Serve with melted butter flavored with herbs and fresh lemon juice.

✔ **Potatoes, carrots, onion, and turnips:** Peel and slice into uniform pieces and precook in boiling water until almost tender. Rinse in cold water to stop the cooking and drain well. Wrap in aluminum foil with seasonings such as olive oil, lemon juice, fresh herbs, and salt and pepper to taste, and grill for 10 to 15 minutes or until tender. (You can also thread them onto skewers before grilling.)

✔ **Tomatoes:** Slice firm, ripe tomatoes into 1-inch-thick slices. Brush with olive oil; sprinkle with dried basil or parsley and salt and pepper. Grill until heated through, about 5 minutes total, turning once.

The Perfect Hamburger

If you want the perfect hamburger — juicy and meaty, moist and not fatty — you have to start with the right meat (check out the yummy-looking burger in the color section to see just what we're talking about). The best all-around meat for hamburgers is ground chuck, which has about 15 to 20 percent fat, just enough to keep it moist. (Supermarkets usually list the percentage of fat on the label.) Also look for coarsely ground meat, which yields a looser patty. Many people think that if they buy the "best" meat, like ground sirloin or ground round, they'll have a superior burger. The flavor may be good, but those cuts are so lean that they tend to be dry.

Hamburgers for the grill should be plump and well seasoned. The ingredients and flavors you can add are limitless: minced onions, minced garlic, minced basil, and chopped thyme or rosemary; soy sauce, seasoned breadcrumbs, and a beaten egg; Worcestershire sauce; minced bell peppers; and Tabasco sauce if you like it hot. And you don't even have to stick to beef; lamb and turkey burgers, or blends of all three, are super, too.

You may enjoy getting your hands (washed, please!) into a mound of rosy ground meat and playing sculptor. But if you get too aggressive when forming your hamburger patties and mold them too firmly, they'll tighten up on the grill. And nobody wants a tight hamburger! To get the most tender burger, keep it loose and don't overwork the meat.

Tools: *Mixing bowl, spatula*

Preparation time: *About 12 minutes, plus time to preheat the grill*

Cooking time: *12 to 15 minutes*

Yield: *4 servings*

Oil for the grill rack	*¼ teaspoon salt, or to taste*	*4 hamburger buns*
1½ pounds ground chuck	*¼ teaspoon black pepper, or to taste*	

1 Oil the grill and prepare a medium fire in a charcoal or gas grill.

2 While the grill is heating, combine in a bowl the ground chuck, the salt, and the pepper. Mix lightly but thoroughly, using your hands. Shape the mixture into 4 patties, each about ¾ inch thick.

3 Place the patties on the oiled grill grid. Grill directly over the heat for 5 to 7 minutes per side for medium, or less for rare or medium rare. (The United States Department of Agriculture suggests an internal temperature of 160 degrees for safety; the inside of the burger should not show any pink.) Make a small incision in each patty to determine doneness — they should be just cooked through and still juicy in the center.

4 Just before the burgers are cooked, toast the buns on the edges of the grill. Serve.

Go-With: *In our opinion, nothing goes better with a great burger than French Potato Salad (see Chapter 12).*

Tip: *Quick and tasty burger toppings include thinly sliced red or yellow onions, tomato slices marinated in a basil vinaigrette dressing, flavored mustards, mango or tomato chutney, tomato-based salsa, grilled peppers, and garlic-grilled mushrooms. (You can find recipes for* *the last dish later in this chapter.)* You can also top a good burger with any kind of cheese: Cheddar, Swiss, mozzarella, and even crumbled bleu cheese are all good choices.

Per serving: *Calories 344 (From Fat 105); Fat 12g (Saturated 4g); Cholesterol 97mg; Sodium 450mg; Carbohydrate 22g (Dietary Fiber 1g); Protein 35g.*

The Perfect Steak

Steak on the grill may be one of summer's nicest luxuries, as long as you cook the steak the right way! A dry, tough steak is disappointing, so don't overcook your steak. Medium or medium-rare yields a more tender steak than well-done. You can also add flavor with a good marinade.

Tools: *Tongs*

Preparation time: *About 5 minutes, plus time to preheat the grill*

Marinating time: *About 30 minutes*

Cooking time: *About 8 to 20 minutes, depending on desired doneness*

Yield: *4 servings*

Oil for the grill rack

2 T-bone, porterhouse, or top loin steaks, about 1 inch thick

½ cup dry red wine (try Merlot or Shiraz)

1 tablespoon Worcestershire sauce

1 large clove garlic, minced or put through a garlic press (about 1 teaspoon)

1 teaspoon ground cumin

¼ teaspoon pepper

1 teaspoon salt

1 Place the steaks in a large resealable plastic bag. Add the wine, Worcestershire sauce, garlic, cumin, and pepper to the bag, seal, and marinate in the refrigerator for about 30 minutes, turning once after about 15 minutes.

2 Oil the grill grid and prepare a medium fire in a charcoal or gas grill.

3 Remove the steaks from the bag and discard the marinade. Put the steaks on the grill.

4 Grill for about 8 minutes for rare, 15 minutes for medium, or 20 minutes for well-done, turning the meat once with the tongs halfway through cooking. Season with the salt and serve immediately.

Go-With: *This steak tastes great with side dishes that are a step above standard picnic fare. Try Penne with Parmesan Cheese and Basil (see Chapter 13), Risotto (see Chapter 4), or a Grilled Vegetable Platter with Fresh Pesto (see Chapter 12).*

Per serving: *Calories 273(From Fat 137); Fat 15g (Saturated 5g); Cholesterol 77mg; Sodium 675mg; Carbohydrate 0g (Dietary Fiber 0g); Protein 30g.*

Barbecued Chicken

Barbecued chicken has a smoky, sweet, tangy flavor that can come from a broiler but that we think tastes even better off the grill. Just be sure the chicken is cooked all the way. Prick the chicken with a fork. If the juices run clear, the chicken is done, but to be really accurate, use a meat thermometer. The internal temperature of chicken parts with the bones should be 180 degrees (be sure the thermometer isn't touching a bone, which can give a falsely high reading). Remember, grill times are approximate, and depending on the heat of your grill and the size of the chicken pieces, you may need to cook the chicken for a shorter or longer time than we list here. To shorten cooking time, you can microwave chicken pieces for about 3 minutes per pound before grilling.

Tools: *Tongs, small bowl, basting brush*

Preparation time: *About 10 minutes, plus time to preheat the grill*

Cooking time: *About 50 minutes*

Yield: *4 servings*

Oil for the grill rack

1 chicken, cut into 4 pieces, or 4 chicken breasts with ribs (about 3 pounds total)

Salt and pepper

1 cup Country Barbecue Sauce (see the recipe in Chapter 7) or store-bought barbecue sauce

1 Oil the grill grid and prepare a medium-hot fire in a charcoal or gas grill.

2 Rinse the chicken pieces in cold water and dry thoroughly with paper towels. Season each piece to taste with salt and pepper on both sides.

3 Put the chicken pieces, bone side up, on the grill. Cook for 30 minutes. Flip chicken pieces with tongs. Cook for an additional 20 minutes or more, as needed.

4 During the last 10 minutes of cooking, brush the chicken pieces with Country Barbecue Sauce. The chicken is done when it's no longer pink inside. (Cut open a piece to check for doneness.)

Go-With: *The assertive flavor of the barbecue sauce marries well with side dishes like French Potato Salad or Bell Pepper Rice Salad (both in Chapter 12), or the traditional Baked Beans, Perfect Corn on the Cob, and All-American Coleslaw (all in Chapter 19).*

Per serving: *Calories 514 (From Fat 253); Fat 28g (Saturated 7g); Cholesterol 134mg; Sodium 452mg; Carbohydrate 21g (Dietary Fiber 0g); Protein 43g.*

○ *Garlic-Grilled Portobello Mushrooms*

Porous vegetables, such as mushrooms and sliced eggplant, need not be marinated before grilling. You simply brush them with a flavorful liquid, as in this recipe, which makes a great replacement for burgers for any vegetarians in the group, or a delicious side dish to any grilled meat. (See the "Grilling Vegetables" sidebar in this chapter for more ideas.)

Tools: *Chef's knife, small bowl, basting brush, tongs*

Preparation time: *About 10 minutes, plus time to preheat the grill*

Cooking time: *About 6 minutes*

Yield: *4 servings*

Oil for the grill rack

1 pound portobello mushrooms

⅓ cup extra-virgin olive oil

3 tablespoons lemon juice

2 large cloves (about 2 teaspoons) garlic, minced

Salt and pepper

2 tablespoons minced fresh parsley (optional)

1 Oil the grill grid and prepare a medium-hot fire in a charcoal or gas grill.

2 Clean the mushrooms by rinsing them and using a damp paper towel to gently brush off any dirt. (The wild varieties especially can be full of sand and dirt.) If the mushrooms are very dirty, rinse more thoroughly with cold water and drain in a colander, wiping away excess moisture with a cloth or paper towel. Be careful not to rinse the mushrooms too long, or they can become water-drenched and mushy. Remove the stems, as shown in Figure 8-1. (You can save them to put in soups or stocks.)

3 In a small bowl, combine the oil, lemon juice, and garlic. Brush the caps with the flavored oil and season to taste with salt and pepper.

4 Place the caps on the grill, top side down, and grill for about 3 minutes. (Do not let them burn.) Turn the caps over and grill for another 3 to 4 minutes, or until you can easily pierce the caps with a knife and the mushrooms are nicely browned.

5 Remove the mushrooms to a platter, garnish with the parsley (if desired), and serve.

Go-With: *Steak — such as the Broiled Skirt Steak, Cajun Style (see Chapter 16) — is the natural accompaniment to these savory mushrooms.*

Per serving: *Calories 213 (From Fat 171); Fat 19g (Saturated 3g); Cholesterol 0mg; Sodium 152mg; Carbohydrate 6g (Dietary Fiber 1g); Protein 2g.*

Figure 8-1:
Trim the stems off the mushrooms before grilling the caps.

How to Trim and Slice Mushrooms

1. wipe away dirt using a paper towel or a dish towel

2. cut off stem

3. slice

Grilled Tuna with Niçoise Dressing

This variation on the classic French dish makes a delicious light lunch. If you don't want to fire up the grill, you can also make it under the broiler. Just keep an eye on the tuna because it may cook more quickly.

Tools: *Chef's knife, spatula, medium mixing bowl, roasting pan*

Preparation time: *about 25 minutes (including time for tuna to marinate in oil), plus time to preheat the grill*

Cooking time: *6 to 7 minutes*

Yield: *4 servings*

1 green onion, trimmed and minced

1 tablespoon finely chopped black olives

1 tablespoon finely chopped capers

2 tablespoons balsamic vinegar

¼ teaspoon pepper

1 teaspoon finely chopped anchovy fillets or anchovy paste (optional)

2 tablespoons chopped parsley

½ cup plus 3 tablespoons olive oil

4 tuna steaks, about 1 inch thick, 1½ pounds total

1 teaspoon minced fresh thyme or ½ teaspoon dried thyme

Salt and pepper

Oil for the grill rack

1 Make the dressing by combining in a bowl the green onion, olives, and capers. Stir in the vinegar and pepper. Beat in the anchovy fillets or paste (if desired) and parsley and then ½ cup of the oil. Set aside.

2 Put the tuna on a roasting pan and add the remaining 3 tablespoons of oil, thyme, and salt and pepper to taste. Turn the steaks to coat well. Let sit, refrigerated for about 15 minutes.

3 Brush the grill grid with oil and heat a gas or charcoal grill to medium-high. Place the tuna on the grill and cook for about 3 minutes. Using a spatula, turn the fillets and grill for 3 minutes on the other side. Remove one of the steaks and test for doneness by making a small incision in the center — some people like grilled tuna very rare, and others medium, so don't overcook it.

4 When the steaks have cooked, transfer them to warm serving dishes. Spoon half of the dressing over the steaks. Serve the remaining dressing on the side.

Go-With: *This entrée salad goes nicely with a soup such as the Carrot Soup with Dill in Chapter 11 or a salad such as Bell Pepper Rice Salad or Cucumber-Dill Salad (both in Chapter 12).*

Vary It! *Other types of fish and shellfish work with this recipe. Choose types that can hold up to grilling, such as firm-fleshed fish like salmon, halibut, swordfish, mako shark, or monkfish. Avoid delicate fish such as sole, which tends to flake and fall apart on the grill and doesn't have enough flavor to match this dressing.*

Per serving: *Calories 454 (From Fat 288); Fat 32g (Saturated 4g); Cholesterol 74mg; Sodium 200mg; Carbohydrate 2g (Dietary Fiber 0g); Protein 38g.*

Bratwurst in Beer

Come October, as the weather gets cooler but nobody is quite ready to go inside yet, try this recipe on the grill. Add some sauerkraut, brown mustard, and a big mug of German beer, and you have an Oktoberfest party!

Tools: *Large saucepan with lid, grill fork or tongs*

Preparation time: *About 10 minutes, plus time to preheat the grill*

Cooking time: *10 minutes*

Grilling time: *About 8 minutes*

Yield: *6 servings*

6 bratwurst (cooked or uncooked)

3 cups medium-bodied or dark beer (not light beer or low-carb beer)

1 tablespoon butter, softened to room temperature

6 buns made for bratwurst, hoagies, or hot dogs (depending on size of bratwurst), split

1½ cups sauerkraut, drained (optional)

6 teaspoons brown mustard (optional)

1 Place the bratwurst and beer in a large saucepan over high heat. Bring to a boil and then reduce the heat. Cover and simmer the bratwurst for 10 minutes, or until cooked through (cut into one to test it).

2 Brush the grill grid with oil and prepare a medium fire in a charcoal or gas grill.

3 Remove the bratwurst from the beer and place them on the grill. Grill for about 8 minutes, or until the bratwurst skin is crisp and golden.

4 Butter the inside of buns and toast by placing the buns around the edge of the grill, butter side down. Serve the bratwurst on the buns, with or without sauerkraut and mustard.

Go-With: *Bratwurst and sauerkraut taste great with potatoes and a salad. Try Skillet Potatoes (see Chapter 5) or wrap baking potatoes in foil and toss them on the grill about an hour before you plan to cook the bratwurst.*

Vary It! *To add extra flavor to your sauerkraut, sauté ¼ cup chopped yellow onions in 1 tablespoon butter over medium-high heat, then add the drained sauerkraut and another half cup of beer. Lower the heat to medium and cook until sauerkraut is heated through. Use it on bratwurst, or just eat it on the side.*

Per serving: *Calories 402 (From Fat 241); Fat 27g (Saturated 10g); Cholesterol 56mg; Sodium 715mg; Carbohydrate 23g (Dietary Fiber 1g); Protein 16g.*

Grilled Shrimp Skewers

Shrimp require minimal cooking time. It takes only a few minutes for those little gray shellfish to turn pink and succulent. Be sure not to overcook them, or they could become rubbery.

Get creative with this recipe by alternating each shrimp with veggies, or even fruit. Try chunks of onion and cherry tomatoes, or cubes of pineapple (as shown in the color section). You can also serve these shrimp skewers with a dipping sauce, such as melted butter with a squeeze of fresh lemon juice, barbecue sauce (store-bought or the Country Barbecue Sauce recipe in Chapter 7), or Asian chili sauce (available in the Asian food section of your grocery store).

Tools: *Chef's knife, small bowl, glass measuring cup with spout, pastry brush, small knife, wooden or metal skewers*

Preparation time: *About 10 minutes, plus time to preheat the grill*

Cooking time: *About 15 minutes*

Yield: *4 servings*

1 pound medium shrimp (the size that equals about 20 per pound)	¼ cup butter, melted 2 teaspoons lemon juice	1 clove garlic, minced or put through a garlic press

1 Oil the grill grid and prepare a medium fire in a charcoal or gas grill.

2 Combine the butter, lemon juice, and garlic in a small bowl. Reserve half the lemon-butter mixture in a glass measuring cup.

3 Peel the shrimp and *devein* them (see the illustration in Chapter 14). You can leave the tails on, or pull them off. Double-thread the shrimp onto 4 skewers, so that the skewer pierces both ends of the shrimp (which prevents the shrimp from sliding off). If you use wooden skewers, soak them for 30 minutes in cold water and cover the tips with foil to prevent burning. (**Note:** Don't pack the shrimp too tightly on the skewers, but allow a little space between each piece to allow the heat to circulate and ensure even cooking.)

4 Brush the shrimp on both sides with the lemon-butter mixture in the bowl. Place skewers on the grate and grill for about 8 minutes, or until golden, turning the skewers once halfway through the cooking time. Remove to a platter and drizzle with the remaining lemon-butter mixture from the glass measuring cup. Serve immediately.

Go-With: *Try this dish with a light accompaniment like Sautéed Spinach Leaves (see Chapter 5), or Roasted Summer Vegetables (in this chapter).*

Per serving: *Calories 188 (From Fat 111); Fat 12g (Saturated 7g); Cholesterol 199mg; Sodium 195mg; Carbohydrate 1g (Dietary Fiber 0g); Protein 18g.*

Chapter 9

Creating Sensational Sauces

*P*robably no aspect of cooking sends a kitchen novice running for a restaurant like sauce making. All this reducing and blending and seasoning and adjusting seems about as arcane as DNA testing.

In fact, sauce making is within the reach of the absolute cooking rookie. Some sauces require nothing more than cooking several ingredients in a pan and tossing them in the blender. We tell you how to do that in this chapter. From there, you can progress to some of the more important basic sauces in American and European cooking, with all kinds of variations. These sauces may seem fancy, and they certainly dress up a piece of meat or fish, but difficult to make? Not necessarily.

While a cream-and-butter-laced sauce is classic in French cooking, not all sauces are designed to clog your arteries. Many sauces in restaurants today are Mediterranean or Californian in style, made with olive oil, aromatic herbs, vegetables, and maybe wine. The gelatin-like *demi-glace,* essentially a heavy, concentrated stock, also adds wonderful flavor to many low-fat sauces today. And let's not forget dessert sauces, made from sweet fruit, creamy custard, or luscious chocolate. Dessert sauces make plain ice cream or unadorned cake something extra special.

Not only are these sauces easier to make than the classic sauces (although we explain the classics because they can be superb in moderation), but they also keep you light on your feet.

Who came up with this saucy idea anyway?

Throughout the Middle Ages and the Renaissance, *gravies,* or thickened pan juices, were served with meat, game, and fowl; they were not the sophisticated sauces we know today, but that doesn't mean they didn't taste good! Besides, what would you expect from people who ate with their hands and tossed bones under the table? It wasn't until the eighteenth century that modern sauces entered the cooking vocabulary. Some of the most famous of French sauces today include *ravigote* (a highly seasoned white sauce), Champagne (white sauce made with Champagne), *bourguignonne* (red wine with mushrooms and onions), *poivrade* (red wine sauce with black pepper),

tomato (red sauce), *raifort* (horseradish and cream), *mayonnaise* (egg yolk and oil emulsion), and Provençale (usually tomatoes along with other ingredients and fresh herbs).

Today, the French cooking repertoire includes several hundred sauces. Annoyingly, most of these sauce recipes are written in French. Add to those the sauces of Spain, Italy, and America, and the list is mind-boggling. But don't fret. Most cooks use no more than a dozen sauces and their variations — and those are within the grasp of anyone who can boil a hot dog and carry on a conversation at the same time.

What Sauce Really Is

Think of a sauce as a primary liquid (chicken stock, beef stock, fish stock, vegetable stock, or wine, for example) flavored with ingredients (sautéed shallots, garlic, tomatoes, and so on) and seasoned with salt and pepper and herbs of choice.

Before it's served, a sauce is often reduced. *Reduced* simply means that the sauce is cooked and evaporated over high heat so that it thickens and intensifies in flavor. Sometimes you strain a sauce through a sieve to eliminate all the solids, such as parsley sprigs or chunks of onion. Other times, you purée everything in a blender.

The best way to understand sauces is to become familiar with their foundations:

- *White sauces* usually contain milk or cream.
- *White butter sauces* are based on a reduction of butter, vinegar, and shallots.
- *Brown sauces* are based on dark stocks like lamb or beef.
- *Vegetable sauces* are made from cooked puréed vegetables, such as tomatoes.
- *Vinaigrettes* are made up of oil, vinegar, and seasonings.
- *Hollandaise* and its variations, like béarnaise sauce, are based on cooked egg yolks and butter.

> ✔ *Mayonnaise* is based on uncooked or slightly cooked egg yolks and oil.
>
> ✔ *Dessert sauces* are typically made with fruits or chocolate and sugar, or have a caramel, butterscotch, or nut base.

Classic White Sauce from ze French

For centuries, béchamel sauce (pronounced besh-ah-mel) has been the mortar that supports the house of French cuisine. With its buttery, faintly nutty flavor, béchamel is also the base of hot soufflés and such homey dishes as macaroni and cheese and pot pies. You can modify béchamel in many ways to suit the dish it garnishes. For example, if you're cooking fish, you can add fish stock to the sauce. If you're cooking poultry, you can add chicken stock.

A *velouté* (pronounced va-loo-tay) is essentially a béchamel made with a stock (fish or chicken) in place of the milk, which gives it extra flavor. Sometimes you enhance a velouté before serving by adding a little cream (for a smoother texture) or some fresh lemon juice (for a little tartness). *Velouté* actually came first, and *béchamel* sauce was invented (officially) when French financier Louis de Bechameil added large amounts of cream to a thick *velouté* sauce, way back in the 17th century.

Variations on béchamel

Bechamel is so basic that it makes the perfect starting point for many different variations. Just add some cheese, horseradish sauce, or boiled vegetables and voila, you have a whole new sauce! Here are some classic variations on béchamel for you to try:

✔ **Mornay sauce:** Add grated cheese, like Gruyère or Parmesan, to the simmering béchamel, along with fish stock (optional) and butter.

✔ **Horseradish sauce:** Add freshly grated horseradish to taste. Serve with game, fish such as trout, or long-braised sinewy cuts of beef from the shoulder and neck.

✔ **Soubise:** Boil or steam yellow onions until they're soft; purée them in the blender and add to the sauce, seasoning to taste with salt and pepper. Slightly sweet from the onions, soubise sauce is suitable for many types of game, poultry, and meat.

But don't feel limited by this list. You can use dozens of other ingredients commonly found in a well-stocked pantry or refrigerator to easily alter the flavor of béchamel. A short list of possibilities includes fresh tomatoes (skinned and finely chopped); sautéed mushrooms, shallots, onions, garlic, or leeks; ground ginger or curry powder; chopped fresh tarragon, dill, parsley, or marjoram; paprika; grated lemon zest; white pepper; and Tabasco sauce. Add them to taste when the béchamel has almost finished cooking.

Like most white sauces, béchamel, in all its incarnations, is based on a *roux*, which is nothing more than butter melted in a pan and then sprinkled with flour (equal quantities of each) and stirred into a paste over low heat. Knowing how to make a roux is the first and most important step in knowing how to make a good French-inspired sauce. Note how, in the first recipe that follows, béchamel begins with a roux.

○ Béchamel

Béchamel and its variations go with all kinds of foods, including poached and grilled fish, chicken, veal, and vegetables like pearl onions, Brussels sprouts, broccoli, and cauliflower. (See Chapter 4 for information about steaming and boiling these vegetables before coating with béchamel.) The thickness of béchamel varies from dish to dish.

Tools: *Small saucepan, medium saucepan, wire whisk*

Preparation time: *About 5 minutes*

Cooking time: *About 8 minutes*

Yield: *About 1 cup, or 8 servings*

1¼ cups milk	*¼ teaspoon ground nutmeg, or to taste*
2 tablespoons butter	*Salt and pepper*
2 tablespoons flour	

1 Heat the milk over medium heat in a small saucepan until almost boiling. (If the milk is hot when you add it to the butter and flour, there's less chance that the béchamel will be lumpy.)

2 Meanwhile, in a medium saucepan, melt the butter over medium heat (don't let it darken or burn). Add the flour and whisk constantly for 2 minutes. (You're cooking the loose paste, or roux, made from the butter and flour.) The roux should reach a thick paste consistency.

3 Gradually add the hot milk while continuing to whisk the mixture vigorously. When the sauce is blended smooth, reduce heat and simmer for 3 to 4 minutes, whisking frequently. The béchamel should have the consistency of a very thick sauce. Remove from heat, add the nutmeg and the salt and pepper to taste, and whisk well.

Tip: *If the butter burns or even gets brown, you should probably start over, or your white sauce will have a brown tint.*

Vary It! *Whipping up some creamed spinach (or creamed vegetables in general) is a good way to try out your béchamel-making skills. Just add béchamel to cooked spinach or other cooked vegetables, such as corn, peas, or sliced carrots.*

Per serving: Calories 56 (From Fat 37); Fat 4g (Saturated 3g); Cholesterol 13mg; Sodium 92mg; Carbohydrate 3g (Dietary Fiber 0g); Protein 2g.

🍅 Velouté

Velouté is wonderful with poached fish, poultry, veal, vegetables, and eggs. This recipe is a simplified version of a classic velouté; variations are endless after you get this technique down.

Tools: *Medium saucepan, small saucepan, wire whisk, waxed paper*

Preparation time: *About 10 minutes*

Cooking time: *About 8 minutes*

Yield: *About 1¾ cups, or 6 servings*

1½ cups homemade or canned chicken or vegetable stock

2 tablespoons butter

3 tablespoons flour

⅓ cup heavy cream or half-and-half

Salt and white pepper

1 Heat the stock almost to boiling in a small saucepan over medium heat.

2 Melt the butter over medium heat in a medium saucepan (don't let it brown or burn). Add the flour and whisk until blended smooth. Reduce heat to low and cook for about 2 minutes, whisking constantly.

3 Raise the heat setting to medium and gradually add the hot chicken broth (watch out — it could splatter), whisking for about 1 minute or until the sauce thickens. Raise the heat and bring to a boil; immediately lower the heat to simmer and cook for about 2 minutes, whisking often.

4 Add the cream and salt and pepper to taste. Raise the heat and whisk constantly while bringing the mixture back to a boil. When it boils, immediately remove the saucepan from the heat and cover with waxed paper (to prevent a thin film from forming on the surface) until served.

Tip: If you forget to cover the velouté with waxed paper and a thin film or skin forms on the sauce's surface, simply whisk it back into the sauce. If the sauce cooks a little too long and gets too thick, add a little more stock or cream.

Per serving: Calories 97 (From Fat 78); Fat 9g (Saturated 5g); Cholesterol 28mg; Sodium 257mg; Carbohydrate 4g (Dietary Fiber 0g); Protein 2g.

Brown Sauces Worth Wearing a Bib For

One major difference between white and brown sauce is that brown sauce is harder to get off your silk tie. Basic brown sauce derives from the 19th century espagnole sauce, so called because a major ingredient was Spanish ham (espagnole being the Spanish word for Spanish ham). It took two or three days to make, which is probably one reason why women's liberation didn't catch on faster in Spain. That's all you need to know about the traditional espagnole sauce — most modern chefs don't bother with it.

Most brown sauces today are based on a reduced stock of beef or veal. When we use the term *stock,* we mean a liquid that results from boiling bones, water, vegetables, and seasonings. The more you reduce the liquid, the stronger the flavor. Extra flavor also comes from browning the bones first in the oven.

If you reduce veal stock to a jelly consistency, it's sometimes called *demi-glace.* If you reduce the liquid so much that it coats a spoon, it's called simply *glace.* Note that, once they've chilled and set, you can cut demi-glace and glace into small pieces and freeze them for later use.

The following recipe uses the deglazing technique. Not sure what deglazing is? Do you ever have a casserole of macaroni and cheese and, when dinner is over, go over and pick at the little semiburned nuggets of cheese and pasta that cling to the dish? Aren't they the best part?

Well, think of deglazing as more or less the same thing. When you sauté a steak or chicken in a hot pan, it leaves behind little particles that stick to the pan. These bits are packed with flavor, and you want to incorporate them into any sauce you make.

For example, when you remove a steak from the pan, you might deglaze the pan with red wine (you generally deglaze with wine or stock of some sort). As the wine or stock sizzles in the pan, you scrape the pan's bottom (preferably with a wooden spoon) to release those tasty little particles. That process is called *deglazing.* After you do that, you finish the sauce and serve.

Basic Brown Sauce

In this recipe, you make the sauce quickly in the same pan you use to brown the pork. The fact that food doesn't stick to nonstick cookware is the one best reason to also have some stainless steel cookware in your arsenal. The stickier the little tasty food particles remaining in the pan, the tastier the sauce that results from deglazing, so make this sauce in a stainless steel skillet, if you have one. Cast iron also works. Traditionally, brown sauce also used a roux as the white sauces above, but then would cook for many hours to get rid of the flour taste. In this recipe, a quick cornstarch infusion thickens the sauce and makes cooking much quicker. Or you can leave out the cornstarch for a thinner, more liquid sauce.

Tools: *Chef's knife, roasting pan, small bowl, wire whisk*

Preparation time: *About 10 minutes*

Cooking time: *About 25 minutes*

Yield: *2 cups, or 8 servings*

¾ cup pan drippings from a beef or pork roast

Enough canned beef broth to add to pan drippings to make ¾ cup, if necessary, plus an additional ½ cup canned beef broth

2 tablespoons butter

½ cup minced yellow onion

½ cup dry red wine, apple cider, or additional beef broth

1 teaspoon cornstarch

Salt and pepper (optional)

1 After roasting meat, pour all the remaining liquid into a large glass measuring cup (one that holds at least four cups of liquid). Let the fat rise to the top and pour off as much of the clear fat as you can. If you have less than ¾ cup of pan juices left, add beef broth to make ¾ cup and then return drippings to the roasting pan and put the roasting pan over one or two burners on the stove, over medium heat.

2 Add the butter to the roasting pan. When it melts, add the onions, stirring and scraping the pan to release more of the cooked bits of meat. Continue until the onions soften, about 2 to 3 minutes. Add the red wine; stir for 1 minute.

3 Combine the cornstarch with the ½ cup beef broth in a small bowl, stirring with a wire whisk until smooth.

4 Add the cornstarch mixture to the roasting pan. Increase the heat to high and reduce the sauce, stirring with the whisk until it evaporates slightly and thickens. Taste and add salt and pepper, if desired. Serve over the roasted meat.

Go With: *Serve the roasted meat and sauce with buttered rice, noodles, or mashed pota-toes (see Chapter 4 for recipes).*

Per serving: Calories 91 (From Fat 38); Fat 4g (Saturated 2g); Cholesterol 38mg; Sodium 75mg; Carbohydrate 1g (Dietary Fiber 0g); Protein 11g.

Dried versus fresh herbs

Unless you live in the southern or western regions of the United States, an area where fresh herbs are available year-round, you may need to substitute dry herbs. Dried herbs generally do in these circumstances, but remember that they're three times as concentrated as fresh. So if a recipe calls for 1 tablespoon of fresh thyme, for example, use 1 teaspoon of the dried herb. (See Chapter 3 for herb and spice charts.)

Egg in Your Sauce

Egg-based sauces are (you guessed it!) based on eggs rather than on meat stock or butter and cream, although most egg-based sauces also contain butter, stock, and/or cream. Hollandaise is the most common of all egg-based sauces. Your first introduction to hollandaise probably came when you went with your parents to a fancy brunch where eggs Benedict was served — hopefully not from the buffet steam table, as egg-based sauces don't have a long buffet life.

Egg-based sauces are typically rich and a little goes a long way, but they're also very versatile, changing with just a few different herbs, vegetables, or cream into all kinds of variations. But most of them start with your basic hollandaise sauce.

☼ Hollandaise

Hollandaise is a good exercise for beginners because if you blow it, you can repair it easily (see the tip at the end of the recipe). The rich, lemon-tinged hollandaise has chameleon-like qualities: Add tarragon and chervil, and you have béarnaise (excellent on salmon); add tomato, and you have Choron (good with steak); fold in lightly whipped heavy cream, and you have Chantilly, also called mousseline (decadently delicious on chicken); add dried mustard, and you have a fine accompaniment to boiled vegetables.

Tools: *Whisk, bowl, double boiler, rubber spatula*

Preparation time: *About 10 minutes*

Cooking time: *About 10 minutes*

Yield: *About ¾ cup, or 6 servings*

4 egg yolks, separated (see illustrated instructions for separating an egg in Chapter 10)

1 tablespoon cold water

½ cup (1 stick) room-temperature butter, cut into 8 pieces

2 tablespoons fresh lemon juice

Salt and white pepper

1 In the top of a double boiler, whisk the egg yolks for about 2 minutes or until they're thick and pale yellow. Add the water, whisking for about another minute, until the mixture easily coats a spoon.

2 Set the top of the double boiler with the egg mixture into the bottom of the double boiler over, but not touching, water that is almost boiling. Heat until just warm, about 3 minutes, stirring constantly with a rubber spatula or whisk.

3 Add the butter 2 tablespoons at a time, whisking vigorously until each batch is incorporated completely. Continue cooking, stirring and scraping the sides of the pot, until the sauce thickens enough to coat the back of a metal spoon. Add the lemon juice and salt and pepper to taste and cook about 1 minute more, or until the sauce is smooth and heated through.

Tip: *You can make a double boiler by setting any heat-resistant bowl snugly into one of your saucepans. Be sure to allow 2 to 3 inches between the bottom of the bowl and the bottom of the pan, for the boiling water.*

Tip: *The most common foul-up that beginners make when preparing hollandaise is leaving the heat on until it curdles. If that happens, or if the sauce becomes too thick, beat in 1 to 2 tablespoons boiling water. Stir vigorously until the sauce becomes smooth. To avoid lumpy hollandaise, reduce the heat to simmer.*

Per serving: Calories 175 (From Fat 167); Fat 19g (Saturated 11g); Cholesterol 183mg; Sodium 104mg; Carbohydrate 1g (Dietary Fiber 0g); Protein 2g.

☞ Béarnaise Sauce

This savory variation on hollandaise goes well with salmon, fillet of beef, or any other rich meat. In fact, it's so good that you may find yourself sopping up the sauce left in the pan with a spare crust of baguette. Go ahead — we won't tell anybody you did it!

Tools: *Small saucepan, glass measuring cup with spout, double boiler or steel bowl, wire whisk, medium saucepan*

Preparation time: *About 5 minutes*

Cooking time: *About 15 minutes*

Yield: *About 1 cup, or 8 servings*

½ cup (1 stick) butter

3 tablespoons dry white wine (such as Chardonnay or Sauvignon Blanc)

3 tablespoons white wine vinegar or tarragon vinegar

1 tablespoon minced white onion

1 teaspoon dried tarragon leaves, or 1 table-spoon fresh chopped tarragon leaves

⅛ teaspoon black pepper

3 large egg yolks (save whites for another use)

1 teaspoon water

¼ teaspoon salt

1 In a small saucepan over low heat (or in a 1-cup glass measuring cup in the microwave), melt the butter, being careful not to burn it. The butter shouldn't heat to the point where it turns brown. Pour the butter into a glass measuring cup made for pouring liquids, if you heated it on the stove.

2 Wipe out the saucepan. Over medium heat, cook the white wine, vinegar, onion, half the tarragon leaves, and pepper, stirring occasionally, until the amount of liquid is reduced by about half. Remove from heat and set aside.

3 Put about an inch of water in a medium saucepan over medium heat. Meanwhile, in the top of the double boiler or in the steel bowl, combine the egg yolks and water. Whip vigorously with the whisk for about 2 minutes, or until the egg yolks begin to look lighter.

4 When the water in the saucepan is just beginning to simmer, set the double boiler or bowl (still containing the egg yolks) over the pan. The water shouldn't touch the bottom of the double boiler or bowl. Continue to beat the yolks. In a slow stream, add the warm (not hot) melted butter to the yolks. Make sure you add the butter very slowly and keep whisking, so you don't scramble the eggs. You want the sauce to remain all liquid. When the butter is completely incorporated, remove from the heat.

5 Stir in the wine mixture, the remaining half of the tarragon leaves, and the salt. Serve immediately.

Per serving: Calories 124 (From Fat 120); Fat 13g (Saturated 8g); Cholesterol 110mg; Sodium 77mg; Carbohydrate 0g (Dietary Fiber 0g); Protein 1g.

Blender Sauces: Impressive in Minutes

For cooks in a hurry, the blender can be an invaluable tool. You can make blender sauces literally in minutes. And they can be more healthful, too, especially if bound with vegetables, low-fat cheeses (like ricotta), yogurt, and the like.

Although food processors are unsurpassed for chopping, slicing, and grating, blenders have an edge when it comes to liquefying and sauce making. Their blades rotate faster, binding (or pulling together) liquids better. The two-level slicing blade on a food processor cuts through liquids instead of blending them, and its wide, flat work bowl is too large for mixing small quantities of sauce. If you don't have a food processor, you can also use the blender for chunkier sauces, like the salsa recipe in this section. Just use the pulse function, which lets you more closely monitor the sauce's consistency.

Blender sauces can be so quick that your dinner guests will suspect that Julia Child is hiding in the pantry. You can transform simple poached fish into something special by combining some of the poaching liquid with wine, fresh watercress, seasonings, and just a dab of cream or ricotta cheese. When mixed in the blender with several pats of butter, these ingredients create a savory and exceptionally smooth sauce. (Read more about the blender in Chapter 2.)

Certain fruit sauces for desserts also work better in a blender than in a food processor, whether it's a purée of raspberries spiked with framboise (French raspberry brandy) or of mango with lime and rum.

Following are two quick and terrific blender recipes.

☞ *Quick and Easy Salsa*

Salsa is one of the most popular condiments today. You can buy all kinds of varieties in the grocery store, but homemade salsa adds a special touch to your meal. It tastes delicious, and it's not that much more difficult than opening a jar.

Tools: *Chef's knife, scissors, blender or food processor*

Preparation time: *About 15 minutes*

Cooking time: *None*

Yield: *About 1½ cups, or 6 servings*

1 tablespoon fresh or jarred jalapeño peppers, minced

¼ cup loosely packed fresh cilantro leaves (cut the stems off with scissors)

1 tablespoon minced red onion

1 clove garlic, minced

1 tablespoon water

1 tablespoon lime juice

1 can (14½ ounces) whole tomatoes, including the juice

½ teaspoon salt

1 Place the jalapeño peppers, cilantro, onion, garlic, water, and lime juice in the blender or food processor fitted with steel blade. Blend on low about 15 seconds, or until everything is well chopped and combined.

2 Add the tomatoes and salt. Pulse briefly to chop but not purée the tomatoes. Serve.

Vary It! *If you want to use fresh tomatoes, this salsa won't be quite as quick or easy, but it will be delicious! Just cut a shallow X in the bottom of each of six medium-sized tomatoes, and then immerse the tomatoes in boiling water for about 30 seconds each. Plunge into cold water, slip off the skins, core the tomatoes, squeeze out the seeds, and use the remaining tomato "meat" in place of the canned tomatoes in this recipe.*

Go-With: *This sauce is delicious spooned over grilled or poached chicken or fish, or as a topping for a quesadilla or any Mexican food. Or just use it as a chip dip!*

Per serving: *Calories 16 (From Fat 1); Fat 0g (Saturated 0g); Cholesterol 0mg; Sodium 296mg; Carbohydrate 4g (Dietary Fiber 1g); Protein 1g.*

🍅 *Pesto Sauce*

Pesto is a favorite summertime sauce that you can make easily in the blender. It goes beautifully with pasta, cold meats, and crudités (raw vegetables). Try swirling a bit of pesto into a sauce of summer tomatoes as a topping for broiled fish or chicken or pasta.

Tools: *Blender, grater, rubber spatula*

Preparation time: *About 15 minutes*

Yield: *About 1 cup, or 8 servings*

2 cups lightly-packed fresh basil leaves, stems removed, about 2 ounces

½ cup extra-virgin olive oil

3 tablespoons pine nuts or walnuts

3 large cloves garlic, coarsely chopped

Salt and pepper

½ cup grated Parmesan cheese

1 tablespoon hot water

1 Rinse and pat dry the trimmed basil leaves.

2 Put the basil leaves in the container of a food processor or blender. Add the oil, pine nuts or walnuts, garlic, and salt and pepper to taste. Blend to a fine texture but not a smooth purée, stopping the motor once to scrape down the sides of the blender container and to force the ingredients down to the blades.

3 Add the Parmesan cheese and water and blend just a few seconds more. Chill until served.

Per serving: *Calories 158 (From Fat 146); Fat 16g (Saturated 3g); Cholesterol 3mg; Sodium 139mg; Carbohydrate 1g (Dietary Fiber 1g); Protein 3g.*

Dessert Sauces to Die For

Many dessert sauces are so easy that you can make them during TV commercials. And you can vary almost all of them in innumerable ways.

Dessert sauces come in two basic types: cream based (with chocolate, vanilla, caramel, butterscotch, and so on) and fruit based. Cream-based recipes usually require cooking, but you can often make the fruit sauces in a blender. In this section, you find some popular sauces and ways to modify them.

☞ *Vanilla Custard Sauce*

This smooth and creamy vanilla sauce dresses up ice cream, fresh strawberries, pound cake, poached pears, soufflés, cold mousses, and more. Keep in mind that when you're making this sauce, as well as custards and yeast breads, you scald milk primarily to shorten the cooking time. To scald milk, heat it in a saucepan over medium-low heat until it foams. Don't bring it to a boil.

Also, be careful not to cook the vanilla sauce too long, to prevent scorching it. Maintain a low to medium-low heat setting to prevent the sauce from curdling, or separating into coagulated solids (curds) and liquids (whey). A curdled sauce is not a pretty sight. If the sauce curdles, whisk it quickly or whirl it in a blender container to cool it rapidly.

Tools: *Electric mixer, heavy saucepan, mixing bowl, wire whisk, wooden spoon, sieve*

Preparation time: *About 15 minutes*

Cooking time: *About 25 minutes*

Yield: *2 cups, or 8 servings*

1 cup heavy cream	*4 egg yolks*
1 cup milk	*¼ cup sugar*
2 vanilla beans, split lengthwise (see the tip at the end of this recipe)	

1 Place the cream, milk, and vanilla beans in a heavy medium saucepan. Scald the milk-cream mixture over medium-low (bring to a foam but do not boil). Remove from the heat and let sit for 15 to 20 minutes.

2 Using a hand-held or stand mixer, beat the egg yolks and sugar in a bowl for several minutes. The mixture should be pale yellow and thick.

3 Return the cream mixture to the heat and scald it again. Pour about one-quarter of the hot cream mixture into the egg yolks and whisk vigorously. Pour the egg mixture into the saucepan that is holding the rest of the cream. Cook over low heat, stirring with a wooden spoon, about 4 to 5 minutes or until it thickens enough to coat the back of the spoon. Strain through a sieve into a bowl, discard the vanilla beans, cover, and chill.

Tip: *To split open a vanilla bean, take a sharp knife and make an incision lengthwise to expose the tiny black seeds; scrape the seeds out with a knife and add them to the recipe. Look for vanilla beans in the spice section of your supermarket.*

Vary It! *Add the flavorings of your choice: rum, Grand Marnier, kirsch, or brandy — 3 to 4 tablespoons should suffice.*

Per serving: *Calories 175 (From Fat 131); Fat 15g (Saturated 8g); Cholesterol 151mg; Sodium 30mg; Carbohydrate 9g (Dietary Fiber 0g); Protein 3g.*

Many recipes for ice cream, custards, puddings, cakes, cookies, and chocolate desserts are flavored with vanilla. You can use either the whole vanilla bean or pure vanilla extract. Although the whole beans are somewhat preferable, because they have much more of an intense flavor than the extract, they're also more expensive and less convenient. (In the following Cracklin' Hot Fudge Sauce recipe, we call for using the more convenient and less expensive pure vanilla extract.) Never purchase "artificial" or "imitation" extracts. Made mostly of paper-industry byproducts treated with chemicals, they have a nasty taste.

ᐸ Cracklin' Hot Fudge Sauce

Cracklin' Hot Fudge Sauce is a twist on regular chocolate sauce and is ideal for ice cream. Because it has butter in it, the sauce turns hard when poured over ice cream and forms a thin, cracklin' crust. You can buy this kind of sauce in the grocery store, but it is laden with hydrogenated fat. This version, while hardly diet food, is free from those trans-fats.

One great thing about this recipe is that you can prepare it up to a week ahead of time and keep it covered and refrigerated. Rewarm it in a double boiler or in the microwave.

Tools: *Sifter, heavy medium saucepan, chef's knife, wooden spoon*

Preparation time: *About 15 minutes*

Cooking time: *About 5 minutes*

Yield: *About 2 cups, or 8 servings*

1 cup confectioners' sugar, sifted (see Chapter 3 for sifting instructions)	½ cup heavy cream	chopped (see the advice at the end of the recipe)
½ cup (1 stick) butter	8 ounces (8 squares) bittersweet chocolate, finely	2 teaspoons vanilla extract

1 In a heavy medium saucepan over medium-low heat, combine the confectioners' sugar, butter, and cream. Stir with a wooden spoon until the butter is melted and the mixture is smooth.

2 Remove the pan from the heat and add the chocolate, stirring until smooth. Then add the vanilla and stir to blend.

Vary It! *If you can't find bittersweet chocolate, substitute the more common semisweet chocolate and reduce the powdered sugar by 2 tablespoons.*

Tip: *Chop chocolate into pieces on a cutting board with a sharp knife or whirl the chocolate in the container of a blender or food processor for a few seconds.*

Per serving: *Calories 354 (From Fat 261); Fat 29g (Saturated 17g); Cholesterol 51mg; Sodium 7mg; Carbohydrate 30g (Dietary Fiber 2g); Protein 2g.*

↻ Whipped Cream

You have no excuse for serving chemical-tasting, aerosol whipped cream. The real thing is so easy and so good that everyone should know how to make it. Spoon sweetened, flavored whipped cream over pies, pudding, cakes, mousses, poached fruit, your cat's nose — anything!

Tools: *Chilled bowl, whisk or electric mixer*

Preparation time: *About 5 minutes*

Yield: *About 2 cups, or 8 servings*

1 cup well-chilled heavy cream

1 tablespoon sugar, or to taste

1 teaspoon vanilla extract, or to taste

In a chilled bowl, combine the cream, sugar, and vanilla. Beat with a whisk or electric mixer on medium speed until the cream thickens and forms peaks. (Do not overbeat, or the cream will become lumpy.)

Vary It! *Add 1 tablespoon unsweetened cocoa powder before mixing; add 1 tablespoon instant coffee; or add 1 or 2 tablespoons Grand Marnier, Kahlúa, Cointreau, crème de menthe, or other liqueur.*

Per serving: *Calories 110 (From Fat 99); Fat 11g (Saturated 7g); Cholesterol 41mg; Sodium 11mg; Carbohydrate 2g (Dietary Fiber 0g); Protein 1g.*

↻ Caramel Sauce

Caramel forms when the moisture is cooked out of sugar and the sugar turns a deep golden brown. Caramel sauce is simply caramel thinned out with a little water, lemon juice, and cream so that it pours easily and has more flavor. It's delicious as a coating on meringue, vanilla cake, and ice cream.

Tools: *Medium saucepan, wooden spoon, whisk*

Preparation time: *About 5 minutes*

Cooking time: *About 10 minutes*

Yield: *1 cup, or 8 servings*

1 cup sugar

⅓ cup water

½ teaspoon fresh lemon juice

⅔ cup heavy cream

1 Combine the sugar, water, and lemon juice in a medium saucepan over medium-low heat. Stir with a wooden spoon, about 3 minutes, until the sugar dissolves.

2 Increase the heat to medium-high and cook until the mixture reaches an amber color, about 3 to 4 minutes. (The mixture comes to a boil rather rapidly.)

3 If you want a medium-colored caramel, remove the mixture from the heat when it is still light golden because it continues to cook and darken off the heat. For darker, more flavorful caramel, remove when medium golden-brown. Remove the pan from the heat and gradually pour in the heavy cream, stirring with a wire whisk. (Be careful: The cream bubbles wildly as you do so.)

4 When all is incorporated, return the saucepan to medium-low heat and stir for 2 to 3 minutes or until the mixture is velvety. Serve warm. To rewarm it after it cools, place it in a microwave or over medium heat on the stove.

Per serving: Calories 166 (From Fat 66); Fat 7g (Saturated 5g); Cholesterol 27mg; Sodium 8mg; Carbohydrate 26g (Dietary Fiber 0g); Protein 0g.

☕ Fresh Strawberry Sauce

Quick sauces made with fresh, seasonal fruit could not be easier. The following technique also works for blueberries and raspberries. (When making raspberry sauces, strain the sauce through a fine sieve before serving to remove the seeds.) This fresh strawberry sauce is wonderful as a topping for ice cream, custards, and puddings.

Tools: *Paring knife, food processor or blender*

Preparation time: *About 10 minutes*

Yield: *About 2 cups, or 8 servings*

1 quart fresh strawberries, hulled (stems removed) and washed

2 tablespoons confectioners' sugar, or to taste, depending on fruit's ripeness

1 tablespoon fresh lemon juice

Place all the ingredients in the bowl of a blender or food processor; purée until smooth. Taste for sweetness and add more sugar, if desired.

Vary It! *For extra flavor, add rum, kirsch, flavored vodka, or other liquor of choice. You also can make this sauce with frozen strawberries. Just thaw them first.*

Per serving: Calories 29 (From Fat 0); Fat 0g (Saturated 0g); Cholesterol 0mg; Sodium 1mg; Carbohydrate 7g (Dietary Fiber 2g); Protein 0g.

Part III
Expand Your Repertoire

The 5th Wave By Rich Tennant

"Anyone for more caramel upside-down cake?"

In this part . . .

*H*ere's where the music starts. You grab your culinary baton and start off slowly, executing the basics. From there, we tell you how to jazz things up — always in a harmonious way.

This part covers various categories of food — from sauces to soups and salads to desserts. We explain the foundations of each category and also give you some ideas for improvising.

After a little bit of practice, you'll be ready to invite volunteer diners over for a meal. Solicit their opinions, always starting with their praise. Consider any suggestions to be great opportunities for more cooking!

Chapter 10

The Amazing Egg

In This Chapter

▶ Choosing fresh eggs

▶ Getting the facts on raw eggs

▶ Perfecting basic egg-cooking techniques

▶ Using eggs to create delicious dishes

*E*ggs just might be the perfect food. What other food is so nutritious and so self-contained? An egg carries its main ingredient (the yolk) and a lightening agent (the white) all in the same convenient package.

Moreover, the repertoire of egg cooking embraces most of the techniques we stress in this book. Making eggs is a great way to start out, especially if your family is big on breakfast. And believe us, the first time you flip that perfect omelet onto a plate or lift that golden-brown meringue out of the oven, you'll be hooked on eggs.

Selecting Fresh Eggs

Freshness is of paramount concern for egg eaters. As an egg ages, the white breaks down, and the membrane covering the yolk deteriorates. So if you cook an older egg, chances are greater that the yolk will break.

Consumers rely on the expiration date on the carton and on the *Julian date,* which indicates the day the eggs were actually packed in their carton. The Julian date should be listed with the expiration date as a three-digit number. A Julian date of 002, for example, means that the eggs were packed on January 2, or the second day of the year. A Julian date of 105 means the eggs were packed on the 105th day of the year, or April 15 (in a non-leap year). As a standard, you should use eggs within 4 to 5 weeks of their Julian date.

What's that spot?

Contrary to what most people believe, blood spots inside a raw egg are not a sign that the egg was fertilized. They are usually the result of a blood vessel rupturing on the surface of the yolk. The spot does not affect flavor, and the egg is perfectly safe to eat. You can remove the blood spot with the tip of a knife, but you don't need to do so.

All about eggs: Grade, size, and color

In the supermarket, you generally see two grades of eggs: AA and A. The differences between the grades are hardly noticeable to the average home cook. Purchase either grade.

Egg size is based on a minimum weight per dozen: 30 ounces per dozen for jumbo eggs, 27 ounces for extra large, 24 ounces for large, and 21 ounces for medium. Most recipes (and all of them in this book) call for large eggs.

Shell color is not related to quality and is simply a function of the breed of hen.

Specialty eggs: Worth the extra bacon?

You may have noticed some additional choices in your supermarket beyond the standard range of size and color. What's with those specialty eggs available today? You know, the ones that say "free-range" or "organic" or "added omega-3s for better health." They sound good but look at that price tag! If you shell out all that extra money for these so-called superior eggs, are you going to end up with egg on your face? The following info may help you decide whether they're worth the higher price:

  ✔ **Free-range eggs:** These eggs come from hens that actually get to peck around outside, even if only in a very small pen, as opposed to hens that live inside in cages. The carton may say "cage-free," which means the same thing. At least these hens get some sunshine and fresh air, even if their outdoor pens are cramped, and theoretically they are treated more humanely. If knowing that makes you feel better about your egg consumption, go for it.

Dollars for eggheads

Here's one to remember in case you are ever on a quiz show and the host says:

"For $500: By spinning an egg on a countertop, you can determine what?"

Tick . . . tick . . . tick . . .

"Okay, Vern! What's your answer?"

"Uh, the gravity in the room?"

"Is that your final answer? Sorry, Vern, the correct answer is whether it's cooked: A hard-cooked egg, which has a solid center, spins quickly and easily; a raw egg, because it has liquid swishing around inside, does not."

✔ **Organic eggs:** These eggs come from chickens that weren't fed any drugs, hormones, or antibiotics and, in many cases, weren't fed any animal by-products, something chickens really aren't meant to eat anyway. Proponents believe this type of diet makes the eggs safer and more pure.

✔ **Eggs with added omega-3s:** These eggs have more of those fatty acids purported to benefit heart health, and they typically have a higher vitamin E content than regular eggs. These benefits result when hens are fed higher-quality grains.

Many brands of eggs have all the above qualities: free-range hens on organic diets producing eggs with extra nutrition. Many people buy these eggs not only because they want to support farmers who treat their hens more humanely but also because the eggs taste better. Many people who have compared the taste of free-range organic eggs with "regular" eggs think that they do indeed taste more flavorful. Try them for yourself to decide whether the improvement in taste is worth the extra money.

Discovering the Real Deal about Raw Eggs

The American Egg Board, a marketing and research organization for the egg industry, does not recommend the consumption of raw or undercooked eggs, yet many recipes call for them. Salmonella, one of several types of bacteria that can cause food poisoning, has been found inside a small number of raw eggs — about 0.005 percent, or 1 in every 20,000 eggs. Though the odds of getting salmonella poisoning from raw eggs are low, we recommend using them only in recipes in which they are essential, like homemade eggnog and Caesar salad. A good substitution for raw eggs is pasteurized liquid egg substitute, which closely resembles fresh eggs. Another safe substitution is egg white powder, to which you add water.

You can't tell by looking whether an egg contains bacteria, but bacteria are destroyed when the egg reaches a temperature of 140 degrees. Never eat an egg whose shell is cracked or broken. Cracked eggs become vulnerable to other types of bacteria, so you should throw them away.

Getting the Techniques Right

Working with eggs means mastering a few techniques: how to break an egg, separate an egg, whip an egg white, and things like that. Before you try any egg recipes, first practice brushing up on how to handle your eggs.

Breaking a few eggs

To make an omelet (or a frittata or a meringue or a cake), you have to break a few eggs. Here's how to do it.

1. **Hold the egg in one hand.**

2. **Tap the egg on the side of a small bowl or glass measuring cup to gently break the shell.**

   Don't tap too hard, or you'll shatter the egg and your egg will be full of shell pieces.

3. **Put your two thumbs inside the crack and gently open the egg so that the yolk and white fall into the bowl or measuring cup.**

   If a piece of shell falls in the egg, use the tip of a knife to nudge it up the side of the bowl and out.

Always break eggs into a separate bowl or cup before adding them to a recipe. That way, you can remove any stray shell pieces before they get lost in, say, the birthday cake batter.

Separating an egg

Many recipes require separated egg whites and yolks. Don't worry; separating an egg really isn't as difficult as it looks. Follow these steps, as illustrated in Figure 10-1, to separate an egg without breaking the yolk. (You don't want any yolk in your whites, or the whites will not beat stiff.)

1. **Hold the egg in one hand above two small bowls.**

2. **Crack the shell on the side of one bowl — just enough to break through the shell and the membrane without piercing the yolk or shattering the shell.**

    This step may take a little practice. Repeat on the other side if necessary.

3. **Pry open the eggshell with both thumbs and gently let the bulk of the white fall into one of the bowls.**

4. **Carefully pass the yolk back and forth from one shell cavity to the other, each time releasing more white.**

5. **When all the white is in the bowl, carefully transfer the yolk to the other bowl (it doesn't matter if the yolk breaks); cover and refrigerate, if not using right away.**

How to Separate an Egg

Figure 10-1:
Recipes often call for separated egg yolks or whites. Follow these steps to get only the part you want.

1. Hold the egg in one hand over two small bowls.

2. Crack the shell on the side of one bowl.

3. Let the white fall into one of the bowls.

4. Pass the yolk back & forth, each time releasing more white.

5. When all the white is in the bowl, drop yolk in the other bowl.

Beating egg whites

Beaten egg whites make soufflés rise. Before beating egg whites, make sure that your mixing bowl and beaters are clean and dry. Even a speck of dirt, oil, or egg yolk can prevent the whites from beating stiff. Beat the whites slowly until they're foamy; then increase the beating speed to incorporate as much air as possible until the whites form smooth, shiny peaks. (If you use a whisk, the same principle applies.) If you're making a sweet soufflé, start beating in the sugar after the whites form soft peaks.

If any of the yolk breaks and falls into the separated whites before you beat them stiff, remove the yolk by dabbing with a piece of paper towel. Also avoid using plastic bowls when beating whites. Fat and grease adhere to plastic, which can diminish the volume of the beaten whites.

If you overbeat the egg whites so that they lose their shine and start to look dry and grainy, add another egg white and beat briefly to reconstitute.

Folding egg whites

To fold egg whites into a batter, a soufflé base, or any other mixture, begin by stirring about one-quarter of the beaten whites into the yolk mixture. (This step lightens the batter somewhat.) Then pile the remaining egg whites on top. Use a large rubber spatula to cut down through the center of the mixture, going all the way to the bottom of the bowl. Pull the spatula toward you to the edge of the bowl, turning it to bring some of the yolk mixture up over the whites. Give the bowl a quarter-turn and repeat this plunging, scooping motion about 10 to 15 times (depending on the amount of batter) until the whites and yolk mixture are combined. Be careful not to overblend, or the beaten whites will deflate. See Figure 10-2 for illustrated instructions of this technique.

Cooking and peeling hard-cooked eggs

Eggs really should never be hard-*boiled* (in their shells), but rather hard-*cooked;* rigorous boiling causes eggs to jostle and crack, leaving the whites tough. The correct technique is to place the eggs in cold water, bring the water to a boil, and then immediately remove the pot from the heat, as in the following steps:

1. **Place the eggs in a saucepan large enough to hold them in a single layer. Add cold water to cover by about 1 inch.**

2. **Cover the saucepan and bring the water to a boil over high heat as fast as possible. Then turn off the heat.**

   If your stove is electric, remove the pan from the burner.

3. **Let eggs stand in the pan, still covered, for 15 minutes for large eggs, 18 minutes for jumbo, and 12 minutes for medium.**

4. **Drain the eggs in a colander and run cold water over them until completely cooled.**

Hard-cooked eggs have numerous uses. Slice them into tossed green salads or potato salads, make deviled eggs, mash them for egg salad sandwiches, or simply peel and eat them with a little salt. Sounds like lunch to us! Always refrigerate hard-cooked eggs and eat them within a week to ten days.

But about peeling that egg. . . . The fresher the egg, the more difficult it is to peel, although running cold water over the eggs as you work can help separate the egg white from the shell slightly, making peeling easier. For perfect peeling, follow these steps:

1. **As soon as your hard-cooked egg is cool enough to handle, tap it gently on a table or countertop to crackle the shell all over.**

2. **Roll the egg between your hands to loosen the shell.**

3. **Peel off the shell, starting at the large end of the egg.**

The copper connection

We won't go into the scientific details of why copper bowls are best for whipping egg whites — just believe us. As far back as the mid-eighteenth century, this was common knowledge. Just remember that if you are making a meringue or other dish that requires whipped whites, whipping the whites in a copper bowl with a balloon whisk yields a fluffier and more stable foam.

A 10-inch copper bowl for whisking costs about $60. If you don't have a copper bowl, a pinch of cream of tartar, added to the egg white, can also stabilize the foam.

How to Fold Egg Whites into a Soufflé Base

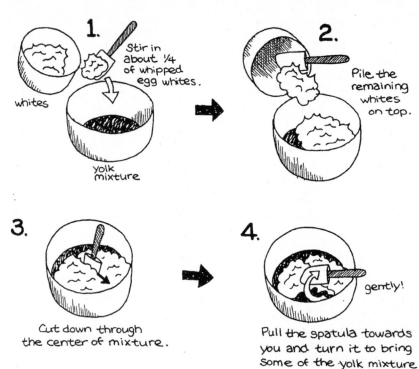

1. Stir in about ¼ of whipped egg whites.

whites

yolk mixture

2. Pile the remaining whites on top.

3. Cut down through the center of mixture.

4. Pull the spatula towards you and turn it to bring some of the yolk mixture over the whites. gently!

Figure 10-2: Folding egg whites into a soufflé base involves a plunging, scooping motion.

5. Give the bowl a quarter turn.

Repeat steps 3 & 4 (about 10-15 times) until the whites and yolk are combined.

CAUTION! Don't overblend or the whites will deflate!

Enjoying Eggs-traordinary Egg Recipes

You can cook a lot of things with eggs, some simple, like the following recipe for egg salad, and some more complex, like meringue or soufflé. Here are some delicious egg recipes to get you started cooking with eggs.

 **Easy Egg Salad**

Egg salad is a classic for picnics and brown-bag lunches. And after you get the basic formula down, you can vary it in countless ways. Let your taste buds and what's available in your refrigerator determine how you dress up this basic egg salad. You can add any number of ingredients to taste, such as flavored mustard, chopped pickles, minced onion, diced celery, fresh or dried herbs (such as parsley, dill, or tarragon), sweet relish, or Tabasco sauce.

Tools: *Medium mixing bowl, fork*

Preparation time: *About 5 minutes*

Cooking time: *About 15 minutes (for cooking the eggs)*

Yield: *2 servings*

4 hard-cooked eggs, peeled   *Salt and pepper*

2 tablespoons mayonnaise (or more to taste)

Mash the hard-cooked eggs in a medium mixing bowl with a fork. Add the mayonnaise and season to taste with salt and pepper. Cover and refrigerate until ready to use.

Per serving: Calories 254 (From Fat 194); Fat 22g (Saturated 5g); Cholesterol 432mg; Sodium 493mg; Carbohydrate 2g (Dietary Fiber 0g); Protein 13g.

ⓢ *Omelet with Herbs*

A plain omelet is quick and easy and cooked on top of the range, whereas a soufflé omelet is lightened with stiff whites and beaten yolks and is finished in the oven.

If you cook the omelet properly, the skin is very smooth and the center is a little moist. You can change the herbs to suit seasonality or personal tastes. And your filling choices are unlimited: cheese, cooked vegetables, ham, hot peppers, and much more. (See the sidebar "Omelet variations" for suggestions.)

You can serve this basic omelet for breakfast, brunch, lunch, or dinner. Various garnishes, such as watercress, parsley, tarragon, or chives, make the omelet more eye-appealing (as shown in the color section).

Tools: *Chef's knife, mixing bowl, 10-inch (preferably nonstick) omelet pan or skillet, rubber spatula*

Preparation time: *About 10 minutes*

Cooking time: *About 1 minute*

Yield: *1 serving*

1 teaspoon chopped tarragon, or ¼ teaspoon dried tarragon	*2 teaspoons chopped parsley, or ½ teaspoon dried parsley*	*3 eggs*
	1 tablespoon chopped chives	*Salt and pepper*
		2 teaspoons butter

1 Combine the tarragon, parsley, and chives in a medium mixing bowl. Remove and set aside 1 teaspoon of the fresh herb mixture for garnish. (If you're using dried herbs, chop extra chives for garnish.)

2 Add the eggs and a few dashes each of salt and pepper to the bowl and beat with a fork, just enough to combine the whites and yolks.

3 Heat a 10-inch omelet pan or skillet over medium-high heat, and then add the butter and melt it, turning the pan to coat evenly. Make sure that the butter is hot and foaming, but not browned, before you add the eggs. (If the butter burns before you add the egg mixture, carefully wipe the pan clean with paper towels and start again, being careful this time not to let the butter brown. Just let it heat up before adding the eggs. Or, if you don't want to waste butter and the butter is just brown, not black and burned, be aware that your omelet will have little brown butter specks in it. Some people don't mind the additional color.) Pour in the egg mixture. It should begin to set at the edges immediately.

4 Using a spatula, gently pull the cooked edges toward the center and tilt the pan so the runny mixture flows to the exposed bottom. When the mixture solidifies, remove the pan from the heat and let it rest for a few seconds. The center should be a little moist because the omelet continues to cook in the hot pan. (If you're making an omelet with a filling, add the filling at this point.)

5 Holding the pan so that it tilts away from you, use the spatula to fold about one-third of the near side of the omelet toward the center.

6 Firmly grasping the pan handle with one hand, lift the pan off the stove, keeping it tilted slightly down and away from you. (Be sure to use a potholder!) Leave a little bit of the handle tip exposed. With the other hand, strike the handle tip two or three times with the side of your fist to swing up the far side of the pan. Doing so causes the far edge of the omelet to fold back on itself, completing the envelope. Use the spatula to press the omelet closed at the seam. Roll the omelet onto a warm dish, seam side down. Sprinkle the remaining herbs on the top. (See Figure 10-3 for illustrated instructions.)

Go-With: *For lunch or a light dinner, serve this omelet with a tossed green salad and Sautéed Skillet Potatoes (see Chapter 5) or the French Potato Salad in Chapter 12.*

Vary It! *Another way to fold an omelet is the half-moon technique. Slide half the omelet onto a serving plate and turn the pan over to flip the omelet into a half-moon shape. This technique is especially helpful if the folding is too difficult or the omelet gets stuck in the pan.*

Tip: *Making an omelet is easier in a pan with nonstick coating. Keep in mind, though, that a nonstick surface can give an omelet a thin "skin," which, to most people, is no big deal.*

Per serving: Calories 294 (From Fat 204); Fat 22g (Saturated 9g); Cholesterol 658mg; Sodium 773mg; Carbohydrate 2g (Dietary Fiber 0g); Protein 19g.

Folding an Omelet

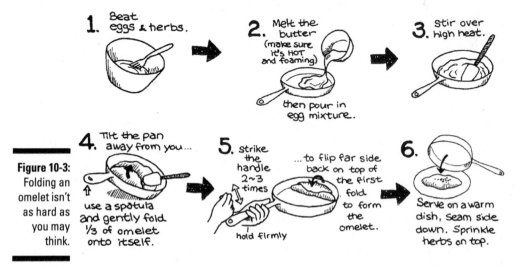

Figure 10-3: Folding an omelet isn't as hard as you may think.

1. Beat eggs & herbs.

2. Melt the butter (make sure it's HOT and foaming) then pour in egg mixture.

3. Stir over high heat.

4. Tilt the pan away from you... use a spatula and gently fold 1/3 of omelet onto itself.

5. strike the handle 2~3 times — hold firmly — ...to flip far side back on top of the first fold to form the omelet.

6. Serve on a warm dish, seam side down. Sprinkle herbs on top.

☺ *Mushroom-Swiss Frittata*

The Italian frittata can get time-pressed cooks out of a jam in no time. A frittata makes a wonderful lunch main course, accompanied by a salad. Making a frittata is simple — and you can dress it up so that it looks great. The fundamental difference between an omelet and a frittata is that an omelet is made with eggs and seasonings, filled with sundry ingredients, and folded; a frittata incorporates the ingredients in the egg mixture. The result is sort of like a cake, slightly thicker and more firm than an omelet. Moreover, an omelet is cooked completely on top of the stove, while a frittata, according to most versions, is finished under the broiler or fully cooked in the oven.

Tools: *Chef's knife, mixing bowl, ovenproof omelet pan or 10-inch cast-iron skillet with lid (make sure the pan you use will fit in your oven), slotted spoon, rubber spatula, whisk*

Preparation time: *About 20 minutes*

Cooking time: *About 20 minutes*

Yield: *4 servings*

8 eggs	Salt and pepper	2 cups sliced white mushrooms
2 tablespoons water	¼ pound Swiss cheese, cut into small cubes	
2 tablespoons finely chopped basil or parsley, or 2 teaspoons dried basil or parsley	2 tablespoons butter	1 small yellow onion, chopped
		1 tablespoon olive oil

1 Beat the eggs and water in a medium mixing bowl with the basil or parsley and the salt and pepper to taste. Add the cheese and set aside.

2 Heat the butter in an omelet pan or 10-inch cast-iron skillet over medium-high heat. Add the mushrooms and onions and sauté for about 7 minutes, until the onions are translucent but not brown and the mushrooms begin to shrink. Remove the mushrooms and onions with a slotted spoon and set aside.

3 Add the olive oil and the egg-cheese mixture to the skillet and cook for about 1 minute. Don't stir, but run a rubber spatula around the edges to make sure it doesn't stick. Spread the mushroom-onion mixture over the top of the eggs and then cover and reduce the heat to medium. Cook for about 4 to 5 minutes, or until the bottom is set and golden brown. The top should still be wet.

4 As the frittata cooks, preheat the oven to 400 degrees.

5 Uncover the skillet and place it in the oven on a middle rack. Bake for an additional 10 minutes, or until the top is cooked solid and golden.

6 To serve, run a rubber spatula around the outside of the frittata. Invert a large, round serving plate over the pan and invert the pan and plate again quickly, letting the frittata fall onto the plate. It should be golden brown. Serve immediately or at room temperature.

Go-With: *For a brunch or lunch, serve this frittata with the Tomato, Red Onion, and Basil Salad or the Bell Pepper-Rice Salad, both in Chapter 12.*

Per serving: Calories 349 (From Fat 243); Fat 27g (Saturated 12g); Cholesterol 466mg; Sodium 348mg; Carbohydrate 5g (Dietary Fiber 1g); Protein 22g.

Classic Quiche Lorraine

Quiche seems to have been relegated to a carry-out food status, but the homemade version, warm from the oven, can be a real treat. This quick version uses a commercial pastry crust, which you can buy in the supermarket. Save any leftover quiche to eat the next day, either cold or reheated in a 325-degree oven for about 15 minutes.

Tools: *Chef's knife, skillet, whisk, mixing bowl, baking sheet*

Preparation time: *About 20 minutes*

Cooking time: *About 50 minutes*

Yield: *4 servings*

3 strips bacon

1 small yellow onion, diced

9-inch frozen, commercial pie crust

½ cup cubed Gruyére or Swiss cheese

2 tablespoons freshly grated Parmesan cheese (optional)

3 eggs, lightly beaten

½ cup heavy cream or half-and-half

½ cup milk

2 tablespoons minced parsley

¼ teaspoon ground nutmeg

¼ teaspoon salt, or to taste

⅛ teaspoon white pepper, or to taste

1 Place the oven rack in the lowest position and preheat the oven to 375 degrees.

2 Heat a medium skillet over medium heat, add the bacon strips, and cook for about 3 to 4 minutes or until crisp, turning frequently. Remove and drain on paper towels. Pour off all but 1 tablespoon of fat from the pan. (Pour the fat into a metal can — not down the sink, where it can clog the drain.) In the same pan, cook the onions over medium heat until they wilt, stirring occasionally, for 2 to 3 minutes.

3 Crumble the bacon and sprinkle it over the pie crust along with the onion and the Gruyère (or Swiss) cheese and, if desired, the Parmesan cheese.

4 In a bowl, whisk together the eggs, cream, milk, parsley, nutmeg, salt, and pepper. Pour this mixture over the bacon, onions, and cheese. Place on a baking sheet and bake for 45 to 50 minutes or until firm.

Vary It! *Replace the bacon with ⅓ to ½ cup of any of the following: cooked cubed zucchini, summer squash, okra, or chopped spinach; roasted bell peppers; diced sautéed mushrooms; chopped sautéed leeks; cubed tomatoes sautéed with garlic and onions; cubed sautéed artichoke hearts; diced baked ham; or blanched asparagus.*

Per serving: Calories 485 (From Fat 344); Fat 38g (Saturated 18g); Cholesterol 232mg; Sodium 624mg; Carbohydrate 20g (Dietary Fiber 1g); Protein 15g.

☺ *Perfect Lemon Meringue Pie*

Lemon meringue pie (shown in the color section) is a classic example of a recipe that uses eggs in two ways: the yolks for the custard, and the whites for the meringue. You can use yolks to make all kinds of custard, from a caramel-laced flan to chocolate pudding to fancy lemon curd, but in this recipe, they make a simple lemon custard. Meringue can top all kinds of things, from key lime pie to chocolate crème pie to baked Alaska, but again, we start simple here. After you get the hang of custards and meringues, you can make all kinds of desserts that look impressive and are actually a lot of fun to construct.

Tools: *Pie plate, medium saucepan, two small bowls for separating eggs, large mixing bowl, electric mixer or wire whisk*

Preparation time: *About 20 minutes, plus 30 minutes cooling time after baking*

Baking time: *About 20 minutes*

Yield: *8 servings*

1 pie crust, purchased (frozen or the refrigerated kind you unfold) or homemade (see the Basic Pastry Crust recipe in Chapter 17)	¼ cup cornstarch	¼ teaspoon cream of tartar
	¼ cup flour	½ teaspoon vanilla
	1 cup boiling water	2 tablespoons confectioners' sugar
4 eggs	2 tablespoons butter	
1½ cups plus ⅓ cup granulated sugar	Juice and zest (the grated, outer peel, just the colored portion) from 2 fresh lemons (organic if possible)	

1 Preheat the oven to 400 degrees.

2 Bake the pie crust for 10 minutes. Remove from the oven and set aside.

3 Separate the eggs, placing the yolks in one bowl and the whites in a larger bowl. (Refer to Figure 10-1 for instructions on separating eggs.)

4 In a medium saucepan, combine the 1½ cups sugar, cornstarch, flour, and boiling water. Stirring constantly, cook over medium-high heat until the mixture comes to a boil. Remove from the heat and allow to cool for 5 minutes.

5 Add the butter, lemon juice, and lemon zest to the sugar mixture. Whisk in the egg yolks until combined. Cook over medium heat until thick, 5 minutes or less, stirring constantly. Pour into the pie crust and set aside.

6 Using very clean, dry whisk-type beaters and a metal or glass bowl, beat the egg whites, cream of tartar, vanilla, the confectioners' sugar, and the remaining ⅓ cup granulated sugar, until stiff peaks form. Completely cover the pie with the meringue, sealing in the lemon mixture.

7 Return to the oven on an oven rack set in the lower third of the oven (to make room for the tall meringue) and bake for 10 minutes, or until the meringue turns a light golden brown. Allow to cool for at least 30 minutes. Serve at room temperature or cold.

Tip: Serve this lemon meringue pie as a dessert following a light lunch or a fancy dinner. It best complements light, fresh summer fare, like salads and fish.

Vary It! Citrus meringue pies are interchangeable. Replace the lemon juice and peel with the juice and peel of three small or two large limes, two or three small tangerines, or two small oranges or one medium orange.

Per serving: Calories 399 (From Fat 111); Fat 12g (Saturated 6g); Cholesterol 119mg; Sodium 132mg; Carbohydrate 69g (Dietary Fiber 0g); Protein 5g.

Omelet variations

To alter the basic omelet recipe in this chapter, omit the herbs and chives and use ½ cup of any of the following ingredients. There's no limit to the type and combination of ingredients, herbs, or seasonings that you can use to fill and flavor an omelet. Be sure to prepare your fillings before you start cooking the eggs.

Grated hard cheese, such as cheddar, Swiss, or Gruyère, and soft and semisoft cheese, such as mozzarella, goat, or Brie, should be added to the egg mixture.

To make the following types of omelets, place the fillings on the omelet a few minutes before folding:

- **Spanish:** Any combination of chopped tomatoes, green bell peppers, onions, and hot sauce, or a couple tablespoons of salsa

- **Vegetarian:** Cooked, chopped asparagus, artichoke hearts, mushrooms, white or sweet potatoes, spinach, broccoli, or cauliflower; slices of avocado; grilled, sliced eggplant; and red peppers

- **Western, also known as Denver:** Chopped ham, onions, and green bell peppers

- **Mediterranean:** Feta cheese, tomatoes, spinach, and onions

- **Seafood:** Smoked salmon or trout, crab meat, or cooked shrimp

- **Meat:** Cooked, crumbled bacon or sausage; diced cooked ham; or salami

- **Mixed greens:** Watercress, arugula, or spinach, with a dollop of sour cream

- **Mushrooms:** Sautéed button, portobello, cremini, or oyster mushrooms

Keep in mind that fresh herbs and dried herbs are similar in flavor but different in potency. Fresh herbs are more delicate; dried herbs are more concentrated. When a recipe calls for, say, 1 teaspoon of fresh thyme and you have only dried thyme, use roughly a third to a half of the quantity, and always taste.

Chapter 11

Stirring Up Soup-er Homemade Soups

In This Chapter

▶ Getting the hang of some basic skills

▶ Using time-tested tips for success

▶ Counting on comfort food soups

▶ Preparing soups with puréed or chunky ingredients

▶ Chilling out with a fruit soup

*N*o offense to the gastronomic wizards at major commercial soup companies, but most 7-year-olds with a recipe and a stepladder can make soup that is superior to the canned version. For one, canned soups are always overcooked. You can't keep vegetables bright and crisp in the sterilization process necessary for canning. What's more, canned soup seasonings typically consist of two things: salt and parsley. Not very interesting, but designed so as to offend the smallest number of people — sort of like American beer.

Homemade soups are easy to make and impressive to serve, and they make a soul-satisfying meal. Homemade soup is nutritious and tastes so good that you'll wonder why you ever ate any other kind. What could be easier than adding meat and vegetables to broth? A soup can be a complete meal or a savory appetizer. In the winter months, a steaming bowl of soup is warming comfort food, and what could be more refreshing in the heat of summer than a bright, sparkling fruit soup? We're getting hungry just thinking about it.

Another great thing about soup is that you can usually whip some up whether you've been grocery shopping or not. Soup is flexible — just add meat, vegetables, dairy products, and/or starches to broth, or even water, and you've got soup! Soup is also a great way to disguise leftovers. Instead of hearing everyone moaning, "Not turkey again!" or "Isn't that the same rice from yesterday?" you'll be more likely to hear, "Mmm, turkey and rice soup with peas and cream. How did you ever think of such a delicious combination?"

Making soup is also a great way to clean out your vegetable crisper. No, you don't want to put that moldy spinach into a soup. Soup isn't magic and won't transform bad ingredients into good ones. But if you aren't sure how to use up that bag of carrots or that whole bunch of celery, soup is the answer! Carrots, celery, an onion, a clove of garlic, some pepper . . . sounds like soup to us. Strain out the vegetables after boiling them for an hour, and you have vegetable stock. Clean and chop the vegetables first, and you'll end up with vegetable soup. Or, for a beautiful orange carrot soup, purée the whole business and stir in a splash of that half-and-half you use in your coffee.

Of course, soup can get pretty fancy and complicated, but for now, just stick to the basics: chicken noodle soup and vegetable beef soup (the quintessential comfort foods), spicy chili perfect for a winter gathering of family or friends, a quick and easy chilled fruit soup for summer meals on the beach, and a few other favorites we know you'll enjoy making. (For even more soup recipes, check out Wiley's *Cooking Soups For Dummies,* by Jenna Holst.) Fear not. Soup is a breeze!

Brushing Up on a Few Essential Soup Skills

Before you start throwing all your leftover vegetables and last night's pot roast into the soup pot, consider a few essential skills. Most soups contain meat and/or vegetables, and while you can boil these, sautéing them first adds a lot of flavor to your soup. Many soups also use garlic, onions, and tomatoes for flavoring, so this section looks at the best ways to prepare these ingredients. Practice the techniques in this section, and the soup recipes that follow will be easy as, well, soup!

What am I eating? Soups defined

Soups come in several different categories. Here are some types of soup you've probably heard about:

Bisque: A thick, rich, puréed soup usually made from shellfish (such as crab or lobster) but occasionally made from vegetables, such as in tomato bisque.

Broth: A clear, flavored liquid made from simmering vegetables, herbs, meats, poultry, or fish bones in water. Strain the solids and serve as a classy appetizer with a garnish (like a basil leaf, a few sliced mushrooms, or a sprinkle of Parmesan cheese) floating on the surface. The French word for broth is bouillon (which is not to be confused with what you get from those salty, processed bouillon cubes, a convenience item that really doesn't belong in a really authentic homemade soup).

Chili: A thick, stewlike concoction of beef or other meat in a tomato base with chili powder and typically onions, peppers, and legumes like kidney or pinto beans. White chili has a chicken- or vegetable-stock base, doesn't contain tomatoes, and usually features chicken or turkey rather than beef.

Chowder: A typically thick and chunky fish soup, usually with vegetables such as potatoes.

Consommé: The "consummate" broth that's completely clear of grease and impurities. A mixture of egg whites, and sometimes finely chopped meat and vegetables, is simmered in the stock. The egg whites cook or solidify, trapping any impurities. After simmering an hour or more, the stock is strained through layers of cheesecloth, resulting in a very clear, pure consommé.

Court bouillon: A broth, usually strained, that simmers for only a short time — no more than 30 minutes — but long enough to draw out the flavor of the vegetables added to the broth. It's used as a poaching liquid for fish, seafood, and vegetables.

Fumet: A strained stock of fish bones, water, vegetables, and herbs. Fumet (French for "fish stock") cooks for about 30 minutes and is used as a flavoring base for soups and sauces.

Gumbo: A soup that typically combines assorted shellfish, poultry, vegetables, a long-cooked dark brown roux of flour and oil, okra, and filé powder (a seasoning made from ground sassafras leaves), which thicken and flavor the soup as it cooks. Gumbo is the African word for okra.

Puréed soup: A soup in which solid ingredients are whirled in a blender or food processor or forced through a food mill. Sometimes the purée is coarse, as in gazpacho (see the recipe later in this chapter). Other times the purée is creamy and velvety, as with a purée of cooked potatoes and leeks. Stock, cream, or a velouté is often added to the vegetable mixture for extra texture and flavor.

Stew: Thicker than your basic soup but thinner than, say, a casserole, stew consists of meat and vegetables simmered in a small amount of broth, or in their own juices.

Stock: The foundation of countless soups. Brown meat bones in the oven before adding to a simmering pot of liquid, vegetables, and herbs. This browning gives the stock a rich caramel color and flavor. You can also make stock from a whole chicken, leftover turkey bones, or any other meat bones. Or just use vegetables like onions, garlic, carrots, celery, and various herbs to make vegetable stock. In most recipes, you can substitute canned broth for stock. What you sacrifice in taste you make up for in convenience. If you have the time, however, just simmer your bones and veggies for a few hours and — *voilà* — homemade stock.

Up the savory quotient: Sautéing meat and vegetables

To *sauté* means to cook meat, poultry, fish, or vegetables in any kind of fat, like butter or olive oil, over medium-high heat until they turn a golden brown. You can use a skillet (a large, round, shallow pan with a long handle), a sauté pan (a round, shallow pan with straight or flared sides), or a saucepan (a round, deeper pan with straight sides). Chapter 5 tells you more about sautéing, but for a quick lesson, you'll be sautéing like a pro if you just follow these steps:

1. **Add the fat (butter or oil) to the pan and turn the heat to medium-high.**

2. **When you can smell the butter or oil, add the ingredients you're sautéing and stir quickly to coat your ingredients with the fat.**

3. **Keep stirring and coating until lightly browned and crispy on the outside.**

   Some chefs sauté by flipping the ingredients in the pan without a spatula, using a practiced jerking of the pan by the handle, but a spatula works just fine and is less likely to result in your beautifully sautéed ingredients flying all over the kitchen.

Whack that clove: Preparing fresh garlic

You can chop it, you can smash it, you can put it through a garlic press, but using fresh garlic really is worth a couple extra minutes of prep time because the flavor is so superior to the stuff that comes prechopped in a jar. That ingredient works in a pinch, however, so it doesn't hurt to keep a jar in the refrigerator.

Garlic comes in buds that break apart into cloves. Buy garlic that feels firm and hard, not soft. Garlic cloves should have very little give when you push on them with your finger. Here's how to prepare garlic for your favorite dishes:

1. **Break off a clove, put it on a cutting board, and smack it with the flat side of your chef's knife.**

   The peel should come off easily.

2. **Mince it (chop it into really tiny pieces) or put it in a garlic press, a handy tool that pushes the garlic through little holes with a squeeze of its handle, doing all the mincing work for you.**

   If you peel the garlic clove first, you can scrape the remaining skin inside the press right into your soup (or whatever you're cooking), using the tip of a knife.

   However, if you don't want to take the time to do this and you have a heavy-duty garlic press, you can squeeze a clove of garlic without peeling it. You need a little more hand strength for this, but it's not a bad way to relieve tension.

Getting to the meat of fresh tomatoes: Peeling and seeding

For many recipes, tomatoes are a staple, but you don't want their peels or seeds. To peel and seed a fresh tomato, follow these steps:

1. **Bring a covered pot of water to a rolling boil over high heat.**

2. **Cut the core out of the tomato.**

3. **Cut an X in the bottom of the tomato, just slicing through the skin, and then put the tomato in a sieve with a handle.**

   If you don't have a sieve, you can use a slotted spoon or even a pair of kitchen tongs for the next step.

4. **Remove the lid from the pot and lower the tomato into the boiling water for 10 to 30 seconds.**

5. **Remove the tomato from the pot, rinse with cold water until cool enough to handle, and then peel off the skin, starting from the X you cut in the bottom.**

   The skin should come off easily, but if it doesn't, return the tomato to the boiling water for another 30 seconds.

6. **Cut the tomato in half.**

7. **Squeeze out the seeds and then chop the remaining flesh.**

Peeling an onion — hold the tears!

Peeling an onion really can make your eyes water, but you can minimize this effect:

1. **Cut off the bud end but not the end with the roots.**

2. **Peel back the skin, just to the roots, pushing it back over the roots, and hold onto it like a handle.**

3. **Rinse the onion under cold water and then slice thinly.**

Following a Few Tricks of the Soup Trade

Besides understanding the basic skills required for concocting a great pot of soup, it helps to know a few tricks of the insiders — the things that professional chefs do to make their soups really special. Follow these soup trade tricks, and your family or guests will marvel at the sparkling flavor and irresistible texture of your homemade soups.

✔ Always add fresh herbs to soups or sauces at the last minute before serving. That way, the herbs remain vibrant and alive with flavor. If you use dried herbs, add them earlier in the cooking process, to help release their flavors.

✓ Don't boil soups containing milk or cream unless the recipe calls for it. Cream soups burn easily, which ruins the taste. Typically, milk or cream is stirred in toward the end of cooking and gently warmed.

✓ If you goofed with the salt, don't dump the soup. If the soup tastes too salty, the simple solution is to add water. If you don't want to add water and thin the soup, try adding paper-thin slices of potato. Cook them until translucent — they tend to soak up salt like little sponges. Leave them in the soup if you like, or fish them out with a fork and discard them. Tomatoes, either fresh or canned (but unsalted!), do the same thing.

✓ If your soup is bland, consider a few high-flavor additions: a teaspoon of salt, a teaspoon of cumin, a teaspoon of chili powder, some freshly ground black pepper, a teaspoon of chili paste, some chopped jalapeño peppers or mild green chiles (the amount depends on how spicy you like it), or some more fresh or dried herbs, such as rosemary, sage, savory, tarragon, or thyme. You also can add a little lemon juice or dry sherry.

Thickening your soup

Sometimes you want to thicken your soup so that it looks more luxurious and tastes richer. You can thicken any soup, although some soups are naturally thick and others you may prefer to be thin (such as a broth-based soup like chicken noodle). You can thicken soup in several ways. For example, you can stir in a teaspoon of butter or cream or add some puréed vegetables.

Here's a classic thickening technique you may want to try:

1. **Take 1 tablespoon of slightly softened butter and work it together with 1 tablespoon of all-purpose flour by mashing both with the back of a spoon or a fork until they form a smooth buttery paste.**

   The French call this a *beurre manié*, but don't worry about that — they have a different word for everything.

2. **Scoop a cup or so of soup liquid into a small bowl and mix in the flour-butter mixture until it has fully melted and been incorporated into the soup liquid.**

3. **Stir this mixture back into the soup pot and cook over medium heat for about 5 minutes, until you notice the soup has slightly thickened.**

Here's another thickening method that's even easier:

1. **Using a fork or a small wire whisk, blend 1 tablespoon all-purpose flour with 2 tablespoons soup broth.**

2. **Stir, add about 1 cup more broth, stir again, and add to the soup.**

3. **Cook over medium heat for 5 to 10 more minutes, or until the soup has slightly thickened.**

Dare we admit it? Instant potato flakes make a great and almost instantaneous thickener! Add a tablespoonful and stir until the soup thickens.

Skimming soups and stocks

When making soup, especially those that contain dried beans or lentils, meat, or poultry, you often need to use a spoon to skim the surface of the simmering liquid to remove and discard any scum or foam that rises to the surface. A spoon with a long handle makes it easier to keep from burning your hand or getting splattered with bubbling soup. Try to skim the surface as soon as the foam forms. If you allow the foam to boil back into the broth, it can affect the flavor.

Sometimes, fat also rises to the surface, especially if your soup contains high-fat meat, such as sausage. As the soup cooks, skim off any fat floating on the surface. Or, if you're making the soup the day before, refrigerate it and, when the fat congeals on the top, skim it off and throw it away before reheating the soup.

Cozying Up to Comforting Soups

Soup makes you feel good inside, all warm and cozy and secure. Certain foods really press those comfort buttons, though. These are soups we remember from childhood, even if some of us remember only the canned versions! Fortunately for you, the homemade versions are easy and taste even better. They also retain more vitamins and have only a fraction of the salt of the canned versions. Try these soups and start a new tradition. Someday your own kids, your friends, or whoever else shares your meals will have some fond soup memories of their own, all because of you.

Comfort food soups are easy to improvise if you follow a few basic steps. You may notice that the three soups in this section are similar in preparation and even in ingredients: beef, chicken, or turkey; barley, pasta, or rice; and an assortment of good, flavorful soup vegetables like onions, garlic, carrots, and celery. With this basic knowledge, you can improvise all kinds of soups. Just follow these steps to make soup for about six people:

1. **Warm a tablespoon or two of cooking oil (olive oil is good for your heart) and cook about a pound of chopped meat, poultry, or fish (or use already cooked leftovers, in which case, skip this step).**

    Sautéing the meat first enhances the flavor, but you can also skip this step and add the meat along with the broth because it will cook in the soup, except in the case of ground meats, which must be cooked first.

2. **Remove the meat to a plate and set aside.**

3. **Melt a tablespoon or two of butter or more oil in the same pan and sauté some chopped vegetables.**

4. **Return the meat to the pan (or add it now if you aren't sautéing it first) and add about 4 cups canned broth and about 4 cups water.**

5. **Season with salt, pepper, and herbs.**

6. **Let it cook for 30 to 60 minutes, and enjoy!**

Vegetable Beef Soup

You can buy the ingredients for this recipe or use leftovers. We've even been known to use leftover restaurant steak or buffet pot roast. When adding the beef, it can be cooked or raw; it works both ways (unless you decide to use ground beef, in which case you must sauté it first). If you add cooked beef, just skip the first two steps, and start with Step 3, to cook the vegetables. When you get to Step 4, add the cooked beef along with the broth.

Tools: *Large saucepan or pot, chef's knife, vegetable peeler*

Preparation time: *About 25 minutes (including time to cook the meat and vegetables)*

Cooking time: *About 1 hour*

Yield: *6 servings*

1 tablespoon cooking oil (a little more if you aren't using a nonstick pan)

1 pound stew meat, cubed, or leftover beef from a pot roast or steak

2 tablespoons butter

1 large yellow onion, chopped

3 carrots, peeled and cut into ¼-inch rounds

3 ribs celery, washed, ends trimmed, and cut into ½-inch pieces

2 small boiling potatoes, about ½ pound total, peeled or not, and cut into ¼-inch cubes

¼ cup pearl barley (the quick-cooking kind that comes in a box in the store or in bulk at health food stores)

4 cups canned beef broth

4 cups water

1 teaspoon salt (optional)

Few dashes of pepper

3 tablespoons chopped fresh parsley, or 1½ tablespoons dried parsley (optional)

1 In a large saucepan or pot over medium-high heat, warm the oil and tilt the pan so the oil covers the bottom.

2 When you start to smell the oil (this should only take about 1 minute), add the beef cubes, unless you're using cooked beef. Stir to coat the meat and keep stirring (this is called sautéing) until the beef is cooked through, about 10 minutes. Remove the beef from the pan and set aside in a small bowl.

3 Pour off any grease from the pan into a heatproof container (you can discard it when it cools and hardens), but don't worry about washing the pan. The beef flavor enhances the flavor of the vegetables.

4 Melt the butter in the same pan in which you were cooking the meat, and add the onion, carrots, celery, and potatoes. Cook, stirring occasionally, until the onions are transparent but not browned, about 11 minutes.

5 Add the barley, beef broth, and water and return the beef to the pot, or add the pre-cooked beef if using leftovers. Add the salt, if desired, and the pepper. Cover and bring to a boil; reduce heat and simmer, uncovered, for about an hour, skimming with a large metal spoon any scum or fat that rises to the surface. Garnish each serving with parsley, if desired.

Vary It! *For a curry flavor, add 1 tablespoon curry powder to the vegetables in Step 4.*

Vary It! *For a chunkier, more stewlike soup (as shown in the color section), cut carrots into 2-inch lengths and quarter potatoes or leave smaller potatoes whole. You can also add different vegetables to this soup, depending on what you have on hand. Try asparagus, turnips, sweet potatoes, or bell peppers.*

Tip: *Leftover soup may thicken, so when warming up this soup the next day, add a little extra water or broth.*

Per serving: *Calories 269 (From Fat 103); Fat 11g (Saturated 5g); Cholesterol 57mg; Sodium 745mg; Carbohydrate 21g (Dietary Fiber 3g); Protein 20g.*

Chicken Noodle Soup

No soup is nicer than chicken noodle soup when you have a cold or just want to warm up. After you have this recipe down, you can get creative by changing the kind of pasta you use, using rice instead of pasta, and altering some of the vegetables. This recipe makes a classic chicken noodle soup, the kind that will make everybody think fondly of your kitchen, except for one change. Once upon a time, our mothers made chicken noodle soup with the whole chicken, extracted the meat, and threw away the bones. This version uses boneless, skinless chicken breasts, which saves time, is less labor intensive, and is also lower in fat. (What's not to like about that?) For this recipe, we prefer to add the chicken into the broth and let it cook there, instead of sautéing it first, because it makes the chicken easy to shred. You can try it both ways after you start feeling adventurous, just to see which method you prefer.

Tools: *Large saucepan or pot, chef's knife, vegetable peeler, wooden spoon*

Preparation time: *About 25 minutes, including time to sauté the vegetables*

Cooking time: *About 50 minutes*

Yield: *6 servings*

2 tablespoons butter	*3 ribs celery, washed, ends trimmed, and cut into ½-inch pieces*	*1½ cups dried egg noodles*
1 large yellow onion, chopped		*1½ teaspoons salt (optional)*
2 cloves garlic, peeled and minced or squeezed through a garlic press	*1 teaspoon dried oregano*	*Dash of cayenne pepper (optional)*
	1 teaspoon dried basil	*Few dashes of black pepper*
3 carrots, peeled and cut into ¼-inch rounds	*8 cups canned chicken broth*	*3 tablespoons chopped fresh parsley or cilantro, or 1½ tablespoons dried parsley or cilantro*
	1 pound boneless, skinless chicken breasts	

1 In a large saucepan or pot over medium heat, melt the butter.

2 Add the onion, garlic, carrots, celery, oregano, and basil. Stir to coat with the butter and cook, stirring every minute or two, until the onions are transparent but not browned, about 5 minutes.

3 Add the chicken broth and chicken breasts. Cover and bring to a boil. Reduce the heat and simmer, uncovered, for about 30 minutes, or until the chicken is cooked all the way through (you can cut it open to check).

4 Increase the heat again and bring to a boil. Add the egg noodles and reduce the heat again, simmering uncovered until the noodles are tender (sample a few to make sure they taste good), about 20 minutes.

5 When the noodles are cooked, remove the chicken breasts to a cutting board and using your chef's knife, chop it into bite-sized pieces or shred it. Return the chicken and any juice to the pot. Season with the salt and cayenne pepper, if desired, and the pepper. Garnish each serving with the parsley or cilantro.

Per serving: Calories 235 (From Fat 102); Fat 11g (Saturated 4g); Cholesterol 66mg; Sodium 1,417mg; Carbohydrate 14g (Dietary Fiber 3g); Protein 19g.

Turkey-Rice Soup

This soup is the perfect way to use leftover turkey from Thanksgiving dinner, or for whatever reason you might have leftover turkey. It's quick, easy, and delicious. If you choose to make this soup from scratch, just add chopped raw or cooked turkey to the broth and, in the case of raw turkey, cook until it's no longer pink in the middle.

Tools: *Large saucepan or pot, chef's knife, vegetable peeler, wooden spoon*

Preparation time: *About 25 minutes, including time to sauté vegetables*

Cooking time: *About 30 minutes*

Yield: *6 servings*

2 tablespoons butter	4 cups canned chicken or (if you can find it) turkey broth	1 cup fresh or frozen green peas
1 medium yellow onion, chopped	4 cups water	1 teaspoon salt (optional)
3 ribs celery, washed, ends trimmed, and cut into ½-inch pieces	1 pound leftover cooked turkey, white and dark meat	Few dashes of pepper
	¾ cup raw white rice	3 tablespoons chopped fresh parsley, or 1½ tablespoons dried parsley (optional)
1 cup white mushrooms, washed, ends trimmed, and sliced	1 cup half-and-half, heavy cream, or whole milk (optional)	

1 In a large saucepan or pot over medium heat, melt the butter.

2 Add the onion, celery, and mushrooms. Stir to coat with the butter and cook, stirring every minute or two, until the onions are transparent but not browned, about 10 minutes.

3 Add the chicken or turkey broth, water, turkey, and rice. Cover and bring to a boil. Reduce heat and simmer, uncovered, for about 30 minutes, or until the rice is cooked (sample it at 30 minutes and cook a little longer if it isn't tender yet).

4 Remove the soup from the heat and add the half-and-half, cream, or milk if you want your soup creamy, along with the peas. Return to the heat until warmed through, about 3 minutes.

5 Season with the salt, if desired, and the pepper. Garnish each serving with parsley, if desired.

Per serving: Calories 358 (From Fat 140); Fat 16g (Saturated 7g); Cholesterol 86mg; Sodium 786mg; Carbohydrate 86g (Dietary Fiber 4g); Protein 28g.

Achieving the Perfect Blend: Puréed Soups

Puréed soups use a blender or food processor to whirl the ingredients into a smooth texture. After you understand the puréeing technique, the variations you can make on this cooking theme are limitless. Asparagus, broccoli, corn, cucumber, mushrooms, parsnips, spinach, rutabaga, tomatoes, winter squash, pumpkin, turnip, and watercress are among the vegetables that purée to a rich and smooth consistency.

If you're going to purée a soup in a blender, let it cool slightly first. Otherwise, the trapped steam could explode and redecorate your ceiling (not to mention burn you!).

Cream of Potato Soup

This simple, quick, and easy soup isn't particularly low in calories or fat, but it sure tastes good! It's also good if you don't purée it and instead prefer a soup with chunks of potato.

Tools: *Chef's knife, large saucepan or pot, wooden spoon or wire whisk, blender or food processor*

Preparation time: *About 15 minutes, to peel and chop vegetables and sauté potatoes*

Cooking time: *About 55 minutes after adding broth*

Yield: *6 servings*

4 tablespoons butter	*4 garlic cloves, peeled (if you don't plan to purée this soup, mince the garlic or put it through a garlic press)*	*½ teaspoon pepper (more or less according to your taste)*
6 medium red potatoes, peeled and quartered (if you don't plan to purée this soup, cut the potatoes into bite-sized pieces)		*6 slices bacon, cooked until crispy and crumbled*
	4 cups chicken broth	*1 tablespoon chopped chives, fresh or dried*
	1 cup heavy cream	
	1½ teaspoons salt (optional)	

1 In a large saucepan or pot, melt the butter.

2 Add the potatoes and garlic cloves and stir to coat. Cook for about 5 minutes. The potatoes won't be tender yet.

3 Add the chicken broth and bring the soup to a simmer. Cook until the potatoes are tender and easy to mash against the side of the pan, about 30 minutes.

4 Remove the soup from the heat and cool for 15 minutes. Spoon the mixture into a blender and purée well.

5 Return the soup to the pot and turn the heat to medium-low. Add the cream and stir constantly until the soup is hot and just barely simmering. If you start to see tiny bubbles, it's done. This should take about 10 minutes.

6 Add the salt, if desired, and pepper and garnish each soup bowl with the bacon and chives.

Go-With: Serve with country bread and a vinaigrette-based salad, such as the Easy Mixed Green Salad in Chapter 12.

Per serving: Calories 425 (From Fat 255); Fat 28g (Saturated 16g); Cholesterol 84mg; Sodium 798mg; Carbohydrate 36g (Dietary Fiber 3g); Protein 8g.

🍅 Tomato Soup

What child doesn't love tomato soup with a grilled cheese sandwich? (For that matter, what adult doesn't love it, during those nostalgic moments?) This soup is almost as easy as opening a can, and it tastes fantastic. It's a great way to use up overflow from a tomato garden in the summer, but canned tomatoes work, too.

Tools: Medium saucepan or pot, blender or food processor, wooden spoon

Preparation time: About 15 minutes for chopping and sautéing vegetables

Cooking time: About 15 minutes, including the cooling time before blending, and blending

Yield: 6 servings

2 tablespoons butter

1 small yellow onion, peeled and chopped

1 clove garlic, minced

3 cups canned chicken or vegetable stock

6 large ripe tomatoes, peeled, seeded, and coarsely chopped, or 2 cans (14 ounces each) tomatoes, undrained and coarsely chopped

2 tablespoons fresh lemon juice

2 teaspoons sugar

Salt and pepper

1 tablespoon chopped fresh cilantro, basil, or tarragon (optional)

1 In a medium saucepan, melt the butter over medium-high heat. Add the onions and garlic and sauté until soft, about 10 minutes.

2 Add the stock and tomatoes to the onion-garlic mixture. Bring to a boil.

3 Remove from the heat and allow to cool 5 minutes. Pour carefully into a blender or food processor. Purée until smooth.

4 Return the mixture to the saucepan; add the lemon juice, sugar, and salt and pepper to taste; and heat over medium until hot again, about 5 minutes, stirring with a wooden spoon. Garnish with the cilantro, basil, or tarragon, if desired.

Go-With: Tomato soup and a salad (try one from Chapter 12) make a filling combination, as shown in the color insert.

Per serving: Calories 102 (From Fat 58); Fat 6g (Saturated 3g); Cholesterol 13mg; Sodium 614mg; Carbohydrate 11g (Dietary Fiber 2g); Protein 2g.

☞ Carrot Soup with Dill

Dill is a natural sidekick to carrots. The following puréed soup usually calls for heavy cream at the end; instead, we use lowfat ricotta cheese, which works just as well at a fraction of the calories. Port (a Portuguese dessert wine) adds a touch of sweetness.

Tools: *Large saucepan or soup pot, chef's knife, colander, blender or food processor, wooden spoon*

Preparation time: *About 15 minutes to chop and sauté vegetables*

Cooking time: *About 1 hour, including time to cool the vegetables*

Yield: *6 servings*

2 tablespoons butter	4 cups homemade or canned chicken or vegetable stock	½ cup lowfat ricotta cheese
1 medium yellow onion, finely chopped	2 cups water	2 to 3 tablespoons port (optional)
1½ pounds carrots, peeled and cut into 1-inch-thick pieces	Salt and pepper	2 tablespoons chopped fresh dill, or 2 teaspoons dried dill

1 In a large, deep saucepan or soup pot over medium heat, melt the butter. Add the onion and cook, stirring often, until it softens, about 5 minutes. Add the carrots, stock, water, and salt and pepper to taste. Cover and bring to a boil. Reduce the heat and simmer, uncovered, for 30 minutes, skimming off any foam that rises to the surface. Cool for 15 minutes.

2 Set a colander over a big bowl or another pot. Carefully pour the soup into the colander. Save the liquid; you need it in Steps 3 and 4.

3 Put the drained carrot-onion mixture into your blender or food processor. Add the ricotta cheese and about a cup of the liquid you're saving. Purée until smooth.

4 Add the purée to the pot holding the remaining cooking liquid and turn the heat to medium-high. Stir well with a wooden spoon until the soup just comes to a boil, about 10 minutes. Remove from the heat, stir in the port (if desired), garnish with the dill, and serve.

Vary It! *You also can use ground ginger as the seasoner in this creamy carrot soup. Ginger is more intense than dill, so you need less. Omit the dill and instead add ½ to ¾ teaspoon ground ginger.*

Vary It! *To turn this soup into a vegetable side dish, simply proceed as instructed, puréeing the cooked vegetables with the ricotta, but adding only as much of the cooking liquid as necessary to produce a thick purée.*

Per serving: Calories 120 (From Fat 42); Fat 5g (Saturated 3g); Cholesterol 15mg; Sodium 588mg; Carbohydrate 15g (Dietary Fiber 3g); Protein 5g.

Chunky Soups to Sink Your Teeth Into

We like chunky soups to be hearty, meaty, and thick with tender morsels of meat, poultry, or fish, and plenty of vegetables. Whether you prefer a savory onion soup or creamy clam chowder, this is the section for you.

French Onion Soup

This restaurant staple is easy to make and elegant enough for parties, but simple enough for a quiet dinner at home.

Tools: *Large pot, 6 ovenproof crocks, sturdy baking sheet, chef's knife, wooden spoon*

Preparation time: *About 20 minutes (for chopping vegetables)*

Cooking time: *About 1 hour, including simmering and broiling time*

Yield: *6 servings*

4 tablespoons butter	7 cups beef broth	6 slices French bread, toasted
4 large sweet onions, like Vidalia, peeled and thinly sliced	1 bay leaf	1 cup grated Swiss cheese

1 Melt the butter over medium heat in a large soup pot. Add the onions. It will seem like a lot of onions, but they'll cook down. Toss to coat the onions with the butter and cook until the onions become transparent, about 10 minutes.

2 Add 1 cup of the beef broth and continue stirring until the broth almost completely cooks away, scraping the pan to keep the caramelized parts moving in the soup, about 35 minutes.

3 Add the remaining 6 cups broth and the bay leaf. Cover and bring to a boil. Reduce the heat and simmer for 15 minutes, stirring occasionally.

4 Remove the bay leaf from the soup and discard. Ladle the soup into 6 ovenproof crocks or bowls. Put a slice of French bread in each bowl and sprinkle each with one-sixth of the cheese. Put the crocks on a sturdy baking sheet.

5 Turn on the broiler of your oven and carefully put the baking sheet under the broiler on the top rack, about 4 inches from the heat source. Watch carefully because food can quickly burn under the heat of a broiler. When the cheese turns golden brown (this should only take a minute or two), carefully remove the baking sheet and serve the soup.

Warning: *When simmering thick soups like this one, occasionally stir and scrape the bottom of the pot with a wooden spoon to prevent the mixture from sticking and burning. Add more water, if necessary. If you do burn food, transfer the unburned portion to another pot.*

Per serving: *Calories 364 (From Fat 131); Fat 15g (Saturated 8g); Cholesterol 37mg; Sodium 1,606mg; Carbohydrate 41g (Dietary Fiber 3g); Protein 16g.*

New England Clam Chowder

Seafood soups of all kinds are quick and easy to make, and this creamy New England chowder is no exception. If you're really ambitious, you can use fresh clams, which you have to steam open and scrub, but for beginners, canned clams work just fine.

If you choose to use fresh clams, buy plump, fresh-looking ones. The old wives' tale that you should only buy clams, oysters, and mussels in the months that contain the letter *r* only applies to wild-caught mollusks. Most clams are raised under controlled conditions and bacterial contamination in the warmer months isn't a factor.

Tools: *Chef's knife; peeler; medium, heavy saucepan or pot*

Preparation time: *About 5 minutes*

Cooking time: *About 55 minutes*

Yield: *4 servings*

1 can (12 ounces) chopped clams (or two 6.5-ounce cans, if this is all you can find)

4 firm potatoes, such as Yukon gold or red potatoes (not baking potatoes), peeled and diced into 1-inch pieces

2 cups bottled clam juice, canned chicken broth, canned vegetable broth, or water

2 tablespoons butter or olive oil

3 garlic cloves, peeled and put through a garlic press

1 medium yellow onion, peeled and chopped

4 cups whole or 2% milk, or 2 cups milk and 2 cups half-and-half or heavy cream

1 tablespoon fresh parsley, or 1 teaspoon dried parsley

½ teaspoon dried thyme

Saltines, oyster crackers, or other good crackers, for garnish

1 Drain the canned clams and put them into a medium saucepan over medium heat. Add the potatoes and the bottled clam juice, broth, or water. Let the mixture come to a simmer, and cook about 40 minutes, until the potatoes are tender enough to spear easily with a fork and the liquid has cooked down to about half of what it was.

2 In a medium skillet, melt the butter or warm the olive oil over medium-high heat. Add the garlic and onion. Sauté until the onions are soft but not brown, about 5 minutes. Add to the clam mixture.

3 Add the milk (or milk and cream), the parsley, and the thyme. Bring to a simmer but not a boil, which should take about 10 minutes if the milk is cold. Serve immediately with the crackers.

Go With: *Serve this delicious soup with bread, such as a hearty loaf of whole-wheat or buttery croissants.*

Vary It! *To add more color to this chowder, add chopped carrots, celery, and chives; sauté them with the garlic and onions in Step 2. Then garnish each bowl with a sprig of fresh parsley (as shown in the color section).*

Per serving: *Calories 374 (From Fat 127); Fat 14g (Saturated 9g); Cholesterol 52mg; Sodium 686mg; Carbohydrate 50g (Dietary Fiber 3g); Protein 13g.*

Getting Sweet with Soup

Soup is for meat and vegetables and savory broths, right? Not always! Not only can soup be served cold, but it can also be made with sweet, juicy fruit. Try the following delectable recipe to cool you on a sultry mid-summer day.

☕ Chilled Fruit Soup

This recipe tastes a little bit like a fruit smoothie in a bowl, and it could hardly be easier, so what excuse do you have not to try it? Use peaches, nectarines, pears, cantaloupe, watermelon, strawberries, blueberries, raspberries, blackberries, or whatever other fruit is freshest and looks the best. Serve this soup for dessert or for a lovely cooling lunch in the heat of the summer.

Tools: *Chef's knife, paring knife, vegetable peeler, food processor or blender, medium bowl*

Preparation time: *About 10 minutes*

Cooking time: *A few seconds to purée and about 1 hour to chill*

Yield: *3 servings*

4 cups ripe, fresh summer fruit (see the recipe introduction for suggestions)	*½ cup vanilla yogurt or heavy cream, plus additional for garnish*
3 tablespoons fresh lime or lemon juice	*Cinnamon or nutmeg for garnish (optional)*

1 Cut the fruit into chunks as if for a fruit salad. Cut off all the parts you wouldn't eat, such as the rinds, stems, seeds, peels, and so on, although for fruits such as peaches and pears, you can leave the peels on if you like.

2 Combine the fruit, juice, and yogurt in a food processor or blender. Blend until smooth. Pour and scrape the mixture into a bowl. Cover with plastic wrap and refrigerate until cold.

3 Just before serving, swirl a spoonful of yogurt or heavy cream over the top of the soup and sprinkle with a little cinnamon or nutmeg, if desired.

Per serving: *Calories 118 (From Fat 9); Fat 1g (Saturated 0g); Cholesterol 2mg; Sodium 28mg; Carbohydrate 27g (Dietary Fiber 5g); Protein 4g.*

Chapter 12

All Dressed Up: Salads and Dressings

A salad can be many things to a meal: a stimu-lating first course, a fresh and crisp accom-paniment to a main dish, or the centerpiece of the meal itself. The key to really great salads is twofold: Use only the freshest ingredients and chop everything into bite-sized portions for easy eating. Who wants to try to fold unwieldy pieces of lettuce dripping with oily vinaigrette onto a fork? If everything is neatly chopped into small pieces, lightly dressed with a delicious homemade or bot-tled dressing, and arranged to present a colorful and attractive plate, you have a spectacular salad.

So Many Dressings, So Little Time

Dressings aren't called that for nothing. A good dressing is a lot like a good outfit. It decorates in a pleasing way, adding flavor to the basic substance. If you go to the supermarket and look at the dressing section, you see many kinds and brands of dressing. You probably tend to reach for the same thing every time: the Italian vinaigrette perhaps, or the creamy ranch dressing, the sweet French, the tangy Thousand Island, or maybe something more trendy, like honey mustard or Caesar. Store-bought dressing can be quite good, but a homemade dressing is something extra special — it has fresh ingredients and a personal touch. Dressings are easy to make, so why not try making yours at home?

When you break them down, dressings are essentially of two kinds: those based on oil and vinegar (vinaigrette) and those based on a creamy mayonnaise (like ranch or Thousand Island). Both types are simple to prepare.

Puckering up for tangy vinaigrettes

Vinaigrette is among the most versatile of dressings. It goes with all sorts of salad greens and grilled vegetables, but it can also work with meat, poultry, and fish, as a marinade or as a light and tasty sauce. The advantage of vinaigrette-based dressing is that you can make a large quantity and store it, sealed, in an old wine bottle or Mason jar. Homemade vinaigrette in a fancy bottle makes a great gift, too.

Vinaigrette has two essential ingredients: vinegar and oil. Add herbs, spices, and other flavorings, and you can give your vinaigrette its unique character. But before you try to get too fancy, take a look at the basic ingredients that make up a high-quality homemade vinaigrette.

The skinny on olive and other salad oils

Some people say that a salad dressing is only as good as the oil it contains, and few oils make a more delicious, complex, and interesting salad dressing than olive oil. But buying olive oil in the supermarket has become as confusing as ordering coffee, what with all the nationalities and fancy labels and terminology in baffling languages. Do you get Italian or Greek or Spanish olive oil? What color and what brand do you buy? Don't worry about all that. The most important thing to look for in olive oil is its *grade,* which is usually printed right on the front of the bottle. In ascending order of quality, you'll find *pure, virgin,* and *extra-virgin.*

The grade has to do with the oleic acid content of the oil, with the finest oils having the least acidity. All three varieties of olive oil come from the olive's first *pressing* (the crushing process that releases the oil from the olives), but extra-virgin is the highest quality. Extra-virgin olive oil usually has the richest aroma and strongest flavor. Pure olive oil can come from both the first and second pressing of the tree-ripened olives and may be blended with 5 to 10 percent virgin olive oil to enrich its flavor.

Don't be misled by olive oil sold as "light." The "light" has nothing to do with its fat content; instead, it refers to its pale color and extremely bland flavor, a result of the way it's processed. One tablespoon of any oil contains the same 120 calories.

Lemonade (Chapter 19)
© Royalty-Free/Corbis

Grilled Shrimp Skewers (Chapter 8)
© Corbis Digital Stock

Spicy Chicken Wings (Chapter 20)
© Burke/Triolo/Brand X Pictures/PictureQuest

New England Clam Chowder (Chapter 11)
© Corbis Digital Stock

Tomato Soup (Chapter 11)
© Royalty-Free/Corbis

Easy Mixed Green Salad (Chapter 12)
© PhotoDisc, Inc.

Vegetable Beef Soup (Chapter 11)
© PhotoDisc, Inc.

American Macaroni and Cheese
(Chapter 14)
© StockFood/FoodCollection

Homemade Mashed Potatoes (Chapter 4)
© Lois Ellen Frank/Corbis

Roasted Pork Ribs with
Country Barbecue Sauce
(Chapter 7)
© Corbis Images/PictureQuest

The Perfect Hamburger
(Chapter 8)
© PhotoDisc, Inc.

Fried Chicken for a Crowd (Chapter 19)
© Burke/Triolo/Brand X Pictures/PictureQuest

Roasted Turkey (Chapter 21)
© Corbis Digital Stock

Smoked Ham with Apricot Glaze (Chapter 7)
© PhotoDisc, Inc.

Spaghetti with Quick Fresh
Tomato Sauce (Chapter 13)
© ROYALTY-FREE/CORBIS

Omelet with Herbs (Chapter 10)
© PHOTODISC, INC.

Family Lasagna (Chapter 13)
© PHOTODISC, INC.

Perfect Lemon Meringue Pie (Chapter 10)
© ROYALTY-FREE/CORBIS

Lemon Granité (Chapter 15)
© PHOTODISC, INC.

Apple Pie (Chapter 17)
© ROYALTY-FREE/CORBIS

Double Chocolate
Pudding
(Chapter 15)

Lemon Bars (Chapter 15)
© Royalty-Free/Corbis

Summer Berry Smoothie
(Chapter 19)
© Royalty-Free/Corbis

Balsamic: The world's most expensive vinegar

Traditional balsamic vinegar is a dark, sweet, syrupy, aged liquid that is worth its weight in gold. The real thing is made in the area around Modena, Italy, and nowhere else (the word "Modena" should be on the label). Virtually all those large bottles of balsamic vinegar you see in supermarkets are imitations — some aged, some not — made to look like the real thing. This "fake" balsamic vinegar is not necessarily bad, just different.

Recognizing real balsamic vinegar is easy: You start to hyperventilate upon seeing the price. Real balsamic vinegar is sold only in little bulb-shaped bottles — they look like perfume. It is usually more than 25 years old and costs $100 and up for a tiny portion. Such rarefied vinegar is not to be tossed around in salads. Italians use it for sauces or just drizzle some on fresh fruit (strawberries are best).

Other salad oils include walnut, hazelnut, sesame, corn, peanut, safflower, and soy. Each has its place. The neutral flavors of corn, peanut, and safflower oils can be mixed with equal amounts of olive or nut oils for a different flavor. Walnut, hazelnut, and sesame oil are strong, so use them sparingly, as flavorings to other, lighter-tasting oils.

Fancy food markets and gourmet shops are increasingly stocking oils flavored with herbs, lemon, peppercorns, and sun-dried tomatoes. These oils can add just the right seasoning touch to a tossed green salad, and they're delicious drizzled over pizza, French bread, goat cheese or Brie, roasted vegetables, or toasted croutons.

The shelf life of oil depends on its variety. Olive oils should keep for up to a year if tightly capped and stored out of the sun in a cool, dark place. But nut oils last only a few months, so purchase them in small quantities.

What puts the vinegar in vinaigrette?

Oil in a salad dressing needs an acidic counterpoint — a tart ingredient that stimulates the palate and cuts through the richness of oil. In most cases, vinegar is the choice, but fresh lemon juice also carries a pungent bite.

Vinegar comes in many different forms. Although red or white wine is the most common liquid base, anything that ferments can be used to make vinegar:

- **Cider vinegar:** Made from apples, this strong, clear, brown vinegar holds up well with pungent greens and is especially good sprinkled on meat, fish, or fruit salads. It's also excellent with ginger or curry dressings.

- **White vinegar:** Colorless and sharp, white vinegar is distilled from assorted grains, and it's terrific in cold rice or pasta salads.

- **Red or white wine vinegar:** Made from any number of red or white wines, this vinegar is full bodied and perfect for dressing pungent, dark greens.

✔ **Rice vinegar:** Common to Japan and China, rice vinegars are less tart than white vinegars and combine well with sesame oils. They're also good in seafood salads.

Experiment with different vinegars to find ones with flavors you enjoy. Your unique choices will make your homemade vinaigrette dressing all yours.

ᕙ *Vinaigrette Dressing*

The proportions in this vinaigrette recipe are only approximations. You must taste it as you go along to balance the vinegar and olive oil flavors. If you're not a red or white wine vinegar fan, specialty shops and even supermarkets sell all kinds of flavored vinegars. Or you can substitute 2 tablespoons fresh lemon juice for the vinegar.

Tools: *Small bowl, whisk*

Preparation time: *Less than 5 minutes*

Yield: *6 servings, or about ½ cup*

2 tablespoons red or white wine vinegar	*⅓ cup olive oil*
1 teaspoon Dijon-style mustard	*Salt and pepper*

1 Place the vinegar and mustard in a bowl. Whisk to blend well.

2 Add the olive oil in a stream while whisking. Season with salt and pepper to taste.

Per serving: Calories 107 (From Fat 106); Fat 12g (Saturated 2g); Cholesterol 0mg; Sodium 119mg; Carbohydrate 0g (Dietary Fiber 0g); Protein 0g.

ᕙ *French Potato Salad*

A delicious European-style potato salad hinges on a good vinaigrette. This version barely resembles the mayonnaise-laden American-style potato salad, and it makes a surprising and pleasing side dish for a fancy dinner as well as an informal picnic. This potato salad is delicious warm or chilled.

Tools: *Chef's knife, medium saucepan, small bowl, serving bowl, whisk*

Preparation time: *About 15 minutes*

Cooking time: *About 30 minutes*

Yield: *4 servings*

2 pounds red potatoes, well scrubbed

6 tablespoons olive oil

1 tablespoon white vinegar

½ cup red onion, chopped

¼ cup finely chopped parsley

1 large clove garlic, finely chopped

Salt and pepper

¼ cup dry white wine at room temperature, or ¼ cup white grape juice or 2 tablespoons cider vinegar

1 In a medium saucepan, cover the potatoes with lightly salted cold water and bring to a boil. Boil for 20 minutes or until the potatoes are tender when pierced with a knife, but not until they fall apart. Drain and let stand until cool enough to handle. (You should assemble the salad while the potatoes are still warm.)

2 As the potatoes cook, make the dressing. Whisk together the oil and vinegar in a small bowl. Whisk in the red onion, parsley, garlic, and salt and pepper to taste.

3 Peel the cooked potatoes and cut them into ¼-inch slices. (Or leave the skins on for more color.) Layer the slices in a shallow serving bowl, sprinkling the wine between the layers.

4 Pour the dressing over the potatoes and gently toss to blend well. Let the salad stand about 30 minutes to blend the flavors. Stir from the bottom before serving, either chilled or at room temperature.

Go-With: *This potato salad is a natural for picnics because its tangy flavor complements milder picnic fare such as sandwiches and cold chicken. It also goes with the Sautéed Chicken Breasts with Tomatoes and Thyme (see Chapter 5).*

Vary It! *Add ¼ cup minced green onions; 2 tablespoons chopped herbs like rosemary, chervil, or basil; or 1 cup diced, roasted bell peppers.*

Per serving: Calories 401 (From Fat 186); Fat 21g (Saturated 3g); Cholesterol 0mg; Sodium 167mg; Carbohydrate 47g (Dietary Fiber 5g); Protein 6g.

Diversifying your dressing

Who wants to eat the same old salad dressing every day? Vinaigrette is a basic formula to which you can add many different ingredients for color, flavor, texture, and taste. Following are some variations on the basic Vinaigrette Dressing recipe in this chapter:

✔ Replace 2 tablespoons of the olive oil with 2 tablespoons of walnut or hazelnut oil to give the vinaigrette a distinctive, nutty flavor. Serve with mixed green salads or salads with grilled poultry.

✔ Add 1 teaspoon drained capers and 1 tablespoon chopped fresh chervil, tarragon, basil, or lemon thyme. This herby vinaigrette really enlivens a cold pasta salad.

✔ Place one small ripe tomato in a blender or food processor container with the rest of the dressing and blend well.

✔ To thicken the vinaigrette, combine it in a blender with 1 to 2 tablespoons of ricotta cheese. Lowfat ricotta enriches just like cream, with far fewer calories.

Concocting creamy dressings

A creamy dressing can enhance various greens, complementing bitter or pungent flavors with the mellow flavor of mayonnaise. Creamy dressings also go well with cold shellfish, meat, and poultry. One downside to creamy dressings is that they spoil more quickly than vinaigrettes, so be sure to keep them refrigerated and use them within a week or so.

⟳ Homemade Ranch Dressing

We add sour cream to this homemade ranch dressing because it adds a nice, sharp edge. You can use all mayonnaise if you prefer. Drizzle this on your salad, or add 1 teaspoon horseradish (or to taste) and use it as a sandwich spread for cold meats such as turkey or ham. Or, for a delicious low-carb option, spread the dressing on a piece of cold meat and roll it up in a leaf of lettuce.

Tools: *Chef's knife, bowl, whisk*

Preparation time: *About 5 minutes*

Yield: *6 servings, or about 1¼ cups*

½ cup mayonnaise	2 tablespoons minced fresh or dried parsley
⅓ cup sour cream	2 teaspoons dried dill
¼ cup buttermilk or regular milk	1 teaspoon salt
¼ cup minced yellow onion	¼ teaspoon pepper
1 teaspoon garlic powder	

Combine all ingredients in a bowl and whisk well. Adjust seasonings to taste.

Vary It! *Try jazzing up this dressing in any of the following ways: For a seafood salad, add 1 tablespoon drained capers and 1 tablespoon (or to taste) minced tarragon, or 1 teaspoon dried tarragon. For a cold meat dish or for a chicken or shrimp salad, make a curry dressing by adding 1 teaspoon curry powder (or to taste) to this dressing. For cold vegetable salad, crumble ½ cup or more blue cheese or Roquefort and mix it into the dressing.*

Per serving: *Calories 169 (From Fat 157); Fat 17g (Saturated 4g); Cholesterol 17mg; Sodium 221mg; Carbohydrate 3g (Dietary Fiber 0g); Protein 1g.*

The Soul of the Salad: Crisp, Fresh Greens

A salad demands the freshest greens and herbs and the tastiest vegetables you can find. If at all possible, buy produce that is in season and then speed home with your lights flashing. Better yet, grow some in your yard, if you have one and your climate is appropriate (greens grow in most climates in the summer).

Getting your greens squeaky-clean

Did you ever fall asleep at the beach with your mouth open and the wind blowing sand in your direction? Well, that's what unwashed salad can taste like. To make sure that you get all the sand out of lettuce, remove the leaves and soak them briefly in cold water, shaking occasionally. Then run them under the tap, being careful to rinse the root ends thoroughly.

Drying lettuce completely is critical, or else the dressing slides right off. Towel drying works, but it's a nuisance. The easiest method is to use a salad spinner that dries with centrifugal force.

Buying and storing greens

When buying greens, avoid those that are wilted or limp. A fresh head of romaine should look like a bouquet of green leaves, clumped tightly together without any rust-colored edges or signs of decay. Pass up the watercress if its leaves are yellowing. Brown spots on iceberg lettuce indicate rot. Greens sold in bunches, such as arugula and dandelion, are especially delicate and prone to quick decay; consume them within a few days of purchase. And don't believe (just because you watched your mother do it) that wilted greens revive when plunged into cold water.

Store rinsed and dried greens in the extra-cold crisper drawer of the refrigerator, wrapped in damp paper towels. You can place bunches of watercress, arugula, parsley, and other fresh herbs in a full glass of water, stem ends down, like fresh-cut flowers. Greens are not long-storage items, so consume them within a few days of purchase.

Now that prebuttered rolls and pregrilled chicken are commonly available at supermarkets, you shouldn't be surprised to find prepackaged salad greens complete with dressings, croutons, and other "instant" salad ingredients. Bagged salads are convenient, and some are organic. You may be able to find greens you couldn't find otherwise in your supermarket. However, the bagged salad greens are more expensive. If you want to spend the extra cash for the convenience of dumping your greens, preplucked and washed, from bag to salad bowl, that's great. Bagged greens may not taste quite as fresh as greens from the produce bin, but if that's the only way you're going to eat your greens, then we say go for it.

A glossary of greens

Greens range in taste from mild to pungent and even bitter. Mild greens like iceberg, Boston, and Bibb lettuce should be used as a base for more assertive, full-strength ingredients and seasonings. Use bitter or tart greens like radicchio, arugula, and escarole sparingly as a contrasting accent. Composing a salad of tart radicchio with a sharp vinaigrette is like catching baseballs without a glove — ouch! You may prefer counterbalancing pungent greens with cream-style dressings.

Supermarkets and produce markets carry an array of greens 12 months of the year, allowing you to combine different types in one bowl. Don't limit yourself to a bland iceberg lettuce, which lacks the higher flavor and nutritional content of more deeply colored greens. The more variety of greens in the bowl, the better.

Our favorite salad greens, some of which are pictured in Figure 12-1, include those listed in the following sections.

Don't overdress

A common mistake with salads is overdressing them, which is like overdressing for dinner. Drizzle just enough dressing over the greens to lightly coat them when tossed well. And when you toss, really toss. Using salad tongs or a large fork and spoon, mix those leaves up really well. The dressing should be evenly distributed on every piece of greenery.

Figure 12-1:
Our favorite
salad
greens.

Mild greens

Typically crunchy and slightly sweet, these greens are easy to eat and go well with a highly flavored vinaigrette:

- ✔ **Bibb (or limestone lettuce):** Tender, rippled leaves form a small, compact head. Bibb has the mildness of Boston lettuce, but more crunch. It tends to be expensive, but a little makes a big impression.

- ✔ **Boston:** Buttery textured, this lettuce looks like a green rose. Mixes well with all varieties and stands well alone topped with sliced, ripe summer tomatoes.

- ✔ **Iceberg:** The white bread of the salad world, iceberg is common to salad bars and political banquets. Iceberg has more texture than flavor, and, if wrapped, can be used for foul-shot practice.

TIP

To remove the core of iceberg lettuce, smash the head (core side down) on a cutting board or countertop. The hard core should then twist out easily.

- ✔ **Loose-leaf lettuce:** This green is also called red leaf or green leaf lettuce, depending on its color. Its long, curly leaves are buttery and almost sweet. Add the red leaf variety to green salad for an elegant contrast or mix red and green leaf together in one bowl.

- ✔ **Red oak leaf lettuce:** Named for the oak tree leaves it resembles, this green is sweet and colorful. It's good mixed with Boston or Bibb lettuce and makes a pretty plate garnish.

- ✔ **Romaine:** The emperor green of Caesar salad, romaine has dark-green exterior leaves with a pale-yellow core. It mixes well with other greens. One advantage of romaine is that it keeps well for up to a week in the refrigerator. Like other dark, leafy greens, romaine is a good source of vitamin A.

Pungent greens

These more pungent greens have a bite. Use them to add interest to milder greens, or serve them with a mild creamy dressing, such as the Homemade Ranch Dressing in this chapter.

- ✔ **Arugula:** You can practically taste the iron in arugula's dark green leaves. The peppery flavor mixes well with any mild lettuce or toss with grilled, portobello mushrooms, red onions, and a lemon vinaigrette.

- ✔ **Belgian endive:** Its pale yellow and white leaves are packed tightly together, in a cigarlike shape. This green has lots of crunch and a slightly bitter taste. Pull the leaves away from the base and tear them into pieces in green salads, or use an entire leaf as a serving base for various cheese and vegetable spreads and fillings.

- **Cabbage:** Red or green, cabbage is a great salad addition and amazingly inexpensive. Tear or shred leaves with a knife and toss with other greens to add color and texture. Cabbage is a long-storage vegetable and a good source of vitamin C.

- **Curly endive (sometimes called chicory):** Similar to escarole in flavor, this green has very curly leaves.

- **Dandelion:** A green that you can probably harvest off your front lawn (if you don't have dogs and don't spray your yard with chemicals), dandelion leaves arrive on the market in the spring. Italians cherish its bitter, crunchy qualities. Choose young, tender leaves; the older ones are too bitter and tough. Toss in a mixed green salad with chopped, hard-cooked eggs and a vinaigrette dressing. Dandelion greens are a good source of vitamin A, vitamin C, and calcium.

- **Escarole:** You can consume this green raw in salad or sauté it in olive oil and garlic. A member of the endive family, escarole is also rather tart and stands up to strong-flavored dressings.

- **Frisée:** Mildly bitter, this pale-yellow green also has prickly-shaped leaves. Mix it sparingly with other greens for contrasting texture and taste. It's similar to curly endive in appearance, but with a more delicate taste.

- **Mesclun (pronounced *mess-clan*):** This type of green is a salad mix that usually contains frisée, arugula, radicchio, red leaf lettuces, mustard, and other delicate greens. Mesclun is very expensive, so purchase only if it appears very fresh, or the greens will wilt before you get home. It's best to buy a small amount to mix with other less expensive salad greens.

- **Radicchio:** A small, tightly wound head with deep magenta leaves that can add brilliant splashes of color to a bowl of greens, radicchio is extremely pungent and comparatively expensive. Use it sparingly. It keeps well in the refrigerator (up to two weeks), especially if wrapped in moist paper towels. Like cabbage, radicchio also may be grilled, baked, or sautéed.

- **Spinach:** These deep green, slightly crumpled leaves are full of iron. Discard the thick stems. The leaves of baby spinach are smaller, oval shaped, smooth, and buttery. Rinse all spinach thoroughly to rid the leaves of sand. Dry well. Mix with milder greens like Boston, Bibb, or loose-leaf.

- **Watercress:** Its clover-shaped leaves lend peppery crunch to any salad. Snap off and discard the tough stems and be sure to rinse well. Watercress makes a pretty soup or plate garnish.

♻ *Easy Mixed Green Salad*

Depending on where you live, different greens are better than others at different times of the year. If you see dark green arugula leaves in the market, try mixing them with other greens like romaine, red leaf, or chicory (curly endive). Arugula has a nice, tart snap that enlivens any salad. It can be sandy, so rinse it well. Try different chopped vegetables, too, depending on what looks fresh. You might try halved cherry tomatoes, cucumber slices, and endive leaves (as shown in the color section), or radish slices, bell pepper strips, or even apple wedges. In the winter, try adding preserved vegetables, such as olives and marinated artichoke hearts.

Tools: *Salad spinner or paper towels, chef's knife, small bowl, salad bowl*

Preparation time: *About 20 minutes*

Yield: *6 servings*

6 cups mixed lettuces, such as romaine, red leaf, Boston, or mixed spring greens

⅓ cup coarsely chopped red onion

2 carrots, scraped and grated (cut off the tips and ends first)

1 rib celery, minced

½ cup grated red or green cabbage (optional)

1½ tablespoons red or white wine vinegar

½ teaspoon dried basil or oregano

Salt and pepper

¼ cup olive oil

1 Rinse the lettuce leaves in a large pot of cold water or in the sink. (Change the water several times, rinsing until no sand remains and the greens are thoroughly cleaned.) Pick over the leaves, removing the tough stems. Spin the greens in a salad spinner or lay them flat on paper towels and pat dry. (Greens may be washed and dried up to one day ahead of serving time and stored in plastic bags in the refrigerator.)

2 Tear the greens into bite-sized pieces and put them in a salad bowl. Add the onion, carrots, celery, and, if desired, the cabbage.

3 Put the vinegar in a small bowl and add the basil or oregano and the salt and pepper to taste. Start beating while gradually adding the oil. Pour the dressing over the salad and toss to evenly coat.

Vary It! *Try one of the following ideas for a little variety: For a fresh taste with just a little extra effort, substitute freshly squeezed lemon juice for the vinegar in Step 3. Add 2 teaspoons mayonnaise, yogurt, or sour cream for a creamy vinaigrette. Whisk 2 teaspoons Dijon-style mustard into the vinaigrette. Add minced herbs, such as tarragon, thyme, chervil, sage, or savory, to taste. Crumble goat cheese or blue cheese over the greens.*

Per serving: *Calories 107 (From Fat 82); Fat 9g (Saturated 1g); Cholesterol 0mg; Sodium 133mg; Carbohydrate 6g (Dietary Fiber 2g); Protein 1g.*

Ten Quick Salads . . . So Easy You Don't Need a Recipe

Salads are easy to improvise. Simply follow the advice of your taste buds to create your own salads. Need some inspiration to get you started? Try a few of these simple combinations, but don't be afraid to substitute, experiment, or add different vegetables or dressings according to your taste:

✔ **Tomato, Red Onion, and Basil Salad:** Slice ripe, red tomatoes ¼ inch thick and layer on a platter with diced red onion and 4 or 5 large chopped fresh basil leaves. Drizzle with oil and vinegar and season with salt and pepper. This salad tastes great with fresh mozzarella cheese, too.

✔ **Bell Pepper-Rice Salad:** Combine about 3 cups cooked white rice with 1 cup cooked green peas and 2 cups seeded, cored, and chopped red, green, or yellow bell peppers (or any combination of colors). Toss with enough herb-vinaigrette dressing to moisten the ingredients sufficiently, add salt and black pepper to taste, and chill before serving.

✔ **Cucumber-Dill Salad:** Toss peeled, sliced, and seeded cucumbers in a dill-flavored vinaigrette. (See the recipe for Vinaigrette Dressing in this chapter for a starting point.)

✔ **Cherry Tomato and Feta Cheese Salad:** Toss 1 pint cherry tomatoes, rinsed and sliced in half, with 4 ounces crumbled feta cheese and ½ cup sliced, pitted black olives. Season with vinaigrette dressing to taste (see the recipe for Vinaigrette Dressing in this chapter).

✔ **Pasta Medley Salad:** Combine about 2 cups of your favorite pasta, cooked, with ½ cup chopped, sun-dried tomatoes. Season lightly with oil, vinegar, and black pepper to taste.

✔ **Garbanzo Bean Toss:** Combine 1 can (15½ or 16 ounces) drained garbanzo beans, ½ cup chopped red onion, 1 or 2 cloves crushed garlic, and the grated zest of 1 lemon. Toss with lemon-vinaigrette dressing. (See the recipe for Vinaigrette Dressing in this chapter for a starting point.)

✔ **Layered Cheese and Vegetable Salad:** Arrange alternating thin slices of ripe tomatoes and mozzarella cheese on a round platter. Fill the center with slices of avocado sprinkled with fresh lemon juice to prevent discoloration. Drizzle with olive oil and lemon juice; garnish with fresh basil.

✔ **Grilled Vegetable Platter with Fresh Pesto:** Arrange any assortment of grilled vegetables (see Chapter 8) on a platter. Serve with spoonfuls of fresh pesto (see Chapter 9).

✔ **Fruit Salsa:** Combine 1 ripe, peeled, pitted, and chopped avocado; 2 ripe, peeled, seeded, and chopped papayas; ½ cup chopped red onion; and 1 teaspoon seeded, chopped jalapeño pepper with a dressing of 1 table-spoon honey and the grated zest and juice of 1 lemon. Serve as a side salad with broiled hamburgers, chicken, or fish.

✔ **Three-Berry Dessert Salad:** Combine 2 pints rinsed and hulled strawber-ries, 1 pint rinsed blueberries, and 1 pint rinsed raspberries in a bowl. Toss with a dressing of ½ cup heavy cream sweetened with confection-ers' sugar to taste.

Chapter 13

Pastamania

Most people love pasta, whether it's a plate of spaghetti or a bowl of mac-and-cheese. You can toss it with vegetables, mix it with meat, and drizzle it with all manner of sauces. You can eat it hot, cold, or at room temperature. Pasta tastes good and makes for a meal. If you stick to moderate portions, pasta is low in calories and fat. (One big ladleful of Alfredo sauce can easily destroy all that, but don't blame us!) Pasta is even a complex carbohydrate, so if you're on a low-carb diet, pasta is better for you than a candy bar or a piece of white bread, particularly when the pasta is made from whole grains, such as whole wheat.

Americans learned to love pasta when Italian-Americans brought classic dishes to the United States. These classics eventually became modified so that Italian-American cuisine is among the most beloved in this country today. Whether you like your pasta steaming with just a little butter or olive oil or drenched in a meaty meatball-spiked sauce, enjoy discovering more about how to cook pasta yourself, so you don't have to rely on restaurants to give you the pasta you crave.

Don't Sweat the Fresh Stuff: Dried versus Fresh Pasta

America's attics and closets must be jammed with pasta-making machines. In the late 1970s and early 1980s, anyone who knew how to boil water wanted to make fresh pasta. Somehow — maybe through a conspiracy of glossy food magazines — people started believing that if you didn't roll your own pasta, you were somehow unpatriotic. Young couples spent weeknights in the kitchen with flour flying all over, eggs spilling, and dough falling on the floor. They cranked and cranked and cranked some more. Then they hung the pasta overnight to dry on chairs, books, tables, and lampshades.

This trend didn't last long. But you can always spot the lapsed pastamaniacs — they're the ones who always remark in Italian restaurants, "Oooh, fresh pasta. We love making fresh pasta! Say, we haven't done that in a while."

The truth is that fresh pasta is not inherently better than dried; it's just different. Many fine dried pastas are available, and the choice between fresh and dried is really a matter of personal taste. Homemade pasta — that is, well-made homemade pasta — is definitely lighter and more delicate. Dried pasta tastes more substantial — and because a wide range of flours is used, flavors vary. The better dried pastas use semolina flour, made from nutritious durum wheat. (Homemade pasta is usually made from plain white flour.)

Specialty food markets and many supermarkets now sell fresh pasta in the refrigerator section, so you really don't need to make your own if you don't have the time or the inclination. Fresh pasta is good, but you pay a premium. For purposes of this chapter, we concentrate on dried pasta because it is widely available, lasts longer in the pantry, and is more economical. In any case, the sauce is what really elevates pasta from ordinary to sublime.

Pasta Tips and Tricks

Cooking pasta isn't difficult, but a few pieces of select pasta knowledge make the job easier and ensure perfectly cooked pasta every time.

- ✔ **Al dente is not the name of an Italian orthodontist.** It is a sacred term in Italy that means "to the tooth" or "to the bite." In cooking, *al dente* means "slightly firm to the bite." Cook pasta to this point, not until it is soft all the way through. When pasta cooks too long, it absorbs more water and becomes mushy. The time-tested method for checking pasta for doneness is still the best: Scoop out a strand or two with a fork, take the pasta in hand, jump around and toss the scorching pasta in the air, and then taste it. (You don't really have to toss it in the air, but it makes the process more fun.) Some people swear by the old method of throwing a piece of pasta against the wall. If it sticks, it's done. If it slides down onto the floor and the dog eats it, it isn't ready yet.

- ✔ **Use a lot of water (5 to 6 quarts of water for a pound of pasta) and an 8-quart pot.** Pasta, like a tango dancer, needs room to move. If you don't have a pot large enough to hold that much water and still be three-fourths full or less, splitting pasta into two pots of boiling water is better than overloading one pot. An overloaded pot will splash boiling water all over the stovetop.

A large pot of boiling water is one of the most dangerous elements in any kitchen. Use a pot with short handles that cannot be tipped easily and set it to boil on a back burner, away from small and curious hands.

✔ **Salt the water to add flavor and to help the pasta absorb the sauce.** As a general guideline, 5 quarts of water takes about 2 teaspoons of salt, and 6 quarts of water calls for 1 tablespoon of salt.

✔ **Oil is for salads, not pasta water.** You don't need to add oil to the water if you use enough water and stir occasionally to prevent sticking.

Stir the pasta immediately and thoroughly after adding it to the water, to prevent it from sticking together.

✔ **Cover the pot to hasten heat recovery.** After you add pasta to the water, the water ceases to boil. When the water begins boiling again, remove the lid and finish cooking.

✔ **Save a cup of the cooking liquid when the pasta is done.** You can use some of the liquid to add moisture to the sauce. The starch in the water binds the sauce, helping it adhere to the pasta.

✔ **Do not rinse pasta.** When the pasta is al dente (tender but firm), pour it gradually into a colander. *Do not rinse!* You want starch on the pasta to help the sauce adhere to it. The only exceptions are if you're making a cold pasta salad or a casserole such as lasagna where the ingredients are layered.

✔ **After draining it, you may want to place the pasta in the pan in which the sauce is cooking and stir well.** This method coats the pasta better than spooning the sauce on top. Serve from the saucepan.

✔ **Never combine two types or sizes of pasta in the same pot of water.** Fishing out the type that is done first is a real nuisance.

✔ **Always have the sauce ready and waiting before the pasta is cooked.** Cooked pasta needs to be sauced immediately after it's drained, or it becomes stiff and gluey. In many of the recipes in this chapter, you work on the sauce as the water for the pasta boils or the pasta cooks. This way, you can ensure that your pasta and sauce will be ready at about the same time. Then all you need to do is drain the pasta (or add the pasta to the pan holding the sauce) and toss well.

✔ **In general, figure about 2 ounces of dried pasta per person.** You can figure less if the pasta is a side dish or you're watching your carbs, or make more if you have lots of big eaters. In other words, on average, a pound of pasta will feed about four people. The pasta box or bag tells you how many servings it includes.

You can also buy a little plastic gadget to help you measure spaghetti servings. It has different-sized holes, and you just stick the spaghetti through the hole that corresponds to the number of people you're serving.

✔ **Don't try to speak broken Italian when you serve your pasta.** "Bonissimo! Perfect-amente mia amigas, Mangia, Mangia!" You will sound silly and irritate your guests.

Name That Pasta: Pasta Types and Cooking Times

Italian pasta comes in two basic forms: macaroni and spaghetti.

Macaroni has distinctive shapes, hollows, and curves. *Spaghetti,* which means "little strings," is pasta cut into delicate strands. Sometimes linguine and fettuccine noodles are identified apart from spaghetti because their strands are flattened. Figure 13-1 depicts some common pasta shapes, also described in the following sections.

Figure 13-1:
Various
shapes
of pasta.

Macaroni

Also known as *tubular pasta*, macaroni is served with thick, rich sauces. (Find a recipe for American Macaroni and Cheese in Chapter 14.) Table 13-1 describes the different types of tubular pastas and tells you how to cook and sauce them.

Table 13-1		The Macaroni Family
Italian Name	*Translation*	*Description and Approximate Cooking Time*
Cannelloni	"Large reeds"	Stuffed with meat or cheese and baked smothered in sauce. Cooks in 7 to 9 minutes.
Ditali	"Thimbles"	Smooth and short. Used in soups and cold pasta salads. Cooks in 8 to 10 minutes.
Penne	"Quills"	Best coated all over with rich sauces. Cooks in 10 to 12 minutes.
Rigatoni	"Large grooves"	Large, wide tube that is excellent with tomato, meat, and vegetable sauces. Cooks in 10 to 12 minutes.
Ziti	"Bridegrooms"	Narrow tube shape that is excellent in rich, baked casseroles with thick tomato sauces. Cooks in 10 to 12 minutes.

Strand pasta

Strand pasta is best served with thin, flavorful sauces that are rich in oil, which keep the very thin pasta from sticking together. Table 13-2 shows the best way to cook each type of strand pasta.

Table 13-2		The Spaghetti Family
Italian Name	*Translation*	*Description and Approximate Cooking Time*
Capelli d'angelo	"Angel hair"	The thinnest pasta of all, Capelli d'angelo is good in soups. Excellent with thin cream or tomato sauces. Cooks quickly in 3 to 4 minutes.
Cappellini	"Little hairs"	Slightly thicker than angel hair. Cooks in 4 to 5 minutes.
Spaghetti	"Little strings"	Long, medium-thick strands. Cooks in 10 to 12 minutes.
Vermicelli	"Little worms"	Thin strands. Cooks in 5 to 6 minutes.

Flat ribbon pasta

Flat ribbon pasta is excellent with rich, creamy sauces such as Alfredo or with simple butter sauces with fresh sautéed vegetables. To find out the best way to cook different types of flat ribbon pasta, see Table 13-3.

Table 13-3		Flat Ribbon Pastas
Italian Name	*Translation*	*Description and Approximate Cooking Time*
Fettuccine	"Small ribbons"	Flat strands. Cooks in 8 to 10 minutes.
Linguine	"Little tongues"	Long, thin ribbons. Cooks in 8 to 10 minutes.
Tagliatelle	"Little cuts"	Like fettuccine, but a bit wider. Cooks in 7 to 8 minutes.

Stuffed pasta

Filled with meat, cheese, fish, or vegetables, stuffed pastas are best coated with simple tomato or light, cream-based sauces. The dough is often flavored and tinted with spinach, tomato, mushrooms, or *saffron*, a fragrant spice. Typically, stuffed pastas are fresh or frozen. Frozen stuffed pasta takes longer to cook than fresh. Table 13-4 gives the cooking times for frozen, stuffed pastas. If buying fresh, just follow the directions on the package.

Table 13-4		Frozen Stuffed Pastas
Italian Name	*Description*	*Stuffing and Approximate Cooking Time*
Agnolotti	Half-moon shaped	Stuffed with meat or cheese. Cooks in 7 to 9 minutes.
Ravioli	Little square pillows	Stuffed with meat, cheese, fish, or vegetables. Cooks in 8 to 10 minutes.
Tortellini	Ring-shaped little twists	Stuffed with meat or cheese. Cooks in 10 to 12 minutes.

Sundry other shapes

Table 13-5 lists a grab bag of other pastas that don't quite fit into any of the other categories.

Table 13-5		Miscellaneous-Shaped Pastas
Italian Name	*Translation*	*Great Accompaniments and Approximate Cooking Time*
Conchiglie	"Shells"	Wonderful with a simple butter-basil sauce and a grating of Parmesan cheese. Cooks in 10 to 12 minutes.
Farfalle	"Butterflies"	Pretty tossed into cold salads with fresh vegetables. Cooks in 10 to 12 minutes.
Fusilli	"Twists"	Corkscrew shaped and good with chunky sauces. Cooks in 10 to 12 minutes.
Orecchiette	"Little ears"	Wonderful in chicken soups and clear broths. Cooks in 7 to 9 minutes.
Orzo	"Barley"	Rice-shaped pasta, good in dishes like cold-chicken-and-sun-dried-tomato salad with vinaigrette. Cooks in 8 to 10 minutes.
Rotelle	"Small wheels"	Fun-shaped favorite of children. Cooks in 8 to 10 minutes.

Sauces: Pasta's Best Friends

Pasta sauces come in many forms and flavors, from light to rich, creamy to tangy, and everything in between.

Before you serve up a sauce, check out these tips for making foolproof sauces:

- Figure about ½ cup of sauce per person.
- Stir sauces often to prevent sticking.
- A tablespoon of olive oil adds flavor and a rich texture to tomato-based sauces.

✔ Sauces are a great place to hide puréed vegetables. The kids will never know!

✔ For added sweetness, try a grated carrot instead of sugar.

✔ To jazz up a canned pasta sauce, add one or two of the following: sliced green or black olives, sautéed chopped shallots, a drained can of tuna, 1 cup of white beans, 4 slices of crumbled bacon, sliced smoked sausage, ½ pound of small cooked shrimp, or ¼ cup freshly grated Parmesan cheese.

Name that sauce: Classic sauce types

Italian pasta sauces are as inventive and varied as pasta shapes. We briefly describe the classic ones, so the next time you dine at an expensive trattoria where the puttanesca is $24 a plate, you'll know what you're paying for.

✔ **Carbonara:** Crisply cooked bacon (usually Italian pancetta) combined with garlic, eggs, Parmesan cheese, and sometimes cream.

✔ **Fettuccine Alfredo:** A rich sauce of cream, butter, Parmesan cheese, and freshly ground black pepper tossed over fettuccine.

✔ **Marinara:** The basic Italian tomato sauce, slow cooked and infused with garlic and Italian herbs like oregano and basil, is easy to adapt to different recipes by adding mushrooms, ground meat, or vegetables.

✔ **Pesto:** Fresh basil leaves, pine nuts, garlic, Parmesan cheese, and olive oil blended to a fine paste.

✔ **Primavera:** A mixture of sautéed spring vegetables, such as sweet red pepper, tomatoes, asparagus, and snow peas, and fresh herbs.

✔ **Puttanesca:** A pungent sauce of anchovies, garlic, tomatoes, capers, and black olives.

✔ **Ragù alla Bolognese:** A long-simmered sauce of meat (usually ground beef, veal, or pork) and tomatoes, named for the city of Bologna, where it was invented. For a true Bolognese, you brown the meat lightly and then cook it in a small amount of milk and wine before adding tomatoes.

✔ **Spaghetti alle Vongole:** Spaghetti tossed with clams, olive oil, white wine, and herbs.

Picking perfect tomatoes

Nothing can compare with a vine-ripened summer tomato for your home-made pasta sauces. But locally grown summer tomatoes are available only a few months of the year in most parts of the United States. One alternative is the hothouse varieties that are picked green, gassed to a pale shade of pink, and then marketed by commercial growers from far away. If a recipe calls for fresh tomatoes when regular tomatoes aren't good, look for plum or Italian tomatoes. Named for the fruit they resemble, plum tomatoes usually ripen fully within a day or two of purchase and are perfect for quick skillet sauces laced with fresh basil and garlic.

For making most soups, sauces, and stews, canned Italian plum tomatoes are not only perfectly fine but even superior to mediocre fresh tomatoes. In the off-season, use canned plum tomatoes, which have lots of flavor.

The best way to ripen tomatoes is to place several in a brown paper bag for one or two days, thereby trapping their natural ripening gases. To hasten the ripening even more, place a banana in the bag.

For a quick lesson on peeling and seeding tomatoes, see the advice later in this chapter in the recipe for Spaghetti with Quick Fresh Tomato Sauce or flip to Chapter 11.

Pasta Creations

Following are some simple pasta recipes that you can vary after you feel more confident. Remember that in this book, pasta is intended to be dry pasta (as opposed to fresh), unless otherwise indicated.

After you can make basic pasta dishes with relative ease, you can begin experimenting with different ingredients. Before you dash down to the store and buy Virginia ham and star fruit to toss into the pan, think first about food pairings. You don't want a single sauce ingredient to bully all the others — turnips, for example, overpower many food combinations. Think of it this way: If you can imagine the ingredients combined and served as part of a non-pasta dinner, then they probably work in a pasta sauce as well.

☺ Spaghetti with Quick Fresh Tomato Sauce

You can use this quick sauce as the foundation for endless enhancements with herbs, vegetables, meat, and more. It takes only a few minutes to make, and its bright, fresh taste works for a main dish or a side dish (shown in the color section). If you can't find good fresh tomatoes, you can substitute approximately 1½ pounds canned tomatoes, drained.

Tools: *Paring knife, chef's knife, large pot, colander, saucepan or skillet, grater*

Preparation time: *About 15 minutes*

Cooking time: *About 15 minutes*

Yield: *4 servings*

5 to 6 ripe plum tomatoes, about 1½ pounds	*2 teaspoons peeled and minced garlic, about 2 large cloves, or 1 teaspoon garlic powder*
Salt and pepper	*2 tablespoons coarsely chopped fresh basil leaves, or 2 teaspoons dried basil*
¾ pound spaghetti or other pasta of your choice	
3 tablespoons olive oil	*3 tablespoons grated Parmesan cheese*

1 Core the tomatoes and peel them by dropping into boiling water for about 10 to 30 seconds. Remove with a slotted spoon and plunge into a bowl of ice water to cool them quickly. After the tomatoes are cool enough to handle, peel them with a paring knife and remove their seeds. Cut them into ½-inch cubes. (See Figure 13-2 for an illustration of this procedure.)

2 Bring 4 to 5 quarts lightly salted water to a boil over high heat in a large, covered pot. Add the spaghetti, stir thoroughly with a long fork to separate the strands, and cook, uncovered, for about 8 minutes or just until al dente.

3 While the spaghetti cooks, heat the oil in a saucepan or skillet over medium heat. Add the garlic. Cook and stir about 30 seconds with a wooden spoon. Do not brown the garlic. Add the cubed tomatoes and salt and pepper to taste. Cook, crushing the tomatoes with a fork and stirring often, for about 3 minutes.

4 When the pasta is ready, drain it and put the pasta in a serving bowl or on individual plates. Ladle the sauce over it. Garnish with a sprig of fresh basil and/or some finely minced fresh basil, and a few shaved pieces of Parmesan cheese or a sprinkle of grated Parmesan. Serve immediately.

Vary It! *You can omit the Parmesan cheese and add a small can of drained, flaked tuna. Or keep the cheese and toss in some sliced black olives and cooked artichoke hearts. A few sautéed shrimp and asparagus spears, or even sautéed chicken livers, also work with this classic sauce.*

Per serving: Calories 418 (From Fat 116); Fat 13g (Saturated 2g); Cholesterol 3mg; Sodium 430mg; Carbohydrate 63g (Dietary Fiber 5g); Protein 12g.

🍅 Penne with Parmesan Cheese and Basil

Sometimes you can forgo a formal sauce and just whip together a quick cheese garnish for pasta. Try this easy recipe for a simple, delicious lunch or no-fuss dinner.

Tools: *Large pot, chef's knife, grater, colander*

Preparation time: *About 10 minutes*

Cooking time: *About 20 minutes*

Yield: *4 servings*

Salt	*¼ cup grated Parmesan or Romano cheese*
½ pound penne	*¼ cup chopped fresh basil or Italian parsley*
2 tablespoons olive oil	*⅛ teaspoon freshly grated or ground nutmeg*
1 tablespoon butter	*Pepper*

1 Bring 3 to 4 quarts lightly salted water to a boil in a large, covered pot over high heat. Add the penne, stir thoroughly to separate the macaroni, and return to a boil. Cook, uncovered, for about 10 minutes or until the pasta is al dente.

2 Just before the penne is done, carefully scoop out ¼ cup of the cooking liquid. When the penne is ready, drain it and return it to the pot. Add the olive oil and butter and toss a bit to coat; then add the cheese, basil, nutmeg, pepper to taste, and the reserved cooking liquid.

3 Toss and blend over medium-high heat for 30 seconds. If necessary, add salt to taste. Serve immediately.

Per serving: Calories 315 (From Fat 107); Fat 12g (Saturated 4g); Cholesterol 12mg; Sodium 156mg; Carbohydrate 43g (Dietary Fiber 2g); Protein 10g.

How to Peel, Seed, and Chop Tomatoes

1. Insert paring knife diagonally. Cut out stem.

2. Cut a shallow "x" on the bottom.

3. Drop into boiling water for about 10 seconds or so.

4. Remove with a long-handled fork. Immerse in cold water.

5. Starting at the "x," peel off the skin. Easy! (Peel peaches and apricots the same way.)

6. Cut in half.

7. Squeeze! Seeds ooze out

8. Chop into desired size.

Figure 13-2: Dropping tomatoes in boiling water for a few seconds makes peeling them much easier.

Seafood Linguine

Linguine and seafood pair up in this elegant recipe. The different textures of seafood and vegetables make a pleasing contrast to the long strands of linguine. You can also make this recipe with spaghetti, fettuccine, or any kind of pasta you have around the house.

Tools: *Large pot, chef's knife, large skillet or sauté pan (at least 12 inches in diameter), colander*

Preparation time: *About 25 minutes (35 minutes if cleaning shrimp)*

Cooking time: *About 25 minutes*

Yield: *4 servings*

Salt

½ pound linguine

4 tablespoons olive oil

1 cup peeled and coarsely chopped yellow onion (about 1 medium onion)

1 medium red bell pepper, cored, seeded, and cut into ½-inch cubes

1 cup sliced white mushrooms

½ teaspoon salt

Few dashes of black pepper

1 pound medium shrimp, peeled and deveined (see instructions in Chapter 14)

½ pound crabmeat (fresh or canned)

½ pound scallops

6 ripe plum tomatoes, cored and cut into ½-inch cubes

1 tablespoon peeled and finely chopped garlic, about 3 large cloves

¼ teaspoon red pepper flakes

¼ cup chopped fresh basil

¼ cup white wine, bottled clam juice, or canned chicken broth

1 Bring 4 to 5 quarts lightly salted water to a boil in a large, covered pot over high heat. Add the linguine, stir thoroughly to separate the strands, and cook, uncovered, according to package instructions. The pasta should be al dente.

2 Start to make the sauce as the water boils. Heat 2 tablespoons of the olive oil in a large skillet or sauté pan. Add the onion, red peppers, mushrooms, ½ teaspoon salt, and black pepper. Cook, stirring often, over medium-high heat until the vegetables are tender, about 10 minutes. Add the shrimp, crabmeat, scallops, tomatoes, garlic, and red pepper flakes. Cook and stir often about 3 to 4 minutes longer, or just until the shrimp are evenly pink and cooked through. Add the remaining 2 tablespoons olive oil, basil, and wine and stir to blend well.

3 Just before draining the pasta, use a measuring cup to carefully scoop out and reserve ¼ cup of the cooking liquid. When the pasta is ready, drain it and return it to the large pot. Add the seafood sauce to the pasta and toss well. If the sauce needs more moisture, add the reserved cooking liquid. Serve immediately.

Vary It! *To make this dish more economical, replace the crab and scallops with 1 pound of imitation crabmeat, a concoction of fish made to look and taste like crab and widely available in supermarkets.*

Per serving: Calories 588 (From Fat 192); Fat 21g (Saturated 3g); Cholesterol 236mg; Sodium 812mg; Carbohydrate 54g (Dietary Fiber 5g); Protein 46g.

Buying shrimp

Unless you live within eyeshot of fishing boats, chances are that the shrimp sold in your supermarket has been frozen in transit.

Much shrimp comes from the Gulf States or the Deep South. Flash-frozen shrimp (which is plunged into a super-deep freeze upon harvest) can be excellent when handled and stored properly. Its shelf life is about six months when well wrapped.

Always buy shrimp in the shell and not pre-cooked. After you remove the shell, pick out the thin, blackish vein that runs down the back, which can have a bitter flavor. (Turn to Figure 14-1 in Chapter 14 for instructions on cleaning and deveining shrimp. Or ask your fish merchant to devein your shrimp when you purchase it.)

☉ *Family Lasagna*

Lasagna is easy to make, especially if you use a good bottled sauce, as we do in this recipe. You can customize the dish by adding ingredients such as ground beef, spinach, mushrooms, or chopped chicken to the sauce. You might also try no-boil lasagna noodles, available in supermarkets, to save even more time. Our simple version feeds at least eight. Reheat leftovers, covered with foil, in a 350-degree oven for about 20 minutes, or in a covered skillet, with a little water, over low heat on the stovetop. You can microwave leftovers as well. If you don't have a good pan for lasagna, you can purchase a cheap aluminum lasagna pan at your local supermarket. Check out the lasagna photo in the color section, sure to make your mouth water.

Tools: *Large pot, colander, 9-x-13-x-3-inch pan, chef's knife, grater, small bowl*

Preparation time: *About 20 minutes*

Cooking time: *About 1 hour*

Yield: *8 servings*

12 lasagna noodles	*⅓ cup plus 2 tablespoons grated Parmesan or Romano cheese*
1 pound mozzarella cheese (reduced-fat variety, if desired)	*Salt and pepper*
2 cups (one 15-ounce container) ricotta cheese (reduced-fat variety, if desired)	*5 cups, more or less, of your favorite brand tomato sauce or jarred red pasta sauce (two 26-ounce jars)*

1 Bring an 8-quart pot filled with about 6 quarts of lightly salted water to a boil over high heat.

2 When the water is boiling, add the lasagna noodles a few at a time. Cover the pot to bring the water back to a boil and then cook uncovered, according to package directions, until barely tender but not so soft that the noodles tear easily.

3 As the noodles cook, preheat the oven to 375 degrees.

4 Cut the mozzarella cheese into ½-inch cubes. In a small bowl, combine the ricotta, ⅓ cup of the Parmesan cheese, and 1 tablespoon of water taken from the boiling pasta pot. Season the mixture with salt and pepper to taste and set aside.

5 When the noodles are cooked, gently drain them in a colander in the sink, and run cold water over them.

6 To assemble the lasagna, spread a heaping cup of the tomato sauce on the bottom of a 13-x-9-x-3-inch ovenproof lasagna pan. Place three noodles over the sauce so that they completely cover the bottom of the pan (the noodles should touch but not overlap).

Spread (or dot by heaping teaspoonfuls) one third of the ricotta mixture evenly over the noodles. Sprinkle one third of the mozzarella cheese cubes over the ricotta. Ladle and spread a heaping cup of the sauce over this layer. Season, if desired, with salt and pepper.

7 Continue making layers, following the same order as Step 6 and ending with a thin layer of sauce. Sprinkle the top layer evenly with the remaining 2 tablespoons Parmesan cheese.

8 Bake in the preheated oven, checking after 30 minutes. If the top layer appears to be dry, cover with foil. Bake for another 20 to 25 minutes, or until the lasagna is piping hot and bubbly. Let stand, covered, for 15 minutes before cutting into squares and serving.

Tip: You can make this recipe (through Step 7) the day before, refrigerate it, and then bake it for about 1 hour before serving.

Vary It! You can make lasagna unique by adding a variety of ingredients to the essential layers of noodles, cheese, and sauce. For example, combine ¼ to ⅓ cup cooked, chopped, drained, fresh or frozen spinach or broccoli with the ricotta cheese mixture. Or, sprinkle the layers with ⅓ to ½ pound cooked ground beef or cooked shredded chicken or turkey. Or, sprinkle the layers with 1 cup cooked chopped vegetables, such as mushrooms, zucchini, or carrots. You can dress up bottled sauces by adding a little red wine to taste, or fresh herbs like chopped oregano, marjoram, or basil. For a spicy version, add chopped, seeded jalapeño or crushed red pepper to taste to the sauce.

Go-With: Lasagna pairs perfectly with a crisp green salad (see some recipe ideas in Chapter 12) and a fresh loaf of Italian bread.

Per serving: Calories 464 (From Fat 216); Fat 24g (Saturated 13g); Cholesterol 73mg; Sodium 1,116mg; Carbohydrate 36g (Dietary Fiber 3g); Protein 27g.

Use your (leftover) noodles

It's easy to overestimate how much pasta you need for a meal, but that's better than underestimating and leaving your guests famished! If you have leftover pasta, you can save it and reheat it the next day, but don't store it more than two or three days. To keep the pasta from sticking and getting gluey, toss it with a little tomato sauce or olive oil and seal it in an airtight container. Store it in the refrigerator. You can reheat it in the microwave or on the stovetop, adding more sauce, a few cubes of good cheese, or just a bit of butter and salt.

Chapter 14

One-Pot Meals

In This Chapter

▶ Simplifying your life with slow cookers and pressure cookers

▶ Having it all — in one pan

▶ Enjoying the benefits of casserole dishes

*W*hy use two pots (or more) when one will do? One pot means less prep time and fewer dishes, and our on-the-go culture has devised many kinds of one-pot meals, including technology to make the one-pot meal even easier via slow cookers and pressure cookers. Whether you want to save time or just love the comfort-food appeal of one-pot meals, this chapter shows you how to become an expert at this delicious form of culinary minimalism.

Savoring the Benefits of Slow Cookers

Slow cookers, which consist of a ceramic crock with a lid that fits into an electric holder, cook food slowly (hence the name) over a period of 6 to 12 hours, so all you have to do is put the food in the slow cooker first thing in the morning. By dinnertime, your hot meal is waiting.

Although you can cook a lot of things in a slow cooker, there are a few rules to remember:

✔ Brown ground meat before putting it into the slow cooker. You can put steak, roasts, poultry, and fish into the slow cooker without cooking them first, but ground meat must be browned first.

✔ Cut vegetables into bite-sized pieces for even cooking.

✔ Rice can cook in the slow cooker, so you can add it raw, but pasta doesn't. If you want to add pasta to your slow cooker meal, cook it first.

✔ Always follow the manufacturer's directions for your individual slow cooker.

Most slow cookers come with a small recipe book to get you started, and you also can find some great recipes and general slow cooking tips in *Slow Cookers For Dummies,* by Tom Lacalamita and Glenna Vance (published by Wiley). Here are two recipes of our own that we love.

Slow Cooker Chicken and Dumplings

This delicious recipe cooks while you spend your time doing other things. Serve it with warm green beans or peas and a small green salad, such as one from Chapter 12.

Tools: *Slow cooker, chef's knife, medium bowl*

Preparation time: *About 15 minutes*

Cooking time: *8 hours (unattended time)*

Yield: *4 servings*

4 skinless, boneless chicken breast halves (about 1 pound), cut into bite-sized pieces

2 cups canned chicken broth

1 medium yellow onion, chopped

3 stalks celery, diced

2 carrots, scraped and sliced

1 cup sliced white mushrooms

1 tablespoon dried parsley

½ teaspoon dried thyme

½ teaspoon pepper

⅛ teaspoon nutmeg

½ cup white wine, white grape juice, or an additional cup of chicken broth

1 cup flour

1 teaspoon baking powder

⅛ teaspoon salt

1 tablespoon butter, melted

½ cup milk or cream, plus an additional ½ cup milk

1 tablespoon cornstarch

1 Add the chicken, broth, onion, celery, carrots, mushrooms, parsley, thyme, pepper, nutmeg, and wine to the slow cooker. Cover, turn on low, and cook for 6 hours.

2 Combine the flour, baking powder, salt, butter, and the ½ cup milk or cream in a medium bowl and mix until smooth. Using your hands, form the flour mixture into ½-inch balls. Drop the dumplings into the hot chicken mixture. Replace the lid and cook for an additional 90 minutes, or until dumplings are cooked through. (To test for doneness, take one out and taste it.)

3 About 30 minutes before serving, stir the remaining ½ cup milk and cornstarch into the chicken mixture to thicken it. Re-cover.

Per serving: Calories 385 (From Fat 108); Fat 12g (Saturated 5g); Cholesterol 84mg; Sodium 1,530mg; Carbohydrate 37g (Dietary Fiber 3g); Protein 31g.

✆ Slow Cooker Ratatouille

Ratatouille is a traditional French vegetable dish cooked until the vegetables form a rich, jammy blend. It makes a great side dish to meat, or serve it over rice as a meat-free main course. Ratatouille is a dish that benefits from long cooking, making it perfect for the slow cooker. It also tastes even better the next day, so save the leftovers!

Tools: *Large skillet, slow cooker, chef's knife*

Preparation time: *About 20 minutes*

Cooking time: *6 to 8 hours (unattended)*

Yield: *6 servings*

3 tablespoons olive oil

1 medium eggplant, peeled and cut into 1-inch cubes

1 medium zucchini, cut into 1-inch cubes

1 medium red onion, chopped

1 large red bell pepper, cored, seeded, and chopped

1 large green bell pepper, cored, seeded, and chopped

2 cloves garlic, minced or put through a garlic press

2 cans (14 ounces each) whole tomatoes

1 teaspoon salt

2 teaspoons dried basil

1 teaspoon dried thyme

½ teaspoon black pepper

1 bay leaf

Hot cooked rice (see Chapter 4)

6 tablespoons grated Parmesan cheese (for garnish)

1 Heat the olive oil in a skillet over medium-high heat. Sauté the eggplant, zucchini, onion, red and green bell peppers, and garlic until the vegetables look golden but not dark brown, about 15 minutes.

2 Put the cooked vegetable mixture, tomatoes, salt, basil, thyme, pepper, and bay leaf in the slow cooker. Turn on low and cook for 6 to 8 hours. Remove the bay leaf and serve over rice. Garnish each serving with 1 tablespoon Parmesan cheese.

Per serving: *Calories 156 (From Fat 79); Fat 9g (Saturated 2g); Cholesterol 4mg; Sodium 682mg; Carbohydrate 17g (Dietary Fiber 5g); Protein 5g.*

Speeding Up the Cooking: Using a Pressure Cooker

The pressure cooker is the slow cooker's polar opposite. While they both cook one-pot meals conveniently, the pressure cooker cooks things extra quickly instead of extra slowly, making dinner ready in minutes. You can cook meat, soup, casseroles, rice, vegetables, and many other dishes in the pressure cooker. Always follow the manufacturer's instructions for use and safety.

Try the previous recipe for chicken and dumplings in the pressure cooker. It should cook for about 6 minutes instead of 8 hours. Or, experiment with soups, roasts, chicken, and seafood. The pressure cooker makes fluffy rice and awesome risotto, too! See Chapter 2 for more information about pressure cookers. If you want even more detailed info and lots of great recipes, check out *Pressure Cookers For Dummies* by Tom Lacalamita (published by Wiley). Here's a recipe to get you started pressure-cooking.

☕ Pressure Cooker Wild Mushroom Risotto

The pressure cooker is a great way to make risotto because you don't have to stand over the stove stirring constantly. Sauté the onions in butter and oil, coat the rice, add the liquid, lock on the lid, and in less than 10 minutes, you have a fantastic, creamy creation that will make your family very happy.

Tools: *Small saucepan, small bowl, wooden spoon, fork, paper towel or coffee filter, pressure cooker, chef's knife, wooden spoon*

Preparation time: *About 10 minutes*

Cooking time: *About 8 minutes*

Yield: *6 servings*

½ cup brandy, Madeira wine, or orange juice

¼ cup dried porcini mushrooms

2 tablespoons butter

1 tablespoon olive oil

½ cup finely chopped yellow onions

2 cloves garlic, minced

½ cup portobello mushrooms, chopped

1½ cups arborio rice

4 cups chicken broth, plus extra if necessary

1 teaspoon dried basil

1 cup grated Gruyère or Swiss cheese

½ cup grated Parmesan cheese

½ teaspoon pepper

1 Put the brandy, wine, or juice in a small saucepan over medium-low heat until warm. Remove from the heat and add the porcini mushrooms. Stir to make sure the mushrooms are covered with liquid. Set aside.

2 Turn the pressure cooker on high and heat the butter and olive oil. Sauté the onions, garlic, and portobello mushrooms just until soft, about 5 minutes.

3 Add the rice and stir to completely coat each grain with the butter and oil mixture.

4 Remove the porcini mushrooms from the soaking liquid and put them in a small bowl. Hold a paper towel over the bowl and slowly pour the soaking liquid into the paper towel so the liquid pours into the bowl and any sediment is filtered by your paper towel. (You can also use a coffee filter for this step, pouring the liquid through the filter and letting it drip into the bowl.)

5 Add the chicken broth, porcini mushrooms, the mushroom soaking liquid, and the basil to the pressure cooker. Stir to combine. Lock on the lid to the pressure cooker. Bring to high pressure and cook for 6 minutes. Reduce the pressure, using the quick release method, and check for doneness. The rice should be tender but firm to the bite, and the sauce should be creamy. If the rice isn't cooked, add a little more chicken broth and stir until the risotto is tender and creamy.

6 When the risotto has reached the desired consistency, stir in the cheese and pepper and serve immediately.

> *Go-With: Serve this risotto with any roasted meat (see Chapter 7), or with a green salad (see Chapter 12) for a light lunch.*

Per serving: *Calories 441 (From Fat 164); Fat 18g (Saturated 9g); Cholesterol 39mg; Sodium 860mg; Carbohydrate 51g (Dietary Fiber 3g); Protein 19g.*

From Oven to Table: Simplicity in a Casserole Dish

Maybe you don't have a slow cooker or a pressure cooker, or maybe you'd rather use your good old-fashioned casserole dish for baking one-pot meals. Sounds good to us! Here are some tasty recipes to bake in your oven.

Bacon and Cheese Strata

A *strata*, great for Sunday brunch, is essentially a custard baked around layers of different ingredients, including bread, vegetables, cheese, and seasoning.

Tools: *2½-quart to 3-quart ceramic or glass shallow baking dish, whisk, mixing bowl, chef's knife, skillet*

Preparation time: *About 25 minutes, plus 15 minutes standing time*

Cooking time: *About 35 minutes*

Yield: *6 servings*

Butter to grease the baking dish	*½ cup rinsed, chopped, packed spinach or sorrel leaves*
8-ounce loaf seedless Italian bread	
5 slices bacon	*5 eggs*
1½ cups grated Gouda, Gruyère, or Italian fontina cheese	*2 cups milk*
	2 tablespoons tomato-based salsa
	Salt and pepper

1 Butter the bottom and sides of a 2½- to 3-quart shallow baking dish. (Use a rectangular dish that allows the bread slices to fit snugly in one layer.)

2 Trim and discard about 1 inch off each end of the loaf of bread and cut it into about 16 slices. If the bread is fresh, dry the slices in a 175-degree oven for about 15 minutes. Arrange the slices in the baking dish, overlapping the edges so the slices fit in the dish.

3 Sauté the bacon in a large skillet over medium-high heat, about 5 minutes, or until crisp, turning occasionally. Drain on paper towels. When it's cool enough to handle, crumble it into small pieces.

4 Sprinkle the crumbled bacon over the bread slices and top with the cheese and spinach or sorrel.

5 In a medium bowl, beat together the eggs, milk, salsa, and salt and pepper to taste. Pour the mixture over the layers of bread, bacon, cheese, and spinach. Using a fork, press the bread slices down to soak them in the egg mixture. Let it set for about 15 minutes.

6 Preheat the oven to 350 degrees.

7 Bake the strata about 35 minutes, or just until the custard mixture is firm and lightly browned. Do not overbake, or the custard will be dry. Remove from the oven and serve immediately, cutting into squares.

Per serving: Calories 363 (From Fat 185); Fat 21g (Saturated 10g); Cholesterol 230mg; Sodium 729mg; Carbohydrate 24g (Dietary Fiber 1g); Protein 20g.

Spanish Paella

Because this one-pot meal is so versatile, you can easily change the ingredients to include whatever leftovers you might have, as long as you stick to a few basics: rice, olive oil, and saffron (an herb made from the bright yellow stigmas of a plant, used to color and flavor food).

Tools: *Paring knife, chef's knife, Dutch oven or large saucepan with a lid*

Preparation time: *About 15 minutes*

Cooking time: *About 70 minutes*

Yield: *8 servings*

¼ cup olive oil

1 chicken, cut into pieces (about 2 pounds)

8 ounces kielbasa or other smoked sausage, sliced

1 large yellow onion, chopped

3 garlic cloves, peeled and minced

2 stalks celery, minced, including some of the leaves

5 cups chicken broth

2 cups raw white rice

1 pinch of saffron threads (find them with the herbs and spices at the grocery store)

1 cup frozen peas

1 pound medium shrimp, shelled and deveined (see Figure 14-1 for instructions)

1 In a Dutch oven or large saucepan, heat the olive oil over medium-high heat.

2 Add the chicken pieces and sauté over medium-high heat, turning the chicken to cook all sides, for about 10 minutes. Add the sausage, onion, garlic, and celery and continue to sauté until the chicken is golden brown and the vegetables are soft, about 10 additional minutes.

3 Add the chicken broth, rice, and saffron. Stir to combine. Bring to a boil and then reduce the heat. Add the peas and stir. Cover and simmer over medium-low until the rice is cooked through and has absorbed all the liquid and the chicken is no longer pink inside, about 45 minutes. (Check after the first 25 minutes of simmering time and add more broth if the rice looks dry.)

4 Stir in the shrimp and cook for an additional 3 to 4 minutes, or until the shrimp turns pink. Serve immediately.

Per serving: *Calories 543 (From Fat 241); Fat 27g (Saturated 7g); Cholesterol 151mg; Sodium 1,104mg; Carbohydrate 41g (Dietary Fiber 4g); Protein 33g.*

Cleaning and Deveining Shrimp

Figure 14-1:
How to
clean and
devein
shrimp.

1.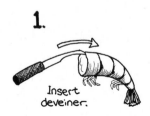

Insert deveiner.

2.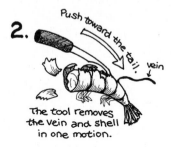

Push toward the tail.

vein

The tool removes the vein and shell in one motion.

3.

Clean under cold water.

Shepherd's Pie

In Ireland, the classic Shepherd's Pie is made with beef, not lamb. We prefer the more distinctive flavor of lamb, so we're giving you this lamb recipe. If you want to try it with beef, simply substitute the same amount of meat.

Tools: *Chef's knife, large pot, potato masher or ricer, large skillet, oval gratin dish, wooden spoon*

Preparation time: *About 1 hour*

Cooking time: *About 45 minutes*

Yield: *6 servings*

2½ pounds baking potatoes

4 tablespoons butter

About 1 cup milk

Salt and pepper

1 tablespoon vegetable oil

1 medium yellow onion, chopped

2 large cloves garlic, peeled and chopped

1½ pounds cooked, chopped lamb
(or raw, ground lamb)

1 tablespoon all-purpose flour

½ cup homemade or canned beef or chicken stock

1 tablespoon chopped thyme or sage, or 1 teaspoon dried thyme or sage

1 tablespoon chopped rosemary leaves, or 1 teaspoon dried rosemary

Dash of ground nutmeg

1 Preheat the oven to 350 degrees.

2 Peel and quarter the potatoes. Put the potatoes in a large pot of lightly salted water and bring to a boil. Cook, covered, until the potatoes are tender, about 20 minutes. Drain well and return the potatoes to the pot.

3 Mash the potatoes with a masher or ricer along with 2 tablespoons of the butter and enough milk to make them smooth and fluffy. Season with the salt and pepper to taste and set aside.

4 Heat the oil in a large skillet over medium-low heat. Add the onion and garlic and cook, stirring often, until the onion is soft and wilted. (Be careful not to let the garlic brown.) Turn up the heat to medium and add the lamb. Cook about 5 minutes, stirring. (If using raw ground lamb, cook over medium heat, stirring often, for about 10 minutes or until it is well browned.) Pour off and discard any fat in the pan.

5 Add the flour and cook, stirring often, for about 2 to 3 minutes. Add the stock, thyme, rosemary, and nutmeg. Reduce the heat to low and simmer, stirring occasionally, for about 15 minutes. Remove from the heat and let cool slightly.

6 Transfer the lamb mixture to an oval gratin dish (about 13 inches long). Spread the mashed potatoes over everything. Dot with the remaining 2 tablespoons butter (which simply means to break up the butter into several small pieces and distribute it evenly) and bake for 45 minutes or until nicely browned. Let cool for 5 minutes before serving.

Go-With: *This dish needs only a simple salad as an accompaniment, such as the Easy Mixed Green Salad in Chapter 12.*

Per serving: Calories 474 (From Fat 173); Fat 19g (Saturated 9g); Cholesterol 125mg; Sodium 589mg; Carbohydrate 38g (Dietary Fiber 4g); Protein 37g.

TIP

Making fresh bread crumbs

You don't need to waste your money by buying bread crumbs. Instead, make your own and store them in an airtight jar.

1. **Lightly toast 6 slices of bread.**

2. **Tear the bread into pieces, place in a food processor or blender, and blend to the consistency of coarse crumbs.**

For variety, add dried herbs of your choice to the blender, or rub the slices of bread with cloves of peeled and sliced garlic before whirling the bread into crumbs.

Chicken and Biscuit Pot Pie

You may remember those frozen chicken pot pies from childhood, but this version is made from scratch and oh-so-much tastier. This recipe takes a little time, but the end result is worth every warm, homey bite. We hope you'll try it.

Tools: *Chef's knife, 4-quart pot with lid, colander, large pot such as a Dutch oven, mixing bowl, 3-quart or 9-x13-inch baking dish, whisk*

Preparation time: *About 15 minutes*

Cooking time: *About 45 minutes*

Baking time: *About 25 minutes*

Yield: *8 servings*

2 pounds skinless, boneless chicken breasts

3 cups chicken broth

1 medium yellow onion, chopped

2 celery stalks, trimmed of leaves and diced

2 cloves garlic, minced or put through a garlic press

3 carrots, trimmed, scraped, and sliced

1 medium boiling potato, peeled and diced

3 tablespoons butter

1 tablespoon all-purpose flour

¼ cup heavy cream

¼ teaspoon ground nutmeg

Salt and pepper

1 cup fresh or frozen peas

1 tablespoon sherry (optional)

1 can (10 to 12 ounces) refrigerated biscuit dough (8 to 10 biscuits)

1 Combine the chicken breasts, broth, onion, celery, and garlic in a 4-quart pot. Add water to just cover the chicken and vegetables. Cover the pot and bring to a boil. Uncover, reduce the heat, and simmer for 15 minutes. Remove the chicken, cut into bite-sized pieces, and return the pieces and any juice to the pot.

2 Add the carrots and potato to the chicken. Bring the broth back to a boil and then lower the heat and simmer 15 minutes more, or until the chicken and vegetables are just tender. Let cool for about 5 minutes in the liquid.

3 Slowly and carefully, pour the broth with the chicken and vegetables into a large colander set over a larger pot (such as a Dutch oven) to catch and reserve the liquid. Put this pot with the liquid back on the stove over medium heat.

4 Melt the butter in a pot or large saucepan over medium heat. (You can use the same pot that you used to make the stock.) Add the flour and cook, whisking constantly, for about 1 minute. Stir in the hot broth, whisking occasionally and cooking about 2 to 3 minutes until the sauce comes to a boil and thickens. Add the cream and nutmeg. Season with salt and pepper to taste.

5 Preheat the oven to 425 degrees.

6 Stir the chicken, vegetables, peas, and, if desired, the sherry into the sauce. Spoon the mixture into a 3-quart or 9-x-13-inch shallow baking dish.

7 Arrange the refrigerated biscuits on top of the chicken mixture and bake for about 25 minutes, or until the biscuits are lightly browned. Serve immediately.

Per serving: *Calories 371 (From Fat 146); Fat 16g (Saturated 7g); Cholesterol 86mg; Sodium 940mg; Carbohydrate 28g (Dietary Fiber 3g); Protein 28g.*

☉ *American Macaroni and Cheese*

This recipe is a classic and simple version of macaroni and cheese (shown in the color section), which you can alter in many ways. You can substitute all kinds of pasta for the elbow macaroni, such as penne, ziti, or shells (see Chapter 13). Mozzarella or Gruyère can replace the fontina or cheddar, or you can use the cheeses in any combination. You can make a spicy version by adding more Tabasco sauce or even crushed red pepper flakes. Add sautéed onion and red bell pepper or cooked broccoli florets and mushrooms to the cheese sauce for a vegetable version. Or sprinkle the top with cooked, crumbled bacon; shredded ham; or Parmesan cheese instead of the bread crumbs.

Tools: 4- or 5-quart pot, small saucepan, large saucepan, whisk, grater, colander, chef's knife, deep 2- to 3-quart casserole dish with lid

Preparation time: About 25 minutes

Cooking time: About 25 minutes

Yield: 4 servings

2 cups elbow macaroni	*2 cups grated sharp cheddar cheese*
2½ cups milk	*Salt and pepper*
5 tablespoons butter	*½ cup cubed Italian fontina cheese*
3 tablespoons all-purpose flour	*1 cup fresh white bread crumbs (see the sidebar "Making fresh bread crumbs")*
½ teaspoon paprika	
Generous dash of Tabasco sauce, or to taste	

1 Preheat the oven to 350 degrees.

2 Bring a 4- or 5-quart pot of lightly salted water to a boil. Add the macaroni and cook for about 6 to 8 minutes, or until just tender. (Be careful not to overcook. The macaroni softens even more when it's baked.)

3 As the macaroni cooks, make the cheese sauce. Heat the milk almost to the boiling point in a small saucepan over medium-low heat.

4 Melt 3 tablespoons of the butter in a large saucepan over medium heat. Add the flour and whisk constantly over low heat for 1 to 2 minutes. Do not let it brown.

5 Gradually whisk in the hot milk and then add the paprika and Tabasco sauce. Cook over medium heat for 2 to 3 minutes or until the sauce thickens, whisking occasionally. Whisk in the grated cheddar cheese and remove from the heat. Season to taste with salt and pepper.

6 Drain the macaroni as soon as it is done, return it to the pot, and add the cheese sauce and the cubes of fontina cheese, stirring well to blend. (If the macaroni cooks before you finish making the sauce, drain and set it aside.)

7 Use 1 tablespoon of the butter to grease a deep, 2- to 3-quart casserole dish fitted with a lid. Add the macaroni and cheese mixture. Cover and bake for 20 to 25 minutes until hot.

8 As the casserole bakes, melt the remaining tablespoon of butter in a small skillet. Add the bread crumbs and sauté over low heat, stirring constantly, until they're moistened but not browned.

9 Carefully remove the casserole from the oven. Raise the oven temperature to broil; spread the bread crumbs evenly over the macaroni and cheese. Return the casserole to the oven, uncovered, and broil for 1 to 2 minutes, or until the crumbs are crisp and browned. Serve immediately.

Go-With: *All this dish needs is a colorful salad, like the Tomato, Red Onion, and Basil Salad in Chapter 12, or even the Three-Berry Dessert Salad in the same chapter.*

Per serving: Calories 732 (From Fat 392); Fat 44g (Saturated 27g); Cholesterol 134mg; Sodium 743mg; Carbohydrate 55g (Dietary Fiber 2g); Protein 30g.

Beef and Turkey Meat Loaf

This slightly untraditional meat loaf (made partly with turkey to cut down on fat) can be a jumping-off point for other creations. If you like, try mixing in a little ground pork or ground veal instead of turkey. Lamb is a nice addition, too. The essential technique is the same for any ground meat. You can serve this meat loaf with a quick tomato sauce, spicy salsa, mustard sauce, or even a jazzed-up sauce of ketchup flavored with Tabasco sauce and Worcestershire sauce.

Tools: *Chef's knife, medium skillet, large bowl, 5- to 6-cup loaf pan, whisk, wooden spoon*

Preparation time: *About 30 minutes*

Cooking time: *About 1½ hours, plus 10 minutes standing time*

Yield: *6 servings*

2 tablespoons olive oil	*1 pound lean ground beef*
1 large yellow onion, chopped	*2 tablespoons chopped thyme, or 2 teaspoons dried thyme*
3 large cloves garlic, finely chopped	
¾ cup milk	*2 tablespoons chopped savory, or 2 teaspoons dried savory*
2 eggs	*2 tablespoons finely chopped parsley*
1½ cups fresh bread crumbs	*¼ teaspoon ground nutmeg*
1 pound ground turkey	*Salt and pepper*

1 Preheat the oven to 350 degrees.

2 Heat the oil in a medium skillet over medium heat. Add the onion and cook, stirring occasionally, for about 3 minutes or until the onion begins to wilt. Add the garlic and cook, stirring often, about 2 minutes more. Do not let the garlic brown. Remove the pan from the heat and set aside.

3 In a large bowl, beat together the milk and eggs with the whisk; stir in the bread crumbs and let stand for 5 minutes. Add the turkey, ground beef, thyme, savory, parsley, nutmeg, salt and pepper to taste, and the sautéed onion and garlic. Combine the mixture thoroughly by using your hands or a wooden spoon.

4 Mold the mixture into a 5- to 6-cup loaf pan. Bake, uncovered, about 1½ hours, draining off any excess grease if necessary. Let the meat loaf stand for about 10 minutes at room temperature before slicing from the pan.

Tip: *A bulb baster is a handy tool for siphoning off undesired grease that can collect in a roasting pan. If you don't have a baster, a large metal spoon also works.*

Per serving: Calories 412 (From Fat 178); Fat 20g (Saturated 6g); Cholesterol 169mg; Sodium 456mg; Carbohydrate 25g (Dietary Fiber 2g); Protein 32g.

Chapter 15

Sweet Somethings

In This Chapter

▶ Measuring ingredients correctly

▶ Whipping up pleasing puddings for all occasions

▶ Chilling out with ice creams and granités

▶ Baking crisps and cobblers

▶ Satisfying everyone's sweet tooth with cookies and cakes

Recipes in This Chapter

- Homey Rice Pudding
- Lemon Granité
- Lime Ice Cream
- Double Chocolate Pudding
- Chocolate Mousse
- Baked Apples with Red Wine
- Apple-Pear Crisp
- Peach-Blueberry Cobbler
- Old-Fashioned Chocolate Chip Cookies
- Lemon Bars
- Divine Brownies
- Lemon Pudding Cake with Fresh Berries
- Free-Form Fresh Fruit Tart
- Perfect Chocolate Cake
- Tiramisù

Desserts are hard for almost everyone to resist. Even if you're counting calories or stuffed after eating a hearty dinner, you still may find it almost impossible to say no to a sweet finish to your meal. The recipes in this chapter, which include cinnamon-scented wobbly puddings, old-fashioned cobblers, luscious baked fruits, and ever-popular chocolate treats, are sure to satisfy your desire for a mouth-watering and irresistible dessert.

This chapter may also help you recall those days when a chocolate chip cookie and a glass of milk were all you needed after school to make the afternoon seem just fine. And what about that perfect chocolate cake your mom made for your birthday or the very first time (probably as an adult) that you ever tasted tiramisù? You can find recipes for all three of those desserts in this chapter to help you relive those sweet memories.

Desserts are great crowd pleasers, so if you want to make a good impression on your family and friends, try your hand at one of the recipes in this chapter. Then just sit back and wait for the adoration.

Half Empty or Half Full: Measuring Techniques

Measuring is important, especially for a beginning cook. Too much salt, and the stew is ruined. Too little baking powder, and the cake doesn't rise. Too much milk, and the pudding never sets. Although you use measuring techniques in all kinds of cooking, measuring in baking is especially important because without precision measuring, your muffins may fall or your bread may rise too much or your cookies will turn out flat or tasteless or far too salty. Baking recipes are formulas that require an exact proportion of dry to wet ingredients, so be extra precise.

But measuring doesn't replace tasting, and the more you cook, the less you need to measure. Experienced chefs are able to sense in their hands the feel of a tablespoon of salt or ½ teaspoon of lemon peel. But this comes with practice. Here are some basic measuring guidelines:

- **Measure dry and liquid ingredients in different cups.** The dry measure is a metal or plastic cup with a handle. To measure flour or rice, dip the measure into the canister or bag, scooping out more than you need. Then use the straight edge of a knife to level off the excess. Work over a piece of wax paper or the bag or canister to catch any excess.

  Measure liquids in a glass or plastic cup with a spout for pouring; do not fill the cup while holding it at eye level. Place the cup on the counter (so that you're sure the liquid is level) and lower yourself to read the mark.

- **Use a kitchen scale to measure dry ingredients accurately when a recipe calls for ounces or pounds.**

- **Use measuring spoons for small amounts of liquid and dry ingredients, such as a teaspoon of vanilla extract or ½ teaspoon of baking soda.** Don't use your table silverware — it's not equivalent to measuring spoons.

- **Don't measure over your working bowl, especially if it's filled with other ingredients.** You may accidentally add too much of an ingredient.

- **Pack brown sugar and solid fats like shortening into a cup.** For butter and margarine packaged in stick form, use the measure marks on the wrapper to slice off a specific amount.

✔ **To easily remove sticky foods like honey, peanut butter, and molasses from a measuring cup, coat the cup first with a small amount of vegetable oil or spray.**

✔ **If the recipe calls for sifted flour, be sure to sift it.** Sifting incorporates air into the flour, and a cup of sifted flour is less — by 2 tablespoons or more — than a cup of unsifted flour, and remember that baking measurements must be precise!

Here's the correct way to get the right amount of sifted flour for your recipes. Using a dry measuring cup, scoop out the approximate amount of flour called for in the recipe and place it in the top of the sifter. Sift the flour into a large mixing bowl or over a piece of wax paper. After sifting, so as not to lose the flour's new "lightness," gently spoon the flour into the appropriate measuring cup, fill to overflowing, and then level it off with the straight edge of a knife.

Cozy Puddings and Elegant Ices

Whether a warm, creamy pudding or a tangy, bracing granité, these desserts in a bowl are sure to be a big hit, and they make a satisfying yet light finish to a meal.

When making any recipe that requires homemade whipped cream, be careful not to overbeat it. Overbeating cream and other ingredients can cause problems, including the following:

✔ **If you overbeat cream, it turns to butter.** Be sure to start with very cold cream, cold beaters, and a cold bowl. Start beating slowly and gradually increase the speed. Don't strive for stiff cream but rather soft, floppy peaks. Always refrigerate whipped cream immediately unless you're serving it right away.

✔ **Overbeating egg whites causes them to dry out.** Beat them so they form peaks that stand on their own. Start beating fairly vigorously and increase to higher speed, adding other ingredients, like sugar. Be sure your beaters and bowls are free of any fat or grease, which makes it more difficult to reach soft peaks.

☺ Homey Rice Pudding

Rice pudding is one of those all-American dishes that you find in roadside diners across the country. It has many incarnations: Sometimes it's firm and custardy, and other times it's creamy and rich. This recipe falls on the rich and creamy side, with a nice sharp bite from cinnamon.

Tools: *Grater, saucepan, whisk, 2 mixing bowls, oval baking dish (approximately 14 x 8 x 2 inches), large baking dish, wooden spoon or spatula*

Preparation time: *About 10 minutes*

Cooking time: *1 hour*

Yield: *8 servings*

5 cups milk	1 cup converted rice	1 tablespoon grated lemon zest
1 cup heavy cream	1¼ cups sugar	
1 vanilla bean, split lengthwise so the inner seeds are exposed (or 1 teaspoon vanilla extract)	¾ cup raisins	1 tablespoon butter for greasing the pan
	3 egg yolks (see Chapter 10 for tips on separating eggs)	1 teaspoon cinnamon

1 Pour the milk and cream into a heavy-bottomed saucepan and add the vanilla bean or extract. Bring the mixture to a boil and stir in the rice and sugar — stir from the bottom to keep the rice from sticking. Reduce the heat to low and simmer, stirring occasionally, until the rice is tender and most of the milk is absorbed, about 30 minutes. Set aside.

2 Meanwhile, put the raisins in a bowl and pour boiling water over them. Let them stand until the rice is cooked.

3 In another bowl, whisk the egg yolks and then blend in the lemon zest. When the rice is cooked, remove it from the heat and slowly whisk in the egg mixture.

4 Preheat the oven to 400 degrees.

5 Drain the raisins and fold them into the cooked rice.

6 Grease an oval baking dish measuring 14 x 8 x 2 inches (approximately). Pour the rice mixture into the dish, sprinkle with the cinnamon, and place in a larger ovenproof dish with sides (like a casserole dish). Pour boiling water into the exterior dish about 2 inches up the sides. Bake for about 30 minutes, or until the custard is set (you can tell it's set when a toothpick inserted into the center of the pudding comes out clean).

Tip: When grating citrus peel, be sure to remove only the colored portion of the skin, called the zest. The white portion underneath, called the pith, is bitter.

Tip: If possible, don't use imitation vanilla extract. Buy pure extracts that, although more expensive, make a big difference in the taste.

Per serving: *Calories 484 (From Fat 176); Fat 20g (Saturated 12g); Cholesterol 145mg; Sodium 94mg; Carbohydrate 71g (Dietary Fiber 1g); Protein 9g.*

🍑 *Lemon Granité*

Granité is the French word for flavored ices. Aside from being pure, healthful, delicious, low-carb dessert options, they require no fancy equipment beyond a fork and a little elbow grease. Essentially, granités are flavored and sweetened water that are frozen. You can use all kinds of fruits to flavor them. Every once in a while during the freezing process, you scrape the ice with a fork to create little crystals. That's it! Granités also make great palate cleansers between courses in a meal. A few bites of lemon granité and you're ready to taste the next course without tasting the previous course. Lemon Granité is shown in the color section of this book.

Tools: *Medium saucepan, shallow freezerproof pan (such as a metal baking pan or shallow plastic freezer container)*

Preparation time: *10 minutes, plus a freezing time of 90 minutes*

Yield: *6 servings*

¾ cup freshly squeezed lemon juice

1 cup water

6 tablespoons sugar

Fresh fruit, such as blueberries, strawberries, kiwis, and pitted cherries

1 In a saucepan, combine the lemon juice, water, and sugar. Stir well. Bring to a boil and remove from the heat.

2 Pour the mixture into a shallow, freezerproof pan. Place in the freezer.

3 After about 30 minutes, remove the trays from the freezer and, using a fork, scrape back and forth over the ice, eventually reaching the bottom of the container. Return the mixture to the freezer. Repeat again after 20 minutes, again after another 15 minutes, and a final time after another 15 minutes. After you're finished, you shouldn't see any big chunks of ice. Serve in chilled bowls, with fresh fruits around it, or serve with cookies and garnish with an edible flower such as a pansy or violet (but be careful to use only flowers you know haven't been sprayed with pesticides), as shown in the color section.

Vary It! *You can make terrific granités with all kinds of fresh fruits and juices, including blueberries, strawberries, Concord grapes, watermelon, cantaloupe, apple juice, oranges, limes, and more. Just extract all of the juice either with a reamer (in the case of citrus) or by putting peeled and pitted fruit in a blender and then straining the juice into the saucepan along with the sugar and water. Fibrous fruits (mangoes, apricots, plums, figs, bananas, and papayas, for example) do not work as well for granités.*

Tip: *When making granités, select the ripest fruit you can find; it can even be a tad overripe. You want as much flavor from the fruit as possible.*

Per serving: *Calories 56 (From Fat 0); Fat 0g (Saturated 0g); Cholesterol 0mg; Sodium 0mg; Carbohydrate 15g (Dietary Fiber 0g); Protein 0g. Without fruit*

☟ Lime Ice Cream

What's special about the following ice cream, aside from its wonderful citrus flavor, is the ease of preparation. You don't need an ice cream maker to prepare it. You simply combine all the ingredients and freeze them until solid. It's creamy, refreshing, and so rich that a small serving is all that you and your guests need.

Tools: *Grater, knife, large bowl, 8- or 9-inch square metal cake pan*

Preparation time: *5 to 10 minutes, plus a freezing time of about 4 hours*

Yield: *About 3 cups, or 4 servings*

2 cups heavy cream	*2 teaspoons grated lime zest*
1 cup sugar	*⅓ cup fresh lime juice*

1 In a large bowl, combine the cream and sugar; stir the mixture until the sugar is dissolved. Stir in the lime zest and juice. The mixture will start to thicken slightly.

2 Pour the mixture into an 8- or 9-inch square cake pan. Cover with foil and freeze until firm, about 4 hours. Scoop or spoon into individual serving bowls with sliced fruit, such as mango, blueberries, kiwi, or strawberries.

Tip: *Grated citrus peel, also referred to as zest, has the unpleasant tendency of clinging to the holes of the grater. To loosen these pieces, brush the holes with a pastry brush so the grated peel falls onto a cutting board or right into the dish you're preparing.*

Per serving: *Calories 610 (From Fat 397); Fat 44g (Saturated 27g); Cholesterol 163mg; Sodium 46mg; Carbohydrate 55g (Dietary Fiber 0g); Protein 3g.*

☟ Double Chocolate Pudding

Put away your packaged pudding mixes forever. This pudding is so rich and delicious that it will be everyone's favorite, and it's a snap to make, too! You can dress it up by spooning it into a tall wine or parfait glass and topping it with sweetened whipped cream and chocolate shavings for a classy garnish (see the color section). Or forget the cream and just indulge in the pure chocolate flavor alone.

Tools: *Medium saucepan, chef's knife, small mixing bowl, wooden spoon, 3- to 4-cup capacity serving bowl or individual serving cups, plastic wrap or wax paper*

Preparation time: *10 minutes*

Cooking time: *6 to 8 minutes*

Yield: *4 servings*

¼ cup water

2½ tablespoons cornstarch

½ cup sugar

⅓ cup unsweetened cocoa powder

Pinch of salt

⅓ cup milk, heated just to warm

2 ounces (2 squares) semisweet chocolate, coarsely chopped

2 cups heavy cream

1¼ teaspoons vanilla extract

Sweetened whipped cream, optional garnish

Chopped pecans or almonds, lightly toasted, optional garnish (see the Tip after this recipe for instructions on toasting nuts)

1 In a small bowl, stir together the water and the cornstarch thoroughly until the cornstarch is dissolved and the mixture is smooth. Set the mixture aside.

2 In a heavy, medium saucepan, mix together the sugar, cocoa, and salt. Using a wooden spoon, stir in the warm milk to make a smooth paste. Place the saucepan over medium heat and bring the mixture to a boil while stirring constantly, about 2 to 3 minutes. Add the chopped chocolate and stir until it completely melts.

3 Gradually stir in the heavy cream. Stir the cornstarch mixture a few times to be sure it's completely dissolved and then stir it thoroughly into the chocolate mixture. Continue stirring over medium heat for about 5 minutes, or until the pudding begins to thicken and boil. (Be sure to sweep the spoon along the bottom and sides of the pan to prevent the pudding from getting lumpy or burning.)

4 Reduce the heat to low and cook for about 1 minute more while stirring constantly.

5 Remove the saucepan from the heat and stir in the vanilla.

6 Pour the pudding into a serving bowl or individual serving cups. To prevent a skin from forming, lay a piece of plastic wrap or wax paper directly on the surface of the pudding. Refrigerate for several hours or until chilled before serving. If desired, garnish each serving with a dollop of sweetened whipped cream and a sprinkling of chopped nuts.

Vary It! *For a mocha-flavored pudding, substitute 1 tablespoon (or to taste) coffee liqueur (like Kahlúa) for the vanilla extract.*

Tip: *Toasting nuts lightly before tossing them into doughs or batters greatly improves their flavor. Simply spread them out on a baking sheet and toast in a 350-degree oven for about 10 minutes or until lightly browned.*

Per serving: *Calories 626 (From Fat 462); Fat 51g (Saturated 32g); Cholesterol 166mg; Sodium 93mg; Carbohydrate 44g (Dietary Fiber 3g); Protein 6g.*

🍑 Chocolate Mousse

You can assemble this popular dessert in just minutes, and it doesn't require the skills of a pastry chef. Mousse is lighter, airier, and less rich than pudding. Because it has less sugar and because the bittersweet chocolate is also relatively low in sugar, chocolate mousse is a good lower-carb option to pudding. It's the perfect ending to a family dinner, and even those watching their weight can have a taste. You can make this simple yet festive dessert days in advance.

Tools: Stainless steel 2-quart bowl, chef's knife, saucepan, whisk, electric hand-held mixer, spatula

Preparation time: About 10 minutes

Cooking time: About 10 minutes (plus several hours chilling)

Yield: 12 servings

8 ounces bittersweet chocolate	*2 cups heavy cream, well chilled*
6 eggs, separated (see Chapter 10 for tips on separating eggs)	*6 tablespoons sugar*
3 tablespoons water	*Whipped cream or grated bittersweet chocolate for garnish*

1 Chop the chocolate coarsely with the chef's knife. Place the chocolate pieces in a saucepan or pot and set the pot over a larger pot holding barely simmering water. Cover the pot containing the chocolate.

2 Meanwhile, put the egg yolks in a saucepan and add the water. Place the saucepan over very low heat while whisking vigorously. When the yolks thicken slightly (to a light sauce consistency), remove the saucepan from the heat.

3 Check the chocolate. When it is melted, stir well with a whisk. Add the melted chocolate to the egg mixture and blend thoroughly. Scrape the mixture into a large mixing bowl.

4 With a hand-held electric mixer, beat the cream in a chilled bowl until it forms soft peaks, adding 2 tablespoons of the sugar toward the end. Fold this into the chocolate mixture.

5 Wash and dry both the bowl and the mixer thoroughly to remove the cream, before proceeding — any fat left on the bowl or mixer will keep the egg whites from getting fluffy. Using the clean mixer, beat the egg whites in the clean bowl until they form soft peaks. Beat in the remaining 4 tablespoons sugar and continue beating until the egg whites form stiff peaks. Fold this into the chocolate mixture.

6 Spoon the mousse into a serving bowl and chill thoroughly before serving. Garnish with whipped cream or grated bittersweet chocolate.

Vary It! *To make this mousse extra elegant, pour about ¼ cup of amaretto or Grand Marnier into the egg yolk and chocolate mixture just before it thickens. You can also garnish the mousse with strawberries or toasted almonds, hazelnuts, or walnuts.*

Warning: *Some raw egg whites may contain salmonella bacteria, which could compromise the health of certain individuals. If you're worried about this risk, use commercially prepared pasteurized egg white product or egg white powder (see Chapter 10).*

Per serving: Calories 293 (From Fat 228); Fat 25g (Saturated 14g); Cholesterol 161mg; Sodium 47mg; Carbohydrate 17g (Dietary Fiber 1g); Protein 5g.

Fruit from the Oven

Who can resist the aroma of baked fruits infusing the kitchen? This section includes a recipe for a cobbler and a recipe for a crisp. What's the difference? *Cobblers* are deep-dish fruit desserts in which sweetened fruits (fresh berries or apples are the traditional choices) are topped with a biscuit dough before baking. Almost any type or combination of fruits can be used, and just about any kind of baking dish — round, square, oval, or rectangular. In a *crisp,* the fruit is baked under a crumbly topping, usually made with flour, butter, and sugar, and sometimes oats, nuts, and spices. Both are terrific in the fall, when apples are in season.

Baked fruit recipes aren't difficult, but a few simple tips will help you to make your baked fruit creations unforgettable:

✔ Baked fruit recipes typically contain spices like cinnamon, ginger, nutmeg, and cloves. Smell the spices that have been sitting on your shelf for months or years. If they've lost their enticing fragrance, throw them out and treat yourself to new ones.

✔ Many baked fruit recipes also use butter. Throughout this book, we call for unsalted butter (and no margarine), and with good reason — margarine doesn't taste as good as butter. Salt (in salted butter) can affect the delicate sweetness of many baked goods. Sometimes, however, margarine is used in combination with butter to add a light and flaky quality to pie crusts (see Chapter 17 for a great pie crust recipe, and notice that we specifically call for butter and margarine).

✔ Baked fruit recipes often use lemon juice to keep the fruit from turning brown. The acid in lemon juice slows the oxidation of fruit when exposed to air. When a recipe calls for fresh lemon juice, never use the bottled reconstituted liquid kind; it tastes more like furniture polish than lemon juice.

☺ Baked Apples with Red Wine

This recipe comes from friends who live in southwestern France — the land of orchards, sunflowers, and the best of the best red wine. It's a quick, home-style dessert that is both light and delicious. Use a quality red wine in the recipe, and you'll be pleased with the result.

Tools: *Paring knife, bread knife, baking sheet, spatula*

Preparation time: *10 minutes*

Cooking time: *20 to 30 minutes*

Yield: *4 servings*

Butter for greasing aluminum foil

4 thick slices country bread

4 apples (Granny Smith or any preferred apple)

¼ cup red wine

6 tablespoons sugar

½ cup vanilla ice cream, or more to taste

1 Preheat the oven to 375 degrees.

2 Using the butter, grease very well a double-thick sheet of aluminum foil that is large enough to hold the four slices of bread. Lay it over a baking sheet. Arrange the bread slices over the foil.

3 With a paring knife, cut a hole in the top of the apples, about ¾ inch in diameter, and deep enough to go about halfway down into the apple. (You want the hole large enough to hold a small scoop of ice cream.) Slice across the bottom of the apples, just enough so that they will stand upright on top of the bread slices. Carefully sprinkle the red wine over the bread slices so that they're thoroughly moistened but not soggy. Sprinkle evenly with 4 tablespoons of the sugar.

4 Place the cored apples on top of the bread slices. Sprinkle the remaining 2 tablespoons sugar into the hollow cores. Place the apples in the oven for 20 to 30 minutes, or until the apples are soft. Use a spatula to carefully remove the apples and bread to a serving plate. Serve with a tablespoon or so of vanilla ice cream placed in the hollow cores, adding a little on top.

Per serving: Calories 287 (From Fat 38); Fat 4g (Saturated 2g); Cholesterol 10mg; Sodium 204mg; Carbohydrate 63g (Dietary Fiber 6g); Protein 4g.

☌ Apple-Pear Crisp

Like some of the other dessert classics in this chapter, this one has been slightly altered — we've added pears to the apple mixture and splashed the fruit with a little brandy. You can assemble this dish before dinner and bake it while you're eating. The vanilla ice cream or sweetened whipped cream is optional, but we recommend it.

Tools: *Apple corer or paring knife, medium mixing bowl, pastry blender or table knives (for combining ingredients), 2-quart glass or ceramic baking dish*

Preparation time: *About 20 minutes*

Cooking time: *40 to 45 minutes*

Yield: *6 servings*

3 large Granny Smith apples

2 large firm, ripe pears

2 to 3 tablespoons brandy or dark rum (optional)

¾ cup flour

⅔ cup granulated sugar

2 tablespoons brown sugar, packed

Grated zest of ½ lemon

¼ teaspoon salt

½ teaspoon ground cinnamon

¼ teaspoon ground nutmeg

½ cup (1 stick) cold butter, cut into small pieces

½ cup toasted chopped almonds or pecans (see the Tip at the end of the Double Chocolate Pudding recipe, earlier in this chapter)

Vanilla ice cream or whipped cream (optional garnish)

1 Position a rack in the lower third of the oven. Preheat the oven to 375 degrees.

2 Peel and core the apples and cut them into 1-inch chunks (for illustrated instructions on coring apples, see Chapter 17). Core the pears and cut them into 1-inch chunks. You don't have to peel them (they have softer skins), but you can if you like the look of the peeled fruit better. Spread the fruit evenly over the bottom of an unbuttered, shallow, 2-quart baking dish. If desired, sprinkle the fruit with the brandy or rum.

3 In a medium mixing bowl, make the topping: Combine the flour, granulated sugar, brown sugar, lemon zest, salt, cinnamon, and nutmeg. Using a pastry blender, two knives, or your fingertips, cut the butter into the dry ingredients until the mixture resembles coarse bread crumbs. Mix in the chopped nuts.

4 Spread the topping evenly over the fruit. Bake for 40 to 45 minutes, or until the fruit is tender and the crust is lightly browned. Serve warm, if desired, with vanilla ice cream or sweetened whipped cream (see the recipe for whipped cream in Chapter 9).

Tip: *To keep your brown sugar from hardening after opening, place the box in a resealable, airtight plastic bag and refrigerate.*

Vary It! *If desired, add ½ cup of fresh, rinsed cranberries to the apple-pear mixture before spreading on the sugar topping. Or, for a summer crisp, substitute peaches and nectarines for the apples and pears.*

Per serving: *Calories 445 (From Fat 184); Fat 21g (Saturated 10g); Cholesterol 41mg; Sodium 101mg; Carbohydrate 66g (Dietary Fiber 5g); Protein 4g.*

☺ Peach-Blueberry Cobbler

For best results with this recipe, be sure the fruit is very close to fully ripe. Taste the sweetened fruit mixture before covering it with the biscuit dough. If the fruit isn't quite ripe (or tart), you may need to sprinkle on a little more sugar. Some recipes call for removing the skins of the peaches by blanching them in boiling water for 1 minute and then peeling them off. However, we don't think doing so is necessary. And note that nectarine skins, which are thinner than peach skins, do not need to be removed.

Tools: Chef's knife, grater, large mixing bowl, 2-quart glass baking dish, fork, rolling pin, biscuit cutter or cookie cutter, medium mixing bowl, electric mixer

Preparation time: 35 to 40 minutes

Cooking time: 45 minutes

Yield: 8 servings

2 pounds firm, ripe nectarines or peaches (or a combination of both)	*Grated zest and juice of ½ lemon*
1 cup blueberries or blackberries, rinsed, picked over, and stemmed	*7 tablespoons cold butter, cut into small pieces*
⅓ cup (or according to taste and ripeness of fruit) plus 2 tablespoons granulated sugar	*2 teaspoons baking powder*
	½ teaspoon salt
2 tablespoons light brown sugar, packed	*1 teaspoon fresh lemon juice*
1½ cups plus 2 tablespoons all-purpose flour	*8 to 10 tablespoons heavy cream or half-and-half, plus ¾ cup heavy cream, well chilled*
½ teaspoon cinnamon	*Confectioners' sugar*
	½ teaspoon vanilla extract

1 Preheat the oven to 375 degrees.

2 To make the fruit filling, cut the nectarines or peaches in half and remove the pits. Cut each half into 4 to 5 wedges and place in a large mixing bowl. Add the blueberries, ⅓ cup of the granulated sugar, the light brown sugar, 2 tablespoons of the flour, cinnamon, and the grated lemon zest and juice. Toss to mix well. Taste the fruit and see if it's sweet enough. If necessary, add more sugar. Turn the fruit mixture into a 2-quart baking dish that's 2 inches deep. Dot the top of the fruit with 1 tablespoon of the butter and bake for 10 minutes.

3 As the fruit bakes, prepare the topping. In a medium mixing bowl, toss together the remaining 1½ cups flour, the remaining 2 tablespoons sugar, baking powder, and salt. Add the remaining 6 tablespoons butter and, using a pastry blender, 2 knives, or your fingertips, cut the butter into the dry ingredients until the mixture resembles coarse bread crumbs. Sprinkle the mixture with the 1 teaspoon lemon juice.

4 Using a fork, wooden spoon, or rubber spatula, gradually stir in just enough of the 8 to 10 tablespoons of heavy cream or half-and-half to moisten the dough so that it holds together and can be rolled or patted. Gather the dough into a ball and place it on a lightly floured work surface. Roll out or pat the dough with your hands so it is about ½ inch thick and roughly matches the shape of the top of the baking dish.

5 Using a biscuit cutter, a round cookie cutter, or a knife, cut the dough into 2½-inch circles. (You should have 9 to 10 circles.) Alternatively, you can gently roll small pieces of the dough into balls and flatten each into ½-inch-thick rounds.

6 After 10 minutes, remove the fruit from the oven. Place the dough on top of the fruit.

7 Return the cobbler to the oven and bake 30 to 35 minutes more, or until the topping is golden brown and the fruit is bubbling around the edges.

8 As the cobbler bakes, make the sweetened whipped cream. Pour the ¾ cup heavy cream into a medium mixing bowl. Using an electric mixer, beat the cream just until it starts to thicken. Add the confectioners' sugar to taste and the vanilla and continue beating until soft peaks form. Refrigerate until ready to use.

9 To serve, spoon the warm cobbler into shallow bowls. Spoon some of the cream over each serving; drizzle some of the fruit juices over the cobbler and serve.

Vary It! *Substitute other summer fruits for the peaches and blueberries, such as plums, raspberries, apricots, or blackberries. Add other spices, such as allspice, ginger, or nutmeg, or sprinkle fruit with a fruit liqueur. Substitute vanilla or lemon ice cream for the sweetened whipped cream.*

Per serving: Calories 355 (From Fat 146); Fat 16g (Saturated 10g); Cholesterol 47mg; Sodium 251mg; Carbohydrate 51g (Dietary Fiber 3g); Protein 4g.

Cookie Collection: All You Need Is a Glass of Milk

Cookies make a delicious, fun, informal dessert for kids and adults alike. Cookie dough can be "dropped" (no, not dropped on the floor for the dog to scarf up, but dropped by the spoonful onto a cookie sheet), rolled into a log and sliced, rolled out and cut out with cookie cutters, put through a cookie press, or molded by hand into balls and rolled in sugar, cinnamon, or imprinted with pieces of chocolate. Cookie baking takes some time, as most recipes require baking several batches. To save time, consider bar cookies, which are baked in a baking pan. You can bake drop cookie dough, such as for chocolate chip cookies, in a baking pan simply by adding about five more minutes to the cooking time. Or try the Lemon Bar or Divine Brownie recipes, later in this section.

If you never want your cookie jar to be empty, you can find more recipes in *Cookies For Dummies,* by Carole Bloom (published by Wiley).

Here are a few general tips to help improve your chances of cookie-baking success:

- **Timing:** Every oven is different, so the baking time for cookies is critical. Always check the cookies a few minutes before they're supposed to be done. A slightly underdone (but not raw) cookie is usually tastier than a slightly overdone cookie, especially because cookies continue to bake for a short time after you remove them from the oven.

  The same rule about timing applies to bar cookies, such as this chapter's brownies and lemon bars, which should be moist (but not raw) in the center, because they also continue baking after you remove them from the oven.

- **Baking sheets:** Traditional aluminum sheets can produce cookies with burnt bottoms and pale tops. We prefer insulated baking sheets, which have two layers of aluminum with air space between them, because they're less likely to burn the cookies, or stone cookie sheets (similar to pizza stones but in rectangles), which produce an evenly baked cookie, top to bottom. For bar cookies, glass or aluminum baking pans both work, but dark aluminum cooks faster than lighter, silver-colored aluminum, and both cook faster than glass, so keep an eye on those cookies!

  Nonstick baking equipment makes removing things like cookies, breads, cakes, and other baked desserts much easier.

- **Greasing the sheets:** For recipes that call for a greased cookie sheet, you don't need to regrease baking sheets after you've removed one batch of baked cookies. If you use a nonstick sheet, you don't need to grease the cookie sheet at all — doing so can make your cookies spread out too much and turn out too thin.

  For recipes containing butter, just use the wrapper from the stick of butter to rub on the cookie sheet. Or use cooking spray for a lower-fat nonstick option (as long as your type of bakeware doesn't specifically warn against using cooking spray).

⏱ Old-Fashioned Chocolate Chip Cookies

A chocolate chip cookie manufacturer once told us that the secret to his famous cookie dough was a little bit of grated lemon peel. It makes sense. Lemon zest, loaded with rich, lemony oil and without a trace of sourness, is frequently used by bakers to heighten the flavors of cookies and other sweet desserts. In this recipe, the grated lemon zest punches up the flavor of the chocolate chips, and a little heavy cream in the dough gives the cookie a pleasant, melt-in-your-mouth softness. These cookies freeze very well in covered, plastic containers; they also keep for a week at room temperature in an airtight tin.

For a more traditional-tasting chocolate chip cookie without a hint of lemon flavor, simply omit the grated lemon peel.

Tools: *Medium mixing bowl, electric mixer, grater, chef's knife, wooden spoon or rubber spatula, metal spatula, baking sheet (preferably nonstick)*

Preparation time: *About 20 minutes*

Cooking time: *8 to 10 minutes*

Yield: *About 36 cookies*

1 cup plus 2 tablespoons all-purpose flour	*⅓ cup plus 2 tablespoons granulated sugar*
½ teaspoon baking powder	*1 egg*
½ teaspoon grated lemon zest	*2 tablespoons heavy cream or half-and-half*
¼ teaspoon salt	*½ teaspoon vanilla extract*
½ cup (1 stick) butter, softened	*1 cup (6-ounce package) semisweet chocolate chips*
⅓ cup plus 2 tablespoons light brown sugar, packed	*⅓ cup coarsely chopped walnuts or pecans (optional)*

1 Preheat the oven to 375 degrees.

2 In a medium mixing bowl, stir together the flour, baking powder, lemon zest, and salt.

3 Using an electric mixer at medium speed, cream the butter with the brown and granulated sugars about 3 minutes. (*Creaming* means making a soft paste out of butter so it absorbs flavors better.) Beat in the egg, heavy cream, and vanilla until well blended. (Turn off the mixer and scrape the sides of the bowl when necessary.)

4 Using a wooden spoon or a rubber spatula, stir the flour mixture into the butter mixture until well blended. Stir in the chocolate chips and, if desired, the nuts.

5 Drop heaping teaspoons of the batter onto a greased baking sheet (if you use a nonstick baking sheet, you don't need to grease it), about 1 to 2 inches apart. Bake one sheet at a time, until the cookies are lightly golden on the top with slightly browned edges, about 8 to 10 minutes. Rotate the sheet 180 degrees halfway through baking to ensure even browning. Remove the baking sheet to a wire rack and let the cookies cool for about 2 minutes, or until slightly firm. Using a metal spatula, carefully remove the cookies from the baking sheet and slide them onto a wire rack to cool completely.

Per serving: Calories 84 (From Fat 40); Fat 4g (Saturated 3g); Cholesterol 14mg; Sodium 26mg; Carbohydrate 11g (Dietary Fiber 0g); Protein 1g.

🍋 Lemon Bars

This lemon bar recipe is a Sunkist Growers classic that we've altered just a bit by decreasing the sugar and adding flaked coconut. The results are perfectly chewy bars with intense lemon flavor. You can serve these bars as is or sift powdered sugar over the top for a prettier finish.

Tools: *Chef's knife, citrus juicer, 13-x-9-inch nonstick baking pan, medium mixing bowl, large mixing bowl, whisk or electric mixer, wooden spoon, spatula*

Preparation time: *15 minutes*

Cooking time: *About 35 minutes*

Yield: *24 bars*

½ cup butter, softened	1½ cups plus 3 tablespoons all-purpose flour	¾ cup sweetened flaked coconut
1½ cups plus 6 tablespoons sugar	4 eggs	6 tablespoons freshly squeezed lemon juice (about 2 lemons)
Grated zest of 1 lemon	¼ teaspoon baking powder	1 teaspoon vanilla extract

1 Preheat the oven to 350 degrees.

2 Line a 13-x-9-inch baking pan (nonstick is best) with aluminum foil so the ends extend over the two 9-inch sides of the pan. Butter the foil lining the pan. Set the pan aside. (Lining the pan with foil allows you to lift the baked dessert easily from the pan before cutting into squares. See Figure 15-1 for an illustration.)

3 To make the crust, in a medium mixing bowl cream together the butter, 6 tablespoons of the sugar, and half of the lemon zest, using an electric mixer. Gradually stir in 1½ cups of the flour to form a soft, crumbly dough. (If necessary, use your fingers or a pastry blender to work the butter into the flour mixture.) Turn the dough into the foil-lined pan and press it evenly into the bottom. Bake for 12 to 15 minutes or until the crust is firm and lightly browned.

4 Prepare the filling as the crust bakes. In a large mixing bowl, use an electric mixer or a wire whisk to beat the eggs well. Add the remaining 1½ cups of the sugar, the remaining 3 tablespoons flour, and the baking powder, and beat well to combine. Stir or whisk in the coconut, the lemon juice, the remaining half of the lemon zest, and the vanilla, just until blended.

5 Using a rubber spatula, spread the filling over the hot, baked crust, being sure to evenly distribute the coconut throughout the filling. Return the pan to the oven and bake for about 20 minutes, or until the top is lightly golden and the filling is set. Set the pan on a wire rack to cool completely. Lift the foil by the ends to lift out the bar cookie; then set it on a cutting board. It will come out easily in one piece. Gently loosen the foil along all the sides. With a long, sharp, wet knife, cut into squares. Refrigerate the squares until ready to serve.

Vary It! *You can also cook these bars in two 8-inch round nonstick cake pans or glass pie plates instead of the 13-x-9-inch pan. Then you can cut the bars into wedges instead of squares.*

Tip: *If you're not fond of coconut, you can omit it.*

Per serving: *Calories 151 (From Fat 49); Fat 5g (Saturated 3g); Cholesterol 46mg; Sodium 21mg; Carbohydrate 24g (Dietary Fiber 0g); Protein 2g.*

🍅 Divine Brownies

Many cooks, even good ones, don't consider making brownies from scratch, because so many great commercial mixes are available. But we believe that homemade is almost always better than the mix. So we give you this classic brownie recipe that's easy, rich, moist, and better (we guarantee it!) than any boxed mix you can buy. Plus, the brownies freeze well, so you can bake them ahead of time and save them for an upcoming event.

Tools: *Chef's knife, 9-x-13-inch baking pan, saucepan, large mixing bowl, wooden spoon or rubber spatula*

Preparation time: *25 minutes*

Cooking time: *About 20 to 25 minutes*

Yield: *24 brownies*

1 cup (2 sticks) butter	2 cups sugar	2 teaspoons vanilla extract
1 ounce (1 square) unsweetened chocolate, coarsely chopped	¾ cup unsweetened cocoa powder	1⅓ cups flour
	4 eggs	½ cup chopped walnuts or pecans (optional)

1 Preheat the oven to 375 degrees. Grease and flour a 9-x-13-inch baking pan.

2 In a small, heavy saucepan, over very low heat, melt the butter and unsweetened chocolate, stirring occasionally until the mixture is smooth. Set the mixture aside to cool slightly.

3 In a large mixing bowl, combine the sugar and the cocoa powder; add the melted chocolate-butter mixture and stir well to combine. Add the eggs, one at a time, stirring with a wooden spoon or rubber spatula, only until well blended. Stir in the vanilla. Add the flour, in three batches, stirring after each addition, just until the ingredients are blended. If desired, stir in the walnuts. Do not overmix.

4 Scrape the batter into the prepared pan, spreading it evenly and to the edges. Bake in the top half of the preheated oven for 20 to 25 minutes, until the center is firm to the touch when lightly pressed. Remove the pan to a rack and let stand until completely cool before cutting into squares.

Per serving: *Calories 182 (From Fat 86); Fat 10g (Saturated 6g); Cholesterol 56mg; Sodium 13mg; Carbohydrate 24g (Dietary Fiber 1g); Protein 3g.*

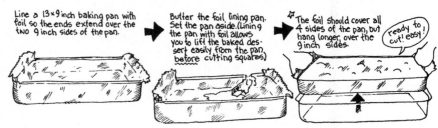

Figure 15-1:
Lining
a baking
pan with
aluminum
foil.

Let Them Eat Cake (Or Tart or Tiramisù)

In this section, we introduce you to several kinds of cakes: pudding cake, shortcake, chocolate cake, and that oh-so-trendy tiramisù. Each is quite different, but they all include valuable cooking techniques.

The fruit tart recipe is really a template for any kind of dessert tart you desire. After you master making the pastry, you're ready to try it with any kind of fruit filling. The same can be said of the recipe for chocolate cake. We experimented with many versions of chocolate cake and found this one to be the hands-down best. Tiramisù, which was originally a simple Italian dessert of ladyfingers or biscuits soaked in coffee and topped with sweetened mascarpone cheese, has metamorphosed, at least in the United States, into a bloated, cloying, chocolate cream cake. Here we give you the authentic Italian recipe. We think you'll appreciate it!

ᗏ Lemon Pudding Cake with Fresh Berries

This recipe produces a two-layered dessert, with a firm, cakelike top and a soft, custardy bottom. Lots of fresh lemon flavor and the complementary textures make this dessert a delight and a surprise. Serve it warm or cold, topped with fresh, sliced, slightly sweetened strawberries.

Tools: 2-quart, 11-x-7-inch ceramic or glass baking dish; medium and large mixing bowls; electric mixer; rubber spatula; grater; large baking pan, teakettle or pot

Preparation time: 20 to 25 minutes

Cooking time: About 50 minutes

Yield: 6 servings

Butter for greasing the baking dish

3 tablespoons butter, softened to room temperature

4 eggs, separated (see Chapter 10 for tips on separating eggs)

¾ cup sugar

¼ cup freshly squeezed lemon juice

3 tablespoons all-purpose flour

¼ teaspoon salt

1 cup milk

Grated zest of 1 lemon

1 pint strawberries, rinsed, hulled, and sliced

2 tablespoons confectioners' sugar, or to taste

1 Preheat the oven to 325 degrees. Heat a teakettle of water to boiling to help with Step 6 of this recipe.

2 Lightly butter a shallow, 2-quart, 11-x-7-inch ceramic or glass baking dish. Set aside.

3 In a large bowl with an electric mixer, beat the 3 tablespoons of butter and egg yolks until well combined. Gradually add ½ cup of the sugar, beating until well blended, about 3 to 4 minutes. Stop the mixer and scrape down the sides of the bowl. Add the lemon juice, flour, and salt; using a wooden spoon or rubber spatula, stir to combine. Gradually blend in the milk and lemon zest. Set aside.

4 In a clean, medium-sized, glass or metal mixing bowl, beat the egg whites until foamy. Gradually add the remaining ¼ cup granulated sugar, and continue beating until soft peaks form.

5 Gently fold the beaten egg whites into the lemon mixture (see Chapter 10 for illustrated instructions for folding egg whites into a batter).

6 Pour the batter into the buttered baking dish. Set the dish in a shallow baking pan filled with ½ inch of hot water. Bake, uncovered, for 45 to 55 minutes, or until the top is lightly browned and firm to the touch.

7 As the pudding cake bakes, toss the sliced strawberries with the confectioners' sugar. Set aside.

8 Spoon the pudding cake, warm or cooled, onto individual serving plates; top each serving with a heaping spoonful of the sweetened strawberries.

Tip: *Did you forget to bring the butter to room temperature? Just grate it on the largest holes of a box grater. It will soften quickly.*

Vary It! *Instead of strawberries, substitute 2 to 2½ cups of other soft fruits, like blackberries, sliced kiwi, mango, papaya, or blueberries. Or sprinkle 1 or 2 tablespoons of a sweet fruit liqueur, such as Cointreau, over the fruit. For a more elegant presentation, spoon the pudding cake into tall wine glasses and then top with the fruit.*

Per serving: *Calories 182 (From Fat 86); Fat 10g (Saturated 6g); Cholesterol 56mg; Sodium 13mg; Carbohydrate 24g (Dietary Fiber 1g); Protein 3g.*

☼ Free-Form Fresh Fruit Tart

This sweet French pastry combines the richness of an egg yolk with the sweetness of a little sugar to make a rich cookielike dough that's easy to roll out.

Rolling out and fitting pie pastry into a pie plate can be a tricky task for the novice cook (see illustrated instructions in Chapter 17). This recipe avoids that step; you simply place the pastry on a large baking sheet. Sliced nectarines and peaches, or a combination of both, are then arranged on the dough and coated with a fruit jam. The open-faced tart is baked until the fruit is tender and the pastry is crisp. We call for less sugar than traditionally used to bake a pie in order to allow the flavors of the fruit to shine through. But if you prefer something sweeter, simply increase the sugar until the fruit slices taste just right to you.

Tools: *Grater, wooden spoon, medium mixing bowl, pastry blender, nonstick baking sheet, rolling pin, knife, small saucepan, 2 mixing bowls, metal spatula, pastry brush*

Preparation time: *About 30 minutes (plus 30 minutes refrigeration for the pastry)*

Cooking time: *30 to 35 minutes*

Yield: *6 servings*

7 tablespoons butter, softened

¼ cup plus 1½ tablespoons (or more to taste) sugar

1 egg yolk

Grated zest of ½ lemon

¼ teaspoon vanilla extract

1 cup all-purpose flour

Pinch of salt

4 to 6 ripe, medium peaches or nectarines, or a combination of both

3 tablespoons apricot or peach jam

1 tablespoon Cointreau or other fruit liqueur (optional)

2 tablespoons finely chopped almonds

¼ cup blueberries or raspberries, rinsed, drained, and stemmed

Vanilla ice cream or whipped cream (see instructions for making whipped cream in Chapter 9), optional

1 To make the pastry, in a medium mixing bowl, use a wooden spoon to blend 6 tablespoons of the butter, ¼ cup of the sugar, egg yolk, lemon zest, and vanilla extract. Add the flour and salt. Use your fingers or a pastry blender to lightly work the butter-egg mixture into the dry ingredients until they form a smooth dough. Press the dough into a ball; enclose in plastic wrap and chill for about 30 minutes.

2 Preheat the oven to 425 degrees. Butter a large, flat baking sheet, preferably nonstick.

3 On a lightly floured counter, use a floured rolling pin to roll out the dough into a free-form rectangle, about 9 inches by 12 inches. Carefully drape the dough over the rolling pin and transfer it to the buttered baking sheet. Fold up and lightly crimp the edges of the dough all around to form a neat rim. Set aside.

4 Halve and pit the fruit; slice each half into 4 to 5 thin wedges. Starting at one corner, arrange the fruit slices side by side on the dough, overlapping and fitting them snugly, until the surface of the pastry is completely covered (see Figure 15-2 for an illustration of this technique).

5 In a small saucepan over low heat, combine the jam and the remaining 1 tablespoon butter, stirring. Cook a few minutes, stirring constantly, until the butter is melted and the jam is runny. Remove the saucepan from the heat and, if desired, stir in the Cointreau. Using a pastry brush, coat the fruit slices with the jam-butter mixture.

6 In another small mixing bowl, combine the remaining 1½ tablespoons of the sugar and almonds. Sprinkle the blueberries or raspberries randomly over the top of the fruit slices and then sprinkle the sugar-almond mixture evenly over the fruit. (Sprinkle with a little more sugar to taste, if desired.)

7 Bake the tart for about 25 to 30 minutes, or until the dough is crisp and golden and the fruit is tender.

8 Cut the tart into 6 pieces. Using a metal spatula, transfer each piece to an individual serving plate. Serve warm or cold, with a little whipped cream or vanilla ice cream if desired. If baked ahead, the tart can be reheated in a 375-degree oven for about 10 to 15 minutes.

Vary It! Try substituting ripe plum slices for some of the peaches and/or nectarines.

Warning: Overbeating doughs, pie crusts, and batters toughens them. Beating triggers the protein in flour and forms gluten — a toughening agent. The more you knead or beat the dough or batter, the tougher it becomes. (Kneading dough is necessary for properly developing the dough of yeast breads, but not for making delicate desserts.) Therefore, use a light touch when making any pastry dough, biscuits, cakes, and cookies. Beat until the liquid and dry ingredients are blended — no more.

Per serving: Calories 316 (From Fat 140); Fat 16g (Saturated 9g); Cholesterol 71mg; Sodium 31mg; Carbohydrate 42g (Dietary Fiber 2g); Protein 4g.

Figure 15-2:
Arrange fruit in an attractive manner over the bottom of the pan, slightly overlapping the fruit slices.

Free-Form Fresh Fruit Tart

On a lightly floured counter, use a floured rolling pin to roll out the dough into a free-form rectangle (about 9×12 inches).

Carefully drape dough over the rolling pin and transfer to a buttered baking sheet. Fold up and crimp edges of dough all around to form a neat rim.

Halve and pit the fruit. Slice each half into 4 or 5 thin wedges. Start at one corner, arrange slices side by side on dough, overlapping + fitting them snugly, until the surface is completely covered.

cozy...

🍑 Perfect Chocolate Cake

This cake may not be completely foolproof, but it is only slightly more involved than using a cake mix, and its homemade character sets it apart as something truly special. Although this cake is delicious enhanced with walnuts (for added texture) and a little cinnamon, you can leave out both, if you wish. The cake will still be good — so good, in fact, that it doesn't even need frosting!

The recipe calls for parchment paper, a thick, durable paper that is heatproof and used to line cake pans and the like. Parchment paper prevents cakes and cookies from sticking to metal pans.

Tools: *Chef's knife, mixing bowls, rubber spatula, electric mixer, double boiler or two pots, whisk, 9-inch cake pan, parchment paper, sieve, spatula*

Preparation time: *About 15 minutes*

Cooking time: *About 30 minutes*

Yield: *8 to 10 servings*

6 ounces bittersweet chocolate (Lindt, Valrhona, and Callebaut are the best brands), chopped into small pieces

½ cup butter (1 stick)

5 eggs, separated (see Chapter 10 for tips on separating eggs)

½ cup sugar

½ teaspoon cream of tartar

½ cup chopped walnuts (optional)

¼ cup flour, sifted

1 teaspoon ground cinnamon

2 tablespoons unsweetened cocoa powder or confectioners' sugar (optional)

1 Preheat the oven to 350 degrees. Line the bottom of a 9-inch cake pan with a circular piece of greased parchment paper. Then grease the sides of the pan.

2 To make a double boiler, fill one pot halfway with water and bring to a boil. Place a second pot on top of the first (they should fit snugly). Place the chocolate and the butter in the top pot and turn off the heat, leaving the pots on the stove. Stir to blend the chocolate and butter together.

3 Meanwhile, using an electric mixer, beat the egg whites, 1 teaspoon of the sugar, and the cream of tartar until nearly stiff. Slowly add the remaining sugar while mixing. Set aside.

4 Beat the egg yolks in a medium bowl. Remove the chocolate mixture from the stove and then whisk the egg yolks into the chocolate. Add the walnuts (if desired), the sifted flour, and the cinnamon and blend well.

5 Fold the egg white mixture into the chocolate. Pour the mixture into the cake pan. Smooth the top with a spatula.

6 Bake for 25 minutes, or until a knife or toothpick inserted into the middle comes out clean. Let the cake cool in its pan.

7 When the cake is cool enough to handle, place a serving plate over the cake pan and then invert them both so the plate is on the bottom. Tap gently to unmold the cake. Using a wide spatula and your hand, reverse the cake again so the top side is up.

8 If desired, decorate the cake with the cocoa powder or confectioners' sugar. Shake either topping through a sieve, dusting the surface of the cake evenly.

Tip: Most kinds of nuts quickly go stale or rancid if left exposed to air at room temperature. To prevent this problem, wrap them well in foil or plastic wrap (or place in a tightly sealed container or a resealable plastic bag) and store them in the freezer. (You don't need to defrost them before using.)

Per serving: *Calories 254 (From Fat 170); Fat 19g (Saturated 10g); Cholesterol 131mg; Sodium 33mg; Carbohydrate 22g (Dietary Fiber 1g); Protein 5g. based on 10 servings.*

☕ *Tiramisù*

This coffee-flavored confection is arguably one of the top three most beloved desserts in U.S. restaurants. Over the years what originally was a simple little treat has been altered, so that the one often served in the United States is more like a cream-drenched, coffee-flavored chocolate cake.

Tiramisù comes from Italy where, as the story goes, older ladies used to play cards in the afternoon, and, after their card games were finished, they made a sweet treat called tiramisù, which means "pick me up." They would take out some biscuits or cookies, drench them with espresso, and then slather some mascarpone cheese on top. And tiramisù was born.

Our recipe, which comes from our friend Bill Yosses, the wizard pastry chef at Citarella in New York City, calls for a combination of sweetened whipped cream, sour cream, and mascarpone cheese. (If you can't find mascarpone, use softened cream cheese or increase the amount of whipped cream and sour cream.) The hallmark of a good tiramisù is a strong coffee flavor. You don't need to make espresso; instant coffee does the trick just fine.

Tools: *Metal spatula, fine sieve, rubber spatula, whisk or electric mixer, wooden spoon, 10-inch circular plate or 9-x-9-inch serving dish, 2 mixing bowls*

Preparation time: *About 20 minutes, plus 3 hours refrigeration*

Yield: *About 8 servings*

3 heaping tablespoons instant coffee crystals or granules	*¼ cup confectioners' sugar*
3 tablespoons granulated sugar	*2 teaspoons vanilla extract*
1 cup water	*⅓ cup mascarpone cheese*
2 packages (6 ounces each) ladyfingers	*2 heaping tablespoons sour cream*
1 pint heavy cream, well chilled	*1 tablespoon unsweetened cocoa powder*

1 In a small bowl combine the instant coffee and granulated sugar. Bring the water to a boil and pour it over the coffee mixture, stirring. Set aside and let cool to room temperature.

2 Place about half of the ladyfingers on the bottom of a 9- or 10-inch square or round serving dish.

3 Using a tablespoon, drizzle half of the coffee mixture evenly over the ladyfingers in the serving dish. Set aside.

4 In a bowl, combine the cream, confectioners' sugar, and vanilla. With a whisk or an electric mixer, whip the mixture until it forms soft peaks. Refrigerate for at least 1 hour.

5 In another bowl, combine the mascarpone and sour cream. Using a wooden spoon, stir the mixture until smooth.

6 Fold half of the whipped cream mixture into the cheese and cream mixture until well blended. Then fold in the rest, being sure not to overmix.

7 Using a metal spatula or spoon, spread half of the mixture over the ladyfingers, and place another layer of ladyfingers, curved side down, over it. Drizzle these ladyfingers with the remaining coffee and cover them with the other half of the cream mixture. Using a sieve, sprinkle the cocoa powder evenly over the top. Refrigerate for 2 hours before cutting into pieces to serve.

Tip: Ladyfingers vary in width and length from brand to brand. Therefore, the number of cookies to complete a layer in a 9-x-9-inch pan will also vary. In general, two 6-ounce packages will complete two layers.

Per serving: Calories 450 (From Fat 281); Fat 31g (Saturated 18g); Cholesterol 251mg; Sodium 93mg; Carbohydrate 37g (Dietary Fiber 1g); Protein 7g.

Baking a better cake

Baking cakes is somewhat of an art and the more experience you have, the more comfortable you will become with the process. To help speed up your learning curve, here are a few cake-baking tips to start you out right:

✔ **Take steps to prevent the bulge that cakes sometimes develop on the top from uneven cooking.** Use "cake strips," which are essentially strips of aluminum-coated cloth that you wet and place around the outside of the cake pan (they come with pins to secure them in place). You can also use strips of old denim to accomplish the same thing. The wet strips slow the heat transfer around the perimeter, thus preventing the bulging.

✔ **Measure ingredients correctly.** Baking is the most precise and scientific part of cooking. Doughs must have the right proportion of liquids to solids to perform correctly when baked; and cakes must have the right flour-liquid-sugar-leavening ratio. Always measure dry and wet ingredients precisely. Level off the tops of dry measuring cups with the flat edge of a knife. Also do this when using measuring spoons to measure dry ingredients like baking powder, flour, or

baking soda. Check out Chapter 2 to read more about the differences between dry and liquid measuring cups.

✔ **Try this fuss-free way to decorate a layer cake without using frosting.** Sprinkle it with a layer of confectioners' sugar. Place the sugar in a fine mesh sieve, hold it over the top of the cake, and tap the strainer lightly with your hand, distributing the sugar evenly over the cake. You can also place a decorative (self-made or store-bought) stencil on the cake, perhaps one with a heart or flower pattern. Sprinkle the sugar over the stencil and then remove it to reveal the design. Powdered semisweet cocoa also works nicely.

✔ **Always check the temperature of your oven when baking.** If a cake looks soupy when the timer has gone off, your oven may not be working correctly. Buy an oven thermometer (the mercury type is best) to determine whether it's accurate; if it's not, adjust the temperature dial as necessary each time you bake. Or better yet, call your range serviceperson or gas company to have your oven properly calibrated.

Part IV
Now You're Cooking! Real Menus for Real Life

The 5th Wave   By Rich Tennant

Eat your dinner, young man! That's your father's special recipe for broccoli-bean casserole made in the slow cooker.

Not slow enough...

In this part . . .

*J*ust because you can cook and like to cook doesn't always mean you have the time, space, or energy to cook the most elaborate of meals. We all have to contend with limited time, ringing phones, leaking washing machines, traumatized tots, and begging dogs. What's an aspiring home cook to do?

In this part, we address the critical element of time. Recipes in this part are designed for real-life situations: when you're trying to plan what to feed your family for the coming week or when you have guests coming in an hour and need to put together a meal, for example. We also offer some tips for becoming a savvy shopper and plan-ahead chef, so that you can make low-cost meals taste like top-of-the-line fare, and so that you can make one good cooking session last for several meals. Leftovers have never tasted so delicious!

Chapter 16

Champagne Dishes on a Beer Budget

In This Chapter

▶ Making filling, satisfying main dishes on the cheap

▶ Using vegetables, beans, and greens in thrifty side dishes

To understand how much money the average shopper wastes every week, just stand around any supermarket checkout counter. Instead of flipping through the intellectual journals on sale ("Liz to Marry an Alien; Honeymoon on Pluto"), take an inventory of customers' shopping carts. Even discounting the usual fatty snack food, you'll find that the average cart is loaded with high-priced (for what you get) frozen dinners, sugared-up prepared sauces, prebuttered bread, precut vegetables, frozen pizzas, boxed croutons (stale bread, only $3.99 a box!), and more.

In an experiment done several years ago, a Tennessee newspaper gave $10 to noted chef and cookbook author Jacques Pépin and asked him to prepare a dinner for four. Not only did he pull it off, but he served beef and came back with 35 cents in change. The meal consisted of salad, flank steak in red wine sauce, sautéed cabbage, mashed potatoes, and poached pears with orange sauce — and yes, he even bought a bottle of wine.

Of course, preparing that meal takes great skill. But by rethinking your shopping habits and getting acquainted with less common cuts of meat, poultry, and fish — and with beans, legumes, and seasonal fresh vegetables — you can approximate this economic approach and eat better (and healthier!), too.

Frugality is no reason to forgo elegance, as the recipes in this chapter demonstrate.

Big Dishes for Small Bucks

Whether you're using inexpensive cuts of beef, stretching chicken with heaps of veggies and rice, or taking advantage of a weekly special at the supermarket, a little attention to detail and presentation can make any meal fit for a, well, family. Just because your meal didn't cost a fortune doesn't mean you should eat off paper plates or gulp it all down without tasting it. Economical meals can be delicious, expertly spiced, and even more nutritious than meals that cost four times more.

A few key concepts can help you to eat more economically all the time:

- ✔ Old food isn't a bargain. If your store has expired food on sale or that bargain meat just doesn't look very good, skip it.

- ✔ Rice, pasta, cornmeal, and other grains typically cost far less than meat. Serve small amounts of meat with pasta, rice, or polenta (hot cooked cornmeal) and fill up for less.

- ✔ Grow your own food. An abundance of produce in the backyard costs very little compared to an abundance of produce from the supermarket. Plus, the veggies are fresher and will last longer on the vine or in the ground than in your crisper, so you can pick your dinner just before you eat it.

- ✔ Soups and stews make meat, veggies, and grains all stretch far beyond the number of people they would feed if they weren't bobbing about in a steamy, savory broth.

- ✔ And don't forget salads! A big bowl of salad with a little meat (or cheese or egg) for flavor costs a lot less than a big plate of meat with a little salad on the side. Plus, you'll be more likely to get your requisite five servings of daily vegetables.

All the main dish recipes in this section also make delicious leftovers — a blessing for busy cooks.

Crowd-pleasing chili

Few words spark gastronomic brouhaha like chili, whether it's rich Texas-style chili con carne, fiery Arizona-style chili, or one of the myriad variations in between. Maybe it's not a glamorous meal, but chili is a real crowd pleaser, and you'd be surprised how festive you can make it look with some thought to presentation. Plus, you can feed your whole football team for about ten bucks.

Chili probably originated in Texas more than 100 years ago, in the days of cowboys. Chili made sense for these hard-riding buckaroos because it was quick, filled with protein, and cheap — beef was not exactly scarce for the herders. The degree of fire in the form of hot peppers became a matter of cowboy competition.

In New Mexico, another state famous for chili, it was made with lamb or mutton rather than beef, and red beans were popular. In Cincinnati, chili has a Greek-influenced personality, with the addition of cinnamon for the famous Cincinnati chili often served over spaghetti. And of course, vegetarian chili is full of juicy vegetables and beans but no meat.

In fact, you can make endless variations on chili. Many champion chilis in competitions around the United States combine beef and pork, one for flavor and the other for texture, as in the following recipe. If you like, you can add lamb, too. Vegetarians can increase the amount of vegetables and skip the meat altogether or add chopped mushrooms or *tempeh,* a texturized soy product that mimics the texture of meat.

Stoke the chili as much as you want with extra red pepper flakes and chili powder. Be careful, though, because pepper flakes intensify as they cook.

Southwestern Chili

This classic Southwestern chili recipe can easily be doubled or even tripled to serve 8 or 12 people. If you have a plastic squeeze bottle (available in restaurant supply stores), you can squirt flavored sour cream in the shape of Texas or Cleveland. You can really get carried away with this idea.

Leave out the meat for a vegetarian version or vary the kinds of meat you use. Ground turkey lowers the fat content somewhat.

Tools: *Chef's knife, deep pot or Dutch oven, wooden spoon*

Preparation time: *About 25 minutes*

Cooking time: *About 40 minutes*

Yield: *4 servings*

1 tablespoon olive oil	*¾ cup homemade or canned beef stock*
1 large yellow onion, finely chopped	*½ cup red wine or water*
1 small green bell pepper, seeded, cored, and finely chopped	*2 teaspoons tomato paste*
	¼ teaspoon red pepper flakes, or to taste
2 large cloves garlic, finely chopped	*Salt and black pepper*
½ pound lean ground beef	*1 can (15 ounces) red kidney beans, drained and rinsed*
½ pound lean ground pork	
1 tablespoon chili powder, or to taste	*4 cups cooked long-grain rice (optional)*
1 teaspoon ground cumin	*Sour cream (optional)*
½ teaspoon ground coriander	*Chopped cilantro or parsley (optional)*
2 cups ripe, diced tomatoes, or 1 can (14½ ounces) diced tomatoes	

1 Heat the oil in a large, deep pot or Dutch oven. Add the onion, green pepper, and garlic and cook for 2 to 3 minutes over medium heat, stirring occasionally.

2 Add the ground beef and pork and cook for another 3 minutes or until browned, stirring to break up any lumps. Add the chili powder, cumin, and coriander. Stir well.

3 Stir in the tomatoes, beef stock, wine (or water), tomato paste, red pepper flakes, and salt and pepper to taste. Bring to a boil, reduce heat to a simmer, and then cook for 25 to 30 minutes, stirring often. Add the kidney beans and cook 5 to 10 minutes more. If desired, serve over rice (see Chapter 4) and garnish with sour cream and cilantro or parsley.

Tip: *If the chili gets too dry while cooking, add a little more beef stock or water or even some liquid from the canned kidney beans.*

Go-With: *Chili calls for colorful side dishes like the Avocado and Tomato Salad in Chapter 17 or the Bell Pepper-Rice Salad in Chapter 12.*

Per serving: *Calories 317 (From Fat 103); Fat 12g (Saturated 3g); Cholesterol 71mg; Sodium 358mg; Carbohydrate 23g (Dietary Fiber 7g); Protein 31g.*

Stir-fry for pennies

Stir-fry is great nutrition for the budget-conscious. Because of all the vegetables and the rich oil, you can stretch a little bit of meat for a lot of people. You don't need a wok to make stir-fry. Just be sure that the pan is hot, the oil is hot, and you cook the vegetables just long enough to be bright and crisp. You can whip up a stir-fry whenever you like, using beef, pork, chicken, fish, or whatever you have on hand, plus whatever fresh vegetables are waiting in your refrigerator. A little oil, a little sizzle, some spices, and you've got dinner. Serve stir-fry alone or over hot cooked rice or thin Chinese noodles (available in the Asian food section of your grocery store).

Chicken Stir-Fry with Peanuts

This inexpensive, quick-cooking stir-fry needs even less chicken than a traditional chicken stir-fry that contains just chicken and vegetables, because the peanuts offer a substantial texture, a dose of protein, and an interesting taste. The recipe calls for bok choy, an Asian green leafy vegetable commonly available in most grocery stores

Tools: *Chef's knife, large sauté pan or wok, tongs, small bowl, whisk*

Preparation time: *About 25 minutes*

Cooking time: *About 20 minutes*

Yield: *8 servings*

3 tablespoons canola or peanut oil (or some of both)

1 pound boneless chicken breasts, cut into strips, or chicken tenders

1 large yellow onion, finely chopped

1 cup chopped bok choy

1½ cups broccoli, chopped (stems and florets)

1 cup zucchini, cut into ½-inch cubes

1 cup sliced white mushrooms

2 large cloves garlic, finely minced

1 bell pepper, any color, cored, seeded, and cut into 1-inch strips

2 ribs celery, trimmed and sliced

1 carrot, scraped, ends removed, and sliced

1 can (4 ounces) water chestnuts

½ cup shelled peanuts

¼ cup soy sauce

¼ cup water

1 teaspoon cornstarch

1 teaspoon sugar

¼ teaspoon hot pepper flakes

1 Heat the oil in a large sauté pan or wok. When the oil is very hot, add the chicken and cook over medium-high heat, about 7 to 10 minutes, or until browned all over, turning frequently with tongs.

2 Remove the chicken from the pan and drain on paper towels. Return the pan to the heat. Add the onion, bok choy, broccoli, zucchini, mushrooms, garlic, bell peppers, celery, carrots, water chestnuts, and peanuts, if desired. Sauté quickly until the onions are soft and the broccoli is bright green, about 7 minutes.

3 In a small bowl, whisk together the soy sauce, water, cornstarch, sugar, and hot pepper flakes. Add the chicken back to the stir-fry ingredients and then pour the soy sauce mixture over the stir-fry and toss to coat, sautéing for an additional 3 minutes. Serve immediately, alone or over hot cooked rice (see Chapter 4).

Vary It! *Substitute any vegetables you like or have on hand for this stir-fry. Also try it with steak or shrimp instead of chicken.*

Vary It! *For an added dose of flavor, marinate the raw chicken strips in soy sauce for an hour or two before cooking. Just put the chicken and about ¼ cup soy sauce in a sealed plastic bag and let it sit in a bowl in the refrigerator until you're ready to start cooking.*

Per serving: *Calories 179 (From Fat 91); Fat 10g (Saturated 1g); Cholesterol 31mg; Sodium 514mg; Carbohydrate 8g (Dietary Fiber 3g); Protein 14g.*

Super Sidekicks

Inviting side dishes are another great way to dress up your meals. Following are some inexpensive but tasty recipes.

Root vegetables

Root vegetables such as potatoes, carrots, turnips, and beets are hearty, filling, super-nutritious, and — you guessed it — cheap! Root vegetables make great side dishes, including the traditional (see the recipe for Homemade Mashed Potatoes in Chapter 4) and the unusual (raw julienned kohlrabi sticks, anyone?). Root vegetables stretch a soup, stew, or stir-fry, and they can also be good raw with a dip (try mixing equal parts nonfat plain yogurt and sour cream with some minced garlic and dill, or just dip them in ranch dressing). Potatoes can add creamy or thick texture to many dishes, and potato side dishes alone number in the hundreds. Try potatoes scalloped, twice baked, layered with cheese, or baked on the grill. If you're partial to sweet potatoes, consider using them to make fries, pie, or a purée . . . we could go on and on.

Deeply colored orange root vegetables are particularly high in vitamins. Here's an easy and delicious root vegetable side dish to try.

☺ Carrots in Cumin Butter

Cumin, a spice most often associated with Middle Eastern and Indian cooking, has an affinity for sweet carrots, as this recipe demonstrates. These exotic-tasting carrots are best paired with a mild-flavored dish, such as Roasted Chicken (see Chapter 7) or Poached Salmon Steaks with Béarnaise Sauce (see Chapter 4).

Tools: *Chef's knife, medium saucepan*

Preparation time: *About 10 minutes*

Cooking time: *About 15 minutes*

Yield: *4 servings*

1 pound carrots, peeled and cut in 1-inch pieces

Salt

2 tablespoons butter

¼ teaspoon ground cumin

2 tablespoons chopped cilantro or parsley

1 Put the carrots in a saucepan and add cold salted water to cover. Bring to a boil and simmer until the carrots are tender, about 15 minutes.

2 Drain the carrots and return them to the saucepan. Add the butter, cumin, and cilantro or parsley and toss well. Serve immediately.

Per serving: *Calories 102 (From Fat 51); Fat 6g (Saturated 4g); Cholesterol 15mg; Sodium 205mg; Carbohydrate 12g (Dietary Fiber 3g); Protein 2g.*

Dried beans

We find it rather amazing that Americans don't cook more with dried beans, which are so inexpensive, healthful, and delicious. You can use dried beans in a side dish, as in the following recipe, or as part of a main course. Whether or not you're cooking on a tight budget, becoming familiar with all kinds of legumes, each of which has a special texture and flavor, is definitely worthwhile. Table 16-1 lists several common types of dried beans.

Table 16-1	Beans
Bean	**Description**
Black beans	Often used in South American and Caribbean dishes and mixed with rice and spices. Sweetish flavor.
Black-eyed peas	Traditional ingredient in the cooking of the American South — black-eyed peas and collard greens, black-eyed peas with ham. Earthy.
Borlotto beans	Large, speckled beans. Mostly puréed and turned into creamy dips.
Boston beans	See "White beans, small (navy and pea)."
Chickpeas	Large, semifirm beans sold dried and canned. Used in casseroles, soups, and stews. Puréed and seasoned in Middle Eastern cuisine. Also known as garbanzo beans.
Kidney beans/ red beans	The traditional beans used in chili and other earthy casserole dishes and soups. A white kidney bean, called *cannellini,* is used in many northern Italian dishes. A staple in Mexican cooking as well. Faintly sweet.
Lentils	A tiny legume. Boiled with vegetables and other seasonings for side dishes, soups, and stews. No soaking is required before cooking.
Lima beans	Eaten as a side dish with mild seasonings. Also good in casseroles, especially with ham. Sweet flavor.
Pinto beans	The base of Mexican refried beans. Frequently used in highly spiced dishes. Earthy, mild flavor.
Split peas	Often used in soups, especially with ham. Sweet. Like lentils, no soaking is required.
White beans, large	Used in stews and casseroles. Often simmered with ham bones or other flavorful stocks. Neutral flavor.
White beans, small (navy and pea)	Foundation of Boston baked beans and the French *cassoulet.* Neutral flavor.

Before cooking dried beans, sort and rinse them. Look over the beans carefully, picking out and discarding any that are withered. Rinse them thoroughly in cold water until the water runs clear, removing any beans or other substances that float to the surface.

White Beans with Tomatoes and Thyme

White beans are among the most likable of dried beans, appealing to almost everyone, from kids to grown-ups. This side dish relies on bacon, onions, garlic, tomatoes, and herbs to add panache to this mild and inoffensive legume.

Tools: *Chef's knife, large pot, large skillet or sauté pan, colander or strainer, wooden spoon*

Preparation time: *About 20 minutes, plus time to soak the beans*

Cooking time: *About 50 minutes*

Yield: *4 servings*

1 cup dried white beans (such as Great Northern or navy beans), rinsed

2 whole cloves

2 medium yellow onions

1 quart water

3 slices bacon

1 large carrot, peeled and cut in half lengthwise

1 bay leaf

Salt and pepper

2 teaspoons butter or oil

1 large clove garlic, minced

1 teaspoon fresh chopped thyme, or ½ teaspoon dried thyme

1 can (14½ ounces) diced tomatoes, drained

2 tablespoons chopped parsley

1 Place the beans in a large pot and add cold water to cover by about 1 inch. Soak overnight or boil for 2 minutes and then let stand for 1 hour. (See the Tip at the end of this recipe.)

2 Stick the cloves into 1 onion and chop the other onion finely.

3 Drain the beans and return them to the pot. Add the 1 quart water, the onion stuck with cloves, the bacon, carrot, bay leaf, and salt and pepper to taste. Cover the pot and bring it to a boil over high heat. Reduce the heat to medium-low, and simmer, partially covered, for 45 minutes to 1 hour, or until the beans are tender. (Different varieties require different cooking times.)

4 Remove the bacon strips and chop them into small pieces.

5 Heat the butter or oil in a large skillet or sauté pan over medium heat and sauté the chopped bacon until golden brown, stirring. Add the chopped onion, garlic, and thyme and cook for about 2 to 3 minutes, or until the onions wilt. Add the tomatoes and cook for 2 to 3 minutes, stirring frequently. Remove from the heat.

6 Remove and discard the carrot, onion with cloves, and bay leaf from the pot of beans. Carefully scoop out and reserve half of the bean liquid and drain the beans. Add the beans to the tomato mixture and stir gently. If the mixture seems dry, add a little of the reserved liquid. Adjust seasoning with salt and pepper. Serve the beans hot, sprinkled with the parsley.

Tip: *You soak most dried beans before cooking to shorten the cooking time, which is important if you cook them with other ingredients. If you don't have time to soak the beans overnight, use this shortcut: Place the beans in a deep pot covered with lots of water. Bring to a boil and cook for 2 minutes. Remove the pot from the heat, cover, and let stand for 1 hour. Or, for an even quicker version, substitute one 14-ounce or 16-ounce can of white beans, drained and rinsed, for the dried beans.*

Per serving: Calories 194 (From Fat 43); Fat 5g (Saturated 2g); Cholesterol 9mg; Sodium 315mg; Carbohydrate 28g (Dietary Fiber 9g); Protein 12g.

☺ *Lentils with Balsamic Vinegar*

The sweet edge of the balsamic vinegar performs magic on the nutty flavored lentils in this recipe. Unlike many other dried beans, lentils don't require soaking and boil tender in 20 to 25 minutes.

Tools: *Chef's knife, large pot or saucepan, large sauté pan*

Preparation time: *About 20 minutes*

Cooking time: *About 30 minutes*

Yield: *4 servings*

1½ cups lentils, rinsed	*2 sprigs fresh thyme, or ½ teaspoon dried thyme*	*1 large clove garlic, finely chopped*
1 quart water	*1 tablespoon butter*	*1 tablespoon balsamic (or red wine) vinegar*
Salt	*1 tablespoon olive oil*	*Pepper*
2 cloves	*1 large carrot, peeled and finely diced*	
2 small yellow onions		
1 bay leaf		

1 Put the lentils in a large pot or saucepan. Add the water and salt to taste. Cover and bring to a boil over high heat. Stick the cloves into 1 onion and chop the other onion finely. Add the onion with cloves to the saucepan, along with the bay leaf and thyme. Reduce the heat, and simmer, partially covered, for about 20 minutes or until the lentils are tender.

2 Before draining the lentils, carefully scoop out and reserve ½ cup of the cooking liquid. Drain the lentils. Remove and discard the onion with cloves, bay leaf, and thyme sprigs.

3 Heat the butter and olive oil in a large sauté pan or skillet over medium-high heat. Add the carrot, chopped onion, and garlic. Cook, stirring often, until the onion wilts, about 3 to 4 minutes. (Do not brown the garlic.) Add the vinegar and the reserved ½ cup cooking liquid. Cover, reduce the heat, and simmer for about 5 minutes, or until the vegetables are tender.

4 Stir the lentils into the vegetable mixture, cover, and cook over medium heat for about 2 minutes more, just to blend the flavors. Season with salt and pepper to taste and serve.

Per serving: Calories 309 (From Fat 63); Fat 7g (Saturated 2g); Cholesterol 8mg; Sodium 161mg; Carbohydrate 45g (Dietary Fiber 17g); Protein 19g.

Seasonal vegetables

Root vegetables aren't the only vegetables that can help fill out a budget-conscious meal. Using seasonal produce in your cooking is not only economical but also follows the venerable tradition of European cooking: People cook what they grow or what they can buy in the local market that was grown nearby and picked that morning. The following recipe, featuring highly nutritious and economical greens (in many places, greens are available all year), gets you started. Choose the greens that look the freshest.

Southern Greens

This variation on traditional Southern greens uses bacon instead of salt pork, and lemon wedges instead of apple cider vinegar, but the soul-food spirit is the same. For a real Southern meal, serve this dish with fried chicken (see Chapter 19), grits (you can buy instant grits in the grocery store), and frozen black-eyed peas — simply cook them in the microwave according to package directions.

Tools: *Chef's knife, sauté pan with lid, wooden spoon*

Preparation time: *About 15 minutes*

Cooking time: *About 20 minutes*

Yield: *6 servings*

2 pounds collard greens, kale, turnip greens, or mustard greens, trimmed of tough stalks	*4 slices bacon, diced* *1 medium yellow onion, finely chopped* *3 large cloves garlic, minced*	*1 cup water* *1 bay leaf* *Salt and pepper* *6 lemon wedges*

1 Wash the greens thoroughly in a sink full of cold water or a large pot. Do not dry. Strip the leaves from the tough center ribs (discarding the ribs) and cut out any blemished areas.

2 In a sauté pan, cook the bacon over medium heat for about 4 to 5 minutes. Add the onion and cook until the bacon is lightly browned. Add the garlic, greens leaves, water, bay leaf, and the salt and pepper to taste. Cover, reduce the heat to low, and cook for 15 minutes, or until tender, stirring occasionally. Discard the bay leaf and serve with lemon wedges.

Per serving: *Calories 80 (From Fat 25); Fat 3g (Saturated 1g); Cholesterol 4mg; Sodium 182mg; Carbohydrate 11g (Dietary Fiber 5g); Protein 5g.*

Chapter 17

Honey, I'm Bringing the Boss Home for Dinner . . .

In This Chapter

▶ Planning your menu when you have all day

▶ Assembling a meal when guests are coming in one hour

▶ Getting dinner on the table in 30 minutes

Recipes in This Chapter

▶ Salmon Marinated in Ginger and Cilantro

▶ Osso Buco

↻ Braised Cabbage with Apples and Caraway

↻ Basic Pastry Crust

↻ Apple Pie

↻ Avocado and Tomato Salad

▶ Broiled Skirt Steak, Cajun Style

↻ Indian Rice with Ginger, Walnuts, and Raisins

↻ Warm Blueberry Sauce

↻ Fresh Tomato Quesadillas

↻ Hummus Dip

▶ Spicy Shrimp Kebabs

↻ Guacamole

↻ Sun-Dried Tomato Spread

▶ Smoked Chicken Slices with Coriander Sauce

▶ Snapper Fillets with Tomatoes

*I*f you haven't received the actual phone call, you've probably seen the scenario enacted on television: "Honey, I'm bringing the boss home for dinner." Yikes! Sometimes, you need to throw together a respectable dinner in just a few minutes. Sometimes you have all day, or even a few days to prepare. But the simple fact is that if you're cooking for company, no matter how much time you have, you want everything to turn out just right. This is no time to char the pot roast or boil the vegetables into oblivion. This is a time for careful planning.

If you're lucky enough to have all day Saturday to prepare for a dinner party, indulge in it. We give you some great ideas for that luxury. But if you have only one hour — or less — the foods you prepare, by necessity, are totally different. That doesn't mean they're any less delicious. But, for example, instead of making a braised shoulder of pork for your spouse's boss that takes three hours to cook, you might broil skewers of shrimp, which take only about 10 minutes.

Regardless of how much time you have, the important thing is to use it well. With the right scheduling strategies and planning, you can whip up a dinner party and still be composed when your guests arrive. The trick is in getting the techniques down and then planning your menus accordingly. Cooking as the timer ticks isn't so bad, especially when you're prepared with a few quick and easy yet elegantly impressive meals in your repertoire. Ready? Set? Go!

If You Have All Day

If you have all day, relax. Enjoy yourself. You may want to try something different. But don't lose track of the clock. The danger with having plenty of time on your hands is forgetting that you still have a schedule and a deadline (the guests are going to show up eventually) and going overboard on what you think you can prepare in a day. Go ahead and run errands while the main dish roasts, but don't forget to be back in time to adjust that oven temperature or stir that side dish. And make a list before you start so that you don't find yourself at the end of a day's happy cooking without a crucial part of your menu because you forgot all about it. If you plan the day, at least roughly, before you get started, you'll be sure to have a leisurely day in the kitchen, and everything you want to serve will be ready by dinnertime.

Classy hors d'oeuvres

One nice menu planning option, if you have time, is to start your meal with an appetizer that involves marinating, such as the spectacular salmon infused with ginger and coriander in the following recipe. Appetizers add an air of elegance and class to any dinner, and a marinated appetizer implies that you've been preparing this special dish for hours (even if the actual work time isn't very long).

Here are a few other ideas for hors d'oeuvres:

- Bell Pepper Rice Salad (see Chapter 12)
- French Onion Soup (see Chapter 11)
- Warm Artichoke-Spinach Dip (see Chapter 21)
- Grilled Vegetable Platter with Fresh Pesto (see Chapter 12)
- Spicy Chicken Wings (see Chapter 20)

Salmon Marinated in Ginger and Cilantro

This dish works well for putting everything together in the early afternoon and ensuring that it will be ready by dinnertime. It has a tangy, herbaceous, pungent quality that will wake up the palate, preparing it for the dinner to follow. In some cases throughout this book, we give a dried substitute for a fresh herb. However, substitutions don't work with a few ingredients, including the fresh gingerroot in this recipe. You can't substitute powdered ginger for fresh gingerroot, or dried cilantro for fresh. The fresh ingredient tastes entirely different from the dried one. Dried parsley is another herb that has its limitations. Always use fresh, chopped parsley when sprinkling it on a dish as a garnish.

Remember, marinating fish can be tricky business. The acid in the marinade — which comes from the lime and vinegar — actually "cooks" the fish. Be sure to leave the fish in the marinade exactly as long as the recipe indicates (4 to 5 hours, in this case). Too long and the fish won't taste good. Not long enough, and the fish will still be raw. This marinade doesn't have the same effect on dense cuts of meat or poultry, so don't try "cooking" chicken this way!

Tools: *Chef's knife, grater, large nonreactive bowl (glass, plastic, or ceramic, but not metal), tweezers for bone removal, if necessary*

Preparation time: *About 25 minutes*

Marinating time: *4 to 5 hours*

Yield: *8 appetizer servings*

2 pounds skinless salmon fillets (have your fishmonger remove the skin and bones)

½ cup fresh lime juice

1 large yellow onion, thinly sliced

3 tablespoons white wine vinegar

3 tablespoons olive oil

2 tablespoons chopped fresh cilantro

1 tablespoon grated fresh gingerroot

¼ teaspoon red pepper flakes

Salt and black pepper

Lettuce for garnish

1 Using a pair of tweezers or your fingers, remove any small bones (called pin bones) in the salmon fillets.

2 Slice the salmon thinly (¼ inch or less) widthwise, leaving strips about 2 inches long. Place the strips in a large bowl.

3 Add the lime juice, onion, vinegar, oil, cilantro, gingerroot, red pepper flakes, and salt and pepper to taste. Stir gently and cover with plastic wrap. Refrigerate for 4 to 5 hours. Taste for seasoning. (You may need more salt; if so, blend it in thoroughly.)

4 Line small serving plates with lettuce of your choice and place a serving of salmon over the lettuce. Discard the onion-marinade mix.

Per serving: *Calories 174 (From Fat 76); Fat 9g (Saturated 1g); Cholesterol 62mg; Sodium 68mg; Carbohydrate 0g (Dietary Fiber 0g); Protein 23g.*

Elegant entrees

After you've whetted everyone's appetite with your delicious, home-cooked hors d'oeuvres, you can impress them even further with the following elegant entree, the Osso Buco. The entree in this section takes longer to cook but is oh-so-worth the wait!

Try these other time-consuming-and-worth-it main dishes when you have the luxury of a day for cooking:

✔ Poached Salmon Steaks with Béarnaise Sauce (see Chapter 4)

✔ Old-Fashioned Beef Stew (see Chapter 6)

✔ Roasted Chicken (see Chapter 7)

✔ Pot Roast with Vegetables (see Chapter 6)

✔ Glazed Leg of Lamb with Pan Gravy and Red Currant Glaze (see Chapter 7)

✔ Roasted Fillet of Beef (see Chapter 7)

✔ Roast Loin of Pork (see Chapter 7)

✔ Family Lasagna (see Chapter 13)

✔ Chicken and Biscuit Pot Pie (see Chapter 14)

✔ Shepherd's Pie (see Chapter 14)

Osso Buco

This glorious dish of braised veal shank with garlic, tomato, and other ingredients will surprise and delight your guests. The meat on the shank is exceptionally succulent, and the sauce that simmers in the meat juices is packed with herbal flavors and lemon.

Many cooks don't know it, but one traditional ingredient in Osso Buco is anchovies. Their intense saltiness, when added in moderation, adds a special depth to the flavor of Osso Buco. If you're one of those people who pick anchovies off pizza, simply omit them from the recipe (or try it anyway — you probably won't even taste them, except to notice the deliciously enhanced flavor of this dish!).

Ideally, Osso Buco should be made a day or two in advance, chilled, and then reheated — the flavors meld and intensify that way. Because you have all day to make this meal, you can prepare it at midday, cool it, and then reheat it for the dinner party.

Tools: *Chef's knife, grater, Dutch oven (cast iron is best)*

Preparation time: *About 40 minutes*

Cooking time: *1 hour and 30 minutes*

Yield: *4 servings*

4 meaty slices of veal shanks cut across the bones (each about 2 inches thick), about 3½ pounds total

Salt and pepper

½ cup all-purpose flour for dredging

2 tablespoons olive oil

1 large yellow onion, finely chopped

2 to 3 large carrots, peeled and chopped

1 stalk celery, chopped

3 large cloves garlic, finely chopped

4 canned anchovy fillets, drained and mashed with a fork (optional)

½ teaspoon dried marjoram

2 sprigs fresh thyme, or 1 teaspoon dried thyme

1½ cups canned crushed tomatoes

1 cup dry white wine or white grape juice

1 bay leaf

1 teaspoon finely grated lemon peel

1 teaspoon finely grated orange peel

¼ cup finely chopped parsley

1 Sprinkle the veal shanks with salt and pepper to taste and then roll them in the flour to give them a light coating, patting to remove excess flour. (This technique is called *dredging*.)

2 Heat the oil over medium-high heat in a heavy Dutch oven large enough to hold the veal shanks in one layer with the bones upright. Brown the veal all around, turning often, about 10 minutes. Remove the shanks from the pan and reserve them on a plate.

3 Lower the heat to medium and add the onion, carrots, and celery to the pan. Cook, stirring often, until the onions wilt, about 2 or 3 minutes. Add the garlic, mashed anchovies (if desired), marjoram, and thyme. Stir and add the tomatoes, wine, bay leaf, and salt and pepper to taste. Return the veal shanks to the pan with any juices that have accumulated in the plate. Cover, reduce the heat to low, and simmer for about 1 hour, or until the meat is tender. (The meat should easily separate from the bone when prodded with a fork.)

4 Sprinkle the lemon and orange zest over the veal and stir to blend. Cover and cook about 15 minutes more. Remove the bay leaf, spoon some of the vegetable mixture on each serving plate, and then place a veal shank on top; sprinkle with the parsley.

Go-With: *You can serve this dish with garlic mashed potatoes, buttered rice, buttered noodles, or any other hot, grain-based side dish. Try the Basic Rice Pilaf or Risotto in Chapter 4 or the Penne with Parmesan Cheese and Basil in Chapter 13.*

Per serving: *Calories 447 (From Fat 125); Fat 14g (Saturated 3g); Cholesterol 195mg; Sodium 378mg; Carbohydrate 24g (Dietary Fiber 4g); Protein 54g.*

Suave side dishes

A perfect side dish for all roasts is mashed potatoes — chefs today like to call them "puréed potatoes," as if they're something more sophisticated. But how can you improve on something so basic and so delicious? You can enhance mashed potatoes (see the recipe in Chapter 4) in many ways. You can add mashed parsnips, carrots, baked garlic, turnips, chopped green onions, minced yellow onions, or fresh herbs. Or, try other cooked vegetables as side dishes, as in the recipe in this section.

Here are some other side dishes that go well with any of the main courses in this chapter:

- Basic Wild Rice (see Chapter 4)
- White Beans with Tomatoes and Thyme (see Chapter 16)
- Risotto (see Chapter 4)
- Crispy Roasted Root Vegetables (see Chapter 7)
- Sautéed Skillet Potatoes (see Chapter 5)
- Southern Greens (see Chapter 16)
- Homemade Mashed Potatoes (see Chapter 4)
- Braised Cabbage with Apples and Caraway (see the following recipe)

🍎 Braised Cabbage with Apples and Caraway

The slight crunch of cabbage makes a fantastic accompaniment to Osso Buco (see the preceding recipe) and also goes particularly well with roasted pork. This recipe brings the lowly cabbage to life, giving it a sweet personality with apples, and a bit of spice with caraway.

Tools: *Chef's knife, paring knife, large skillet or sauté pan with lid, wooden spoon*

Preparation time: *About 25 minutes*

Cooking time: *About 25 minutes*

Yield: *4 servings*

3 tablespoons vegetable oil

1 medium yellow onion, coarsely chopped

1 large clove garlic, minced

1 medium apple

1 small head green cabbage, about 1½ pounds, halved, cored, and coarsely shredded

½ cup homemade or canned chicken or vegetable stock

1 tablespoon white vinegar

1 teaspoon caraway seeds

Salt and pepper

1 Heat the oil in a large skillet or sauté pan over medium heat. Add the onion and garlic and cook, stirring often, until the onion is wilted, about 2 to 3 minutes; remove from the heat. (Do not brown the garlic.)

2 Peel, core, and cut the apple into thin slices. Add the apple, cabbage, chicken or vegetable stock, vinegar, caraway seeds, and salt and pepper to taste to the skillet.

3 Raise the heat to high and bring to a boil. Cover, reduce the heat to low, and simmer for 15 to 20 minutes, or until the cabbage is crisp-tender, stirring occasionally. Uncover. If a lot of liquid is still in the pan, raise the heat to high and cook, stirring, for about 1 to 2 minutes or until most of the liquid is evaporated.

Per serving: Calories 163 (From Fat 97); Fat 11g (Saturated 1g); Cholesterol 0mg; Sodium 254mg; Carbohydrate 16g (Dietary Fiber 5g); Protein 3g.

Irresistible desserts — easy as pie

Okay, it's dessert time. You didn't think we'd forget, did you? Without getting involved in stratified layer cakes or chocolate concoctions with various tag names implying a pleasurable demise, you can make plenty of easy desserts that are suitable for entertaining. Knowing how to make a basic sweet pastry crust is always a good idea. Make the recipe over and over again until you can make it in your sleep. Then when fresh fruit is in season, or when you want to make a lemon or chocolate mousse pie, all you have to concentrate on is the filling. And that's a cinch.

An essential ingredient in pie crust is shortening, an ingredient you may be hesitant to use these days because it contains trans fat. Solid vegetable shortening, including margarine, is made out of this hydrogenated fat, which uses a chemical process to make liquid vegetable oil into solid vegetable oil. The latest news says hydrogenated, trans fats are even worse for heart health than the saturated fats found in animal products like beef and eggs. If you don't want to use this artificial shortening, you might even consider reverting back to good old-fashioned lard (solid pork fat), the pie-making staple your grandmother probably used. Lard makes pie crusts super flaky, but not everybody wants to use it. Alternatively, you can use all butter (you'll have a less flaky crust) or try some of the new nonhydrogenated shortenings available in health food aisles, although you may have to experiment a bit to get a really flaky crust.

☺ Basic Pastry Crust

All you have to know about a basic pastry crust is that butter makes it sweet and short-ening (like Crisco) makes it flaky. Many cooks split it down the middle and use equal amounts of butter and shortening or lard to make the dough. You can also use stick margarine, but don't use the softer, tub margarine, which contains too much water and/or liquid oil to work in a pie crust.

See how you like this pastry dough and then modify it, if you want, with suggestions that follow this recipe.

Tools: *Food processor or mixer, wire pastry blender (if making by hand), rolling pin, 9-inch pie pan*

Preparation time: *About 1½ hours (includes time to chill dough)*

Yield: *Enough pastry for a 9-inch double-crust pie*

⅓ cup plus 1 tablespoon cold butter, cut into small pieces

⅓ cup plus 1 tablespoon vegetable shortening (like Crisco or stick margarine)

2 cups all-purpose flour

¾ teaspoon salt

4 to 5 tablespoons ice water

1 In the bowl of a food processor fitted with a steel blade, cream the butter and shorten-ing, which takes about a minute. (Stop the motor as necessary to push the mixture with a rubber spatula toward the blade.) Add the flour and salt and process just a few sec-onds, until the dough resembles coarse cornmeal. With the motor running, add the cold water a little at a time, just enough to hold together the dry ingredients. (The exact amount of water required depends on the humidity of the day.) Do not overblend or the dough will get tough. Shape the dough into a ball.

To make the dough without a food processor, as shown in Figure 17-1, cream the butter and shortening in a large bowl with an electric mixer. Add the flour and salt. Using a pastry blender or your fingers, work the flour mixture into the butter and shortening, making a dough that resembles coarse cornmeal. Sprinkle enough ice cold water to form soft but not sticky dough. Shape the dough into a loose ball.

2 Divide the dough into two equal halves, wrap both in plastic, and refrigerate for at least 1 hour. (As the dough is chilling, prepare the filling from the following Apple Pie recipe.)

3 When ready to make your pie, preheat the oven to 450 degrees.

4 Lightly flour a large cutting board or counter and roll out one dough ball into a circle that is a few inches larger in diameter than the pie plate — that is, about 11 inches. (See Figure 17-2 for illustrated rolling instructions.)

5 Loosely drape the dough around the rolling pin and transfer it to the pie plate. Unroll the dough flat onto the bottom and gently press it against the sides and rim of the pie plate. Trim off any excess dough with a knife. Lightly press any excess dough into the remaining ball. (Fill the pie shell or, if the recipe calls for it, bake the pie shell before fill-ing it. For an apple pie filling, see the following recipe.)

6 Roll out the second ball of dough the same way and lay it over the filled bottom crust, leaving an overhang of about ½ inch. Tuck the overhang under the lower crust to form a neat edge; crimp firmly by pressing the tines of a fork all around the edge. Prick the top a few times with a fork before baking. (See the following Apple Pie recipe for baking instructions.)

Per serving: Calories 281 (From Fat 173); Fat 19g (Saturated 8g); Cholesterol 24mg; Sodium 220mg; Carbohydrate 24g (Dietary Fiber 1g); Protein 3g. based on eight servings.

Making Pie Dough by Hand

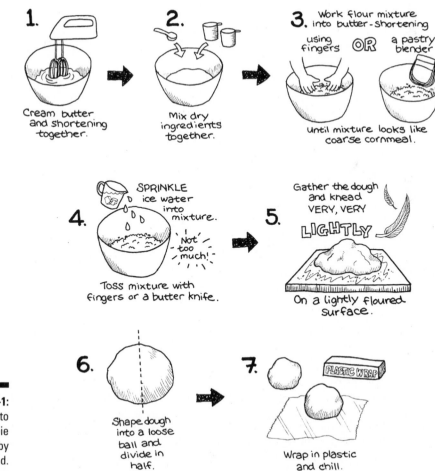

Figure 17-1:
How to make pie dough by hand.

How to Roll Dough

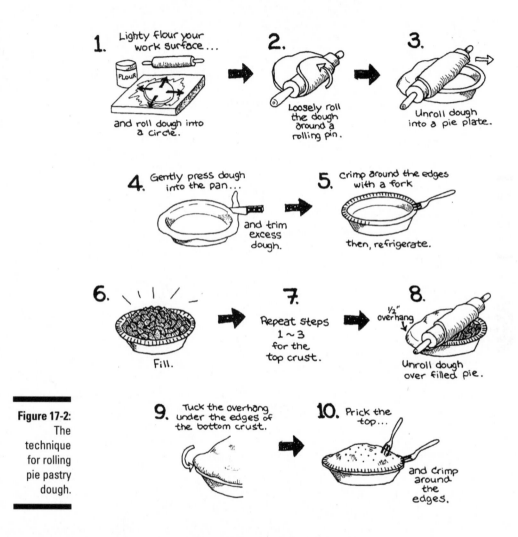

1. Lighty flour your work surface... and roll dough into a circle.

2. Loosely roll the dough around a rolling pin.

3. Unroll dough into a pie plate.

4. Gently press dough into the pan... and trim excess dough.

5. Crimp around the edges with a fork then, refrigerate.

6. Fill.

7. Repeat steps 1 ~ 3 for the top crust.

8. ½" overhang Unroll dough over filled pie.

9. Tuck the overhang under the edges of the bottom crust.

10. Prick the top... and crimp around the edges.

Figure 17-2:
The technique for rolling pie pastry dough.

Variations to this pastry crust include the following:

- **Nuts:** Add ¼ cup ground pecans, hazelnuts, almonds, or walnuts to the flour mixture before you process or blend by hand.

- **Spice:** Add some cinnamon, allspice, or ground ginger to the flour.

- **Citrus:** Add 2 teaspoons of finely grated lemon or orange zest to the flour.

- **Sweet:** Add 1 tablespoon sugar to the flour-salt mixture.

> ✔ **Single-crust pie:** If you're making a recipe that calls for prebaked crust (usually custard or other soft fillings), cover the pie shell with aluminum foil and pour dried beans or other weights inside, as shown in Figure 17-3. Bake the crust for 15 minutes in a 400-degree oven; then lower the heat to 350 degrees and bake another 10 minutes. Be careful that the crust doesn't get too brown.

For a Single Crust

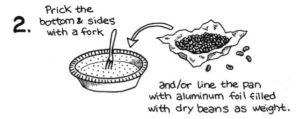

Figure 17-3:
Preparing
dough for a
single crust.

1. Follow "How to Roll Dough," steps 1 ~ 5.

2. Prick the bottom & sides with a fork

and/or line the pan with aluminum foil filled with dry beans as weight.

Rolling dough is a skill that takes a little practice. Don't be discouraged if, after your first try, your pie crust looks like a relief map of Antarctica. If, while rolling, your pastry starts to break apart at the edges, overlap the pieces a little bit. Then gently roll over the overlapping edges until smooth, moistening them first with a drop of water. If that doesn't work, reshape the pastry into a ball and roll again. But remember, the more you handle the pastry dough, the tougher it becomes.

Remember these other tips for rolling pastry dough:

> ✔ Work on a lightly floured counter or board. Dust the rolling pin and your dough *lightly* with flour, using a little more flour *only* if the dough sticks to the counter or the pin.

> ✔ Roll the dough from its center out to the edges and turn it frequently (about one-quarter turn) to keep it from sticking to the counter.

> ✔ Try to work quickly so that the dough remains chilled. Room-temperature dough is more difficult to roll, which is why it's important to chill dough thoroughly before rolling out.

> ✔ If the dough sticks to the counter, run a long metal spatula underneath to loosen it.

> ✔ Do not stretch the dough when transferring it from the counter to the pie plate.

Here's a recipe to help you practice your pie-crust skill.

🍑 Apple Pie

What could be more down-home than homemade apple pie? This dessert is the ultimate comfort food and will make your guests feel warmly welcomed. The taste and texture of a homemade crust are superior to any packaged mix, but when you don't have the time to make the pastry yourself, using a box of pie crust mix or frozen pie shells is better than having no pie at all! Making the filling from scratch makes this pie special, no matter the crust.

Tart-style apples are best for this pie. For suggestions on apple varieties to use, see the sidebar "Which apples are best for baking?" in this chapter.

Tools: *Paring knife, large bowl, 9-inch pie plate, wire rack*

Preparation time: *About 30 minutes, plus time to prepare pie crust dough*

Cooking time: *About 1 hour*

Yield: *8 servings*

6 medium tart-style apples, peeled, cored, and sliced about ½-inch thick (see Figure 17-4)

¾ cup sugar

2 tablespoons all-purpose flour

1 tablespoon fresh lemon juice

¾ teaspoon cinnamon

½ teaspoon grated lemon zest

⅛ teaspoon nutmeg

9-inch pie plate covered with pastry dough plus 1 uncooked sheet of pastry dough, about 11 inches in diameter (see the preceding recipe)

1 tablespoon butter

About 2 tablespoons milk or water (optional)

About 1 teaspoon sugar (optional)

1 Preheat the oven to 450 degrees.

2 Combine the apples, sugar, flour, lemon juice, cinnamon, lemon zest, and nutmeg in a large bowl. Toss gently to evenly coat the apples with sugar and seasonings.

3 Fill the uncooked pie shell with the apple mixture. Dot with the butter. Fit the top crust over the apples, trim off excess, and crimp the edges firmly (refer to Figure 17-2).

4 Prick the top crust several times with a fork to provide a vent for steam to escape. (For a shiny crust, use a pastry brush to brush the crust lightly with milk or water and then sprinkle sugar over it.)

5 Bake for 15 minutes. Reduce the heat to 350 degrees and bake another 45 minutes, or until the pie crust is golden brown. Cool the pie on a wire rack for at least 20 minutes before serving.

Vary It! *You can substitute fruits such as peaches, strawberries, apricots, and berries. You may want to vary the seasonings, but the idea is essentially the same. Pick a fruit and think about how to enhance it. For example, toss peaches with sugar, vanilla extract, and maybe a touch of rum. For pears, use sugar, cinnamon, maybe clove, and, if you like, vanilla extract. A dash of rum or brandy doesn't hurt, either. Adding ¼ cup brown sugar gives the filling a slightly caramelized flavor.*

Tip: *You also can use the basic pie crust for individual ramekins (single-serving, porcelain baking dishes) and fill them with fruits. The cooking time is less, of course — approximately half the cooking time for a 9-inch pie.*

Vary It! *Cheese and apples make a classic pairing. Try melting a slice of American or cheddar cheese on top of your slice of apple pie (see the color section).*

Per serving: *Calories 430 (From Fat 189); Fat 21g (Saturated 9g); Cholesterol 28mg; Sodium 220mg; Carbohydrate 59g (Dietary Fiber 3g); Protein 4g.*

Peeling and Coring an Apple

Figure 17-4:
You peel and core apples before slicing them into a pie.

1. Quarter the apples.

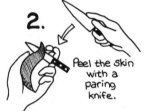
2. Peel the skin with a paring knife.

3. Cut out the core.

TIP

Which apples are best for baking?

Tart, crisp apples that hold their shape are best for pie making. Fall or early winter is the ideal time to bake an apple pie because the apple crop is fresh. With the exception of Granny Smiths (tart, green apples that are available all year), apples found in markets in the spring and summer have been stored since the fall harvest and do not have the same taste or texture as fresh apples.

The following varieties are among the best for baking in pies: Baldwin, Cortland, Granny Smith, Gravenstein, Jonathan, Macoun, Newtown Pippin, Northern Spy, Rhode Island Greening, Rome Beauty, and Winesap.

If You Have One Hour

One hour is actually a good chunk of time in which to put together a meal — that is, if you are organized, have all the shopping done, and can focus without interruptions. One phone call can throw off your pace, so take the phone off the hook or designate another family member to answer it, if it rings. Don't be tempted to run out to the mailbox or get involved in answering e-mail when you're in the middle of a one-hour dinner prep, and do think in advance about how long each dish needs at each stage so that one doesn't burn while another is still cold. Your mission is to get all the dishes to the table on cue and perfectly cooked. You can do it! We're here to help.

Getting started: Quickie appetizers

Just because you only have an hour is no reason to jettison the appetizer or order take-out. You can take a lot of heat off the situation by starting with a good mixed salad, like the Avocado and Tomato Salad in this section.

Looking for other quickie start ideas? Try one of these, if you have an hour or less:

- Garlic-Grilled Portobello Mushrooms (see Chapter 8)
- Layered Cheese and Vegetable Salad (see Chapter 12)
- Carrot Soup with Dill (see Chapter 11)
- French Potato Salad (see Chapter 12)
- Garbanzo Bean Toss (see Chapter 12)

○ Avocado and Tomato Salad

This simple, colorful salad is a cinch to prepare, but it tastes extra-luxurious because of the avocados. Use the freshest veggies, locally grown if possible, to make your salad special. This salad will start your meal out with a tangy, vinaigrette-enhanced bang.

Tools: *Chef's knife, paring knife, salad bowl*

Preparation time: *About 25 minutes*

Yield: *4 servings*

2 ripe avocados	¼ cup coarsely chopped cilantro	2 tablespoons red wine vinegar
4 ripe plum tomatoes		
2 hard-cooked eggs, peeled and quartered (optional)	2 large cloves garlic, finely chopped	½ teaspoon ground cumin
		Salt and pepper
1 small red onion, thinly sliced	6 tablespoons olive oil	

1 Halve and pit the avocados. Peel away the skin and cut each half into 4 lengthwise slices and then across into large cubes.

2 Core the tomatoes and cut them into 1-inch cubes.

3 Toss the cubes of avocado and tomato with the eggs (if desired), onion, cilantro, garlic, olive oil, vinegar, cumin, and salt and pepper to taste in a salad bowl and serve.

Per serving: Calories 338 (From Fat 297); Fat 33g (Saturated 5g); Cholesterol 0mg; Sodium 152mg; Carbohydrate 12g (Dietary Fiber 9g); Protein 3g.

Entrée: The short version

Dinner doesn't have to take hours. Plenty of impressive entrees cook up in less than an hour. The Broiled Skirt Steak, Cajun Style recipe in this section will get you started . . . because the clock is ticking!

When you have only an hour, here are a few other main dishes to try:

- ✔ The Perfect Steak (see Chapter 8)
- ✔ Mushroom-Swiss Frittata (see Chapter 10)
- ✔ Seafood Linguine (see Chapter 13)
- ✔ Sautéed Chicken Breasts with Tomatoes and Thyme (see Chapter 5)
- ✔ Sautéed Peppered Sirloin of Beef (see Chapter 5)

Making and storing dressings

To save the time and effort of making a vinaigrette every time you need one, make a large batch and store it in empty wine bottles. Then you can have a mixed green salad with homemade vinaigrette whenever you need one! Here's how:

1. **In a mixing bowl, combine 1 tablespoon or more of Dijon-style mustard with lots of salt and freshly ground black pepper.**

2. **Add about ½ cup olive oil in a slow stream while whisking.**

3. **Gradually whisk in vinegar (roughly a 5-to-2 ratio of oil to vinegar), tasting constantly.**

4. **When you like the results, pour the dressing into the bottle with a funnel.**

   If you like, add fresh herbs or minced garlic to the bottle.

5. **Shake, seal with a cork, and refrigerate.**

Broiled Skirt Steak, Cajun Style

This zesty skirt steak dish (see the sidebar "Skirt steak: Fashionable fare" in this chapter) is an alternative to flank steak, with a down-by-the-bayou kick. Adjust the seasonings — less if you like it a little less spicy, or more if you want to crank up the heat.

Tools: *Chef's knife, mixing bowl, broiler or grill*

Preparation time: *About 35 minutes, including marinating time*

Cooking time: *About 10 minutes, including standing time*

Yield: *4 servings*

4 skirt steaks, ½ pound each	*½ teaspoon ground cumin*	*2 tablespoons butter*
Salt	*½ teaspoon dried thyme*	*2 tablespoons finely chopped fresh parsley*
2 tablespoons olive oil	*¼ teaspoon cayenne pepper*	
1 teaspoon chili powder	*¼ teaspoon black pepper*	

1 Half an hour before broiling or grilling, sprinkle the steaks with salt to taste. In a small bowl, combine the oil, chili powder, cumin, thyme, cayenne, and black pepper and stir well to mix. Brush this mixture all over the steaks. Cover the steaks with plastic wrap but do not refrigerate.

2 Preheat the broiler or set a charcoal or gas grill to medium-high.

3 If broiling, arrange the steaks on a rack and place under the broiler about 6 inches from the heat source. Broil for 3 minutes with the door partly open. Turn the steaks and continue broiling, leaving the door partly open. Broil for about 3 minutes more, for medium-rare, or to the desired degree of doneness. To check for doneness, make a small incision with a sharp knife into the center or thickest part of the steak. Medium-rare meat is bright red and juicy; medium has a light pink center with light brown edges and less juice.

If grilling, put the steaks on a medium hot, oiled grill and cover. Cook for 3 minutes. Turn the steaks, cover, and cook about 3 minutes more for medium-rare, or to the desired degree of doneness.

4 Transfer the steaks to a hot platter and dot with butter. Let them stand in a warm place for 5 minutes to redistribute the internal juices, which accumulate as the steaks stand.

5 Sprinkle with parsley and serve with the accumulated butter sauce.

Per serving: Calories 487 (From Fat 278); Fat 31g (Saturated 12g); Cholesterol 122mg; Sodium 292mg; Carbohydrate 1g (Dietary Fiber 1g); Protein 49g.

Skirt steak: Fashionable fare

Skirt steak, formerly unknown to home cooks, has become a fashionable cut of meat in restaurants, particularly because it works so well in fajitas. Skirt steak goes by many names, including hanger steak, oyster steak, and butcher steak. The last name arose because butchers traditionally kept these exceptionally juicy and flavorful cuts for themselves.

If you know how to cook a skirt steak, it can be delicious and far less expensive (and leaner) than sirloins or fillets. The skirt steak comes from the pad of muscle that runs from the rib cage toward the loin (see the beef chart in Chapter 3). It is usually sold in sections of about 12 ounces each and has a thin, silvery membrane that the butcher should remove.

Because skirt steak contains a lot of moisture, it should be cooked very fast over high heat to sear. For that reason, you should let the steak reach room temperature before broiling or grilling. Also let the cooked steak sit for several minutes before slicing, so the juices can settle. Cut the steak on a bias across the fibrous muscle on a cutting board that can catch the runoff. (*Cutting on a bias* means slicing the meat at about a 45-degree angle to the cutting board — not perpendicular to the board as you would with a loaf of bread. Cutting on a bias gives you a larger, thinner slice for each portion.) Pour the juice back over the steak when serving, or use it in your sauce.

Super-quick side dishes

Don't let those tasty entrees stand alone just because you're pressed for time. Try the Indian Rice with Ginger, Walnuts, and Raisins side dish recipe in this section or one of the following super-quick side dishes to jump-start your dinner preparation:

✔ Green Beans with Shallots (see Chapter 21)

✔ Tabbouleh Salad (see Chapter 4)

✔ Polenta with Herbs (see Chapter 4)

♂ *Indian Rice with Ginger, Walnuts, and Raisins*

This exotic-tasting rice goes well with any steak or poultry dish as long as the sauce doesn't contain the same seasonings.

Tools: *Chef's knife, medium saucepan or sauté pan, grater*

Preparation time: *About 15 minutes*

Cooking time: *About 25 minutes*

Yield: *4 servings*

2 tablespoons butter

¼ cup finely chopped yellow onion

1 cup chopped walnuts

1 teaspoon grated fresh gingerroot

½ teaspoon cinnamon

¼ teaspoon red pepper flakes, or to taste

1 cup raw converted rice (see Chapter 4 for more about converted rice)

1¾ cups homemade or canned chicken or vegetable stock, heated to just below boiling

2 tablespoons brandy or orange juice

½ cup raisins

3 tablespoons finely chopped cilantro or parsley

Salt (optional)

1 Heat the butter in a saucepan over medium heat. Add the onion and cook, stirring often, until the onion is wilted, about 2 to 3 minutes. Add the walnuts, gingerroot, cinnamon, and pepper flakes. Cook, stirring constantly, for about 30 seconds. Stir in the rice, coating the grains in the melted butter, and cook for an additional 1 minute, stirring constantly. Carefully add the hot chicken stock.

2 Cover and simmer over low heat for 20 minutes, or until the rice is tender and all the liquid is absorbed. Meanwhile, pour the brandy or orange juice over the raisins and allow them to soak while the rice is cooking.

3 When the rice is done, stir in the raisins, any remaining brandy or orange juice, and cilantro or parsley and adjust the seasoning just before serving, adding salt if necessary.

Per serving: *Calories 492 (From Fat 229); Fat 26g (Saturated 5g); Cholesterol 15mg; Sodium 279mg; Carbohydrate 60g (Dietary Fiber 4g); Protein 11g.*

Desserts on the double

The key to a quick dessert is sauce. A homemade sauce gives a special touch to ice cream or even store-bought pound cake. Try this sauce, and your guests will feel like you really went to a lot of trouble. (We won't tell.)

Warm Blueberry Sauce

This warm blueberry sauce goes well with ice cream, pastries, or a simple yellow cake. The basic technique works for all fresh berries, so once you've tried blueberries, substitute other berries you enjoy, such as strawberries or raspberries.

Tools: *Saucepan, wooden spoon*

Preparation time: *About 10 minutes*

Cooking time: *About 7 minutes*

Yield: *4 servings*

⅓ cup granulated sugar	¾ cup water	2 tablespoons butter, softened
1 tablespoon cornstarch	2 teaspoons fresh lemon juice	
Pinch of salt	1 cup ripe blueberries, rinsed and stems removed	¼ teaspoon ground cinnamon, or to taste

1 In a saucepan, thoroughly combine the sugar, cornstarch, and salt. Add the water and lemon juice and cook over medium-high heat, stirring frequently, until the mixture thickens, about 3 to 5 minutes.

2 Add the blueberries and lower the heat to medium, stirring frequently, for 1 minute. Remove the pan from the heat and add the butter and cinnamon. Stir well. Keep warm in a double boiler until ready to serve. Stir well before serving.

Per serving: Calories 142 (From Fat 52); Fat 6g (Saturated 4g); Cholesterol 15mg; Sodium 38mg; Carbohydrate 24g (Dietary Fiber 1g); Protein 0g.

If You Have 30 Minutes

What can you possibly accomplish in 30 minutes? Half an aerobics class? Wash the front half of the car? Watch the first part of *60 Minutes?* Not much fun, huh? But you can prepare a meal in this time if you follow our organizational plan. If you don't have the ingredients on hand, you may need to run to the market. But after you start cooking, you'll be able to complete these recipes quickly.

The good news is that you don't have to worry too much about orchestrating your time; the bad news is that you'll be doing everything at once. Before you dive in, give some thought to what tasks, if any, you can combine. Chop all the vegetables together, for example. Do two of your dishes call for celery? Prepare enough for both at one time. Another key timesaver is having all your materials out and ready before you begin so that you don't get thrown off track mid-menu trying to locate the darn marjoram.

Putting a meal on the table in 30 minutes also often means that you have to rely on certain store-bought goods for help and give your timesaving gadgets in the kitchen a real workout. But in the end, you have a real meal.

The following recipes are meant to steer you into a certain way of thinking when the clock's incessant ticking is following you all over the house and your guests will be arriving in no time.

Hungry now? Instant hors d'oeuvres

Appetizers don't have to take much, if any, time at all. Try assembling open-face sandwiches (called tartines in France) topped with cheese, meats, fish, or whatever you already have in your refrigerator. Or, go south of the border and use the same technique on tortillas, either flat, quickly baked, and cut into wedges, or warmed in the microwave for 10 seconds and rolled up with meat, cheese, and greens and then sliced. Or serve antipasto, which is an assembly of meats, cheeses, and fresh and marinated vegetables you arrange on a platter. Use what you have or consult the "Shop and platter: The art of antipasto" sidebar for ingredient ideas.

☉ Fresh Tomato Quesadillas

Quesadillas are quick, easy, and popular appetizers that are easy to eat and make a welcome addition to any hors d'oeuvres tray. For the best results, use the ripest, freshest tomatoes you can find for this recipe.

Tools: *Chef's knife, small skillet, pastry brush*

Preparation time: *About 5 minutes*

Cooking time: *About 15 minutes*

Yield: *8 servings*

2 teaspoons olive oil	1 cup grated Monterey Jack cheese	½ cup chopped fresh cilantro plus extra for garnish
4 flour tortillas, about 8 inches in diameter	1 ripe tomato, cored, seeded, and chopped	

1 In a skillet, heat 1 teaspoon of the olive oil over medium heat. Put one tortilla in the skillet. Top with ¼ cup cheese, half the tomatoes, half the cilantro, another ¼ cup cheese, and the second tortilla. When the bottom tortilla is golden and crisp (lift it up with a spatula to check), flip it over and cook the other side until golden. Remove to paper towels to absorb any extra oil.

2 Repeat with the other 2 tortillas and remaining ingredients, adding more olive oil if necessary. Cut each quesadilla into 8 wedges. Garnish with extra cilantro leaves.

Vary It! *You can vary quesadillas to include whatever you have in the refrigerator. Try adding cooked chicken or beef, different kinds of cheeses, or leftover cooked vegetables.*

Per serving: *Calories 140 (From Fat 63); Fat 7g (Saturated 3g); Cholesterol 13mg; Sodium 202mg; Carbohydrate 14g (Dietary Fiber 0g); Protein 6g.*

With a little practice, you can knock off any of these appetizers in minutes:

- ✔ **Hummus Dip:** Whirl in a blender until smooth a 16-ounce can of drained chickpeas, 1 clove garlic, ¼ cup sesame seeds, the juice and grated zest of 1 lemon, ½ cup water, with salt and pepper to taste. Serve on triangles of toasted pita or with assorted raw vegetables.

- ✔ **Spicy Shrimp Kebabs:** Thread medium or large shrimp and chunks of sweet onions on skewers (preferably metal, which, unlike wooden skewers, don't require presoaking); grill or broil about 2 minutes a side or until done, brushing at the last minute with ¼ cup melted butter mixed with ½ teaspoon hot pepper flakes. Serve hot.

- ✔ **Guacamole:** Mash in a small bowl the flesh from 2 medium, ripe avocados. Add 1 small, finely chopped onion; 1 ripe finely chopped tomato; 2 tablespoons chopped cilantro; half a jalapeño chile, seeded and minced; and the juice and grated zest of half a lemon. Season with salt and pepper and serve with blue or white corn chips.

- ✔ **Sun-Dried Tomato Spread:** Whirl sun-dried tomatoes, garlic, and onions in a food processor or blender container with enough oil to moisten into a coarse spread. Season with white pepper. Serve on Melba toast rounds.

- ✔ **Smoked Chicken Slices with Coriander Sauce:** You can buy smoked chicken and slice it into bite-sized strips, serving the strips over thin slices of French or Italian bread. Brush with a basic vinaigrette seasoned with chopped cilantro and, if you like, a dash of Tabasco sauce.

Main dishes in minutes

Just 30 minutes? Try Snapper Fillets with Tomatoes. Fish cooks quickly, so it's great for a quick but fancy dinner.

Shop and platter: The art of antipasto

When you barely have time to shop, much less prepare a full meal, knowing how to buy and assemble various foods into an attractive spread is an invaluable skill. As a source of inspiration, we recommend an Italian approach that calls for serving an array of cheeses, meats, breads, olives, and vegetables on a large platter.

Assembling an Italian *antipasto* is 50 percent presentation. Think about how the tastes and colors contrast. Antipasto is traditionally served as the appetizer course, but there's no reason you can't make a meal of it. Here is an incomplete list of choices for an antipasto platter that you can purchase about a half-hour before your guests arrive — that is, if you catch all the green lights on the way home from the market.

- Mozzarella, provolone, fontina, Parmesan, or goat cheese (cubed or thinly sliced)

- Thinly sliced ham, prosciutto, and Genoa salami

- Rounds of pepperoni or sopressata salami

- Thin slices of *mortadella* (a garlic-flavored bologna) or capicola (made from cured pork)

- Cooked shrimp (best if tossed in a vinaigrette dressing)

- Canned anchovies, sardines, or tuna packed in olive oil

- Canned chickpeas tossed in vinaigrette dressing (you need to make the dressing)

- Sun-dried tomatoes in oil

- Marinated artichoke hearts, roasted red peppers, and capers

- Assorted black and green olives

- Assorted fresh vegetables, including radishes with tops; carrot, celery, cucumber, and pepper sticks; pieces of fennel; green onions; and whole red or yellow cherry tomatoes

- Arugula, basil leaves, and radicchio for garnishing

- Sliced ripe pears, melon, figs, or small bunches of grapes

- Flavored breads, breadsticks, flatbreads, and warmed Boboli (a brand of flatbread that resembles a thick pizza crust)

Here are a few more super-quick entrees you may want to try:

- Tuna Steaks with Ginger Chili Glaze (see Chapter 5)

- Easy Coq au Vin (see Chapter 6)

- Sautéed Chicken Breasts with Tomatoes and Thyme (see Chapter 5)

- Grilled Shrimp Skewers (see Chapter 8)

- Omelets or frittatas (see Chapter 10)

- Spaghetti with Quick Fresh Tomato Sauce (see Chapter 13)

Snapper Fillets with Tomatoes

This classy main course has some unusual tastes. Find fennel in your produce aisle. The optional addition of anise-flavored liqueur will keep your guests guessing the secret.

Tools: *Chef's knife, paring knife, medium saucepan, sauté pan with lid*

Preparation time: *About 15 minutes*

Cooking time: *About 15 minutes*

Yield: *4 servings*

2 tablespoons olive oil

5 plum tomatoes, peeled, seeded, and chopped

1 large leek, white and light green part only, finely chopped (see Figure 17-5 for info on how to clean and trim leeks)

½ cup chopped fennel bulb

2 large cloves garlic, finely chopped

1 teaspoon turmeric

Salt and pepper

½ cup dry white wine or white grape juice

½ cup fish stock or bottled clam juice

1 bay leaf

4 sprigs fresh thyme, or 1 teaspoon dried thyme

⅛ teaspoon Tabasco sauce

4 snapper fillets with skin on, or other white-fleshed fish, about 6 ounces each

2 tablespoons Ricard, Pernod, or other anise-flavored liqueur (optional)

2 tablespoons chopped basil or parsley

1 In a medium saucepan over medium heat, combine 1 tablespoon of the olive oil and the tomatoes, leeks, fennel, garlic, and turmeric. Season with salt and pepper to taste. Cook, stirring often, about 3 minutes. Add the wine or white grape juice, stock, bay leaf, thyme, and Tabasco. Bring to a boil, reduce heat, and simmer for 5 minutes.

2 In a large sauté pan, add the remaining tablespoon of oil and arrange the fillets of fish in one layer, skin side down. Season with salt and pepper to taste. Pour the leek-tomato mixture evenly over the fish fillets. Sprinkle on the Ricard or Pernod, if desired, cover, and cook over medium heat for about 5 minutes, until the fish is opaque in the center. (The exact cooking time depends on the thickness of the fillets.) Discard the bay leaf and sprinkle with the basil or parsley before serving.

Per serving: Calories 264 (From Fat 85); Fat 9g (Saturated 1g); Cholesterol 61mg; Sodium 302mg; Carbohydrate 9g (Dietary Fiber 2g); Protein 35g.

Figure 17-5:
Cleaning
and
trimming
leeks.

Sides of veggies in a flash

Need a side dish in a jiffy? Try these extra-quick dishes to accompany your
main course when you have only a half-hour to get ready:

- Sautéed Spinach Leaves (Chapter 5)
- Steamed Broccoli with Lemon Butter (Chapter 4)
- Carrots in Cumin Butter (Chapter 16)

Or microwave a package of frozen vegetables according to package directions
and then dress them up with a teaspoon of olive oil or butter and some fresh
herbs mixed in.

Speedy sweets

As for dessert, you can always serve fresh fruit and a really good-quality ice
cream. Or, you can make a nice, quick ice cream sauce with frozen strawberries (or fresh, of course, if they're in season). See Chapter 9 for a recipe for
Fresh Strawberry Sauce. The Caramel Sauce and Cracklin' Hot Fudge Sauce
from Chapter 9 are also great with ice cream.

It doesn't take too long to assemble the Tiramisù in Chapter 15, which can
add real class to a quick dinner. You can skip the 2 hours chilling time, and
the dessert will still be tasty! Or, if you have only 30 minutes, you also can try
sweetened Whipped Cream (see Chapter 9) to add on top of the fresh fruit
you just found at the farmers market. Now go, go, go!

Chapter 18

Cook Once, Eat Thrice: Making the Most of Leftovers

In This Chapter

▶ Making one pork, lamb, or chicken recipe last several days

▶ Figuring out how to stir-fry like a pro

*N*o matter how crazy about cooking you become as you read this book, you'll undoubtedly be too busy to cook every single day.

This chapter emphasizes one basic concept: cooking once in order to make food for three different meals. This concept is all about the inspired use of leftovers — leftovers so resourcefully put to use that nobody even notices they're leftovers!

Thinking of new things to do with the rest of last night's dinner can be fun. But just in case you aren't too confident about your cooking creativity just yet, this chapter serves as your guide.

Making the Most of a Pork Shoulder

The first group of meals we recommend starts with a great pork recipe and then uses the remaining pork for two more delicious meals. For this recipe series, we recommend buying pork shoulder, which for some anatomically illogical reason is also sold by the name "pork butt." The pork shoulder (or pork butt) is the upper part of a hog's shoulder. Here's the plan:

✔ Meal 1: Smoked Pork with Winter Vegetables

✔ Meal 2: Smoked Pork Hash

✔ Meal 3: Pasta and Bean Soup

Smoked Pork with Winter Vegetables

This recipe calls for cooking the pork and vegetables at the same time. However, if the potatoes start to fall apart in the broth, remove them with a slotted spoon to a buttered baking dish. Cover the dish with foil and keep warm in a 200-degree oven until you need them.

Tools: *Chef's knife, vegetable peeler, large pot, slotted spoon*

Preparation time: *10 minutes (plus 5 minutes for soaking the meat)*

Cooking time: *1½ hours*

Yield: *4 servings (with enough left over for the following two dishes), or 8 servings with no leftovers*

3 pounds boneless smoked pork shoulder (also called smoked pork butt)

1 large yellow onion, peeled and halved

2 bay leaves

10 black peppercorns

6 carrots, peeled and quartered crosswise

6 medium baking potatoes, peeled and quartered

3 large parsnips, peeled and quartered crosswise

½ head green cabbage, cut into 3 to 4 wedges

¼ cup chopped parsley (for garnish)

Salt and pepper

1 stick softened butter (for the vegetables)

Dijon-style mustard (for the meat)

1 Remove the netting from the pork butt and soak the meat in warm water for about 5 minutes to remove excess salt.

2 Place the pork, onion, bay leaves, and peppercorns in a large pot; add cold water to cover. Cover the pot and bring the water to a boil; reduce the heat and simmer for 1 hour and 10 minutes, adding more water if necessary to keep the pork immersed in the liquid.

3 Remove the onion and bay leaves with a slotted spoon and discard. Add the carrots, potatoes, and parsnips to the pot and bring the liquid to a boil again; reduce the heat and simmer for 10 minutes. Add the cabbage and return to a boil; reduce the heat and simmer for another 10 to 15 minutes, or until the pork and vegetables are tender.

4 Remove the meat from the simmering liquid and slice it into serving portions; arrange the slices on a serving platter. Remove the vegetables with a slotted spoon and arrange them around the meat. (Reserve the cooking liquid to make the Pasta and Bean Soup later in this section.) Sprinkle the meat and vegetables with the parsley. Season the vegetables with salt and pepper to taste. Serve with small bowls of butter, to mash into the steaming vegetables, and the mustard, for the pork.

Per serving: Calories 634 (From Fat 373); Fat 42g (Saturated 18g); Cholesterol 128mg; Sodium 2,100mg; Carbohydrate 43g (Dietary Fiber 8g); Protein 28g.

Smoked Pork Hash

After you've served the Smoked Pork with Winter Vegetables, you can use the leftovers to make this delicious meal, which stands on its own as a light supper, perhaps with a green salad and bread. It also makes a great country breakfast with the addition of fried eggs and toasted cornbread muffins.

Tools: *Chef's knife, large skillet (cast-iron is best), metal spatula*

Preparation time: *About 10 minutes*

Cooking time: *About 15 minutes*

Yield: *4 servings*

3 tablespoons vegetable oil

1 cup chopped yellow onion

2 cups cubed cooked smoked pork butt, trimmed of excess fat

2 to 3 cups drained, cubed, leftover vegetables, excluding the cabbage, from Smoked Pork with Winter Vegetables

Salt and pepper

3 tablespoons chopped parsley (for garnish)

1 In a large skillet, heat the oil over medium heat; add the onion and cook, stirring often, until translucent, about 2 to 3 minutes.

2 Gently stir in the cooked pork and the vegetables so they're well mixed; season to taste with salt and pepper. Using a metal spatula, press down on the hash to compress it against the bottom of the skillet. Cook, without stirring, until the bottom is well browned, 10 to 15 minutes. (If desired, place the skillet under the broiler, about 6 inches from the heat, for 3 to 4 minutes, to brown the top.) Using a metal spatula, lift and invert the hash onto individual serving plates. Garnish with the parsley.

Tip: *A well-seasoned cast-iron skillet gives hash a deep brown crust. You can use a non-stick skillet and reduce the oil to 2 tablespoons from 3 because the coating on the pan keeps the crust from burning. But the crust on the hash will be lighter.*

Vary It! *You can really let your creative cooking side go wild and dress up this hash with different seasonings and ingredients: Add 1 to 2 chopped, seeded, jalapeño or other chile peppers or 1 large seeded and chopped green or red bell pepper along with the onions. Add 1 cup of cooked frozen or canned corn or 1 tablespoon chopped fresh herbs, such as rosemary, thyme, or marjoram, with the cooked vegetables. Sprinkle some hot sauce, like Tabasco, over the cooking vegetables.*

Go-With: *Round out this great meal by pairing the hash with Scrambled Eggs (see Chapter 1) or a simple green salad with vinaigrette dressing.*

Per serving: *Calories 318 (From Fat 209; Fat 23g (Saturated 5g); Cholesterol 41mg; Sodium 1,081mg; Carbohydrate 19g (Dietary Fiber 3g); Protein 11g.*

Pasta and Bean Soup

Few kitchen tasks are more satisfying to a home cook (or a professional chef, for that matter) than making a delicious soup that uses rich, homemade broth derived from another dish. The smoked pork butt adds just the right salty, meaty tones to this soup's broth. Pasta and Bean Soup is one dish that tastes even better the next day. You can find different versions of a soup like this all over Italy, where it is called *pasta e fagioli* (yep, "pasta with beans").

Tools: *Chef's knife, vegetable peeler, grater, large pot, ladle*

Preparation time: *10 minutes*

Cooking time: *45 minutes*

Yield: *8 servings*

¼ cup olive oil

1 medium yellow onion, peeled and chopped

2 carrots, peeled and diced

1 stalk celery, diced

1 large clove garlic, peeled and chopped

1 can (14½ ounces) diced tomatoes

7 to 8 cups broth saved from Smoked Pork with Winter Vegetables

1 tablespoon chopped fresh basil, or 1 teaspoon dried basil

1 teaspoon chopped fresh thyme, or ½ teaspoon dried thyme

1 can (15 ounces) cannellini or red kidney beans, rinsed and drained

1 bay leaf

1 cup small dried pasta, such as elbow macaroni

Salt and pepper

Grated Parmesan cheese (for garnish)

1 In a large, heavy-bottomed soup pot or saucepan, heat the oil over medium heat. Add the onion and cook, stirring occasionally, until wilted, about 5 minutes. Stir in the carrots, celery, and garlic and cook over medium-high heat another 5 minutes, or until the vegetables are softened, stirring often.

2 Add the diced tomatoes with their juice, 7 cups of the broth, the basil, and thyme. Cover the pot, bring to a boil, and then reduce the heat and simmer gently for 20 minutes.

3 Carefully ladle 1½ to 2 cups of the soup into a blender container; pulse for just a few seconds. Stir the mixture back into the soup.

4 Add the cannellini or kidney beans, and the bay leaf; cover the pot and simmer another 5 minutes.

5 Add the pasta and cook, partially covered, only until al dente, or firm to the bite, about 10 minutes; stir occasionally. If, after cooking the pasta, too much of the liquid has evaporated and the soup seems a little thick, add enough of the remaining broth to thin to a desired consistency.

6 Remove the bay leaf. Adjust seasoning with salt and pepper to taste. Ladle the soup into bowls; sprinkle each with the grated cheese.

Vary It! *This soup is flexible, and like its incarnations in the Mediterranean, each version differs with the cook. That means you can experiment, adding your favorite ingredients to the base of broth, beans, pasta, and vegetables. Try 1 cup of cooked, chopped cabbage; 1 cup of cooked, diced potatoes; or ½ to 1 cup cooked, diced pork — whatever you have left from the Smoked Pork with Winter Vegetables recipe in this section.*

Go-With: *A salad and bread always go well with a substantial soup. Try a mixed green salad with vinaigrette and a crusty baguette with this recipe.*

Per serving: *Calories 195 (From Fat 73); Fat 8g (Saturated 1g); Cholesterol 0mg; Sodium 515mg; Carbohydrate 23g (Dietary Fiber 4g); Protein 23g.*

On the Lamb: Serving It Three Ways

Lamb is another great meat to stretch over the course of a couple of meals. It tastes great the first night you cook it, but it keeps on tasting great, in all its tender juiciness, for several nights to come. In this section, we give you three dishes, based on a roasted leg of lamb:

- Meal 1: Roasted Leg of Lamb, with or without the glaze (see Chapter 7 for the recipe, where we call it Glazed Leg of Lamb with Pan Gravy and Red Currant Glaze)

- Meal 2: Lamb Curry

- Meal 3: Sliced lamb sandwiches with Red Onion and Mango Chutney

Lamb Curry

A large roasted leg of lamb often has lots of meat left around the bone. This curry is a perfect way to use it. The flavors intensify if the curry is refrigerated overnight. It also freezes well.

Tools: *Chef's knife, grater, large saucepan, wooden spoon*

Preparation time: *About 15 minutes*

Cooking time: *About 45 minutes*

Yield: *4 servings*

1 tablespoon olive oil

½ tablespoon butter

1 large yellow onion, chopped

1 medium red bell pepper, cored, seeded, and diced

2 teaspoons seeded and minced jalapeño or other hot chile pepper (optional)

1 clove garlic, minced

1 tablespoon peeled, grated fresh gingerroot

1 tablespoon curry powder

½ teaspoon ground cumin

1½ cups homemade or canned beef stock

¼ cup plus 2 tablespoons canned coconut milk

1 tablespoon tomato paste

2½ to 3 cups 1-inch cubed cooked lamb, trimmed of excess fat

⅓ cup golden raisins

Salt and black pepper

4 cups cooked long-grain rice

Optional accompaniments: mango chutney, chopped dry-roasted peanuts, chopped parsley or cilantro

1 In a large, deep saucepan, heat the oil and butter over medium-high heat. Add the onion, red pepper, jalapeño pepper (if desired), and garlic, and cook for about 4 to 5 minutes, stirring often, until the vegetables begin to soften. Stir in the gingerroot, curry powder, and cumin; cook about 1 minute, stirring.

2 Stir in the beef stock, coconut milk, and tomato paste; bring to a boil. Stir in the lamb. Reduce the heat, cover, and simmer for 20 minutes. Add the raisins and simmer for another 20 minutes. Season to taste with salt and pepper. Serve over rice with suggested accompaniments, if desired.

Go-With: *Lamb curry is an assertive dish, packed with flavor, so pair it with something mild, such as a Cucumber-Dill Salad (see Chapter 12) or Converted Rice (see Chapter 4).*

Per serving: *Calories 545 (From Fat 156); Fat 17g (Saturated 8g); Cholesterol 83mg; Sodium 252mg; Carbohydrate 62g (Dietary Fiber 3g); Protein 33g.*

↻ Red Onion and Mango Chutney

Leftover cold lamb makes delicious sandwiches, especially when slathered with mango chutney. A good chutney tastes both sweet and savory at the same time, with flavors more complex than a jam or jelly. A mixture of fruits, onions, sugar, and vinegar, chutney makes a great sandwich condiment for strong-tasting meats like pork or beef tenderloin, lamb, or a grilled hamburger. The ingredients for chutney are extremely flexible. In this recipe, you can substitute firm peaches for the mangoes, or add dark raisins or chopped green pepper, if you like.

Tools: *Medium saucepan, wooden spoon, chef's knife*

Preparation time: *About 20 minutes*

Cooking time: *About 25 to 30 minutes*

Yield: *About 2 cups, or about 6 servings*

2 tablespoons vegetable oil	*½ cup plus 2 tablespoons packed brown sugar*
1 cup chopped red onion	*½ cup cider vinegar*
1 to 2 (or to taste) jalapeño peppers, or other hot chile pepper, seeded and minced	*2 large ripe mangoes, peeled and cut into ¼-inch cubes (see Figure 18-1 for instructions)*
2 teaspoons peeled, minced fresh gingerroot	*Salt and black pepper (optional)*
1 clove garlic, minced	

1 In a medium saucepan, heat the oil over medium heat; add the onion and sauté for 4 to 5 minutes, or until slightly browned, stirring often. Add the jalapeño, gingerroot, and garlic, and cook for 1 minute more, stirring. (Do not let the garlic brown.)

2 Remove the saucepan from the heat; stir in the brown sugar and vinegar. Return the saucepan to the heat; bring the mixture to a boil. Reduce the heat and simmer for 3 to 4 minutes. Stir in the mangoes.

3 Raise the heat and bring the mixture to a boil. Reduce the heat and simmer, partially covered, for 15 to 20 minutes, or until the mango is tender. (Exact cooking time may vary, depending on the ripeness of the mango.) Taste and adjust seasoning, if desired, with salt and pepper. Chill and serve as a condiment on lamb sandwiches. It's also good with grilled chicken or beef.

Tip: *A ripe mango is slightly soft to the touch, with at least half of its otherwise green skin tinged with orange, yellow, or red coloring.*

Per serving: *Calories 187 (From Fat 44); Fat 5g (Saturated 0g); Cholesterol 0mg; Sodium 12mg; Carbohydrate 38g (Dietary Fiber 2g); Protein 1g.*

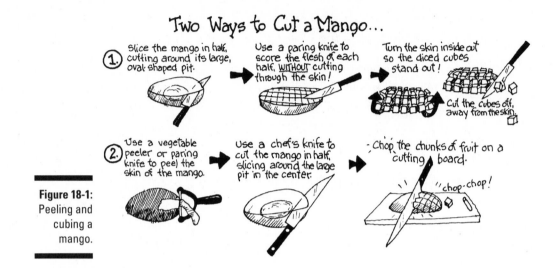

Two Ways to Cut a Mango...

(1.) Slice the mango in half, cutting around its large, oval shaped pit.

Use a paring knife to score the flesh of each half, WITHOUT cutting through the skin!

Turn the skin inside out so the diced cubes stand out!

Cut the cubes off, away from the skin.

(2.) Use a vegetable peeler or paring knife to peel the skin of the mango.

Use a chef's knife to cut the mango in half, slicing around the large pit in the center.

Chop the chunks of fruit on a cutting board.

"chop-chop!"

Figure 18-1:
Peeling and cubing a mango.

Chicken Dinner Times Three

If you roast a large chicken (for example, 4 or 5 pounds), you'll have enough leftovers to make the following three recipes. You may even want to roast two chickens while you're at it! And don't forget about using your slow cooker, which can roast a chicken while you're at work all day. Here's our three-day chicken plan.

- ✔ Meal 1: Roasted Chicken (see Chapter 7)
- ✔ Meal 2: Chicken, Avocado, and Red Onion Salad
- ✔ Meal 3: Chicken and Grilled Vegetable Wrap

Chicken, Avocado, and Red Onion Salad

This chicken salad uses leftover roasted chicken from the recipe in Chapter 7. However, if you don't have 3 cups of leftover chicken, simmer a whole chicken breast (or less depending on what you need) in chicken broth (or in water, seasoned with salt, pepper, and lemon juice) for about 10 minutes, or until the chicken is fully cooked (you can tell the chicken is fully cooked when you slice it in the center and see no pink).

The dressing for this colorful salad is first used as a marinade for the cooked and diced chicken. You can reuse it because the chicken was never raw. (Never reuse marinade used on raw meat, unless you boil it first.) Use generous amounts of salt and pepper in the dressing and on the salad ingredients to pull out the flavors of the fresh vegetables.

Tools: *Chef's knife, medium mixing bowl, whisk*

Preparation time: *20 to 25 minutes, plus 30 minutes refrigeration time*

Yield: *4 servings*

2 tablespoons cider vinegar	*2 cloves garlic, minced*	*2 ripe avocados, peeled, pitted, and cut into ½-inch cubes*
2 tablespoons fresh lemon juice	*Salt and pepper*	
	3 cups cubed cooked chicken	*½ cup crumbled blue cheese (or other favorite cheese)*
1 teaspoon Dijon mustard	*6 cups spinach, rinsed and torn into bite-size pieces*	
½ cup olive oil		*8 slices bacon, cooked and broken into small pieces*
2 tablespoons chopped fresh herbs, such as basil, tarragon, and/or marjoram, or to taste (or 2 teaspoons dried herbs)	*2 cups Boston lettuce, rinsed and torn into bite-size pieces*	*16 cherry tomatoes, stemmed and halved*
		1 small red onion, chopped

1 In a medium mixing bowl, whisk together the vinegar, lemon juice, and mustard. Slowly add the olive oil, whisking constantly to incorporate it into the vinegar-lemon juice mixture. Stir in the herbs, garlic, and salt and pepper to taste. Add the chicken and toss well. Refrigerate for at least 30 minutes.

2 Divide the spinach and lettuce among 4 individual plates. Place equal amounts of the chicken on top of the greens. Reserve the small amount of vinaigrette that remains in the bottom of the mixing bowl.

3 Arrange an equal amount of the avocados, blue cheese, bacon, cherry tomatoes, and red onion around the chicken on each plate; drizzle the remaining marinade over everything. If desired, adjust seasoning with salt and pepper; serve immediately.

Vary It! *You can substitute 16 to 20 pitted black olives for the cherry tomatoes. You can also add 4 chopped, hard-cooked eggs (see Chapter 10) to the base of the greens, or use other types of mixed greens entirely.*

Tip: *When buying an avocado, feel the skin; it should be slightly soft but not mushy. If you want to ripen the avocado quickly at home, place it in a paper bag along with an apple or an orange, close the bag, and let it sit overnight. Oranges emit a gas called ethylene, which causes other fruits — melons, tomatoes, and bananas — to ripen quickly. In fact, avocados, bananas, and tomatoes are usually shipped hard and then placed in rooms filled with ethylene.*

Go-With: *Toasted corn muffins are the perfect accompaniment to this salad. You can also serve this salad with a side dish of Garlic Grilled Portobello Mushrooms (see Chapter 8).*

Per serving: *Calories 747 (From Fat 531); Fat 59g (Saturated 14g); Cholesterol 117mg; Sodium 749mg; Carbohydrate 16g (Dietary Fiber 10g); Protein 43g.*

Chicken and Grilled Vegetable Wrap

A *wrap* is a sandwich made with flatbreads, such as flour tortillas, that roll around a filling of vegetables, poultry, meat, or fish. Unlike a sandwich, the fillings in a wrap are usually diced, shredded, or thinly sliced. In this recipe, we designed a wrap that uses leftover cooked chicken, grilled vegetables, and a sour cream-yogurt dressing. Because you're already grilling the vegetables, you can also use raw chicken breasts for this recipe and cook the chicken along with the veggies. If your grill is too small to hold all these vegetables, you can cook them in two batches instead.

This recipe tastes even better the next day, so it makes for great leftovers on its own, even when it already uses leftover chicken! Just cover the chicken-grilled vegetable mixture and store overnight in the refrigerator before assembling the next day.

Tools: *Chef's knife, charcoal or gas grill, brush for oiling the grill grates, baking sheet, large mixing bowl, blender, small pitcher*

Preparation time: *About 15 minutes*

Cooking time: *25 minutes, or 50 minutes if cooking vegetables in two batches*

Yield: *4 servings*

1 red, yellow, or green bell pepper, cored, seeded, and quartered	1 small zucchini, quartered lengthwise to make 4 long strips	¼ cup chopped basil or parsley
1 large portobello mushroom cap	Oil for coating the vegetables and the grill	Salt and black pepper
1 medium red or yellow onion, cut into ½-inch slices	2 cups cooked chicken, cut into ½-inch cubes, or 2 chicken breasts, raw	¾ cup sour cream
		¼ cup lowfat yogurt
		4 flour tortillas (8 to 9 inches)

1 Prepare a medium-hot fire in a charcoal or gas grill.

2 As the grill preheats, brush the bell peppers, mushroom, onions, and zucchini with the oil, coating all sides. Brush the grill grate with the oil. Place the bell peppers, mushroom, onions, and zucchini on the grill grate. Also place the raw chicken, if using, on the grill grate; grill, turning often, until the vegetables are lightly browned on both sides and the chicken is cooked through, about 25 minutes. (The vegetables may be done before the chicken, so you can remove them and let the chicken continue cooking until no pink remains in the middle. Cut the chicken open to check.) Remove the vegetables and the grilled chicken to a baking sheet and let them stand until they're cool enough to handle.

3 Chop all the vegetables into ½-inch-thick pieces. Chop the chicken, if just cooked on the grill. Transfer the vegetables to a large mixing bowl; add the chicken and 2 tablespoons of the chopped basil or parsley and toss well. Season to taste with salt and pepper.

4 In a blender container, combine the sour cream, yogurt, and the remaining 2 tablespoons of the basil or parsley. Blend a few seconds, or until the dressing is well incorporated; season to taste with salt and pepper.

5 Divide the chicken-vegetable mixture among the tortillas, leaving a 1- to 2-inch border. Drizzle 1 to 2 tablespoons of the sour cream-yogurt dressing over the filling. Transfer the remaining dressing to a small pitcher.

6 On 2 opposite sides of the tortilla, fold the tortilla ½ inch over the filling; then take one of the unfolded sides and start rolling to the end. Serve with the remaining sour cream-yogurt dressing.

Tip: *Warming the tortillas in the microwave for about 30 seconds just before you use them makes the tortillas easier to work with.*

Vary It! *You can make all kinds of wrap fillings based on ingredients in your refrigerator or pantry. Substitute any of these vegetables for the ones in our recipe: tomatoes, radicchio leaves, asparagus spears, or sliced fennel.*

Tip: *If you don't have an outdoor grill or the weather prevents you from using it, you can still grill. All you need is a stovetop grill pan, which looks like a frying pan but has ridges over the cooking surface that provide the great smoky flavor and sought-after marks of an outdoor grill. The pan comes in a variety of shapes and with nonstick or cast-iron surfaces.*

Per serving: *Calories 418 (From Fat 170); Fat 19g (Saturated 8g); Cholesterol 82mg; Sodium 491mg; Carbohydrate 34g (Dietary Fiber 2g); Protein 28g.*

Wok This Way: Stir-Frying

Stir-frying is an easy technique to master and is the perfect way to use up leftover meat, poultry, or vegetables, although uncooked meat also works in the following recipe. When stir-frying, the oil in the wok or skillet should be very hot before adding the ingredients, but not so hot that it begins to smoke. You don't need a wok (a concave, bowl-shaped pan, traditional to Chinese cooking) to stir-fry — a large skillet will do. But if you do have a wok and are looking for more ways to use it, check out *Chinese Cooking For Dummies,* by Martin Yan (published by Wiley).

Before you start stir-frying, have all your ingredients cleaned, chopped, and ready to go. Being prepared, with everything in its place, is called *mise en place* in French cooking. Measure and organize your ingredients, and set them up right next to the stove before you heat the cooking oil (as shown in Figure 18-2). Your aim is to place all the ingredients right at your fingertips for a quick and timely addition to the skillet.

Use two forks or two large wooden spoons to toss the shredded ingredients in the hot oil. The tossing doesn't have to be constant, but tossing thoroughly and often exposes all of the ingredients to the hot oil and causes them to cook quickly. To speed up the cooking, you can cover the wok or skillet immediately after adding the vegetables and pork to the oil, but remove the cover after about 45 seconds so you can watch the mixture to keep it from scorching.

Stir-fry greens

Greens are an essential part of traditional stir-fry. Besides being super-nutritious, greens add texture, crunch, and a pleasingly bitter bite to an otherwise rich stir-fry. The following greens are the ones most often used in stir fry and most traditional to Chinese cooking.

Bok choy, with its long white stem and dark, ribbed leaves, resembles Romaine lettuce in its shape. Bok choy, a staple in Chinese cooking, has a very mild flavor and comes in different sizes. The smaller bok choy is best for stir-frying, while the larger ones are best used in soups. Bok choy is available year-round in well-stocked groceries and Asian markets.

Napa cabbage is a laid-back term for common Chinese cabbage. It comes in two varieties. One variety is stout, with a thick core and wide leaves; the other is longer and narrower, with tall, clinging leaves. The flavor of both is more subtle than that of round cabbage, which makes it excellent for stir-frying. Napa cabbage is widely available in supermarkets.

Improvising with leftovers

What you do with your leftovers is limited only by your imagination — and the knowledge you gain from having a lot of cooking experience! Leftover meat can serve all kinds of functions for future meals. Why just warm it up and serve it the way you had it the night before? Boring! Instead, try these suggestions:

- Serve pieces of leftover cold meat or fish, from beef to chicken to salmon, in a salad.

- Slice leftover cold meat for sandwiches.

- Roll slices of cold meat in a wrap.

- Prepare appetizers of cold meat on crispy crackers or baguette slices spread with a thin layer of cream cheese. Top with a bit of watercress, lettuce, or a fresh cilantro leaf.

Looking for a hot meal that uses leftover meat?

- Mix it with pasta.

- Bake it into a strata (see Chapter 14).

- Fry it with rice and vegetables.

- Scramble it into eggs (see Chapter 1).

- Fold it into an omelet (see Chapter 10).

Any of these options go for leftover veggies, too.

Figure 18-2: Have all your ingredients ready to go before you start to stir-fry.

Pork and Noodle Stir-Fry

Make this stir-fry recipe with pork or substitute leftover chicken, beef, or raw, shelled shrimp (cooking leftover shrimp again will make it too tough). You can also switch out the vegetables, according to what you have. For example, you can use thinly sliced red peppers instead of the carrots. Using light soy sauce, as the recipe calls for, adds a subtle salt flavor, but if you prefer a more intense flavor, use regular soy sauce instead. If you prefer, substitute 3 to 4 cups of cooked rice for the noodles. But don't toss the rice into the stir-fry; use it as a bed on which to place the pork and vegetable mixture. In other words, don't feel bound to the recipe! Remember that the whole point is to use up your leftovers in a delicious way.

Tools: *Chef's knife, grater, vegetable peeler, large pot, colander, mixing bowl, wok or large skillet*

Preparation time: *About 15 minutes*

Cooking time: *About 15 minutes*

Yield: *4 servings*

½ pound dried Chinese noodles (available in Asian groceries), or thin spaghetti or linguini (broken in half)

2 teaspoons sesame oil

3 tablespoons light soy sauce

1 tablespoon dry or medium-dry sherry

2 teaspoons cornstarch

1 teaspoon packed brown sugar

2 cups thinly sliced cooked pork (or raw pork)

2 tablespoons vegetable oil

1 tablespoon peeled and grated gingerroot

3 cups thinly sliced napa cabbage, bok choy, or green cabbage (see the sidebar "Stir-fry greens")

1 cup thinly sliced or shredded carrot

½ cup homemade or canned chicken stock

3 thinly sliced green onions (white and green parts)

1 large clove garlic, peeled and minced

½ jalapeño or red chile pepper, seeded and chopped (optional)

Salt and black pepper

3 tablespoons chopped cilantro

1 Bring a large pot of lightly salted water to a boil; add the noodles and cook according to package directions. (Do not overcook, or the noodles will be mushy.) Drain and rinse the noodles under cold water; drain again. Transfer the noodles to a medium mixing bowl; toss them with the sesame oil to keep them from sticking together. Set aside.

2 In a medium mixing bowl, stir together 2 tablespoons of the soy sauce, the sherry, corn-starch, and brown sugar; add the pork and toss to mix well. Set aside.

3 Place a wok or large skillet over high heat. Add the vegetable oil and heat until the oil is hot but not yet smoking. Add the gingerroot and stir just a few seconds, or until it browns lightly. Add the cabbage, carrots, chicken stock, green onions, garlic, jalapeño pepper (if desired), and pork with all of the marinade. Cook, tossing the ingredients often, for 3 to 5 minutes, or until the vegetables are crisp-tender.

4 Remove the wok from the heat; add the noodles and toss thoroughly. Stir in the remain-ing tablespoon of soy sauce. Season to taste with salt and pepper. Sprinkle with the cilantro before serving.

Tip: *If the mixture in the wok gets dry, add a little more chicken stock and toss well. Always keep your eye on the wok to make sure there's a little liquid in the bottom.*

Go-With: *Soup is a natural starter for this Asian-style dish. You could serve a light Carrot Soup with Dill (see Chapter 11), or stir boiling water into some miso paste (available in the Asian food section) and top with a few slices of green onions, mushrooms, and/or tofu cubes.*

Per serving: *Calories 444 (From Fat 134); Fat 15g (Saturated 2g); Cholesterol 56mg; Sodium 813mg; Carbohydrate 53g (Dietary Fiber 10g); Protein 29g.*

Part V
Special Occasions

The 5th Wave   By Rich Tennant

Hey, Brad! Love the coconut butter on the shrimp!

Where's that suntan lotion?

In this part . . .

*W*ho doesn't like a party? Maybe you didn't, back in the days when you didn't feel quite so comfortable in the kitchen. But with this book in hand, we think you're ready to play host to a whole herd of guests. Whether you're planning a Super Bowl party for the whole gang, or you're hosting a traditional holiday meal, we provide the recipes you need in these chapters. Plus, we help you prepare for the party in advance, guiding you through the process of cooking ahead of time so that you can relax on the day of the party and enjoy yourself.

Chapter 19

Summertime Soiree

In This Chapter

▶ Planning a menu for a summertime party

▶ Making the perfect fried chicken

▶ Serving up summertime side dishes

▶ Whipping up a patriotic dessert

▶ Cooling off with lemonade or a berry good smoothie

Backyard barbecues, beach volleyball bonanzas, pool parties. From Memorial Day in May to Labor Day in September, summer is filled with opportunities for outdoor gatherings. Whether you're celebrating a national holiday or simply surrounding yourself with family and friends just for the fun of it, we have the perfect menu for a summer soiree in this chapter. We even let you know what to make in advance and what to make the day of the party. So sit back and relax with a tall glass of lemonade (if you don't have any on hand, check out the end of this chapter). And leave the planning to us.

Planning the Party

Planning a party can sometimes overwhelm even the most experienced entertainer among us. But often, when you figure out what your menu will look like, the other things fall into place. The menu is the heart of a party. It sets the tone and sometimes even the theme of your entire party. This one is perfect for summertime, but feel free to tweak it for any theme you prefer:

✔ Fried Chicken for a Crowd

✔ Baked Beans

✔ Perfect Corn on the Cob

✔ All-American Coleslaw

- Macaroni and Ham Salad with Mustard Dressing
- Red, White, and Blue Berry Shortcake
- Strawberry Lemonade
- Summer Berry Smoothie

The most important thing you can do to make your party a success rather than an organizational nightmare is to plan ahead. Planning ahead makes all the difference in cooking for large groups. Figure out what you can make a few days before, the day before, the morning of the party, and which things require your last-minute attention. Enlist help when you can, either for cooking or for putting out plates and napkins, setting out food, or keeping the flies out of the punch bowl.

For the menu in this chapter, you can do the following things the day before:

- Assemble the Baked Beans.
- Make the All-American Coleslaw.
- Make the Macaroni and Ham Salad with Mustard Dressing.
- Make the Strawberry Lemonade.
- Place the chicken pieces in the batter marinade (see the recipe for Fried Chicken for a Crowd).

Cover well and refrigerate anything you make ahead of time. You also may want to clean out your refrigerator at least two days before the party to make space for this food.

The morning of your party, start your day off right by doing the following to get your Red, White, and Blue Berry Shortcake started.

- Make the biscuits.
- Hull and slice the strawberries; rinse, pick over, and drain the blueberries.

And you can finish off your cooking the day of the party with the following:

- Make the whipped cream for the Red, White, and Blue Berry Shortcake.
- Make the Fried Chicken for a Crowd and the Perfect Corn on the Cob just before serving.
- Bake the Baked Beans.
- Assemble the Red, White, and Blue Berry Shortcake.

Now your party is off and running! For the nitty-gritty details of actually cooking all that delicious party food, see the following sections.

Making Fried Chicken to Please a Crowd

Deep-frying usually calls for cooking food in at least 2 inches of hot fat. However, in this next recipe, we reduce the fat to about ½ inch. With this method, less fat is absorbed by the chicken, less hot fat splatters, and, most importantly, the skin still develops that yummy, crispy crust.

Here are a few things to keep in mind when frying chicken:

- ✔ **Keep the oil in the pan hot enough (between 350 and 365 degrees) so that the chicken crust is not greasy.** Gauge the temperature with a deep-frying thermometer, which comes with a clip that attaches to the side of the pot. If you don't have such a thermometer, drop a small amount of batter into the hot oil; if it sizzles instantly, the oil has reached 365 degrees. If the batter burns in 5 seconds or so, the oil is too hot. Adjust the heat, as necessary, to raise or lower the temperature of the oil.

- ✔ **Use solid or liquid vegetable oil, like Crisco, when you're deep frying.** Solid vegetable shortening has just the right characteristics to make the chicken skin crispy and the meat moist. Vegetable oil, particularly canola, corn, or peanut oil, works well, too. Don't use butter, which will smoke horribly, or olive oil, which also has a low smoking point.

- ✔ **When frying chicken, be sure the heat is even and doesn't fluctuate.** When the chicken first hits the oil, it causes the temperature to fall. So you need to raise the heat to offset this effect, and then carefully lower it as the oil temperature rises again. Watch the temperature carefully; extreme heat causes the skin of the chicken to look like charred marshmallow.

- ✔ **Use a high-sided fry pan.** Cast-iron frying pans are best, because when they get hot, they stay hot, even long after you remove them from the heat. (That also means don't grab the handle without an oven mitt!)

- ✔ **If you have time, place the chicken pieces in the batter and let them sit overnight in the refrigerator.** Doing so makes the batter cling more readily to the chicken during frying.

- ✔ **You can add all sorts of seasonings to the batter, including paprika, cayenne, nutmeg, cinnamon, garlic salt, garlic powder, and other spices.** Experiment with one or two of these spices at a time and see what you like best. Don't add more than two seasonings at once, though, because too many spices spoil the dish!

- ✔ **Be sure that all your utensils are very dry.** Water and oil are not a good combination; together, water causes the hot oil to splatter and can give you a nasty burn. Use long tongs to turn the chicken pieces when cooking.

Fried Chicken for a Crowd

Fried chicken (shown in the color section) is sinfully rich, so one piece per person may be enough — especially if you're serving other entrees. But at a summer picnic, your guests may be likely to go on a fried chicken binge! If you're feeding only 4 or 5 people, cut this recipe in half. (Or not. Who doesn't love cold fried chicken the next day?)

If you don't want to make this recipe in two skillets, make the fried chicken in batches. Just remember that it tastes best when eaten right away, so serve the first batch while you're making the second batch. Also, replenish the oil before you cook the second batch.

Tools: *2 large, deep skillets (preferably cast-iron), tongs, chef's knife, large bowl, whisk or spoon, baking rack, baking sheet, deep-fat thermometer*

Preparation time: *25 minutes, plus optional 2 to 12 hours for chicken to sit in batter mix*

Cooking time: *About 20 minutes*

Yield: *8 servings*

7 to 8 pounds chicken parts (legs, wings, thighs, and breasts)	3 teaspoons salt, or to taste
3½ cups buttermilk	2 teaspoons garlic powder
1 tablespoon Tabasco sauce, or to taste	1 teaspoon paprika
Salt and pepper	4 to 5 cups solid vegetable shortening (such as Crisco)
3 cups all-purpose flour	Parsley sprigs for garnish (optional)

1 Cut each whole breast in half by running a knife along the breastbone. Trim off any loose fat. Rinse the chicken pieces and pat dry with paper towels.

2 Pour the buttermilk into a large bowl. Stir in the Tabasco sauce and add the salt and pepper to taste. Add the chicken pieces and turn them to coat in the batter. If you have time, cover and refrigerate for 2 to 12 hours, turning occasionally.

3 In a large bowl or shallow baking dish, combine the flour, 3 teaspoons salt, pepper to taste, garlic powder, and paprika. Lift the chicken pieces out of the batter. Roll each piece in the seasoned flour several times, or until well coated all around. (Or place the seasoned flour in a 1-gallon resealable plastic bag, add the chicken pieces one at a time, and shake the bag until the chicken is well coated. Repeat with the remaining pieces.)

4 Set the coated chicken pieces on a dish for about 15 minutes to let the coating dry and adhere to the chicken.

5 Place 2 large and deep heavy skillets over medium-high heat; add enough of the Crisco or vegetable oil to each skillet to make a ½-inch layer of oil. Heat until the oil registers 350 degrees on a deep-frying thermometer or until a small amount of batter sizzles and bubbles when dropped into the pan.

6 Gently add the chicken pieces to the pan, skin side down, in a single layer. Do not crowd the pan. Cover and cook over medium heat for 10 minutes, checking after 5 minutes to see if the pieces are browning evenly. Move them around if necessary and turn the heat down if they're browning too quickly.

7 Gently turn the pieces and cook, uncovered, another 10 to 12 minutes or until done. (The wings should be removed after about 7 minutes.) To test for doneness, remove a thigh or leg and carefully make a small incision in the center of each piece; the juices should run clear, and the meat should be white with no trace of pink.

8 Drain the cooked pieces on a rack set over paper towels or on a baking sheet. If not serving immediately, the chicken may be kept warm by placing the rack on a baking sheet in a 200-degree oven. Chicken that is to be served from 30 minutes up to 1 hour later can be safely left on the rack at room temperature, loosely covered with wax paper, and reheated in a 350-degree oven. (It is also delicious cold.)

9 Serve the chicken on a large platter or in a basket lined with colorful napkins. Garnish with parsley sprigs, if you want.

Vary It! *If you like hot, spicy flavors, push up the level of the Tabasco sauce in the batter. We use up to ¼ cup of Tabasco sauce with delicious results. Tabasco also makes a garlic pepper sauce that divinely accents the chicken.*

Per serving: Calories 789 (From Fat 376); Fat 42g (Saturated 12g); Cholesterol 161mg; Sodium 929mg; Carbohydrate 42g (Dietary Fiber 1g); Protein 58g.

Serving Up Sides and a Sweet Finish

Just as important as the main dish are the accompaniments. What's a summer party without macaroni salad, savory-sweet baked beans, and, of course, good old-fashioned corn on the cob? Be sure to have plenty of side dishes for hungry guests. With these choices, you're bound to have people clamoring for second helpings.

Round off your party with a delicious, not-too-filling dessert. Nobody wants to feel too loaded down while wearing shorts or a bathing suit! The light and whimsically patriotic dessert we offer here fits the bill perfectly.

Baked Beans

Classic baked bean casseroles call for cooking dried beans for hours on end, as much as all day. If that isn't your idea of fun, we spare you that effort without sacrificing much flavor by using canned and frozen beans in this recipe. You can assemble and refrigerate this dish a day or two ahead and then bake it the day you serve it. Leftovers are also terrific. Just reheat the casserole, covered, in a 350-degree oven for about 15 minutes, or until warmed through. Add a little more water if the sauce needs to be thinned. You can use almost any precooked canned beans in this recipe. The ones listed here are just suggestions (and the ones we enjoy).

Tools: *Large skillet, saucepan, deep baking dish with cover, chef's knife, tongs, wooden spoon*

Preparation time: *15 minutes*

Cooking time: *About 1 hour and 15 minutes*

Yield: *8 servings*

¼ pound thickly sliced bacon (about 4 slices)	*¼ cup water*
1 large yellow onion, chopped	*1½ tablespoons cider vinegar*
1 to 2 jalapeño peppers, or other hot chile peppers, seeded and chopped	*1½ tablespoons Worcestershire sauce*
	Black pepper
1 large clove garlic, minced	*1 package (10 ounces) frozen baby lima beans*
½ cup molasses	*1 jar or can (16 ounces) baked beans*
½ cup chili sauce	*1 can (16 ounces) red kidney beans, drained and rinsed*
½ cup ketchup	

1 Preheat the oven to 375 degrees.

2 In a large skillet, cook the bacon over medium heat until lightly browned, turning occasionally, about 10 minutes. Drain on paper towels, reserving the bacon drippings in the pan. When the bacon is cool enough to handle, tear it into small pieces and set aside.

3 Add the onion, jalapeño peppers, and garlic to the skillet and cook over medium heat until the onions are transparent, about 3 to 4 minutes, stirring often. Stir in the molasses, chili sauce, ketchup, water, vinegar, Worcestershire sauce, and black pepper to taste. Bring to a boil, reduce the heat, and simmer for 5 minutes, stirring occasionally.

4 Bring a medium saucepan of lightly salted water to a boil, add the lima beans, and cook for about 3 to 4 minutes, or until just tender, and then drain.

5 Place the lima beans, baked beans, and kidney beans in a large, deep baking dish. Add the molasses-onion mixture and stir well to combine. Sprinkle the reserved bacon pieces over the top. Cover and bake for 30 to 35 minutes or until bubbly; remove the cover and bake for about 25 minutes more to thicken the sauce slightly.

Go-With: *In addition to tasting great with fried chicken, baked beans go well with hamburgers. Check out Chapter 8 for our Perfect Hamburger recipe.*

Per serving: *Calories 308 (From Fat 64); Fat 7g (Saturated 3g); Cholesterol 18mg; Sodium 1,341mg; Carbohydrate 51g (Dietary Fiber 8g); Protein 11g.*

○ *Perfect Corn on the Cob*

How hard can it be to cook the perfect ear of corn? Not so hard if you follow a few simple tips. First, buy corn still in its husk, if possible, rather than the plastic-wrapped, fully shucked kind you often see in the store. Second, do not shuck the corn until cooking time. The silk and husk help keep the kernels moist. If you have to store corn, put it in a plastic bag and refrigerate. Finally, don't overcook your corn. About 5 to 6 minutes, just until the corn is heated through, is plenty for young, tender ears. Older ears may take up to 10 minutes.

This recipe calls for one ear of corn per person, but if you have more guests or you think your guests may eat more than one ear each, just add more to the pot. The cooking time remains the same.

Tools: *Large pot, tongs*

Preparation time: *5 minutes*

Cooking time: *About 5 to 6 minutes*

Yield: *8 servings*

8 ears fresh sweet corn

Salt and pepper

½ cup (1 stick) butter

1 Bring a large pot of water to a boil. While waiting for the water to boil, husk the corn.

2 When the water boils, carefully drop the ears, one at a time, into the pot. Cover and boil for about 5 minutes, or until the corn is warmed through. Using tongs, remove the ears from the water and set them on a plate to drain. Serve immediately with salt, pepper, and 1 tablespoon of butter per ear.

Vary It! *For a change of pace, flavor the butter with assorted spices and herbs. For example, you can soften the butter to room temperature and mix in a little lemon or lime juice, chopped cilantro or chervil, or chopped fresh basil.*

Per serving: *Calories 178 (From Fat 112); Fat 12g (Saturated 7g); Cholesterol 31mg; Sodium 88mg; Carbohydrate 17g (Dietary Fiber 2g); Protein 3g.*

As American as . . . corn?

Americans in particular have always fancied themselves as corn connoisseurs. Every summer, on picnic tables across the land, culinary Olympic judges rate the current crop as if it were a high-dive competition. "This is pretty good — I give it an eight. But it's not like the ones we had last Labor Day." Soil, sun, and freshness are critical in producing superior corn. True corn-on-the-cob aficionados say that fresh corn should be picked as close to cooking time as possible. The sugar in corn quickly converts to starch after picking, making it lose its sweetness. However, the corn industry has made a lot of progress in recent years to develop strains of corn that hold their sweetness for several days.

Corn comes in colors ranging from almost white to deep yellow, and the ears and individual kernels can be big or small. Size and color have nothing to do with flavor. Corn in a store or market should look fresh. The husks should be green with no sign of dryness or splotching. The silk at the tip of the husk can be dark, but the silk inside should be moist.

☺ All-American Coleslaw

Not a huge coleslaw fan? Maybe that's because you think of coleslaw as the gloppy, overly sweetened stuff so often displayed in giant bowls at the delicatessen. Give this recipe a try. Our homemade coleslaw is not heavily coated with mayonnaise, which means that the flavors of the cabbage and other vegetables shine through.

Tools: *Chef's knife, grater (or food processor or mandoline), large bowl, small bowl, whisk*

Preparation time: *15 to 20 minutes, plus 2 to 3 hours refrigeration*

Yield: *8 servings*

1 medium head green cabbage (about 2 pounds), tough outer leaves removed	2 red bell peppers, cored, seeded, and diced	⅓ cup sugar
4 carrots, peeled and grated	1 medium yellow onion, diced	⅓ cup cider vinegar
	1½ cups mayonnaise, or to taste	Salt and black pepper

1 Using a large chef's knife, halve the cabbage crosswise; cut out the hard, solid core; and then quarter the remaining chunks of leaves. Slice the cabbage, starting at one end, as thinly as possible. Then chop the slices crosswise to make short lengths. (You can do this quickly in a food processor by using the shredding blade, or with a mandoline, as shown in Figure 19-1.) You should have about 16 cups of loosely packed cabbage. Place the cabbage, carrots, bell peppers, and onion in a large bowl.

2 In a small bowl, using a wire whisk or fork to blend, combine the mayonnaise, sugar, vinegar, and salt and black pepper to taste. Pour the dressing over the cabbage mixture and toss thoroughly to coat. Taste to see whether it needs more salt and pepper. Cover the bowl with plastic wrap and refrigerate for 2 to 3 hours before serving to blend the flavors, stirring occasionally.

Tip: Try using lowfat or nonfat mayonnaise to lower the calorie and fat content of this recipe.

Per serving: Calories 360 (From Fat 263); Fat 29g (Saturated 4g); Cholesterol 22mg; Sodium 329mg; Carbohydrate 23g (Dietary Fiber 5g); Protein 3g.

Macaroni and Ham Salad with Mustard Dressing

The ham in this salad adds a bit of distinctive saltiness and is a nice counterpoint to the cold macaroni.

Tools: Chef's knife, citrus juicer, large pot, large bowl

Preparation time: 15 to 20 minutes, plus 2 hours refrigeration

Yield: 8 servings

½ pound elbow macaroni

1 cup mayonnaise

2 tablespoons Dijon-style mustard

Juice of 1 lemon

1 cup diced (about ¼-inch cubes), fully cooked, smoked, or boiled ham

⅓ cup chopped fresh basil leaves

1 large clove garlic, minced

⅔ cup diced green or red bell pepper

⅔ cup diced fennel bulb or celery

¼ cup minced red onion

Salt and black pepper

1 Bring a large pot of salted water to a boil, add the macaroni, and cook until just tender, about 6 to 8 minutes. Drain, rinse under cold water, drain again, and place in a large bowl.

2 In a small bowl, combine the mayonnaise, mustard, and lemon juice.

3 Add the mayonnaise mixture, ham, basil, garlic, bell pepper, fennel bulb, red onion, and salt and black pepper to taste to the macaroni. Toss well to combine. Refrigerate, covered, for at least 2 hours before serving.

Vary It! For a vegetarian version of this macaroni salad, omit the ham and add 2 chopped, hard-cooked eggs or 1 cup canned white beans, drained and rinsed.

Tip: You can cut the calories and fat in the recipe by using lowfat or fat-free mayonnaise.

Per serving: Calories 333 (From Fat 211); Fat 23g (Saturated 4g); Cholesterol 25mg; Sodium 562mg; Carbohydrate 25g (Dietary Fiber 2g); Protein 8g.

Figure 19-1:
How to
use a
mandoline.

Place the mandoline on a cutting board. Choose a slicing blade and adjust it to a desired thickness...

..If your vegetable is too bulky to fit into the box under the handle, cut it down to size. Place the lid firmly down on the vegetable and run rapidly up and down over the slicing blade. The slices will fall onto the counter!

Red, White, and Blue Berry Shortcake

With its strawberries, blueberries, and whipped cream, this patriotic cake is especially well suited for a Fourth of July or Memorial Day celebration. Not only does it look patriotic, but it's a light, refreshing dessert that won't make everybody feel weighed down in the heat of summer. You can make all the components of this cake — the berry mixture, the cream, and even the biscuits — a few hours before serving and then assemble them while someone is whisking the dinner dishes off the table. To make this recipe even easier, use easy-bake biscuits that come in a tube in the refrigerated section of the grocery store.

Tools: *Paring knife, medium and large mixing bowls, electric mixer, spatula, baking sheet, serrated knife, wire rack*

Preparation time: *40 minutes*

Cooking time: *About 15 minutes*

Yield: *8 servings*

2 pints strawberries, rinsed and hulled

2 cups blueberries, rinsed and drained

⅓ cup (or more, to taste) plus 3½ tablespoons granulated sugar

1 tablespoon Cointreau (optional)

1¼ cups heavy cream

2 tablespoons confectioners' sugar, or more, to taste

½ teaspoon vanilla extract

2⅔ cups self-rising cake flour

¼ teaspoon salt

10 tablespoons chilled butter, cut into small pieces

1 cup plus 1 to 2 tablespoons milk

1 Preheat the oven to 400 degrees.

2 Set aside 8 of the most perfect strawberries for a garnish. Crush half of the remaining strawberries with a fork or the back of a spoon; cut the rest in half the long way, from core to tip.

3 In a medium mixing bowl, combine the sliced and crushed strawberries, blueberries, ⅓ cup granulated sugar, and, if desired, the Cointreau. Taste the fruit mixture and add more sugar if necessary. Refrigerate until ready to assemble the shortcake.

4 In a bowl, using an electric mixer, whip the cream with the confectioners' sugar and vanilla until stiff. Cover and refrigerate until you're ready to assemble the shortcake.

5 In a large mixing bowl, combine the flour, the remaining 3½ tablespoons granulated sugar, and salt. Cut the chilled butter into the flour mixture, using two knives, your fingertips, or a pastry blender, until the mixture resembles coarse breadcrumbs. Work quickly so the butter doesn't melt or form a paste.

6 Make a well in the center of the flour mixture and add 1 cup of the milk. Mix gently with a fork, rubber spatula, or wooden spoon just until most of the dry ingredients are moistened and a very soft dough is formed. Do not overmix.

7 Drop the dough, in eight equal portions 1 to 2 inches apart, onto an ungreased baking sheet. Lightly brush the tops of the rounds with the remaining 1 to 2 tablespoons of milk.

8 Bake the biscuits on the center rack of the oven for 15 to 17 minutes, or until golden brown. (Do not overbake, or the bottoms may darken or burn.) Transfer to a wire rack to cool. Finished shortcakes may be served warm or cold.

9 To assemble, using a serrated knife, carefully slice the shortcakes in half crosswise. Transfer each bottom half to an individual serving plate. Spread a generous dollop of whipped cream over the bottom of each biscuit; top with about ⅓ cup of the fruit mixture. Cover with the other half of the shortcakes. Spoon over more cream and berries, and drizzle with any berry juices that have accumulated. Garnish each serving with a reserved whole strawberry. Don't despair if berries fall around the cakes; it's part of the charm. Serve immediately.

Vary It! *If you like, make this recipe in its more traditional Strawberry Shortcake incarnation by using only strawberries. Or, substitute ½ pint each of raspberries and blackberries or 1½ cups sliced bananas (sprinkled with a little lemon juice to keep them looking fresh) for the blueberries.*

Per serving: *Calories 522 (From Fat 269); Fat 30g (Saturated 18g); Cholesterol 94mg; Sodium 621mg; Carbohydrate 59g (Dietary Fiber 4g); Protein 7g.*

Mixing Fruity Drinks for Thirsty Crowds

Summer heat makes party guests thirsty! Every party needs some beverages, and if you're serving beer, wine, or fruity umbrella drinks, you'll also want some delicious drinks for kids and people who prefer nonalcoholic beverages.

Two great options are homemade lemonade and homemade smoothies. Classic lemonade becomes even more exciting when flavored with other fruit purées like strawberry and watermelon. Smoothies look great in a margarita glass and are just thick enough to hold that little paper umbrella.

🍓 Strawberry Lemonade

Don't feel limited by the "strawberry" in the title. This lemonade tastes great made with any kind of fresh berry, or even without berries in its unadorned, homemade goodness. People can tell that this is the real thing, not something you mixed up from a powder, so expect this recipe to be popular. Lucky for you that it's so easy to make more! (For seconds, just skip the chilling stage and serve over plenty of ice.)

Tools: *Strainer, blender or food processor, paring knife, large pitcher*

Preparation time: *10 to 15 minutes, plus 2 hours chilling*

Yield: *8 servings*

1½ cups fresh lemon juice, strained of pits (9 to 10 large lemons)	*6 cups water*	*Lemon slices for garnish (optional)*
	1 pint strawberries, rinsed and hulled	*Mint sprigs for garnish (optional)*
1½ cups sugar		

1 Combine the lemon juice, sugar, and water in a large pitcher. Stir well.

2 Place the hulled strawberries in a blender or food processor; add a little of the lemonade from the pitcher, and blend until smooth.

3 Pour the strawberries into the lemonade, stir, and chill for 2 hours. Stir well before serving. Pour into ice-filled glasses, garnishing each, if desired, with a lemon slice or a sprig of fresh mint.

Vary It! To make classic lemonade, simply omit the strawberries (as shown in the color section). Or try other fruit flavors, such as watermelon (use 3 cups of watermelon chunks with seeds removed) or peaches (use 2 cups of fresh peach slices).

Per serving: Calories 168 (From Fat 1); Fat 0g (Saturated 0g); Cholesterol 0mg; Sodium 1mg; Carbohydrate 44g (Dietary Fiber 1g); Protein 0g.

Summer Berry Smoothie

Smoothies can be a meal in themselves (check out the smoothie photo in the color section). Thick and nutritious, smoothies use the whole fruit, not just the juice, so you get all the benefits of the fiber as well as the vitamins. They're filling and a great way to cool off in the middle of a hot summer day. They can also stand in for daiquiris, margaritas, piña coladas, or any other blender drink.

Blend up a pitcher and invite the neighbors over. Using frozen fruit keeps the smoothie thick and creamy and doesn't dilute the drink the way ice does when it melts. Buy a bunch of bananas, peel them, and store them in individual plastic bags in the freezer so you can whip up smoothies anytime, or keep frozen strawberries handy. If you don't have any frozen fruit, use fresh fruit and add two cups of ice to the blender. Or, use frozen yogurt instead of regular yogurt. This recipe makes 4 small servings, as before-dinner drinks or a dessert. Or, if your smoothie is your entire meal (it makes a great breakfast!), this recipe serves 2.

Tools: *Blender or food processor, paring knife, large pitcher*

Preparation time: *About 15 minutes*

Yield: *4 servings*

1 cup fresh or frozen berries, such as strawberries, blueberries, raspberries, or blackberries	*1 cup vanilla yogurt (nonfat, lowfat, or regular)*
1 frozen, peeled banana	*½ cup orange juice, lemonade, or milk, plus more for thinning if necessary*

1 Combine all the ingredients in a blender.

2 Blend on high until smooth. Add more liquid if the smoothie is too thick. Serve immediately.

Vary It! *Smoothies are easy to adapt to whatever fruit you have. Try adding different flavors of yogurt or other flavorings, such as a teaspoon of instant coffee, a dash of cinnamon, 2 tablespoons of chocolate or maple syrup, or some crushed peppermint leaves. You're limited only by your imagination!*

Per serving: *Calories 118 (From Fat 3); Fat 0g (Saturated 0g); Cholesterol 1mg; Sodium 44mg; Carbohydrate 26g (Dietary Fiber 2g); Protein 4g.*

Chapter 20

Super Bowl Buffet

Any armchair athlete worth his or her salted, buttered bowl of popcorn knows that sitting in a reclining chair with a glass of beer or wine while watching football stirs the appetite as much as actually playing on the field. No, really! It's been scientifically proven. In this chapter, we give you everything you need to keep your "team" going at full force from the kickoff through the last seconds on the clock. Our menu will definitely tempt you to pay attention to the food between plays.

This menu is also ideal for any party or gathering where serving warm and hearty foods helps chase away the chills of fall or winter. These foods are ideal for a Labor Day party, a tailgating party, the basketball season play-offs, election day, Veterans Day, or — what the heck — a party for the end of day-light savings time. Or maybe, like us, you don't need an excuse to throw a party. Just do it!

But for now, we'll just say that the recipes in this chapter are designed especially for your Super Bowl party. Our satisfyingly spicy menu is guaranteed to keep your guests on the edges of their seats — reaching for seconds, not cheering on their favorite team.

Bowling 'Em Over with a Super Menu

A Super Bowl party is all about camaraderie, competition, and the kind of food you can eat out of a bowl or a casserole or pick up with your fingers. After a meal consisting of the following menu items, you'll feel so satisfied that you probably won't mind quite as much if your team loses.

- ✔ Crunchy Party Nibbles
- ✔ Spicy Chicken Wings
- ✔ Taco Casserole
- ✔ Spanish Rice
- ✔ Old-Fashioned Bread Pudding

Now, we know perfectly well that you don't want to miss the beginning of the game because you're too busy doing last-minute cooking chores in the kitchen. To pull off this menu with ease, do these things the day before the party:

- ✔ Make the Crunchy Party Nibbles.
- ✔ Assemble the Taco Casserole, except for the tortilla chips and cheese that make up the topping — add that right before baking.
- ✔ Make the Warm Brandy Sauce.

A few hours before the big game, check these things off your list:

- ✔ Remove the tips from and season the chicken wings. Refrigerate about 2 hours before roasting.
- ✔ Make the Spanish Rice.
- ✔ Bake the Taco Casserole.
- ✔ Assemble the Old-Fashioned Bread Pudding.

Just before the game starts and you're ready to eat, finish your preparations by doing the following:

- ✔ Roast the Spicy Chicken Wings.
- ✔ Bake the Bread Pudding.

At halftime, just reheat the Warm Brandy Sauce, and you're ready to serve dessert during the second half.

Ready by Halftime: Making Your Meal

These recipes are all easy to make and fun to eat, from the Crunchy Party Nibbles to the comforting bread pudding. Stock the fridge full of beer or make a big pitcher of margaritas or fruit smoothies (see Chapter 19) and you're ready to go! Remember to assemble as much food as possible ahead of time (see the preceding section) and put dishes in the oven a couple hours before you need them so that you can join the party, too. Because what's the fun of having a Super Bowl party if you have to miss the game?

Depending on how many raw vegetables you include with the wings, you may want to also serve a simple green salad (see Chapter 12) along with the casserole and rice, just to add something crisp and cool to the meal.

☺ Crunchy Party Nibbles

This recipe is a great snack to eat in front of the TV, and it has two distinct advantages over other similar treats: First, it tastes better than the stuff you buy in the grocery store, and second, you can make it ahead of time, so it's almost as convenient as the packaged stuff.

Tools: *Large roasting pan, large spoon or rubber spatula*

Preparation time: *About 15 minutes*

Cooking time: *30 to 35 minutes*

Yield: *About 5 cups, or 5 servings*

2 tablespoons butter

1½ teaspoons vegetable oil

1 tablespoon Worcestershire sauce

½ teaspoon ground cumin

¼ teaspoon Tabasco sauce

¼ teaspoon paprika

¼ teaspoon garlic salt

¼ teaspoon garlic powder

¼ teaspoon salt, or to taste

4 cups assorted bite-sized cereals (Shredded Wheat, Chex, and so on.)

1 cup mixed nuts (pecan halves, whole natural almonds, unsalted peanuts, and so on)

1 cup unsalted pretzel rounds

1 Preheat the oven to 300 degrees.

2 In a large roasting pan, heat the butter and oil in the oven (just long enough to melt the butter). Take the pan from the oven and add the Worcestershire sauce, cumin, Tabasco, paprika, garlic salt, garlic powder, and salt; stir well to combine. Add the cereal, nuts, and pretzels and toss thoroughly to coat.

3 Return the pan to the oven and bake for 30 to 35 minutes, or until lightly toasted, stirring every 10 to 15 minutes. Let the mixture cool to room temperature. Store in an airtight container.

Per serving: Calories 363 (From Fat 188); Fat 21g (Saturated 5g); Cholesterol 12mg; Sodium 223mg; Carbohydrate 40g (Dietary Fiber 6g); Protein 9g.

Spicy Chicken Wings

This appetizer (shown in the color section) is not only easy to make but is also easy on your pocketbook — a big plus when serving a crowd of ravenous football fans. Serve these zesty chicken wings informally, perhaps with Tabasco sauce on the side, and with bottled blue cheese and/or ranch dressing (for a homemade ranch dressing recipe, see Chapter 12). Stack an assortment of colorful raw vegetables (carrot sticks, bell peppers, celery, broccoli, and so on) alongside the wings, to help offset the wings' spicy flavor.

Tools: *Chef's knife, citrus juicer, grater, large plastic bag or mixing bowl, large roasting pan, rack, cutting board*

Preparation time: *20 minutes, plus 2 hours chilling time before roasting*

Cooking time: *About 45 minutes*

Yield: *8 appetizer servings*

3 pounds chicken wings	2 teaspoons ground cumin	1½ teaspoons salt, or to taste
3 tablespoons olive oil	1 teaspoon dried oregano	Black pepper
3 tablespoons fresh lemon or lime juice	2 teaspoons paprika	1 teaspoon hot chili powder
4 large cloves garlic, minced	2 teaspoons peeled, grated ginger	½ teaspoon cayenne pepper
		Tabasco sauce (optional)

1 Remove the tips of the chicken wings by laying the wing on a cutting board. With a heavy knife, locate the joint between the bony tip and the main part of the wing. Cut down firmly. Discard wing tips or freeze for later use in chicken broth. Rinse the chicken wings under cold tap water and pat them dry with paper towels.

2 Combine the olive oil, lemon juice, garlic, cumin, oregano, paprika, ginger, salt, black pepper, chili powder, and cayenne pepper in a large, resealable plastic bag (or mixing bowl), shaking (or stirring) well to blend. Add the chicken wings; toss well to coat. Seal the bag (or cover the bowl) and refrigerate for about 2 hours.

3 Preheat the oven to 400 degrees. Arrange the chicken wings in a single layer on a rack in a large roasting pan; roast in the oven for 40 to 45 minutes, or until sizzling, crispy, and browned. Turn them once after 20 to 25 minutes. If you want them spicier, serve the wings with Tabasco sauce on the side.

Warning: *Hot chili powder is to regular chili powder what a bonfire is to a cigarette lighter, so use it sparingly. We suggest you add hot chili powder incrementally, stir it in well, and stand back. If nothing happens, approach the bowl and continue cooking. (And keep tasting — you don't want to make the wings so hot that people won't eat them!)*

Per serving: *Calories 204 (From Fat 127); Fat 14g (Saturated 4g); Cholesterol 55mg; Sodium 164mg; Carbohydrate 1g (Dietary Fiber 0g); Protein 18g.*

Taco Casserole

This hearty dish is ideal for casual parties where the food and the conversation tend toward the spicy. Essentially a chili baked with cheese and chips, this casserole is filling and appeals to a wide variety of people, including kids, who might prefer the casserole without the salsa and sour cream garnish. You can assemble this recipe quickly, so you can make it even after the guests arrive.

Tools: *Chef's knife, large skillet, 3-quart oven-safe casserole or 9-x-13-inch baking dish, wooden spoon or spatula*

Preparation time: *15 to 20 minutes*

Cooking time: *25 minutes*

Yield: *8 generous servings*

2 pounds ground chuck or other lean ground beef, or ground turkey	*1 can (15 ounces) pinto beans, drained and rinsed*
½ medium yellow onion, chopped	*3 cups slightly crushed tortilla chips*
1 package taco seasoning mix	*2 cups shredded cheddar cheese*
1 can (8 ounces) tomato sauce	*2 cups store-bought salsa*
1 can (14 ounces) crushed tomatoes	*½ cup sour cream*
2 cans (4 ounces each) mild green chiles, drained and chopped, or ½ cup jarred jalapeño peppers, drained	*2 green onions, chopped, including some of the green part*

1 Preheat the oven to 350 degrees.

2 Put the ground meat and onion in a large skillet. Cook over medium heat until the meat is browned, about 10 minutes. Drain.

3 Stir in the taco seasoning mix, tomato sauce, crushed tomatoes, green chiles, pinto beans, and 2 cups of the tortilla chips. Put into a casserole or baking dish. Top with the cheese and the remaining 1 cup tortilla chips.

4 Bake the casserole for 25 minutes, or until the cheese is melted and the casserole is hot and bubbly. Serve immediately, garnishing each serving with salsa and sour cream sprinkled with the green onions.

Tip: *If you make this casserole a day ahead (as suggested in the previous section), keep in mind that casseroles that are assembled and refrigerated the day before either need a little more baking time to remove the chill, or they need to be brought almost to room temperature before baking.*

Per serving: *Calories 476 (From Fat 230); Fat 26g (Saturated 12g); Cholesterol 114mg; Sodium 1,154mg; Carbohydrate 28g (Dietary Fiber 6g); Protein 35g.*

✍ Old-Fashioned Bread Pudding with Warm Brandy Sauce

Bread puddings fall into two distinct categories. In the first version, bread is immersed in a custard mixture and baked over a pan of hot water. This "water bath" keeps the oven moist and prevents the custard from becoming grainy. In the second version (which uses more bread relative to custard), *all* the custard is soaked up into the bread during baking, so it doesn't need a water bath.

In this recipe, we opt for the latter version. This recipe is wonderfully rich and slightly dense and has fewer than 50 calories per serving (just kidding — but it's a Super Bowl Party, so counting calories is against the rules). Serve this bread pudding with the heady Warm Brandy Sauce. If you have any left over, bread pudding makes a great breakfast, with or without the booze.

Tools: *Bread knife, whisk, mixing bowl, 9-x-13-inch baking pan, baking sheet, saucepan, whisk, small bowl*

Preparation time: *About 20 minutes*

Cooking time: *1 hour and 15 minutes for drying the bread and baking the custard, 5 minutes for cooking the brandy sauce*

Yield: *8 servings*

About 1 tablespoon butter for greasing the baking pan	2 tablespoons packed brown sugar
1 loaf (16 to 18 ounces) of brioche, challah, or other egg bread	2½ cups milk
	2 cups light cream or half-and-half
½ cup raisins	1 tablespoon vanilla extract
3 eggs	½ teaspoon grated orange peel
1 cup granulated sugar	½ teaspoon ground cinnamon
	¼ teaspoon ground nutmeg

1 Preheat the oven to 200 degrees. Butter a 9-x-13-inch baking pan.

2 Cut the bread into 1-inch-thick slices; place the slices in a single layer on a baking sheet and dry them in the oven (about 15 minutes, turning once). Or lay the bread slices in one layer on a baking sheet and let them dry at room temperature overnight.

3 Turn the oven up to 325 degrees.

4 Tear the bread into 1½-inch pieces (you should have about 12 cups). Transfer the bread pieces to the buttered baking pan. Scatter the raisins over the bread.

5 In a large mixing bowl, whisk together the eggs and the granulated and brown sugars until well blended. Whisk in the milk, cream, vanilla extract, orange peel, cinnamon, and nutmeg. Pour this custard mixture over the bread. Press the bread with your fingers so it absorbs the liquid thoroughly; cover and refrigerate for about 1 hour before baking. Let stand at room temperature about 20 minutes to take off some of the chill.

6 Place the pudding, uncovered, on the center oven rack and bake until the surface is lightly browned and the custard is firm in the center (about 1 hour). Remove it from the oven and let it cool for 15 minutes before cutting into squares. Serve with Warm Brandy Sauce. Leftover pudding can be refrigerated and served cold or reheated. To reheat, cover with foil and bake in a 325-degree oven for about 20 minutes.

Warm Brandy Sauce

¾ cup granulated sugar

¼ cup water

¼ cup butter

¼ cup brandy or cognac, or orange juice or apple juice

1 egg

⅛ teaspoon ground nutmeg

1 In a medium saucepan, combine the sugar, water, butter, and brandy or juice. Simmer, whisking until the butter is melted and the sugar is dissolved. Remove from the heat.

2 In a small bowl, whisk the egg with the nutmeg until light and foamy, about 1 minute. Pour the egg mixture into the brandy mixture while whisking vigorously.

3 Set the saucepan over low heat and bring to a simmer, stirring constantly. Cook until the sauce is thickened, about 1 minute. Do not allow it to boil rapidly or the egg may curdle. Spoon the sauce over individual portions of the bread pudding. (This sauce can be made ahead and refrigerated for up to 2 days. Reheat over low heat, stirring constantly).

Vary It! This brandy sauce can be modified in many ways. If you like, substitute an equal amount of dark rum, Grand Marnier, or Kahlúa for the brandy.

Per serving: *Calories 648 (From Fat 245); Fat 27g (Saturated 15g); Cholesterol 204mg; Sodium 376mg; Carbohydrate 89g (Dietary Fiber 2g); Protein 13g.*

Spanish Rice

This flavorful side dish is a good accompaniment to taco casserole because it offers a savory but nonspicy foil to all the spicy stuff in the rest of your menu. Or, if you can't get enough fire, you can always stir in a few chopped jalapeño peppers or some hot red pepper flakes.

Tools: *Chef's knife, large nonstick saucepan with a lid or a Dutch oven or stockpot with a lid*

Preparation time: *About 10 minutes*

Cooking time: *About 30 minutes*

Yield: *10 servings*

1 tablespoon olive oil	½ teaspoon thyme
2 cups converted rice (see Chapter 4)	2 bay leaves
½ medium yellow onion, chopped	1 can (14 ounces) diced tomatoes
2 cloves garlic, peeled and minced	1 teaspoon salt
1 teaspoon oregano	4 cups chicken broth

1 In a large nonstick skillet or Dutch oven, heat the olive oil over medium-high heat. Add the rice, onion, garlic, oregano, thyme, and bay leaves. Sauté until the rice is coated and onions are translucent, about 5 minutes.

2 Add the tomatoes, salt, and chicken broth. Bring the mixture to a boil. Reduce the heat to medium-low, cover, and simmer until all the broth is absorbed, about 20 minutes. Add more broth if the rice looks dry. Remove the bay leaves and serve hot.

Per serving: Calories 175 (From Fat 27); Fat 3g (Saturated 1g); Cholesterol 2mg; Sodium 683mg; Carbohydrate 33g (Dietary Fiber 1g); Protein 4g.

Chapter 21

Thanksgiving Dinner

In This Chapter

▶ Previewing your holiday menu

▶ Starting out with delicious dips

▶ Cooking the big bird

▶ Serving up stuffing and veggies

▶ Concluding with pumpkin pie

*B*eginning cooks often chicken out at the prospect of cooking a turkey, let alone an entire Thanksgiving dinner! All those relatives, all those friends . . . what will they think of you if you char the bird, scald the gravy, drop the mashed potatoes, set the kitchen on fire . . . yikes!

Hey, relax! Thanksgiving dinner isn't all that much different from cooking an ordinary dinner. Sure, you want a feast with a lot of different dishes, but that doesn't mean they have to be all that complicated. In fact, the basic traditional dishes of Thanksgiving are pretty easy. The hard part is in the planning. If you try to do everything at once, you're certainly courting a disaster. But if you plan and construct the meal in easy steps, starting a few days before, the whole experience can be a breeze. Aunt Gertrude will wonder how you learned to cook so well. Uncle John will ask for thirds. Your mother will claim you inherited your skills from her. And everyone will get along famously. (Well, maybe we're being a bit optimistic, but good, well-cooked, homemade food does seem to have that effect on people — even relatives!)

Planning Your Thanksgiving Menu

Half the fun of Thanksgiving is in planning the menu. Well, maybe not half, but a lot of the fun! Thanksgiving isn't quite Thanksgiving without some mouthwatering appetizers to get everybody's digestive systems geared up for dinner. A perfectly roasted, golden turkey is, of course, the crowning glory of the meal, but side dishes make Thanksgiving seem truly bountiful. And don't forget dessert! You can certainly create your own Thanksgiving menu or adapt the one we've provided here to suit you and your family and friends, but just to get you started, here's a Thanksgiving meal we've tried. It tastes great, offers a wide array of delicious foods, and really isn't all that hard to put together. Here is our suggestion for your Thanksgiving menu:

- ✔ Warm Artichoke-Spinach Dip
- ✔ Apple Curry Dip
- ✔ Roasted Turkey with Cornbread, Sausage, and Apple Stuffing
- ✔ Madeira Pan Gravy
- ✔ Fresh Cranberry-Orange Relish with Walnuts
- ✔ Green Beans with Shallot Butter
- ✔ Mashed Potatoes (recipe in Chapter 4)
- ✔ Rum-Baked Sweet Potatoes
- ✔ Praline Pumpkin Pie

Does that sound so overwhelming? It does? Just remember, if you start cooking in advance, you can save yourself a lot of stress. Plan out your schedule. Do the meal in steps. Here's how to break it down, assuming you have a few days ahead of time to prepare and that you plan to eat in the mid-afternoon:

Two days before your meal, make the following:

- ✔ Praline Pumpkin Pie
- ✔ Rum-Baked Sweet Potatoes
- ✔ Fresh Cranberry-Orange Relish with Walnuts (but wait to stir in the walnuts until just before serving)
- ✔ Cornbread for the stuffing

The day before your big meal, do these tasks:

- ✔ Wash and trim the green beans, wrap them in a paper towel, and seal them in a plastic bag.
- ✔ Make the shallot butter.
- ✔ Make and chill the dips.

On Thanksgiving morning, do the following:

- ✔ Whip the cream for the pie.
- ✔ Make the Cornbread, Sausage, and Apple Stuffing.
- ✔ Roast the turkey.

After you take the turkey out of the oven and it is sitting, covered, allowing the juices to sink into the meat, do your final tasks:

- ✔ Make the Madeira Pan Gravy.
- ✔ Cook the Green Beans with Shallots.
- ✔ Make the mashed potatoes.

What's left? Sit down and enjoy your bountiful dinner!

Warming Up for the Feast with Fresh Dips

Serving substantial hors d'oeuvres, like aged cheeses or puff pastries filled with meat, is not a good way to save room for dinner! We favor light, tasty starters like fresh raw vegetables and the dips described in this section. These dips can be jazzed up in many ways with various dried or fresh herbs, hot sauces, and so on.

Warm Artichoke-Spinach Dip

This classic dip is perfect to tantalize everyone's palate for the big meal. Serve it in a bread bowl (pull pieces from the middle of a round loaf for dipping and fill the center of the loaf with the dip) or with tortilla chips, good crackers, or thin toasted slices of French bread.

Tools: *Medium saucepan, chef's knife, citrus juicer, whisk, ovenproof casserole dish or oval gratin dish, colander*

Preparation time: *About 15 minutes*

Cooking time: *About 20 minutes*

Yield: *12 servings, or about 3 cups*

2 boxes (10 ounces each) frozen spinach, thawed

2 tablespoons butter

¼ medium yellow onion, minced

2 cloves garlic, peeled and minced

2 tablespoons flour

1½ cups whole milk or half-and-half

3 tablespoons canned chicken broth

1 teaspoon freshly squeezed lemon juice

½ teaspoon Tabasco sauce

¼ teaspoon salt

½ cup grated Romano cheese

⅓ cup lowfat sour cream

⅔ cup shredded Monterey Jack cheese

1 large ripe plum tomato, cored, seeded, and chopped

1 can (12 ounces) artichoke hearts (not the marinated kind), drained and coarsely chopped

1 Preheat the oven to 350 degrees.

2 Put the thawed spinach in a colander and cover with paper towels. Squeeze to remove as much moisture as possible. Set aside.

3 In a medium saucepan, melt the butter over medium-high heat. Sauté the onion and garlic until the onion is soft and translucent but not brown, about 5 minutes. Add the flour and cook, stirring, for 2 minutes.

4 Slowly whisk in the milk or half-and-half and the chicken broth. Bring to a boil and then remove from the heat. Immediately add the lemon juice, Tabasco sauce, salt, and Romano cheese. Stir to combine and then set aside.

5 Combine the sour cream, Monterey Jack cheese, tomatoes, artichokes, and spinach. Fold into the warm cream mixture and pour the dip into an ovenproof casserole dish. Bake in the oven for 10 minutes, or until warmed through but not browned. Serve immediately.

Vary It! *Add more spice to this dish by upping the amount of Tabasco sauce, or make it milder by eliminating the Tabasco altogether. If you do the latter, try adding ½ teaspoon dried dill or 1 tablespoon fresh, chopped cilantro leaves.*

Per serving: *Calories 96 (From Fat 55); Fat 6g (Saturated 4g); Cholesterol 19mg; Sodium 231mg; Carbohydrate 6g (Dietary Fiber 2g); Protein 5g.*

🍎 Apple Curry Dip

This unusual dip packs a surprising combination of flavors: the tart sweetness of green apples and the exotic spiciness of curry powder. Serve it with good crackers or raw vegetables such as carrots, celery, and cucumber slices.

Tools: *Paring knife, chef's knife, mixing bowl*

Preparation time: *10 minutes*

Yield: *About 1 cup, or 4 servings*

1 Granny Smith apple, peeled, cored, and grated	*2 to 3 teaspoons curry powder, according to taste*
½ cup mayonnaise	*Salt and pepper*
½ cup lowfat plain yogurt	*2 tablespoons chopped parsley (as a garnish)*

In a bowl, stir together the apple, mayonnaise, yogurt, curry powder, and salt and pepper to taste; transfer the mixture to a small serving bowl and chill until served. Garnish with the parsley before serving.

Vary It! *Not a big fan of curry? You can make a sweeter version of this dip. Use 1 cup yogurt instead of using half mayonnaise. Replace the curry powder with ½ teaspoon ground cinnamon, ¼ teaspoon ground nutmeg, and 2 tablespoons honey. Skip the salt and pepper, and instead of garnishing with parsley, garnish with a drizzle of honey and a few cinnamon sticks artfully arranged on top of the dip. Serve with slices of fruit and sticks of carrots and celery.*

Per serving: *Calories 239 (From Fat 204); Fat 23g (Saturated 4g); Cholesterol 18mg; Sodium 324mg; Carbohydrate 8g (Dietary Fiber 1g); Protein 2g.*

Roasting the Turkey

Turkey is an ideal main course for entertaining a crowd — it is easy to cook, ranges in size, and looks great on the table. But which one should you buy and how do you cook it? Don't worry. That's just why we're here with you, to guide you along the way. Here are some important turkey tips to remember before you start cooking.

- ✔ Most supermarket turkeys are frozen; fresh ones are better, so it's worth asking around to find one. Here's why: When a turkey is frozen, its juices turn to ice crystals; when thawed, these crystals disrupt the protein cell membranes in the flesh and cause some of the juices to leak out — that's the reddish stuff you see in the packaging when you open it. A frozen turkey is never as moist as a fresh one, which is why many frozen turkeys are injected with a broth/sugar solution to replace the lost moisture. Wouldn't it be nice to just keep the original juiciness inside the turkey instead? This is why we prefer fresh.

- ✔ If you do buy a frozen turkey, let it defrost in the refrigerator (allow about 24 hours for every four to 5 pounds).

- ✔ When you're trying to decide what size turkey to buy, consider that an 18- to 20-pound bird feeds 14 or more. A 25-pound bird could easily serve 20 or more. (One general guideline recommends 1 pound of turkey per person.) Also, be sure you know the dimensions of your oven and that the bird you buy will fit.

- ✔ Basting a turkey during roasting gives it a golden and crisp skin; however it doesn't penetrate the skin, so it has no effect on the moisture of the meat, despite what your Aunt Gertrude may have told you.

- ✔ If your turkey starts to get too brown during cooking, cover it loosely with aluminum foil.

- ✔ Check out Table 21-1 for roasting times for a fresh or thawed turkey at 325 degrees. These times are approximate and should be used only as a guide; factors that can alter cooking time include the accuracy of your oven, the temperature of the bird when it goes into the oven, and the number of times the oven door is opened during roasting. Always use a meat thermometer to be sure of the temperature.

- ✔ If you don't want to stuff your turkey, you can cook the stuffing in a casserole in the oven (see the recipe later in this chapter) instead of cooking it in the bird. Doing so decreases the turkey's cooking time as well as the chance of salmonella bacteria growing in the cavity. If you do want to stuff the bird, that's fine. Just be sure to keep the turkey well chilled until just before stuffing it, and stuff the turkey immediately before baking, not hours before. Then you should be fine.

✔ If you choose to stuff the turkey, stuff it loosely; this way, the stuffing cooks faster and more thoroughly than if you pack it in tightly.

✔ Always test the stuffing for doneness. It should register 160 degrees on an instant-read thermometer. If the bird is done but your stuffing is not, remove the turkey from the oven, spoon the stuffing into a buttered casserole, and continue to bake it (as the bird rests).

Table 21-1	Turkey Roasting Chart	
Weight	*Cooking Time (Unstuffed)*	*Cooking Time (Stuffed)*
8 to 12 pounds	2¾ to 3 hours	3 to 3½ hours
12 to 14 pounds	3 to 3¾ hours	3¼ to 4 hours
14 to 18 pounds	3¾ to 4¼ hours	4 to 4½ hours
20 to 24 pounds	4½ to 5 hours	4¾ to 5¼ hours

Turkey roasting resources

The following organizations are available to provide information about turkey roasting — in case you need a little help around the holidays:

✔ **The National Turkey Federation:** Visit www. eatturkey.com for over 600 recipes, as well as information about purchasing, storing, and cooking a turkey. The site even gives tips for using leftovers.

✔ **The USDA Meat and Poultry Hotline:** Visit the USDA on the Web at www.fsis.

usda.gov for food and safety tips about meat, poultry, and eggs. You can also call toll-free at 800-535-4555.

✔ **Butterball Turkey:** Between November 1 and December 23, you call 800-323-4848 for tips on roasting, storing, stuffing, and so on. Or, visit Butterball online at www.butterball.com for recipes, tips, and a list of the ten most frequently asked questions, along with the answers, of course!

Roasted Turkey

Roasting a turkey is somewhat of an art and somewhat of a science. Certain rules apply, but then again, the experience seems to differ every time and can become largely a matter of individual style. In this recipe, the stuffing is baked separately, not in the turkey, but you can also stuff the turkey with stuffing and bake it (see the color section). Just spoon stuffing loosely into the cavity right before cooking. Then tie the legs together and increase the cooking time (see Table 21-1). Before serving, scoop out the stuffing into a bowl.

Tools: *Chef's knife, vegetable peeler, large roasting pan, roasting rack, meat thermometer (unless the turkey comes with one), kitchen string or twine, carving board*

Preparation time: *15 minutes*

Cooking time: *3 to 3½ hours (for a 12-pound turkey)*

Yield: *12 servings*

1 fresh or thawed frozen turkey (about 12 pounds)	2 carrots, peeled and quartered	Salt and pepper
1 medium yellow onion, quartered	2 large cloves garlic, crushed	Madeira Pan Gravy (see the recipe later in this section)
	2 tablespoons vegetable oil	

1 Preheat the oven to 325 degrees, with the oven rack on the lowest rung.

2 Set a wire roasting rack in a large roasting pan. Remove the giblets and neck from the turkey cavity and reserve for the stock; discard the liver. (While the turkey is roasting, you can prepare a quick turkey stock with the giblets and neck; this is used for the pan gravy recipe later in this chapter). Remove any excess fat from the turkey. Rinse the turkey inside and out with cold water and pat dry.

3 Place in the turkey cavity the onion, carrots, and garlic. Tie the legs together with kitchen string. If desired, bend the wing tips back and fold them underneath the turkey.

4 Set the turkey, breast side up, on the roasting rack. Rub the turkey all over with 2 tablespoons of the oil. Season generously with salt and pepper. Add 1 cup of water to the roasting pan. If using a meat thermometer, insert it into the thickest part of the thigh, close to the body, without touching any bone.

5 Roast for about 3 to 3¾ hours, or until the thigh temperature registers 180 degrees. Add another ½ cup of water to the roasting pan if it gets dry. To brown the turkey evenly, turn the pan laterally about midway through the roasting. If the turkey turns brown before the roasting time is over, cover it loosely with aluminum foil to shield the skin. Start checking for doneness during the last 30 minutes of roasting, and baste with the pan drippings 2 to 3 times during the last hour.

6 Remove the turkey from the oven, transfer it to a carving board, and cover loosely with aluminum foil, letting it rest for 20 minutes while you make the gravy. Remove the vegetables from the cavity and discard. Carve (see Figure 21-1). Serve with the Madeira Pan Gravy.

Vary It! *You can season a turkey in all sorts of ways to add flavor and color to the skin. For example, mix 2 tablespoons molasses or maple syrup with 2 tablespoons reduced-sodium soy sauce; baste the turkey with this mixture, along with the pan juices, during the last hour of cooking — but no sooner! Never baste a turkey with a sugar-based mixture for more than an hour or the sugar will burn.*

Vary It! *For an attractive presentation, garnish the turkey platter with fruits and other attractive produce. Try a heap of fresh cranberries, piles of leafy greens or fresh herbs (such as whole basil), a few kumquats or orange slices, or red and green grapes dusted in sugar.*

Per serving (with gravy): Calories 505 (From Fat 173); Fat 19g (Saturated 6g); Cholesterol 204mg; Sodium 598mg; Carbohydrate 2g (Dietary Fiber 0g); Protein 76g.

Per serving (without gravy): Calories 404 (From Fat 122); Fat 14g (Saturated 4g); Cholesterol 171mg; Sodium 206mg; Carbohydrate 0g (Dietary Fiber 0g); Protein 66g.

Figure 21-1:
How to
carve a
turkey.

Madeira Pan Gravy

We love this recipe for the kick it gets from Madeira (a sweet Spanish dessert wine). Everyone always asks for more and raves about the taste! However, you can also make it without the Madeira, or substitute white wine or a little extra chicken broth.

Tools: *Chef's knife, vegetable peeler, degreaser (optional), medium saucepan, roasting pan (from the turkey), whisk, wooden spoon, measuring cup, sieve or cheesecloth*

Preparation time: *10 to 15 minutes*

Cooking time: *About 30 minutes*

Yield: *12 servings, or about 3 cups*

4 cups canned chicken broth	2 carrots, quartered	½ cup Madeira (optional)
Turkey giblets (liver discarded) and neck	2 stalks celery, quartered	3 tablespoons flour
	1 bay leaf	Salt and pepper
1 medium yellow onion, peeled and quartered	Turkey pan drippings	

1 To make the turkey stock, in a medium saucepan, combine the chicken broth, turkey giblets and neck, onion, carrots, celery, and bay leaf. Cover and bring to a boil. Reduce the heat to low and simmer, partially covered, for 30 minutes. Strain the stock through cheesecloth or a fine sieve into a large measuring cup. (You should have between 1½ and 2 cups. If the stock has evaporated more than this, add water or additional chicken broth.) Refrigerate until ready to make the pan gravy. When the broth is chilled, skim off and discard any fat that rises to the surface. (Stock can be made several days ahead if you want to pull out the turkey giblets before cooking the turkey.)

2 Pour the drippings from the roasting pan into a 2-cup glass measuring cup or a degreaser. Spoon off and discard all but 3 tablespoons of fat from the drippings. Reserve the fat in a small cup.

3 Strain the skimmed drippings through a fine sieve into a second 2-cup glass measuring cup or bowl. Set aside.

4 Add the Madeira to the roasting pan and cook over medium-high heat, stirring and scraping the bottom for about 1 minute; strain this into the cup holding the skimmed pan drippings.

5 Add the 3 tablespoons of the reserved fat to the roasting pan. Set two burners to medium heat under the pan and heat the fat. Add the flour to the pan and stir constantly with a wire whisk, about 1 to 2 minutes, to blend the flour into the fat. The roux (a thickening paste of fat and flour) should turn golden brown.

6 Slowly whisk in the Madeira pan drippings; whisk for about 1 minute, stirring and scraping the bottom of the pan. Continue whisking and gradually add the turkey stock, 1 cup at a time. Use only enough stock to reach a gravy consistency. Season to taste with salt and pepper.

Per serving: Calories 102 (From Fat 52); Fat 6g (Saturated 2g); Cholesterol 32mg; Sodium 392mg; Carbohydrate 2g (Dietary Fiber 0g); Protein 10g.

Making Scrumptious Stuffing

When most people think of roasted turkey, they think of stuffing as well. Take a look at the following tips about stuffing before you begin, and you'll be sure to leave your guests happily stuffed (pardon the pun!).

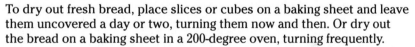

✔ **Whenever making stuffing for your roasted turkey (whether it is cooked in the bird or separately), make sure that the bread you use is very dry, even stale.** Two-day-old bread (left out uncovered) yields the best result; fresh, moist bread can leave it gummy. Just be sure to slice it before you dry it, or it can get too hard to work with.

To dry out fresh bread, place slices or cubes on a baking sheet and leave them uncovered a day or two, turning them now and then. Or dry out the bread on a baking sheet in a 200-degree oven, turning frequently.

✔ **As a general guideline, you need about ¾ to 1 cup of stuffing per pound of bird.** This amount also leaves you with delicious leftovers.

✔ **When making stuffing, overmixing and packing it too densely into the bird's cavity can cause the stuffing to cook more slowly and crumble when served.** If you're not baking it inside the bird's cavity, bake your stuffing in a well-buttered, covered baking dish for about 45 minutes. Try to time the cooking so that the stuffing comes out of the oven as the bird is being carved.

✔ **Drizzle a little chicken stock, a little white wine, or some of the turkey pan drippings over it for extra flavor and moisture.**

Cornbread, Sausage, and Apple Stuffing

In this stuffing recipe, we use poultry seasoning, which is a commercial blend of ground sage, rosemary, thyme, marjoram, savory, and salt. However, you can experiment and substitute any of your favorite herbs (see the herb chart in Chapter 3). Be sure the poultry seasoning isn't too old — one telltale sign is a faded, yellowish label with a promotional quote like "Eleanor Roosevelt's favorite!" Dried spices can lose potency within a year of opening.

Stuffing cooked separately from the turkey may need a little extra moisture. The stuffing in our recipe is kept moist with pork sausage, eggs, and an assortment of fruits and vegetables. However, if after 30 minutes in the oven, the stuffing becomes a little dry, simply add a little more chicken stock or warm water and then return it to the oven to finish baking. If you need a little more liquid to hold the stuffing together, use a little more stock or warm water. If you can't find bulk pork sausage, purchase sausage links and remove the casings.

Tools: *Chef's knife, apple corer, large skillet, slotted spoon, whisk, ovenproof baking dish, large mixing bowl, small bowl*

Preparation time: *20 minutes*

Cooking time: *About 1 hour*

Yield: *12 servings*

About 7 to 8 tablespoons butter	2 hot chile peppers or jalapeño peppers, seeded and diced (optional)	⅓ cup chopped parsley
1 pound bulk pork sausage (mild or hot, to taste)	8 cups cornbread cubes (see the cornbread recipe later in this section)	2 teaspoons poultry seasoning, or to taste
1 large yellow onion, diced		1 teaspoon sugar
1 cup diced celery	4 cups stale French bread, cut into ⅓- to ½-inch cubes	Salt and black pepper
1 large red bell pepper, cored, seeded, and diced	2 Golden Delicious apples, peeled, cored, and cut into small cubes	1 can (14½ ounces) chicken stock, or 2 cups homemade stock
		2 eggs, lightly beaten

1 In a large skillet, melt 2 tablespoons of the butter over medium-high heat. Add the sausage and cook until browned, about 5 minutes, stirring frequently to break it up. Using a slotted spoon, remove the sausage to a large mixing bowl.

2 Add to the skillet 4 more tablespoons of the butter with the onion, celery, red bell pepper, and, if desired, the hot peppers. Cook, stirring occasionally, about 4 to 5 minutes, or until the vegetables are cooked but still a little firm. Stir the vegetables into the sausage.

3 Add the cornbread and French bread cubes, apples, parsley, poultry seasoning, sugar, and salt and pepper to taste; toss well.

4 In a small bowl, whisk together the chicken stock and eggs; add this to the stuffing, about 1 cup at a time, stirring well. Add enough egg-broth mixture to moisten the stuffing so that it holds together when lightly pressed between the palms of your hands.

5 Transfer the dressing into a well-buttered baking dish with a lid; dot with the remaining 1 to 2 tablespoons of butter. Cover and bake at 325 degrees for 45 to 55 minutes, or until heated through.

Vary It! *You can substitute some white wine for some of the chicken stock to add more flavor. Instead of using poultry seasoning, substitute 2 to 3 tablespoons fresh chopped herbs, such as sage, marjoram, thyme, or any combination.*

Per serving: *Calories 360 (From Fat 204); Fat 23g (Saturated 8g); Cholesterol 86mg; Sodium 675mg; Carbohydrate 31g (Dietary Fiber 2g); Protein 9g.*

Cornbread for Stuffing

Cornbread mixes and cornbread muffins are often too moist and sweet to use as a base for stuffing. This cornbread recipe holds its shape when combined with the other stuffing ingredients. You can make it ahead of time and freeze it, or wrap it and keep it in the refrigerator for a few days. It's perfect for stuffing but too hard and dry to cut into squares and serve on its own.

Tools: *Measuring cup, large bowl, wire whisk, 8- or 9-inch square baking pan, wooden spoon or spatula*

Preparation time: *5 minutes*

Cooking time: *20 minutes*

Yield: *About 8 cups cornbread cubes*

1 cup yellow cornmeal	*2 teaspoons sugar*	*1 egg*
1 cup flour	*½ teaspoon salt*	*⅓ cup corn oil or vegetable oil*
1 tablespoon plus 1 teaspoon baking powder	*1 cup buttermilk*	

1 Preheat the oven to 425 degrees.

2 In a large bowl, combine the cornmeal, flour, baking powder, sugar, and salt; stir to mix.

3 With a wire whisk, stir in the buttermilk, egg, and oil; beat just until the mixture is combined — do not overmix. Spread the batter in a buttered 8- or 9-inch square baking pan. Bake for 20 minutes, or until the top of the bread springs back when touched. Cool in the pan on a wire rack. If you're not using the cornbread right away, cut the bread into big pieces, wrap tightly, and refrigerate until ready to make the stuffing. Slice the cornbread into ¼ to ½-inch cubes for turkey stuffing.

Per cup: *Calories 227 (From Fat 95); Fat 11g (Saturated 1g); Cholesterol 28mg; Sodium 376mg; Carbohydrate 28g (Dietary Fiber 2g); Protein 5g.*

Fresh Cranberry-Orange Relish with Walnuts

We dress up this relish recipe by adding some Cointreau or Grand Marnier (sweet orange-flavored liqueurs), but they're optional. So are the walnuts, but they add interesting texture.

Tools: *Paring knife, food processor, wooden spoon*

Preparation time: *10 minutes, plus about 1 hour to chill*

Yield: *12 servings, or about 3 cups*

1 navel orange

1 package (12 ounces) fresh or frozen cranberries

1 cup sugar

2 teaspoons Cointreau, Grand Marnier, brandy, or other orange liqueur (optional)

½ cup chopped walnuts (optional)

1 Starting at the stem end of the orange, remove the peel, working in a spiral fashion with a sharp paring knife; take care to leave behind the bitter white pith (the soft, white layer that lies beneath the orange peel). Set the orange peel aside.

2 Peel away and discard the layer of white pith from the orange; coarsely chop the fruit.

3 Put the orange pieces, the orange peel, and the cranberries into the bowl of a food processor. Pulse 4 or 5 times, or until the fruit is coarsely chopped. Transfer the cranberry-orange mixture to a bowl or a glass serving container. Stir in the sugar and, if desired, the brandy or orange liqueur and the walnuts. Chill until ready to serve.

Per serving: Calories 85 (From Fat 0); Fat 0g (Saturated 0g); Cholesterol 0mg; Sodium 0mg; Carbohydrate 22g (Dietary Fiber 1g); Protein 0g.

Preparing Holiday Vegetables

The turkey is great, but everybody also loves all the delicious side dishes that come with Thanksgiving dinner. Don't forget the mashed potatoes (Chapter 4) so you can make full use of that delicious gravy you made with the turkey. Add to that the following two irresistible vegetable side dishes, and you'll have a meal that is almost complete — that is, until all your guests get their second wind and want dessert! (And for that, just check out the recipe at the end of this chapter.)

☁ Green Beans with Shallots

This recipe is simple and elegant; it also lends a nice green color to your menu, which is dominated by shades of orange. And where many of the other side dishes are sweet, this bean dish is savory. You can make it at the last minute, although you can save time by trimming the beans and mincing the shallots ahead of time.

Tools: *Chef's knife, large pot, large skillet, colander*

Preparation time: *15 minutes*

Cooking time: *About 20 minutes*

Yield: *12 servings*

3 pounds fresh green beans, rinsed and trimmed	*1 cup shallots, sliced crosswise into thin rounds*
6 tablespoons butter	*2 teaspoons fresh lemon juice (optional)*
	Salt and pepper

1 Place the beans in a large pot. Add cold salted water to cover. Cover the pot and bring to a boil over medium-high heat; cook until just tender but still firm, about 10 to 15 minutes. (Actual cooking time will depend on the tenderness and size of the beans.) Check for doneness after about 8 minutes.

2 As the beans cook, melt the butter in a large skillet. Add the shallots and cook over medium heat for 3 to 4 minutes, stirring often, until golden. Set aside.

3 Drain the beans well and add them to the skillet with the shallots. Stir to combine and heat briefly just before serving. If desired, stir in the lemon juice. Season to taste with salt and pepper.

Vary It! *An elegant alternative for this dish is thin, French string beans, also called haricot verts. If making this variation, reduce the cooking time to 4 to 6 minutes, or until tender.*

Per serving: *Calories 99 (From Fat 54); Fat 6g (Saturated 4g); Cholesterol 15mg; Sodium 54mg; Carbohydrate 11g (Dietary Fiber 4g); Protein 3g.*

♂ *Rum-Baked Sweet Potatoes*

Remember that bottle of dark rum you bought impulsively at the duty-free store in the airport? If you're like us, that bottle is sitting, unopened, in your kitchen. Well, get out the bottle . . . here's a great way to use it.

These terrific sweet potatoes can be baked very quickly — you can put them in the oven as you're removing the turkey to rest. The sweet potatoes are first parboiled (which softens them slightly and makes the second cooking much quicker) for about 15 minutes, and then they bake for about 20 minutes to finish cooking.

Tools: *Chef's knife, large pot, large skillet, baking dish*

Preparation time: *5 to 10 minutes*

Cooking time: *About 45 minutes*

Yield: *12 servings*

6 medium sweet potatoes (about 3½ pounds), peeled

⅓ cup butter

1½ cups packed dark brown sugar

⅔ cup dark rum (or use ⅓ cup molasses mixed with ⅓ cup pineapple juice and ¼ teaspoon almond extract or rum extract)

⅓ cup fresh orange juice

¾ teaspoon ground allspice

Salt and pepper

1 Preheat the oven to 350 degrees.

2 Place the potatoes in a large pot of lightly salted boiling water. Cover and boil for 15 to 20 minutes, or until still slightly firm when pierced with a fork. (Don't overcook, or they'll fall apart. You want them slightly *under*cooked. Check for doneness after 10 minutes.) Drain and cut each sweet potato in half lengthwise and then widthwise into quarters. Place the potatoes in a single layer in a 9-x-13-inch baking pan (or a ceramic baking dish that can be brought right from the oven to the table). Set aside.

3 In a large skillet, melt the butter over medium heat; add the brown sugar, rum, and orange juice. Bring to a boil, stirring occasionally to break up any lumps of sugar. Reduce the heat and simmer for 7 to 8 minutes, stirring occasionally, until the sauce is thickened and slightly caramelized. Stir in the allspice.

4 Drizzle the rum mixture over the sweet potatoes. Gently turn the potatoes in the glaze to coat all sides. Season the potatoes well with salt and pepper. Bake for 20 to 25 minutes, or until the sauce is bubbly and the potatoes are heated through and tender.

Per serving: Calories 261 (From Fat 48); Fat 5g (Saturated 3g); Cholesterol 14mg; Sodium 73mg; Carbohydrate 53g (Dietary Fiber 2g); Protein 2g.

Who Has Room for Dessert?

Thanksgiving is hardly Thanksgiving without the traditional slice of pumpkin pie. Although some people make all kinds of desserts for Thanksgiving, we would rather fill up on the savory stuff, so we offer just this one classic, with a new twist. You just may find a new family tradition in this very special recipe. If your family likes a variety of desserts, however, you can find plenty of choices in Chapter 15 or in *Desserts For Dummies,* by Bill Yosses and Bryan Miller, or *Baking For Dummies,* by Emily Nolan (both published by Wiley).

🍑 Praline Pumpkin Pie

This uncommon pumpkin pie uses a sweet, delicious, and thin bottom crust of crunchy pecans and brown sugar. The pecan layer is a nice contrast to the semisweet pumpkin filling. The crust recipe calls for a food processor — the best and quickest way to make pie pastry. But of course you can use a pastry blender or two knives to work the butter and shortening into the flour and salt. (See Chapter 17 for complete instructions and illustrations.)

If your dinner is for 12, we suggest making two pies. Try two of these, or one pumpkin and one apple pie (for a homemade apple pie recipe, see Chapter 17). If you make two kinds of pie, don't be surprised if people ask for "just a *tiny* piece of both!"

Tools: *Food processor, rolling pin, 9-inch pie pan, scissors (or sharp knife), aluminum foil, chef's knife, pan, saucepan, 2 medium mixing bowls, large mixing bowl, rubber spatula, hand-held mixer (optional), wire cooling rack*

Preparation time: *5 to 10 minutes for the pastry crust (a little more if mixing by hand), 15 minutes for the filling, 1 hour chilling*

Cooking time: *13 minutes for the pastry crust plus 50 minutes for the filling*

Yield: *8 servings*

3 tablespoons butter, chilled (for the pastry)	3 tablespoons butter (for the filling)	1 teaspoon ground ginger
3 tablespoons vegetable shortening (such as Crisco) or chilled margarine	⅔ cup coarsely chopped, lightly toasted pecans (see the tip at the end of the recipe)	1 teaspoon ground cinnamon
1 cup flour		½ teaspoon ground nutmeg
¼ teaspoon salt	1½ cups canned pumpkin	1 can (5 ounces) evaporated milk
2 to 3 tablespoons ice water	3 eggs, lightly beaten	¼ cup whole milk
1 cup packed light brown sugar	1 tablespoon granulated sugar	2 teaspoons vanilla extract
		1 cup lightly sweetened whipped cream (optional)

Pastry Crust

1 In the bowl of a food processor, cream the butter and shortening until light and fluffy, about 2 minutes. Stop the motor, if necessary, and use a rubber spatula to scrape the mixture toward the blade. Add the flour and salt and process just a few seconds until the dough resembles coarse cornmeal. (If you don't have a food processor, turn to Chapter 17 for instructions and illustrations on how to make pie dough by hand.) Add the cold water a little at a time, pulsing just enough to bind the dry ingredients. The exact amount of water required depends on the humidity of your kitchen. *Do not overblend* or the dough will get tough. Shape the dough into a ball, wrap entirely with plastic wrap, and refrigerate for at least 1 hour.

2 Before baking the pie crust, preheat the oven to 450 degrees.

3 Lightly flour a large cutting board or counter and, with a rolling pin, roll out the dough into a circle that is about 12 inches in diameter. Loosely drape the dough around a rolling pin and position it over the pie pan. Unroll the dough onto the bottom of the pie plate and gently pat it flush against the sides. With scissors or a sharp knife, trim the overhanging pastry to ½ inch beyond the edge of the plate. Flute the crust by pinching the dough all around the edge. Do not prick the bottom. Line the bottom with a double thickness of aluminum foil. Bake for 8 minutes. Carefully remove the foil. Bake for 4 to 5 minutes more or until the bottom of the crust is set and dry. Let cool.

Filling

1 Preheat the oven to 375 degrees.

2 In a small pan, combine ⅓ cup of the brown sugar with the 3 tablespoons butter. Cook over medium heat for a few minutes, stirring constantly until the butter is melted and the brown sugar is dissolved. Stir in the pecans. With a spatula or spoon, spread this hot mixture over the bottom of the cooled pastry shell; set aside to cool to room temperature.

3 Meanwhile, in a large mixing bowl, combine the pumpkin with the remaining ⅔ cup brown sugar; add the eggs, granulated sugar, ginger, cinnamon, and nutmeg and beat lightly with a whisk or hand-held mixer on low speed until well blended. Whisk or beat in the evaporated milk, whole milk, and vanilla extract, blending well. Pour the filling over the cooled pecan mixture in the pie shell.

4 Bake the pie for 45 to 50 minutes, or until a knife inserted into the center comes out clean. Cool on a wire rack. Cover and refrigerate until ready to serve. If desired, spoon a heaping tablespoon of lightly sweetened whipped cream over each portion before serving (see Chapter 9 for a great whipped cream recipe).

Tip: *Be sure to flute the pastry crust high over the edge of the plate; the filling of this pie comes all the way to the top. A deep dish pie plate makes spillage less likely.*

Tip: *To toast the chopped pecans, heat a cast-iron pan over medium-high heat. Add the chopped pecans and stir constantly until the pecans turn a golden brown.*

Vary It! *If you want to make a pumpkin pie without nuts (some people don't like them or are allergic to them), just leave out the pecans. The pie will still have a thin, sweet, brown-sugary bottom layer, and why would anybody object to that? Chocoholics can even replace the pecans in this recipe with chocolate chips. Who are we to stop you?*

Per serving: Calories 427 (From Fat 217); Fat 24g (Saturated 9g); Cholesterol 109mg; Sodium 131mg; Carbohydrate 48g (Dietary Fiber 3g); Protein 7g.

Part VI
The Part of Tens

"I really wish you wouldn't wear that thing when you chop vegetables."

In this part . . .

Think of this part as a cheat sheet to use after finishing your own personal cooking course. You can refer to these lists for specific reminders or just for fun. (We had fun writing them, anyway.)

Here, you'll find information about common kitchen disasters and how to avoid them (they happen to the best of us!). You'll also discover ways to think like a chef by absorbing some classic cooking wisdom.

And be sure to refer to the helpful appendixes that follow the fun Part of Tens chapters. These cover cooking terms you may have heard but always wondered about, substitutions for common ingredients, and other helpful at-your-fingertips information.

Chapter 22

Ten Common Cooking Disasters and How to Deal with Them

*N*o matter how careful you are and no matter how experienced a home cook you are, you're bound to encounter the occasional kitchen disaster. It happens to the best of us! That's why we devote this chapter to ten common cooking disasters, and what you can do to a) deal with the disaster, and fast; and b) prevent it from happening again (or preferably, prevent it from happening in the first place!).

You Started a Fire

When you have a flare-up in the kitchen, you need to act fast to keep the fire from getting out of control. But how you act depends on what kind of fire you have and where it is. Most small fires don't require a call to the fire department, let alone a fire extinguisher, but just in case, always have an ABC-certified fire extinguisher handy! These fire extinguishers can put out fires caused by electrical appliances as well as grease fires.

If you do have a kitchen fire, don't panic. Instead, memorize these instructions for putting out kitchen fires:

✔ If you have a fire in the oven, shut the door and turn off the oven. The lack of oxygen will douse the flames. If your oven continues to smoke as if a fire is still going on in there, call the fire department.

✔ If you have a fire in a cooking pan and you can safely put the lid on the pan, do so. Use an oven mitt, clap on the lid, move the pan off the burner, and turn off the stove. The oxygen will douse the flames in a pot just like it will when you shut the oven door. If you can't safely put the lid on a flaming pan or you don't have a lid for the pan, use that fire extinguisher! That's what it's there for.

✔ To use a fire extinguisher, pull out the pin, hold the fire extinguisher firmly with one hand, point the nozzle at the fire, squeeze the trigger, and sweep the spray back and forth over the fire.

✔ Don't use water to put out grease fires. Water repels grease and can spread the fire by splattering the grease. Instead, smother the fire with a wet towel or use that fire extinguisher.

✔ If the fire is spreading and you can't control it, get out of the house and call 911! Make sure everybody in your family knows how to get out of the house safely in case of a fire. Practice your fire escape route. Kids, especially, should practice how to get out of the house safely on their own, in case of fire.

As for prevention, you can do a lot to prevent kitchen fires by doing the following:

✔ Keep your appliances serviced, clean, and in good repair. Unplug wayward appliances and have them repaired or replace them.

✔ Install a smoke detector near, but not in, the kitchen (you don't want the small amount of smoke sometimes generated from cooking to constantly trigger the alarm).

✔ Use caution when lighting the pilot light or burner on a gas stove. Follow the manufacturer's instructions.

✔ Don't use metal in the microwave. The sparks can turn into fire or can seriously damage your microwave.

✔ Don't overfill pots or pans with oil or grease. Wipe up spills and don't cook on a dirty stove.

✔ Always roll up long sleeves and tie back long hair when cooking so they don't catch on fire!

You Burned Yourself

Whether you accidentally touch a hot burner, pick up a hot pot handle without an oven mitt, or burn the back of your hand on the oven coils when taking a pie out of the oven, burns hurt! Treat burns by running cold water over them for five minutes. If your skin is seriously blistering, see a doctor. Otherwise, follow up your cold-water rinse with an ice pack for pain and, when the pain eases, apply antibiotic and/or burn cream and an adhesive bandage. For larger burns or burns that aren't healing quickly, look inflamed or infected, or ooze fluid, see your doctor for treatment.

Prevent burns by following these tips:

- ✔ Always use oven mitts when taking things out of the oven or removing things from the stove.

- ✔ Never touch or put anything other than pots and pans on the stovetop, especially if you aren't sure whether the burners are still hot.

- ✔ Stand back from hot pans when you remove the lid, to avoid steam burns.

- ✔ Be careful when draining hot pasta or pouring hot liquids from a pot into a bowl or a blender. A splatter can burn you.

- ✔ Never mix hot liquids in a blender. They can explode out of the blender container, even with the lid on. Allow liquids to cool to lukewarm before blending.

- ✔ Stand back from spattering grease (such as when you are cooking bacon or deep-fat-frying) and vigorously boiling liquids, including water, which can also spatter and burn you.

- ✔ Keep pot handles turned inward, not out over the edge of the stove, where someone could bump them and send a pan full of hot food flying.

- ✔ Teach kids to stay away from the stove, oven, and microwave, and to never touch anything on the stove or in the oven.

You Burned the Food

Sooner or later, most cooks accidentally burn food when they get distracted while cooking. The phone rings, the kids need something, or the dog has to go out, and before you know it, smoke is pouring out of the oven, and the pot roast looks like a shiny black lava rock.

The best way to avoid burning food is, of course, to keep an eye on it! But if you do overcook something, here are a few suggestions:

- ✔ If you do burn a large piece of meat, you may be able to cut off the burned sections and save the rest. It may not be pretty, but it may be edible. Or cut off the burned sections, chop up the rest of the meat, and stick it in a nice soup. Will anyone know the difference? Probably not (unless you then proceed to burn the soup!).

- ✔ If you burn soup, pour the unburned soup into a separate pot, removing any blackened pieces, and reheat.

- ✔ As for your poor burned pots and pans, a good soaking and some elbow grease along with a steel wool scrubber (if it's safe to use on your particular type of cookware) can go a long way toward rescuing them, but sometimes, you can't do much other than buy a new pan. If your roaster looks like it has been lined in black, shiny volcanic rock, you probably need a new roaster. Just be thankful you didn't start a fire!

You Cut Yourself

Knives (or cheese graters or mandolines or . . .) can be very dangerous, whether they're super sharp or too dull. Use them carefully and always keep your fingers curled under when chopping with a knife. Better to ding a knuckle than slice a fingertip! Also, don't ever slice things freehand over the sink. Slice that raw carrot on the cutting board, not against your own hand! Secure your cutting board if it doesn't have rubber feet by putting a towel under it when cutting. If you do cut yourself, wash the cut and apply pressure to stop the bleeding. Fingertip cuts can bleed a lot. Raise your hand above your head as you press on the cut with a cloth or paper towel until the bleeding stops. Then put antibiotic cream on the cut and bandage it. If the cut won't stop bleeding after a few minutes or if it is very deep, see your doctor or an emergency care facility. You may need stitches.

Your Recipe Misses the Mark

Sometimes, no matter how closely you follow the recipe, the food you cook just doesn't taste very good. It hardly seems fair, after you've taken all the time to buy the ingredients and do exactly what the recipe writer instructed. But food that doesn't taste good can sometimes be made to taste better. Here are some tips:

✔ Add salt. Salt makes a lot of things taste better, from a bland soup or too-dry pork chop to a less-than-juicy watermelon. (If you have to watch your salt intake due to doctor's orders, just ignore this step.)

✔ Sprinkle disappointing fruit with sugar to bring out the natural juices, and let it sit for a few minutes. Or, drizzle fruit with honey or cream.

✔ Add herbs and spices to any savory dish. Herbs and spices can add interesting flavor to bland casseroles, meats, fish, egg dishes, soups, stews, and salads. Try adding Italian-inspired combinations like oregano, basil, and thyme to tomato-based or egg dishes. Creamy soups can taste great with some dill, marjoram, or tarragon. To meaty dishes, add chili powder, cumin, paprika, or some of the hotter spices like cayenne pepper or hot pepper flakes, for some jazz. (See Chapter 3 for more ideas on using herbs and spices.)

✔ For boring soups, enhance the flavor by stirring in any of the following: 2 tablespoons butter or olive oil, ¼ cup cream, ½ cup puréed tomatoes, or a bouillon cube. (But keep in mind that the latter is high in salt.)

✔ Boring desserts may taste better with some added cinnamon, nutmeg, or a tiny pinch of cloves.

✔ Ho-hum cookies perk up with a little frosting or jam. Try making them into sandwiches with peanut butter filling or dipping them in melted dark or white chocolate and letting the chocolate harden.

✔ If your cake is too dry, poke tiny holes all over it with a toothpick or a skewer and soak each layer with a quarter cup of sweet liqueur such as Kahlúa, amaretto, Kirsch, or Grand Marnier, or for a nonalcoholic version, drizzle with a little warmed honey, chocolate syrup, or strong coffee. Add some homemade whipped cream (see Chapter 9), and suddenly you have a very special dessert.

Your Barbecue Is Ablaze, and Other Grill Disasters

Just because you're cooking outside instead of inside is no guarantee that you won't experience culinary misfortune. Here are a few tips for keeping your outdoor cooking experiences safe, sound, and savory:

✔ Before lighting the grill, make sure it's a safe distance (four feet or more) from deck railings, roof eaves, patio umbrellas, or anything else that might catch on fire.

✔ Use extreme caution when using lighter fluid to soak briquettes. Never let children use lighter fluid.

✔ Keep matches and lighters out of the reach of children.

✔ If the grill fire gets too high, cover the grill and close the vents to smother the flame.

✔ Always know where the fire extinguisher is, just in case the flames get out of control.

✔ Always follow manufacturer's instructions for grill usage, especially for gas grills and propane tanks.

✔ Use long-handled tongs, spatulas, and other grill tools rather than the regular tools you use in the kitchen to keep your hands farther away from the heat.

✔ Don't overcook food on the grill. Charred food could pose a health risk, and it certainly doesn't taste very good!

You're Out of an Ingredient

If you suddenly realize that you're out of an ingredient you need for a recipe, think twice before substituting something else. Ounce for ounce, grain for grain, baking soda and baking powder are not the same thing. Flour and cornstarch are not the same thing. Neither are wine and vinegar, eggs and mayonnaise, condensed milk and evaporated milk, or brown sugar and white sugar.

The safest way to go about substituting ingredients is to check reliable cooking resources so that you're sure that your substitute ingredients won't adversely affect the recipe. For more advice on smart substitutions, check out Appendix B in this book.

You Have Too Many People and Not Enough Food

It's always a compliment to have more people show up to your party, or even your regular family dinner, than you expected. Perhaps they've heard rumors about your new culinary skills? But what do you do when the good food you have prepared, or are in the process of preparing, doesn't quite stretch? Try these tricks for making your dinner stretch to feed a few more mouths:

✔ Transform your menu. If you planned to serve each guest a chicken breast or steak, cut the meat into bite-size portions and mix with rice or pasta and lots of veggies sautéed in butter or olive oil. Or, put everything into a wok with hot oil for a delicious stir-fry. See Chapter 18 for one example of a delicious stir-fry recipe.

✔ Soup it up. Throw meat and rice into a soup pot with some canned chicken broth and all the fresh veggies you can find in the crisper, sautéed in a little butter and added to the pot. Let it all simmer for 30 to 45 minutes and serve. See Chapter 11 for some easy soup recipes.

✔ Add a course. Serve smaller portions of the entrée and add a salad, a simple soup, a dish of pasta with butter and herbs or a simple sauce, a bowl of creamy risotto (see Chapter 4), or a stir-fry of fresh vegetables. Look for ingredients you already have on hand.

✔ Layer ingredients into a strata. See Chapter 14 for a strata recipe.

✔ Set up a buffet instead of serving everyone at the table. Put out the dishes you had planned to serve and then fill out the meal with more items you already have on hand: a bowl of fruit cut into bite-sized pieces, chips and salsa, or a salad mix topped with bottled dressing.

You Damaged Your Kitchen Counter

If you accidentally scorch, scratch, knick, or otherwise mar your kitchen counter, don't despair. Some of these goofs can be repaired. You can also do a lot to prevent wrecking your kitchen counter. Here are some tips:

✔ Always cut on a cutting board to prevent nicks and scratches.

✔ Clean up spills immediately to prevent stains. If you do get a stain, try a bleach-water solution, a bleach pen, or vinegar. Certain enzyme-based stain-removing products can also work well.

✔ Avoid scorching by setting hot pots and pans on your stovetop or on a heat-resistant ceramic or metal trivet.

✔ If your countertop does seem irreparably stained, scorched, scratched, or otherwise marred, consult a countertop repair specialist to see whether the countertop can be refinished or repainted, or whether it needs to be replaced. Every surface is different, so it pays to have a specialist advise you, but get several estimates so you can best assess what needs to be done.

You're Such a Good Cook That You Have to Do All the Cooking

Okay, maybe this isn't such a huge disaster. Sure, being a great cook is a tough job. It can get lonely at the top. But for the sake of good eating, somebody has to do it. Aren't you just a little bit glad that it's you? In the meantime, here are a few tips to make sure that you don't spend *all* your time in the kitchen (even if you wouldn't really mind all that much):

- ✔ Plan your meals a week in advance to avoid wasting time trying to decide what to make, or running to the market at the last minute to pick up the necessary ingredients.

- ✔ Take requests — within reason. Nobody should have to cook a different menu for each family member.

- ✔ Enlist others to help. Even the most kitchen-challenged can tear lettuce leaves, chop veggies, or fetch meat from the freezer.

- ✔ Share cleanup chores. Even young kids can rinse their plates and put their own dinner dishes in the dishwasher.

- ✔ Take a break now and then. Just because you *can* cook doesn't mean you always *must* cook. There is no shame in the occasional take-out or a visit from the pizza delivery guy. Everyone does it.

- ✔ Accept the kudos. Maybe you aren't used to people telling you what a great cook you are. But now that you *are* a great cook, be gracious. You may be tempted to respond to culinary praise with self-deprecating phrases like, "Oh, it wasn't so great" or "Oh, I really don't know how to cook very well." When someone tells you the meal you just cooked was great, respond with a smile and a polite (now practice with us here) "Thank you very much!" Was that so hard? We didn't think so.

Chapter 23

Ten Ways to Think Like a Chef

. . . .

In This Chapter

▶ Sniff your way through the spice rack

▶ Save those chicken bones!

▶ Build dishes from the bottom up

. . . .

*I*n observing and interviewing many chefs, we found a consensus among them about how to progress as a cook. The ten points in this chapter reflect their thoughts.

Know the Basic Techniques

Cooking is so much more fun — and successful — when you approach it with confidence. Chefs say that confidence arises from knowing your techniques so well that they're second nature.

Use Only the Freshest Ingredients

Use only the freshest ingredients and buy in-season fresh fruits and vegetables. Seasonal produce offers the highest quality and supply and the lowest price. Why make an apple pie in the summer from mealy apples held in storage all year when you can make one with fresh, ripe peaches or juicy plums? Let what's fresh and available at the market help you spontaneously decide what's for dinner.

Get It Together

So much of cooking, even for professionals, is preparation — slicing, peeling, dicing, and so on.

The French call this preparation *mise en place,* which translates to "everything in its place." Get the chopping, mincing, deboning, and washing chores out of the way in order to create an even, efficient flow of cooking steps.

That way, when the butter or oil is hot and sizzling in the skillet, you don't need to stop suddenly to peel and mince onions and garlic that are supposed to be sautéed in the hot fat.

With This Basil, I Thee Wed

Learn about herbs, both fresh and dried, so that you can season without always relying on a book or recipe. Chefs base some of the world's great cuisines on the combination of a few simple herbs and spices.

For example, Italian cooking relies heavily on the flavors of garlic, olive oil, tomatoes, Parmesan cheese, and basil. The French use a basic seasoning blend called *mirepoix* — a sautéed mixture of chopped onions, carrots, and celery. Many chefs begin their soups, stews, stuffings, and pan sauces with these simple, sautéed ingredients. Louisiana home cooks have their own version, which adds chopped bell pepper and garlic to the mix. You can vary this base by adding bacon, ham, fresh herbs, or even curry. In a perfectly made *mirepoix,* the vegetables cook slowly for a long time, causing them to caramelize slightly and sweeten.

All the Plate's a Stage

Think of the choreography of food on a plate. People eat with their eyes first. The food should be colorful and attractively arranged, with fresh herbs as a colorful garnish.

Plan Your Menus in Advance

Before cooking, think about contrasting flavors, textures, and colors. If the appetizer is a salad of grilled portobello mushrooms, then mushrooms in the entree is not an interesting choice. Keep the courses balanced and don't overload yourself. If you serve a time-consuming and complex appetizer, serve a simple entree or one that needs only reheating, like a tasty stew. If your appetizer is cold, be sure that the entree is hot.

Take a good look at the timing of the meal, too. Figure out how much cooking and preparation time are needed so that your diners don't feel like they are getting the bum's rush or have to wait too long between courses.

Be Thrifty

Throw out nothing (unless, of course, it's spoiled). Every morsel of food is usable for soups, stocks, salads, and so on. You can sometimes make great meals from leftovers (see Chapter 18 for ideas for using leftovers).

Learn about different cuts of meat and how to cook them so that you don't have to rely on more expensive cuts. Hone your knife skills so that you can save money by purchasing whole chickens, ducks, fish, and so on and then cutting them up yourself.

Don't Be a Slave to Recipes

Use a good, basic recipe that you like as a starting point, but don't consider it written in stone. Say that you have a recipe for basic stew. You make it once and decide that it could use more garlic, so the next time you double the amount. Or instead of turnips, you think that the sweet effect of chopped carrots would work, so you substitute one vegetable for the other. With experience and good technique, and by discovering how ingredients work together, you can simply glance at a recipe and make adjustments to suit your taste.

Simplify, Simplify

Too many spices spoil the broth. If you stick to no more than four basic flavors in a dish, they work together to provide complexity, yet each flavor maintains its individuality. Don't load up your dishes with everything you can find. Sometimes the most perfect, delicious dishes are the simplest.

Above All, Have Fun

Take a cooking course, buy yourself a cookbook, or make a new dish that you've always wanted to try. Cooking, like golf, should be fun — something you look forward to. So what if you slam one into the rough every now and then! It's all part of the game.

Try new things. Stretch your skills. Take risks. Try again. You can experiment with other sauces, mousses, soups, casseroles, and more. Heard about a fascinating new ethnic dish? Try it! Wish you knew more about classic French cooking? Plunge into the research and start practicing. The world of cooking is vast and fascinating, forever yielding new wonders, flavors, mysteries, and surprises. What could be more fun than that? Cooking offers the adventure of a lifetime. We know that you'll come to love it as much as we do. Bon appétit!

Glossary of 100 (Plus) Common Cooking Terms

• •

*C*ooking and recipe writing have their own distinct language. Before you roast a chicken, for example, you need to know what *trussing* means. To make a soufflé that rises above the rim of the dish, you need to understand *whipping* and *folding* egg whites. This appendix gives you a list of basic terms. Most of them are thoroughly described and illustrated elsewhere in the book.

Adjust: To taste the dish before serving and add seasoning (such as salt and pepper), if necessary, as in, "Taste the soup and adjust for seasonings." *Adjust* could also mean to raise or lower heat while cooking.

Al dente: An Italian phrase meaning "to the tooth" that describes the tender but still firm texture of perfectly cooked pasta. (See Chapter 13 for pasta recipes.)

Au gratin: A dish, usually topped with buttered bread crumbs, grated cheese, or both, that has been browned in the oven or under the broiler.

Bake: To cook in the dry heat of an oven. (See Chapter 15 for easy baking recipes.)

Barbecue: Any food cooked on a charcoal or gas grill over an indirect fire (opposed to grilling, which occurs directly over the fire). Also refers to the process of cooking foods in a pit or on a spit for a long time, or as a descriptive term for the particular spicy tomato-based sauce used to baste grilled meat.

Baste: To add flavor and moisture by brushing food with pan drippings, fat, or a seasoned liquid as it cooks.

Batter: An uncooked, semiliquid mixture usually containing beaten eggs, flour, liquid, and a leavening ingredient, such as baking soda or baking powder, that makes the batter rise when cooked.

Beat: To mix ingredients briskly in a circular motion so that they become smooth and creamy. A hundred hand-beaten strokes generally equal one minute with an electric mixer, if you're the type who counts these things. (See Chapter 10 for information about beating egg whites.)

Beurre manié: A butter-flour paste used to thicken soups and stews. (Turn to Chapter 11 for instructions for making this paste.)

Bind: To bring together a liquid mixture, such as a sauce, with a thickening ingredient, such as cream or butter.

Blanch: To plunge vegetables or fruits into boiling water for a short time to loosen their skin or preserve their color. (See Chapter 4.)

Blend: To mix or combine two or more ingredients with a spoon, whisk, spatula, or electric mixer.

Boil: To bring the temperature of a liquid to 212 degrees for water at sea level, causing bubbles to break at the surface. (See Chapter 4.)

Bone (or debone): To remove the bones from meat, fish, or poultry.

Bouquet garni: A package of mixed herbs (often tied in cheesecloth) that is used to season stocks, soups, and stews to impart flavor. A typical combination is parsley, thyme, and bay leaf.

Braise: To brown meat or vegetables in fat and then cook, covered, in a small quantity of liquid over low heat, usually for a long time. The long, slow cooking both tenderizes and flavors the food, especially tough cuts of meat. Braising can take place either on the stovetop or in the oven. (See Chapter 6 for braising and stewing recipes.)

Bread: To coat a piece of food with crackers or bread crumbs to seal in moisture and give it a crisp crust. The piece of fish, poultry, meat, or vegetable is usually first dipped into a liquid, such as beaten egg or milk, to make the crumbs adhere.

Broil: To cook food under a hot oven coil, as opposed to grilling, in which the heat is underneath. (See Chapter 8.)

Brown: To cook food briefly over high heat, usually in fat and on top of the stove, to impart a rich brown color to its skin or surface. Food also may be browned in a very hot oven or under the broiler.

Brush: To coat the surface of food with a liquid ingredient such as melted butter, egg, or fruit glaze.

Butterfly: To split food down the center (removing bones if necessary), leaving the two halves joined at the seam so that the food opens flat to resemble a butterfly.

Caramelize: To heat sugar until it melts into a liquid, syrupy state that ranges from golden to dark brown in color (320 degrees to 350 degrees on a candy thermometer). See Chapter 9 for a recipe for Caramel Sauce. Also, to cook onions and other vegetables until they become soft and brown (the sugars they contain caramelize).

Chill: To put food in a cool place, typically the refrigerator, to bring it to a cold (but not frozen) state.

Chop: To cut food into small pieces by using a knife or food processor.

Clarify: To make a cloudy liquid clear by removing the impurities. For example, you can clarify a stock or broth by simmering raw egg whites or eggshells for 10 to 15 minutes to attract impurities. You then very gently strain the liquid through a sieve lined with cheesecloth.

Cool: To allow hot or warm food to stand at room temperature or in a cool place such as a refrigerator, to bring the temperature down typically to room temperature.

Core: To cut out the core of a food, usually a fruit or vegetable such as an apple or pepper.

Cream: To beat one ingredient, such as butter, with another, such as sugar, until soft and smooth.

Crimp: To press together with your fingers or a fork (see Chapter 17) and seal the rim of a double-crust pie to form a double thickness of dough that you can then shape into a decorative pattern.

Crumble: To break up or crush food, such as dried herbs or crackers, into small pieces with your fingers.

Cube: To cut food into ½-inch square pieces. Cubed food is larger than diced food. See also *dice*.

Cure: To preserve food such as meat or fish by salting, drying, and/or smoking.

Cut in: To use a knife to mix hard fat (like butter) into dry ingredients (like flour). For example, "Cut the butter into the flour until it resembles coarse crumbs."

Dash: See *pinch.*

Deglaze: To add liquid, usually wine or broth, to a hot skillet or roasting pan and scrape up the browned bits clinging to the bottom of the pan that pieces of sautéed meat, fish, or poultry left behind. You then reduce and season the pan sauce. See Chapter 5 for recipes that use this technique.

Degrease: To skim the fat off the surface of a soup or gravy with a spoon. Also done by chilling the mixture, turning the liquid fat into a solid, which you can then easily lift off the surface.

Demi-glace: A rich, brown sauce made by boiling down meat stock until it's reduced to a thick glaze that can coat a spoon. (See Chapter 9.)

Devein: To remove the vein from shrimp or other shellfish. (See Chapter 14 for illustrated instructions for cleaning shrimp.)

Devil: To season foods with hot and spicy ingredients such as Tabasco sauce, mustard, or red pepper flakes.

Dice: To cut into small (⅛-inch to ¼-inch) cubes.

Dilute: To thin a mixture by adding water or other liquid.

Disjoint: To sever a piece of meat at its joint, as when you separate a chicken leg from its thigh.

Dot: To distribute small portions or pieces of food (such as bits of butter) over the surface of another food.

Drain: To remove the liquid from a food, often in a colander. Also, to pour off liquid fat from a pan after you brown a food (such as bacon or ground meat).

Dredge: To coat the surface of a food by dragging it through flour, cornmeal, or crumbs.

Drizzle: To pour a liquid such as melted butter, sauce, or syrup over a food in a thin, slow stream.

Dust: To give the surface of food a thin coating of flour or confectioners' sugar.

Fillet: As a verb, to cut the flesh away from the bones of a piece of meat or fish. As a noun, a piece of meat, fish, or poultry that has the bones removed.

Flake: To peel off or form into flakes, usually with a fork, as in the process for determining if fish is done (when you can flake the fish with a fork, it is cooked).

Flambé: To ignite food that is drenched in alcohol so that it bursts into a dramatic flame just before serving. (See Chapter 5 for a recipe for Sautéed Peppered Sirloin of Beef, which includes a flambé option.)

Flute: To form into a decorative pleated groove, as in fluting a pie crust before baking.

Fold: To combine a light mixture, such as beaten egg whites or whipped cream, with a heavier mixture, such as sugared egg yolks or melted chocolate, by using a gentle mixing motion. (See Chapter 10 for illustrated instructions.)

Fricassee: A white stew in which meat or poultry is not browned before cooking.

Fry: To cook or sauté food in fat over high heat. Deep-fried foods are submerged in hot fat and cooked until crisp.

Fumet: A concentrated fish stock that is used as a flavoring base for sauces.

Garnish: An edible plate adornment, ranging from a simple wedge of lemon to a fancy chocolate leaf.

Glaze: To coat the surface of a food with syrup, melted jelly, an egg wash, or other thin, liquid mixture to give it a glossy shine.

Grate: To rub a large piece of food (such as a block of cheese) against the coarse, serrated holes of a grater.

Grease: To spread a thin layer of fat, usually butter, on the inside of a pan to prevent food from sticking as it cooks.

Grill: To cook food over a charcoal or gas grill, or to cook on an iron (or other) grill pan on the stovetop. (See Chapter 8.) Relatively high heat is used to sear food and add depth of flavor.

Hull: To trim strawberries by plucking out their green stems.

Julienne: To cut foods into thin (⅛ inch or less) strips.

Knead: The technique of pushing, folding, and pressing dough for yeast breads to give it a smooth, elastic texture. You can knead by hand or with an electric mixer equipped with a bread hook or a bread machine.

Marinate: To soak or steep a food such as meat, poultry, fish, or vegetables in a liquid mixture that may be seasoned with spices and herbs in order to impart flavor to the food before it is cooked. (See Chapter 8.) The steeping liquid is called the marinade.

Mash: To press food, usually with a potato masher or ricer, into a soft pulp.

Mince: To cut food into tiny pieces.

Mirepoix: A combination of finely chopped sautéed vegetables, usually carrots, onions, and celery, that is used as a seasoning base for soups, stews, stuffings, and other dishes. (See Chapter 23.)

Parboil: To partially cook foods, such as rice or dense vegetables like carrots and potatoes, by plunging them briefly into boiling water. (See Chapter 4.)

Pare: To remove the skin from fruits or vegetables.

Pickle: To preserve food in a salty brine or vinegar solution.

Pinch or dash: A small amount of any dry ingredient (between $\frac{1}{16}$ and $\frac{1}{8}$ teaspoon) that can be grasped between the tips of the thumb and forefinger.

Poach: To cook foods in a simmering, not boiling, liquid. (See Chapter 4.)

Pound: To flatten food, especially chicken breasts or meat, with a meat mallet or the flat side of a large knife (such as a cleaver) to make it uniform in thickness. Has some tenderizing effect.

Preheat: To turn on the oven, grill, or broiler before cooking food to set the temperature to the degree required by the recipe.

Purée: To mash or grind food into a paste by forcing through a food mill or sieve or by whirling in a food processor or blender. Finely mashed food also is called a purée.

Ream: To extract the juice from fruit, especially citrus.

Reconstitute: To bring dehydrated food, such as dried milk or juice, back to a liquid state by adding water.

Reduce: The technique of rapidly boiling a liquid mixture, such as wine, stock, or sauce, to decrease its original volume so that it thickens and concentrates in flavor.

Render: To cook a piece of meat over low heat so that its fat melts away.

Roast: To cook in the dry heat of an oven. (See Chapter 7.)

Roux: A cooked paste of flour and fat such as oil or butter that is used to thicken soups, stews, and gumbos. (See Chapter 9.)

Sauté: To cook food quickly in a small amount of fat, usually butter or oil, over very high heat. (See Chapter 5.)

Scald: To heat milk to just below the boiling point when making custards and dessert sauces to shorten the cooking time and add flavor.

Score: To make shallow cuts (often in a crisscross pattern) on the exterior of a food (such as meat, fish, or bread) so that it cooks more evenly.

Sear: To brown quickly in a pan, under the broiler, or in a very hot oven. (See Chapter 7.)

Season: To flavor foods with herbs, spices, salt, pepper, and so on.

Shred: To reduce food to thin strips, usually by rubbing it against a grater.

Shuck: To remove shells from shellfish, such as clams, oysters, and mussels or to remove husks from fresh corn.

Sift: To shake dry ingredients, such as flour or confectioners' sugar, through a fine mesh sifter to incorporate air and make them lighter.

Simmer: To gently cook food in a liquid just below the boiling point or just until tiny bubbles begin to break the surface (at about 185 degrees). (See Chapter 4.)

Skewer: To thread small pieces of food on long, thin rods made of bamboo or metal to hold meat, fish, or vegetables for grilling or broiling.

Skim: To remove the fat and bits of food that rise to the surface of a soup or stock with a spoon. (See Chapter 11.)

Soft peaks: A term describing whipped egg whites, at the stage when they form soft peaks that curl over when the beater is lifted out of the egg whites.

Steam: To cook over a small amount of simmering or boiling water in a covered pan so that the steam trapped in the pan cooks the food. (See Chapter 4.)

Stew: To simmer food for a long time in a tightly covered pot with just enough liquid to cover. The term *stew* also can describe a cooked dish. (See Chapter 6.)

Stiff peaks: A term describing whipped egg whites, at the stage when they form stiff, upstanding peaks that stay erect when the beater is lifted out of the egg whites.

Stir-fry: The Asian cooking technique of quickly frying small pieces of food in a wok with a small amount of fat over very high heat while constantly tossing and stirring the ingredients. The term stir-fry also can refer to a dish prepared this way.

Stock: The strained, flavorful liquid that is produced by cooking meat, fish, poultry, vegetables, seasonings, or other ingredients in water. (See Chapter 4.)

Strain: To separate liquids from solids by passing a mixture through a sieve.

Stuff: To fill a food cavity, such as the inside of a chicken, turkey, or tomato, with various types of food.

Tenderize: To soften the connective tissue of meat by pounding or cooking very slowly for a long time. See also *braise*.

Toss: To turn over food a number of times to mix thoroughly, as when a green salad is mixed and coated with dressing.

Truss: To tie meat or poultry with string and/or skewers to maintain its shape during roasting. (See Chapter 7 for illustrated instructions for trussing a chicken.)

Whip: To beat air into ingredients such as eggs or cream with a whisk or electric beater to make them light and fluffy.

Whisk: A hand-held wire kitchen utensil used to whip ingredients like eggs, cream, and sauces. When used as a verb, the term *whisk* describes the process of whipping or blending ingredients together with a wire whisk.

Zest: As a noun, the colored, grated outer peel (the colored portion only) of citrus fruit that is used as a flavoring ingredient in dressings, stews, desserts, and so on. As a verb, the process of removing the colored, grated outer peel.

Appendix B
Common Substitutions, Abbreviations, and Equivalents

• •

*E*ven experienced chefs sometimes end up in the middle of a recipe with the realization that they don't actually have *evaporated* milk, or quite enough brown sugar, or that the box of baking soda in the cupboard is empty. You might also wonder what certain cooking abbreviations are, that you run across in other cookbooks or recipes you find in magazines or on the Internet. And what about that recipe you are dying to try from your friend in Canada, that turns out to be all in metric measurements?

This is the Appendix for you! In it, we have listed all kinds of ingredients to substitute for the ingredients you need but don't have, we decode the most common abbreviations, and we give you a list of English to metric equivalencies. We hope you refer to this appendix often as your skill grows.

Substituting in a Pinch

Say that you're making a vinaigrette dressing for a salad and suddenly realize that you're out of vinegar. But you do have lemons, which are an acceptable substitute. How much lemon do you use? Or you may not have whole milk for a gratin dish, but you do have skim milk. Is skim milk okay? Situations like these are what this section is all about.

Some ingredients are almost always interchangeable: For example, you can substitute vegetable or olive oil in most cases for butter when sautéing or pan frying; lemon juice for vinegar in salad dressings and marinades; almonds for walnuts in baked breads and muffins; vegetable stock for beef or chicken stock in soups, stews, or sauces; and light cream for half-and-half.

But sometimes there is no acceptable substitution for an ingredient. Other times, the substitution is very exact and specific. This is most often the case for baked goods, where you need to follow a formula to produce a cake, soufflé, pastry, or bread with the perfect height, density, and texture.

Most of the following substitutions are for emergency situations only — when you have run out of an essential ingredient and need a very specific replacement.

For thickening soups, stews, and sauces:

- 1 tablespoon cornstarch or potato flour = 2 tablespoons all-purpose flour

- 1 tablespoon arrowroot = 2½ tablespoons all-purpose flour

For flour:

- 1 cup minus 2 tablespoons sifted all-purpose flour = 1 cup sifted cake flour

- 1 cup plus 2 tablespoons sifted cake flour = 1 cup sifted all-purpose flour

- 1 cup sifted self-rising flour = 1 cup sifted all-purpose flour plus 1¼ teaspoons baking powder and a pinch of salt

For leavening agents in baked goods:

- ¼ teaspoon baking soda plus ½ teaspoon cream of tartar = 1 teaspoon double-acting baking powder

- ¼ teaspoon baking soda plus ½ cup buttermilk or yogurt = 1 teaspoon double-acting baking powder in liquid mixtures only; reduce liquid in recipe by ½ cup

For dairy products:

- 1 cup whole milk = ½ cup unsweetened evaporated milk plus ½ cup water

  or 1 cup skim milk plus 2 teaspoons melted butter

  or 1 cup water plus ⅓ cup powdered milk

  or 1 cup soy milk

  or 1 cup buttermilk plus ½ teaspoon baking soda

✔ ¾ cup whole milk plus ⅓ cup melted butter = 1 cup heavy cream (but not for making whipped cream)

✔ 1 cup skim milk =1 cup water plus ¼ cup nonfat powdered milk, or ½ cup evaporated skim milk plus ½ cup water

✔ 1 cup sour milk = 1 cup buttermilk or plain yogurt or 1 cup minus 1 tablespoon milk, plus 1 tablespoon lemon juice or white vinegar after standing 5 to 10 minutes

✔ 1 cup sour cream = 1 cup plain yogurt

For eggs:

✔ 2 egg yolks = 1 egg for thickening sauces and custards

✔ 4 extra-large eggs = 5 large eggs or 6 small eggs

For sweetening:

✔ 1 cup sugar = 1 cup molasses (or honey) plus ½ teaspoon baking soda

✔ 1 cup brown sugar = 1 cup white sugar plus 1½ tablespoons molasses

Miscellaneous substitutions:

✔ 1 cup broth or stock = 1 bouillon cube dissolved in 1 cup boiling water

✔ 1 square (1 ounce) unsweetened chocolate = 3 tablespoons cocoa plus 1 tablespoon butter, margarine, or vegetable shortening

✔ 1 square (1 ounce) semisweet chocolate = 3 tablespoons cocoa plus 1 tablespoon butter, margarine, or vegetable shortening plus 2 tablespoons sugar

✔ 1 2- to 3-inch piece of vanilla bean = 1 teaspoon pure vanilla extract

✔ 1 tablespoon fresh chopped herbs = ¾ to 1 teaspoon dried herbs

✔ 1 medium garlic clove = ⅛ teaspoon garlic powder

✔ 1 cup red wine = 1 cup apple cider, cranberry juice, or beef broth

✔ 1 cup white wine = 1 cup apple juice, apple cider, white grape juice, or chicken broth

Taking a Quick Look at Abbreviations

Although we spell out measurements in this book, many cookbooks use abbreviations. Table B-1 lists common abbreviations and what they stand for.

Table B-1	Common Abbreviations
Abbreviation(s)	*What It Stands For*
C, c	cup
g	gram
kg	kilogram
L, l	liter
lb	pound
mL, ml	milliliter
oz	ounce
pt	pint
t, tsp	teaspoon
T, TB, Tbl, Tbsp	tablespoon

Looking Up Conversions and Metric Equivalents

Cookbook writers have a penchant for practical jokes. Just when you're getting the hang of cups and tablespoons, they throw you a recipe in ounces and pounds. Tables B-2 and B-3 list common equivalent measures. All measurements are for level amounts.

Note: Some metric measurements are approximate. The recipes in this cookbook were not developed or tested using metric measures. There may be some variation in quality when converting to metric units.

Table B-2	Conversion Secrets	
This Measurement . . .	*. . . Equals This Measurement*	*. . . Equals This Metric Measurement*
Pinch or dash	less than ⅛ teaspoon	0.5 mL
3 teaspoons	1 tablespoon	15 mL
2 tablespoons	1 fluid ounce	30 mL
1 jigger	1½ fluid ounces	45 mL
4 tablespoons	¼ cup	50 mL
5 tablespoons plus 1 teaspoon	⅓ cup	75 mL
12 tablespoons	¾ cup	175 mL
16 tablespoons	1 cup	250 mL
1 cup	8 fluid ounces	250 mL
2 cups	1 pint or 16 fluid ounces	500 mL
2 pints	1 quart or 32 fluid ounces	1 L
4 quarts	1 gallon	4 L

Table B-3	Food Equivalents
This Measurement . . .	*. . . Equals This Measurement*
3 medium apples or bananas	about 1 pound
1 ounce baking chocolate	1 square
2 slices bread	about 1 cup fresh bread crumbs
1 pound brown sugar	2¼ cups packed
4 tablespoons butter	½ stick
8 tablespoons butter	1 stick

(continued)

Table B-3 *(continued)*

This Measurement . . .	. . . Equals This Measurement
4 sticks butter	1 pound
6 ounces chocolate chips	about 1 cup
1 pound confectioners' sugar	about 4½ cups sifted
1 pound granulated sugar	2 cups
½ pound hard cheese (such as cheddar)	about 2 cups grated
1 cup heavy whipping cream	2 cups whipped cream
1 medium lemon	3 tablespoons juice, 2 to 3 teaspoons grated zest
1 pound macaroni	4 cups raw, 8 cups cooked
4 ounces nuts	about ⅔ cup chopped
1 large onion	about 1 cup chopped
1 cup uncooked rice	4 cups cooked
1 pint strawberries	about 2 cups sliced
1 large tomato	about ¾ cup chopped
3 to 4 tomatoes	about 1 pound
1 pound all-purpose flour	about 4 cups sifted

Tables B-4 through B-7 show you a variety of metric conversations: volume, weight, measurement, and temperature. Use them if you need to convert a recipe, but again, remember that these are approximate and results could vary.

Table B-4   Volume

U.S. Units	Canadian Metric	Australian Metric
¼ teaspoon	1 mL	1 ml
½ teaspoon	2 mL	2 ml
1 teaspoon	5 mL	5 ml
1 tablespoon	15 mL	20 ml
¼ cup	50 mL	60 ml

U.S. Units	Canadian Metric	Australian Metric
⅓ cup	75 mL	80 ml
½ cup	125 mL	125 ml
⅔ cup	150 mL	170 ml
¾ cup	175 mL	190 ml
1 cup	250 mL	250 ml
1 quart	1 liter	1 liter
1½ quarts	1.5 liters	1.5 liters
2 quarts	2 liters	2 liters
2½ quarts	2.5 liters	2.5 liters
3 quarts	3 liters	3 liters
4 quarts	4 liters	4 liters

Table B-5	Weight	
U.S. Units	Canadian Metric	Australian Metric
1 ounce	30 grams	30 grams
2 ounces	55 grams	60 grams
3 ounces	85 grams	90 grams
4 ounces (¼ pound)	115 grams	125 grams
8 ounces (½ pound)	225 grams	225 grams
16 ounces (1 pound)	455 grams	500 grams
1 pound	455 grams	½ kilogram

Table B-6	Measurements
Inches	Centimeters
½	1.5
1	2.5
2	5.0

(continued)

Table B-6 (continued)

Inches	Centimeters
3	7.5
4	10.0
5	12.5
6	15.0
7	17.5
8	20.5
9	23.0
10	25.5
11	28.0
12	30.5
13	33.0

Table B-7 — Temperature (Degrees)

Fahrenheit	Celsius
32	0
212	100
250	120
275	140
300	150
325	160
350	180
375	190
400	200
425	220
450	230
475	240
500	260

Index

● **C** ●

• *S* •

• *U* •

• *V* •

SINESS, CAREERS & PERSONAL FINANCE

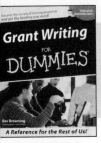

0-7645-5307-0

0-7645-5331-3 *†

Also available:

- Accounting For Dummies †
  0-7645-5314-3
- Business Plans Kit For Dummies †
  0-7645-5365-8
- Cover Letters For Dummies
  0-7645-5224-4
- Frugal Living For Dummies
  0-7645-5403-4
- Leadership For Dummies
  0-7645-5176-0
- Managing For Dummies
  0-7645-1771-6

- Marketing For Dummies
  0-7645-5600-2
- Personal Finance For Dummies *
  0-7645-2590-5
- Project Management For Dummies
  0-7645-5283-X
- Resumes For Dummies †
  0-7645-5471-9
- Selling For Dummies
  0-7645-5363-1
- Small Business Kit For Dummies *†
  0-7645-5093-4

ME & BUSINESS COMPUTER BASICS

0-7645-4074-2

0-7645-3758-X

Also available:

- ACT! 6 For Dummies
  0-7645-2645-6
- iLife '04 All-in-One Desk Reference
  For Dummies
  0-7645-7347-0
- iPAQ For Dummies
  0-7645-6769-1
- Mac OS X Panther Timesaving
  Techniques For Dummies
  0-7645-5812-9
- Macs For Dummies
  0-7645-5656-8

- Microsoft Money 2004 For Dummies
  0-7645-4195-1
- Office 2003 All-in-One Desk Reference
  For Dummies
  0-7645-3883-7
- Outlook 2003 For Dummies
  0-7645-3759-8
- PCs For Dummies
  0-7645-4074-2
- TiVo For Dummies
  0-7645-6923-6
- Upgrading and Fixing PCs For Dummies
  0-7645-1665-5
- Windows XP Timesaving Techniques
  For Dummies
  0-7645-3748-2

OD, HOME, GARDEN, HOBBIES, MUSIC & PETS

0-7645-5295-3

0-7645-5232-5

Also available:

- Bass Guitar For Dummies
  0-7645-2487-9
- Diabetes Cookbook For Dummies
  0-7645-5230-9
- Gardening For Dummies *
  0-7645-5130-2
- Guitar For Dummies
  0-7645-5106-X
- Holiday Decorating For Dummies
  0-7645-2570-0
- Home Improvement All-in-One
  For Dummies
  0-7645-5680-0

- Knitting For Dummies
  0-7645-5395-X
- Piano For Dummies
  0-7645-5105-1
- Puppies For Dummies
  0-7645-5255-4
- Scrapbooking For Dummies
  0-7645-7208-3
- Senior Dogs For Dummies
  0-7645-5818-8
- Singing For Dummies
  0-7645-2475-5
- 30-Minute Meals For Dummies
  0-7645-2589-1

NTERNET & DIGITAL MEDIA

0-7645-1664-7

0-7645-6924-4

Also available:

- 2005 Online Shopping Directory
  For Dummies
  0-7645-7495-7
- CD & DVD Recording For Dummies
  0-7645-5956-7
- eBay For Dummies
  0-7645-5654-1
- Fighting Spam For Dummies
  0-7645-5965-6
- Genealogy Online For Dummies
  0-7645-5964-8
- Google For Dummies
  0-7645-4420-9

- Home Recording For Musicians
  For Dummies
  0-7645-1634-5
- The Internet For Dummies
  0-7645-4173-0
- iPod & iTunes For Dummies
  0-7645-7772-7
- Preventing Identity Theft For Dummies
  0-7645-7336-5
- Pro Tools All-in-One Desk Reference
  For Dummies
  0-7645-5714-9
- Roxio Easy Media Creator For Dummies
  0-7645-7131-1

SPORTS, FITNESS, PARENTING, RELIGION & SPIRITUALITY

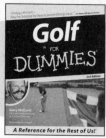

0-7645-5146-9

0-7645-5418-2

Also available:
- Adoption For Dummies
  0-7645-5488-3
- Basketball For Dummies
  0-7645-5248-1
- The Bible For Dummies
  0-7645-5296-1
- Buddhism For Dummies
  0-7645-5359-3
- Catholicism For Dummies
  0-7645-5391-7
- Hockey For Dummies
  0-7645-5228-7

- Judaism For Dummies
  0-7645-5299-6
- Martial Arts For Dummies
  0-7645-5358-5
- Pilates For Dummies
  0-7645-5397-6
- Religion For Dummies
  0-7645-5264-3
- Teaching Kids to Read For Dummies
  0-7645-4043-2
- Weight Training For Dummies
  0-7645-5168-X
- Yoga For Dummies
  0-7645-5117-5

TRAVEL

0-7645-5438-7

0-7645-5453-0

Also available:
- Alaska For Dummies
  0-7645-1761-9
- Arizona For Dummies
  0-7645-6938-4
- Cancún and the Yucatán For Dummies
  0-7645-2437-2
- Cruise Vacations For Dummies
  0-7645-6941-4
- Europe For Dummies
  0-7645-5456-5
- Ireland For Dummies
  0-7645-5455-7

- Las Vegas For Dummies
  0-7645-5448-4
- London For Dummies
  0-7645-4277-X
- New York City For Dummies
  0-7645-6945-7
- Paris For Dummies
  0-7645-5494-8
- RV Vacations For Dummies
  0-7645-5443-3
- Walt Disney World & Orlando For Dummies
  0-7645-6943-0

GRAPHICS, DESIGN & WEB DEVELOPMENT

0-7645-4345-8

0-7645-5589-8

Also available:
- Adobe Acrobat 6 PDF For Dummies
  0-7645-3760-1
- Building a Web Site For Dummies
  0-7645-7144-3
- Dreamweaver MX 2004 For Dummies
  0-7645-4342-3
- FrontPage 2003 For Dummies
  0-7645-3882-9
- HTML 4 For Dummies
  0-7645-1995-6
- Illustrator CS For Dummies
  0-7645-4084-X

- Macromedia Flash MX 2004 For Dummies
  0-7645-4358-X
- Photoshop 7 All-in-One Desk Reference For Dummies
  0-7645-1667-1
- Photoshop CS Timesaving Techniques For Dummies
  0-7645-6782-9
- PHP 5 For Dummies
  0-7645-4166-8
- PowerPoint 2003 For Dummies
  0-7645-3908-6
- QuarkXPress 6 For Dummies
  0-7645-2593-X

NETWORKING, SECURITY, PROGRAMMING & DATABASES

0-7645-6852-3

0-7645-5784-X

Also available:
- A+ Certification For Dummies
  0-7645-4187-0
- Access 2003 All-in-One Desk Reference For Dummies
  0-7645-3988-4
- Beginning Programming For Dummies
  0-7645-4997-9
- C For Dummies
  0-7645-7068-4
- Firewalls For Dummies
  0-7645-4048-3
- Home Networking For Dummies
  0-7645-42796

- Network Security For Dummies
  0-7645-1679-5
- Networking For Dummies
  0-7645-1677-9
- TCP/IP For Dummies
  0-7645-1760-0
- VBA For Dummies
  0-7645-3989-2
- Wireless All In-One Desk Reference For Dummies
  0-7645-7496-5
- Wireless Home Networking For Dummies
  0-7645-3910-8